Waves of Opposition

THE HISTORY OF COMMUNICATION

Robert W. McChesney and John C. Nerone, editors

A list of books in the series appears at the end of this book.

Waves of Opposition

LABOR AND THE STRUGGLE FOR DEMOCRATIC RADIO

Elizabeth Fones-Wolf

UNIVERSITY OF ILLINOIS PRESS

URBANA AND CHICAGO

♾ This book is printed on acid-free paper.
Library of Congress Cataloging-in-Publication Data
Fones-Wolf, Elizabeth A., 1954–
Waves of opposition : labor and the struggle for democratic radio /
Elizabeth Fones-Wolf.
p. cm. — (The history of communication)
Includes bibliographical references and index.
ISBN-13: 978-0-252-03119-9 (cloth : alk. paper)
ISBN-10: 0-252-03119-9 (cloth : alk. paper)
ISBN-13: 978-0-252-07364-9 (pbk. : alk. paper)
ISBN-10: 0-252-07364-9 (pbk. : alk. paper)
1. Labor unions and radio—United States—History—20th century.
2. Labor unions—Public relations—United States—History—20th century.
3. Mass media and business—United States—History—20th century.
4. Radio broadcasting—Political aspects—United States—20th century.
I. Title. II. Series.
HD6490.R352U648   2006
384.54'43   2006000327

(( ))

CONTENTS

(( ))

ACKNOWLEDGMENTS

WRITING A BOOK is never a solitary activity, and I owe much to many friends, colleagues, and institutions. Steven J. Ross read the manuscript at an early stage and offered invaluable criticism and guidance, which has made this a better book. Nathan Godfried has been a longtime coconspirator in the study of labor and broadcasting. He shared ideas and sources, joined me in presenting our research at conference sessions, and read and critiqued the final manuscript. I am also grateful to Gerd Horten, whose valuable suggestions improved the manuscript. Deb Weiner provided moral support throughout the research and writing process and effectively applied her editorial red pen to the manuscript.

I would like to thank librarians and archivists at the State Historical Society of Wisconsin, the Broadcast Pioneers Library at the University of Maryland, the George Meany Memorial Archives, the Kheel Labor-Management Documentation Center at Cornell University, Historical Collections and Labor Archives at Pennsylvania State University, the Library of Congress, the Department of Archives and Manuscripts at the Catholic University of America, the Hagley Museum and Library, National Archives and Records Center at College Park, Special Collections and University Archives at Rutgers University, the United Electrical Workers Archives at the University of Pittsburgh, and the Seeley G. Mudd Library at Princeton University. I extend special thanks to the Interlibrary Loan staff at West Virginia University, especially Judi McCracken, and to my friends at the Walter Reuther Library at Wayne State University: Mike Smith, Margaret Raucher, Louis Jones, William

LeFevre, and the rest of the staff welcomed me and provided wise counsel and unflagging support.

I am grateful to the National Endowment for the Humanities and the West Virginia Humanities Council for summer research grants and to WVU's history department and the Eberly College of Arts and Sciences, which supported the project with grants and sabbatical leaves. I would also like to thank Joe Turrini, Sean Adams, Greg Wood, Stephen Mihm, Ron Applegate, Ken Robinson, and Kate Kadlec for invaluable archival research assistance. At the University of Illinois Press, editor Kerry Callahan provided steady encouragement, and the manuscript benefited from Matt Mitchell's careful copyediting.

Friends, colleagues, and family provided help in a variety of important ways. Inger Stole and Bob McChesney hosted me while researching in Madison, Wisconsin, and Bob's enthusiasm for the project and encouragement kept me working. I am pleased to be contributing again to his History of Communication series at the University of Illinois Press. David Anderson and Irwin Marcus shared research, and I benefited from the interest of fellow radio and communications scholars: Kathy Newman, James Baughman, Michele Hilmes, Cathy McKercher, and Vinny Mosco. Greg and Ginny Field provided a warm welcome while I researched in the Detroit area, and my sister and brother-in-law, Julie and Elliott Maizels, opened their home to me and made my trips to Maryland enjoyable. My friends in the Bike Club—Deb Weiner, Maryanne Reed, Elizabeth Engelhardt, Marya Outterson, Katherine Aaslestad, Annastella Vester, and Sharon Ryan—provided important encouragement as we rode the rail trails of Morgantown.

Most of all, I want to thank my family. My children, Colin and Kasey, grew up with the book and are now beginning their own scholarly endeavors. As always, my biggest debt is to Ken, my partner, colleague, advisor, and best friend, without whom I would never have completed this book.

IN THE MID 1950S, following afternoons of play, a young Rich Klimmer would burst into his family's small home in a working-class Chicago neighborhood eager to share the events of his day with his family. If he happened to arrive after 6:00 P.M., his great aunts greeted him impatiently: "Shush, Richard, be quiet—it's the voice of labor." Retired union glove workers, his aunts were devoted listeners of the Edward P. Morgan radio show, an AFL-CIO-sponsored nightly network news and commentary program that aired in Chicago over the ABC affiliate WCFL. The Klimmer family organized its evening around the program. Dinner came after the show's conclusion, and conversation around the table in this working-class household often revolved around the issues raised by Morgan, whose liberal commentary stood in stark contrast to the conservative voices that inundated much of the media.[1]

Morgan's show was one of several labor-oriented programs on the air on WCFL, the nation's only union-owned station. At midcentury, listeners throughout the nation could hear a wide array of union-sponsored radio programs that promoted labor's political and economic agenda. Moreover, as regular participants on public affairs and news programs, union leaders were familiar voices and faces on network radio and television. These broadcasting initiatives helped organized labor to defend itself against a well-orchestrated postwar business campaign that sought to attack liberalism and undermine union power. At the same time, they strengthened union identity among working-class families like the Klimmers, provided support for labor's collective-bargaining goals, and promoted a liberal democratic political agenda. Today, in an era in which the media has rendered organized labor largely invisible, it is almost impossible to imagine that unions had a significant voice in the media that vigorously promoted labor and liberalism. Fifty years ago, at the height of its economic and political power, labor invested considerable resources into broadcasting in an effort to compete with business for the loyalty of the working class and the support of the rest of society.

This book explores how labor (in competition with business) used broadcasting from the rise of industrial unionism in the 1930s through the peak of its power in the late 1950s. It argues that radio, a powerful new medium of communication, helped spark labor's growth during the Depression and over the ensuing two decades became an important weapon in the ideological and cultural war between labor and business. Throughout much of the twentieth century, labor and business offered Americans two contrasting views of the world. While unions and their allies promoted a vision of society that emphasized equal rights, industrial democracy, economic equality, and social justice, business sought to sell Americans on the virtues of individualism, freedom, consumerism, and the centrality of the free enterprise system to the American way of life. That business had greater resources that often overwhelmed labor's voice does not diminish the significance of this struggle. Since the 1980s, business's individualistic ethos has so dominated America's political culture that it is easy to ignore the fact that unions contested the corporate exercise of cultural hegemony.

My earlier work, *Selling Free Enterprise,* examined this ideological struggle from 1945 to 1960, a period in which the business community, threatened by the growth of organized labor's power and the changes unleashed by the New Deal, launched an aggressive campaign to recast the political economy of America and to reeducate the public in the principles and benefits of the free enterprise system. This campaign filled much of America's cultural space with a series of selectively distorted symbols that helped lay the groundwork for containing organized labor and legitimating the conservative ideology that came to dominate America in the late twentieth century. Unions, however, fought back in creative ways in an effort to defend the liberal-labor vision. *Selling Free Enterprise* explores the variety of realms in which this ideological contest took place, including the mass media, the workplace, the community, recreation, schools, and houses of worship.[2]

This new study focuses more closely on the mass media and particularly the role of radio. Susan J. Douglas writes that "radio is arguably the most important invention of the century." From its inception in the 1920s, radio exerted a powerful influence on American society, transcending spatial boundaries, blurring the private domestic and public spheres, and reshaping American culture and politics. Warren Susman has suggested that broadcasting in the 1930s helped "create or reinforce uniform national values and beliefs in a way that no previous medium ever had before." It pulled the country together by making possible shared experiences and common access to ideas and culture. Although overshadowed in broadcasting history by television, for thirty years radio was the most important medium of mass communication, supplanting the press and even movies. Michele Hilmes observes that government regulation contributed to radio's unique influence. The creation of radio broadcasting "as a government-regulated extension of the public sphere gave the experience of 'listening in' more weight and influence than going to the movies or reading a popular magazine." Surveys showed that listeners placed more trust in what they heard on the radio than what they read in the press.[3]

This book begins at a point when business and labor began to grasp the impact of radio on American society. Although a few union leaders in the 1920s had recognized its "unique power, reach, and influence" and had urged labor to use radio broadcasting to reach workers and the broader public, unionists, particularly within the newly formed Congress of Industrial Organizations (CIO), did not attempt to fully exploit the possibilities inherent in the new medium until the 1930s. They understood that radio, which reached directly into homes, could serve as a integral tool for organizing and union building and as a means of constructing an oppositional community among a working-class audience. Unionists took to the air, and radio helped fuel the massive upsurge of organized labor in Depression-era America. Labor broadcasting also contributed to what Michael Denning has called a "laboring of American culture," an effort by writers, artists, and intellectuals to infuse culture with themes of social democracy and racial equality.[4]

Yet, as Douglas has observed, radio was "hardly an unfettered vehicle for the democratic expression of diverse American voices." It quickly developed into a corporate-controlled medium guided by "a set of basic class-bound [and race-bound] assumptions about who should be allowed to exert cultural authority." During the 1920s and 1930s and through most of World War II, commercial broadcasters sharply curtailed labor's access through censorship or explicit denial of airtime. At the same time, they offered radio to business as the "first line of defense" against "radicals stirring up criticism" of the free enterprise system. Corporate America quickly came to understand that radio could sell not only its products but its ideology. Through the sponsorship of institutional programming and radio news commentary, business made radio into an important weapon against organized labor and a more intrusive federal government.[5]

Government was the key to labor's eventual access to the air. Because radio was regulated, there were limitations on business's freedom to monopolize the airwaves. Using the 1934 Communication Act's requirement that radio stations operate in the public interest, during World War II the CIO attacked broadcasting's censorship of labor and challenged radio's negative coverage of unions, particularly by business-sponsored commentators. Like African Americans, who were also "vilified or rendered invisible by radio," unions fought to "make their voices and political claims" heard in the "influential new political space" created by radio.[6] In late 1945, prompted by a vigorous United Auto Workers (UAW) campaign for media equity, the Federal Communication Commission (FCC) mandated that stations cover controversial issues and provide time for all points of view. This decision helped open the airwaves to labor. It became one of the sources of the Fairness Doctrine, which until 1987 served as the most important tool for social reformers seeking to fight prejudice over the air.

Labor's involvement in media reform deepened in the tumultuous postwar years. Unions joined a wide-ranging reform movement that has been largely forgotten. This media-reform movement raised fundamental questions about the American broadcasting system, focusing particularly on the impact of business control over the mass media. The CIO was a major player in this loose coalition, which included public intellectuals, members of the FCC, and leftist elements of the cultural front. In the mid-1940s, these reformers fought unchecked commercialism, promoted public service, and sought to make radio more representative and democratic. A furious corporate counterattack ensued as the broadcasting industry mobilized across a broad front against the reform movement. Exploiting the emerging cold war, broadcasters joined with conservative business and patriotic organizations to delegitimize the reformers, charging that they would destroy radio. By the end of 1948, reformers' hopes for sweeping changes were sharply diminished.

The union commitment to radio in the postwar years remained strong nonetheless. As the business campaign against unions and liberalism intensified at midcentury, and as companies stepped up their use of radio to sell a corporate ideology, important elements of the labor movement embarked on an ambitious plan to use radio aggressively to compete for worker loyalty and public sympathy and to sustain labor's progressive social and economic agenda. Labor pursued two radio strategies: One focused on establishing nonprofit stations and on promoting FM, which labor and other media reformers viewed as a second chance at station ownership by groups excluded from the dominant AM broadcasting system. The second strategy involved purchasing or obtaining free time on the networks and local commercial stations. By the early 1950s, labor's voice was broadcast widely on the airwaves, contributing to the business community's continuing insecurity over its economic and political dominance in the postwar era.

This was not the first time that workers and their allies sought to use the mass media to contest business dominance and advance progressive change. Beginning with newspapers and followed by movies, radio, and television, the mass media has always been an important battleground between business and organized labor in the United States. For the most part, a corporate-controlled media has projected an image of unions as corrupt, greedy, violent, and un-American. Workers, however, have occasionally succeeded in challenging the class bias of mass communications. The large circulation of Socialist newspapers at the turn of the century briefly enabled workers to contest capitalist dominance of the press, providing the means for presenting the public with an alternative political vision. During the silent-film era, labor and the Left made movies viewed by millions of Americans. These films challenged the dominant conservative discourse of individualism and "portrayed collective action . . . as the most effective way to improve the lives of citizens." The rise of the powerful Hollywood studio system and the emergence of the more expensive talkies in the late 1920s brought to a close this era of worker-produced oppositional cinema. Although not produced by organized labor, some radical films of the 1930s continued to question the dominant values of American society and to treat workers sympathetically.[7]

As worker cinema was disappearing, the emergence of noncommercial community-sponsored radio broadcasting offered a similar promise. By the mid-1920s, local ethnic, religious, educational, and working-class groups had taken to the air. In 1926, hoping that radio would help "awaken the slumbering giant of labor," the Chicago Federation of Labor founded WCFL and the Socialist party established WEVD in New York City. However, by the end of the decade, corporate interests had seized control of broadcasting, consolidating the new industry along commercial and national lines and supplanting most community stations. Commercial broadcasters argued that privatization and commercialization were the most democratic methods of organizing the new medium. Business proceeded to use its power over radio to sell its products and to promote its ideology. At the same time, broadcasters excluded organized labor, minorities, and other dissident voices from radio. Yet, as the media scholar Robert W. McChesney has demonstrated, there was nothing natural about the emergence of commercial broadcasting. During the early 1930s, before commercial radio became ideologically entrenched, it faced stiff resistance from an eclectic broadcast-reform movement. A small group of unionists joined educators, theologians, civil libertarians, journalists, and intellectuals in an unsuccessful campaign to preserve a significant portion of the spectrum for nonprofit, noncommercial broadcasting.[8] The failure of this campaign meant that labor access to broadcasting would be attenuated until the CIO broke down the barriers during World War II.

The CIO's quest for access to radio was driven in part by the need for fair coverage of labor by the media. Organized labor in the United States has routinely complained about the mass media's biased treatment of workers and its hostility to unions. Scholars who have analyzed the portrayal of organized labor in the movies, on television, and in the press have corroborated these grievances, contending that the mass media pays little attention to workers or unions except during strikes or dramatic conflicts, when the public is fed a distorted image of labor. Fictional accounts in films and television as well as news coverage have portrayed the working class as either "good-natured but easily manipulated dupes" or an angry, violent collection of reactionaries and bigots. Union leaders often come across as greedy and corrupt. Strikes, in the media's portrayal, are annoying and unnecessary, with stories emphasizing consumer inconvenience instead of a dispassionate analysis of the issues.[9]

We know less, however, about how organized labor has used the mass media in the ideological struggles between capital and labor or about union efforts to gain access and democratize broadcasting. This study is influenced by Roland Marchand and William L. Bird Jr., whose innovative work emphasizes corporate uses of media to enhance the "social and moral legitimacy" of business and to ensure that the corporate vision would be the "mainstay of American political culture." I assert, however, that organized labor vigorously contested the corporate plan. My work also builds upon the scholarship of several historians who have begun to uncover the largely ignored history of organized labor's efforts to use and reform the mass media. Steven J. Ross's book on working-class film in the early twentieth century provides an important comparative perspective to this work on radio. Nathan Godfried has written an important study of WCFL and labor broadcasting as it developed in one specific locale from the 1920s through the 1970s, emphasizing the initially progressive and then increasingly conservative thinking of a city labor council and the American Federation of Labor (AFL). Robert W. McChesney gives us insights into the contributions of labor to the first media reform campaign of the late 1920s and early 1930s.[10] This study takes a more comprehensive look at labor broadcasting, highlighting the ideas and actions of the CIO as well as the AFL in communities across the nation. It also shows that the struggle against the corporate domination of radio broadcasting continued "long after the commercial nature of the airwaves had been established." Groups like the CIO persisted in a struggle for reform within the existing system. Finally, my study suggests the importance of state regulation in enabling a mobilized social institution to challenge corporate control of the media. Organized labor's media reformers relied on a governmental regulatory regime that provided public interest groups with at least the opportunity to fight for a more democratic media. In recent years, deregulation has left us with limited means to wage an effective campaign for media reform. This has dire consequences for the open exchange of ideas in a democratic society.[11]

This book juxtaposes the competing efforts of business groups and labor unions to reach the American people through broadcasting during the apex of radio's political and cultural impact on society and the union movement's unprecedented influence. It explains why, despite some temporary gains, labor was ultimately unsuccessful in matching the financial resources, political support, and cultural capital that corporate interests were able to muster. Defeat in this struggle to contest the political culture of business ultimately left unions at a severe disadvantage in shaping postwar society. Indeed, labor's virtual disappearance from the media helps explain in part why unions have become so marginalized in contemporary America.

This study is divided into three parts. Part 1 begins by examining labor's and business's initial experience with radio in the late 1920s and 1930s. While unionists in Chicago and New York City began broadcasting in the 1920s, labor's early radio forays were fairly limited. This was primarily because the AFL eschewed mass-mobilization tactics and because unions lacked sufficient resources and political clout to envision radio as a tool to alter the national labor-relations climate. Moreover, the conservative AFL leadership accepted the commercial, advertising-driven, network-dominated broadcasting system that emerged in the late 1920s and was complacent about radio censorship. Similarly, until the Depression jolted the nation's confidence in capitalism, corporate America made little use of radio to promote its economic and political ideology. By 1934, however, the New Deal had alarmed business, awakening a determination to counter its liberal, pro-labor bent. Business organizations such as the National Association of Manufacturers (NAM) and leading firms, including Du Pont, Ford, and General Motors, turned to radio—sponsoring institutional programming, propagandistic dramas, and conservative news commentators—to help restore public faith in their leadership and to promote the corporate vision of the American way.

Business sponsorship of programs selling its ideology alerted many in the labor movement to the power of radio. Increasingly concerned about the impact of a hostile press and radio programs promoting business, a revitalized labor movement began to more fully use broadcasting in the late 1930s. CIO leaders in particular believed that radio, which allowed penetration into the private sphere of workers' homes, could serve as an important tool for union building and organizing. Local stations aired a variety of labor programs. Labor leaders had traditionally relied on speeches to help plant the seeds of unionization and to win public support for labor. Radio in the 1930s and 1940s, however, attracted audiences with serial dramas and love stories, thrillers, and musical variety shows. Recognizing the appeal of this kind of programming, some union broadcasters began presenting their political and economic messages in the form of entertainment. They interspersed talk with music but also sometimes presented simple skits and occasionally longer dramatizations, all produced and performed by amateurs.

Throughout the 1930s, there were barriers to labor's access to the air and freedom of speech. Business faced few of these obstacles. While networks and local stations generally found little objectionable about business-sponsored programs, they routinely rejected or censored labor shows. Indeed, commercial broadcasters actively colluded with business to suppress labor's voice. At the end of the decade, the broadcasting industry constructed an even stronger barrier to broadcasting unionism when the National Association of Broadcasters (NAB), radio's trade organization, adopted a code of ethics that virtually knocked labor off the air.

Part 2 focuses on labor's struggle to reform radio during World War II and the immediate postwar years. The war enabled business to more effectively use public relations in its effort to regain the confidence of the American people, and radio played a prominent role in this propaganda effort. Goodwill programs emphasizing business contributions to the war effort enhanced corporate prestige, while business-sponsored news commentators fueled public hostility towards organized labor. Barred from buying radio time from the networks and many local stations, unions had difficulty counteracting this corporate campaign. During the war, the AFL and CIO denounced media attacks on labor's patriotism, but until 1944 the AFL remained relatively complacent about radio's restrictions on labor. An outraged and contentious CIO, however, conducted a multipronged campaign to open the airwaves to labor that succeeded in eliminating the NAB code in August 1945.

The union voice in broadcasting was not entirely silent during the war. Some local stations ignored the prohibitions against selling time to labor. Even the major networks felt a growing pressure to diversify the viewpoints represented on the air. In 1942, in an effort to assuage the flood of union complaints over commentators' attacks on organized labor, NBC offered the AFL and CIO a regular program to focus on labor's contribution to the war effort. "Labor for Victory" was a milestone production that briefly provided unions with a national platform. It also marked labor's first use of professional writers and entertainers in union productions.

In the postwar years, the CIO joined a loose alliance of leftist media reformers associated with organizations such as the Voice of Freedom and the National Citizens Political Action Committee. They fought for diversity in ownership of stations and for locally produced programming. Early postwar battles involved defending radio's political diversity, as the rising tide of the cold war swept liberal and leftist commentators off the airwaves. Worried about corporate monopoly control of broadcasting, reformers also fought for a democratic allocation of FM licenses. Envisioning FM as a second chance to create a democratic and diverse broadcasting medium, they urged the FCC to grant only a quarter of FM channels to existing broadcasting stations and newspapers and the rest to local veteran, farm, cooperative, labor, and other nonprofit groups.

The CIO's involvement in media reform was underpinned by a belief in the concept of "listeners' rights."[12] The CIO argued that the people's ownership of the airwaves gives the public the right to hear a diversity of voices and balanced coverage of controversial issues. CIO unionists became involved in the regulatory process, seeking to intervene in licensing hearings to ensure labor access to broadcasting and greater community control over radio. For a brief period in the mid-1940s, pressured by the CIO and other reformers, the FCC encouraged public participation in the workings of the regulatory system. This was a major, if short-lived, shift in policy. It would be twenty years before the FCC, under pressure from the civil rights movement, would again allow significant citizenship participation in licensing decisions. The course initially charted by the CIO resulted in a burst of citizenship involvement in broadcasting and greater community control over the media in the 1970s.[13]

The final part of the book explores the continuing competition over the air between labor and business in the postwar era. Radio was an important tool in the corporate postwar campaign to undermine organized labor and liberalism and to fully restore its power and prestige. Organized labor challenged the growing business domination of political discourse through its ownership of FM stations and by increasing its presence on network and local AM radio. In 1949, the UAW and the International Ladies Garment Workers Union (ILGWU) launched labor stations in Detroit, Cleveland, Chattanooga, Los Angeles, and New York City. Labor hoped that these stations would serve as a model for a new kind of socially progressive, nonprofit, community-oriented broadcasting. The union experiment with FM, however, was short-lived, and by the end of 1952 all of labor's FM stations were off the air.

Unions were not discouraged, however. After World War II, unions spoke directly to the public with ever greater volume, as labor developed a significant local and national media presence. Unions continued to experiment with embedding the labor message in entertainment and borrowed from the emerging disc-jockey genre, developing programs that mixed labor news with music. Ultimately, however, they settled on old-fashioned, straightforward talk to advance labor's ideology. Unions sponsored their own public-affairs programs, and the labor leaders who appeared on these news shows were familiar to postwar listeners. Borrowing a page from the corporate media strategy, the AFL and CIO also began sponsoring radio commentators who provided liberal voices in a media that catered to conservatives. In the increasingly conservative political atmosphere of postwar America, radio enabled labor to provide an important alternative political perspective that helped nurture unionism and liberalism against a furious business assault. By the 1960s, however, the union voice in the media began to fade, leaving a labor movement unprotected from an increasingly unfettered corporate media that is hostile to workers and their institutions.

PART 1

Labor and Business Broadcasting in the Thirties

1   Putting Class on the Air: Initial Forays into Labor and Business Broadcasting

IN THE DECADE before the Great Depression, radio burst onto the American scene and rapidly became one of the most important avenues of communication. Radio's popularity with the working class encouraged a few forward-thinking individuals in the labor movement to use this exciting new medium to reach a working-class audience. By the end of the 1920s, the trade-union movement had one small radio station in Chicago and close ties with the low-powered Socialist station in New York City. In addition, the American Federation of Labor sponsored several short series of educational programs that were broadcast on the major networks. Beyond these ventures, however, labor's use of radio was fairly limited, in large part because the conservative leadership of the AFL eschewed mass-mobilization tactics and was unable to envision radio as a tool that might influence the economic and political ideas of the American public.

The business community quickly embraced radio's commercial possibilities, but initially it too showed little interest in the power of radio to promote its ideological interests. Corporate America reigned supreme through the 1920s, making concerted use of radio to promote a business agenda seem superfluous. Not until the depths of the Depression jolted the nation's confidence in American capitalism did corporations begin to experiment with radio as a pubic relations tool capable of restoring the credibility of individual companies and, more importantly, shaping public thinking about pressing economic and social questions. In the 1930s, the business community made radio into an important weapon for deflecting criticism from organized labor and keeping at bay a more intrusive federal government.

❖ ❖ ❖

Radio was the most significant leisure-time innovation of the 1920s. Combined with movies, mass-circulation magazines, telephones, automobiles, and chain stores, radio helped propel America into a modern era that emphasized leisure, consumption, and amusement. As the newest instrument of the mass media, radio promoted a "new national self-awareness," which made Americans conscious of themselves as living through a period of vast change. At the same time, it helped forge the consumer culture that exists today. In many ways, radio epitomized this new consumer culture. Entrepreneurs quickly linked radio to advertising, encouraging workers to find satisfaction through consumption and individual self-fulfillment rather than in their labor and their communities. Moreover, the emergence of national networks in the late 1920s helped strengthen radio's power as a homogenizing force. As Lizabeth Cohen has shown, however, workers were not passive recipients of commercialized culture. Because radio had strong local elements, workers helped shape as well as partake of this exciting conveyor of mass culture.[1]

Radio was initially very much a local phenomenon. During the early part of the twentieth century, thousands of radio enthusiasts, mostly young men and boys, operated amateur transmitting stations. These early experiments in broadcasting came to a halt during World War I, when the government ordered the amateurs to shut down. After the war, commercial interests, department stores, newspapers, electrical manufacturers, and even a laundry discovered broadcasting. In November 1920, Westinghouse Electric Company's experimental station in Pittsburgh, KDKA, began transmitting from the top of the firm's factory—the first station to broadcast regularly scheduled programs. The following year, along with twenty-five other stations, it received a license from the Department of Commerce. By 1923 there were 556 mostly small stations on the air, many operated by companies seeking to sell their products. Almost a third of these early stations, however, were owned by churches, universities, and other groups interested in public service.[2]

As Susan J. Douglas observes, early radio programming was "locally produced for local audiences," and it reflected the concerns and talents of local listeners: informational talks, lots of music, local church services, and vaudeville-type entertainment performed by hometown talent. Much of this programming, provided by ethnic, religious, and labor groups, was nonprofit and community-oriented. In urban areas, stations carried "nationality hours" aimed at the largest ethnic groups in the city. Rural stations broadcast vital weather reports, and stations in southern mill towns promoted the talent of local string bands, many of whom were comprised of mill workers. Although offerings were typically unpolished, many listeners enjoyed hearing the voices of local performers. Hearing their own language or their own music helped strengthen and legitimize listeners' sense of ethnic or group identity.[3]

Once businesses realized that there were profits to be made in radio advertising, the medium became increasingly commercialized and nationalized. By the end of the decade, two major commercial networks—the National Broadcasting Company and the Columbia Broadcasting System—had begun operations. Shows produced in New York City and transmitted throughout the nation supplanted local programming. Government regulation accelerated this trend. The Radio Act of 1927 required stations to operate in the "public interest, convenience, or necessity" and established the Federal Radio Commission (FRC) to bring order to the airwaves. The new regulatory commission, which was dominated by commercial broadcasters, argued that nonprofit groups were more likely to spread propaganda. It decided that the public interest would best be served by commercial broadcasters, and it allocated frequencies and power assignments in a way that forced most educational and nonprofit broadcasters off the air. Still, during the 1920s and early 1930s, there was no clear mandate for commercial broadcasting. Reformers advocated a nonprofit and noncommercial model controlled by the public. Mindful of the unease over commercialization of the airwaves, the networks stressed their commitment to public service and trumpeted their cultural and educational programming. This public service programming featured elements of high culture, such as classical music broadcasts and educational talks, including occasional speeches by labor leaders.[4]

After the ascendancy of the networks, when families gathered for the evening around the radio, their listening experience likely differed from the pre-network days. Most often they tuned in to stations affiliated with one of the national networks. Many communities still had small, usually low-powered, non-network stations, but their low-budget offerings had difficulty competing with the elaborate network productions. The staple of network broadcasting shifted from music to comic and dramatic serial narratives such as "The Rise of the Goldbergs," "Amos 'n' Andy," and "Fibber Mc-Gee and Molly." Big-name variety shows such as "The Fleischmann's Yeast Hour" with Rudy Vallee and "The Kraft Music Hall" with Al Jolson and Bing Crosby also attracted large audiences. This format mixed vaudeville humor with concert-hall or nightclub performances. Daytime network broadcasting targeted women and children. By 1936, half of the daytime schedule was

devoted to soap operas, with their complicated stories of intrigue, romance, and betrayal. The 1930s also saw the development of broadcast journalism. Particularly in the latter part of the decade, as tensions heated up in Europe, Americans learned to tune in to the networks for news commentary that brought the world into their living rooms.[5]

First local broadcasting and then network radio caught the imagination of the American public. In 1922, when only 2 percent of households had radio receivers, the *New York Times* observed that "radio phoning has become the most popular amusement in America." The size of the radio audience grew at a phenomenal pace, and radio became an integral part of daily life. By 1930 almost half of American homes had radio receivers, and a survey conducted the previous year found that 80 percent of those who owned a radio listened daily. The Depression proved no detriment to the diffusion of radio. In the early 1930s, set prices dropped dramatically to an average of thirty-four dollars. The 1940 census revealed that radio reached almost 83 percent of American families. With the average listener tuning in for over four hours each day, radio listening was America's favorite pastime.[6]

Many of these listeners were workers. During the 1930s, half of the poorest Americans owned sets. Group listening was common in the pre–World War II era, so even those without receivers often had access to programming. Market research showed that radio particularly appealed to the working class. Lower-income families, for instance, were more likely to listen than those at higher income levels. While radio-ownership levels were highest in the industrial states of the East and Midwest and lower in the South, the historian Jacquelyn Hall found that southern mill workers also were devoted to their favorite shows. In 1930, for instance, textile workers in Gastonia, North Carolina, asked their employer to start the workday earlier so they could be home in time to listen to "Amos 'n' Andy." One textile worker, Ralph Latta, recalled that it was impossible to avoid hearing the show in working-class neighborhoods. "'If it was summertime, or a lot of times in wintertime, because people played their radios pretty loud, I could listen to that all the way. They said that the world was nearer at a standstill during that thirty minutes than any other thirty minutes during the twenty-four hours.'" The historian Richard Butsch writes that destitute families during the Depression, who were forced to sell the radio that had helped make life more bearable during these harsh times, described the loss of this prized possession "as a considerable hardship."[7]

❖ ❖ ❖

During the 1920s and early 1930s, intrigued by radio's potential and aware of its powerful appeal to workers, some unionists began urging the labor movement to explore this new medium. Radio offered labor the opportunity to bypass the more established commercial mass media. Unions already had a long list of grievances against the mass media of the 1920s. They charged, for instance, that the commercial press was dominated by big business and paid little attention to workers or unions except during labor strife, which newspapers routinely misrepresented or condemned. Movie treatment of unions was hardly more favorable. As Steven Ross recounts, ideologically conservative films attacked organized labor and radicals, while liberal films were often sympathetic to individual workers but treated collective action with skepticism.[8]

Radio had the potential to shape public opinion and was not yet under complete corporate control. Unionists hoped it might combat anti-union propaganda while improving the image of organized labor and advancing the causes of social justice and economic democracy. To members of the International Brotherhood of Electrical Workers, radio had become the "unrivaled master of human destiny," overshadowing and "outreaching all other means of communication." The electrical workers predicted that whoever controlled radio would control the nation. Comparing radio to the "air we breathe, or the sunlight that gives us life," they argued that it "must be charged with a public trust" and that no corporation should be permitted to appropriate broadcasting.[9]

Much of the impetus for labor's foray into radio came from unionists who had supported the production of worker-made films in the 1910s. These films mixed entertainment with radical politics and helped give a voice to workers' "desires, dreams, and discontents" while humanizing the image of unionists and radicals. Challenging the dominant conservative discourse of most commercial movies, worker-made films emphasized that strikes and class conflict are the result of employer exploitation of ordinary Americans. Working-class audiences cheered for radicals, strikers, and union leaders on screen, and some workers were inspired to become active in the labor movement. Appalled at the powerful reaction to these movies, state and local government censors fought to keep worker films out of the theaters. Censorship, the rise of the studio system, and the arrival of the talkies, which were much more expensive to make, helped destroy the worker-film movement in the 1920s.[10]

Despite these impediments, some unionists still hoped to use the mass media to present a working-class perspective. Periodically during the 1920s, they introduced resolutions at the AFL's annual conventions proposing that the federation revitalize labor-film making by opening a studio and establishing a chain of labor-owned movie theaters. Other resolutions urged the federation to apply for a license to operate a national labor radio station at the AFL headquarters in Washington, D.C. Concerned about corporate monopolization of radio, unionists also called for sweeping reform of the broadcasting system, including nationalization of the industry, to protect freedom of the air.[11]

AFL leaders repeatedly rejected all these proposals as too costly. Believing that the commercial broadcasting system could effectively serve labor's interests, they encouraged local unions to use existing radio stations. Relatively few local unions actually took up the suggestion. In late 1925, the AFL Executive Council surveyed central labor bodies across the nation; four reported that they had sponsored programs, and others thought that they might be able to obtain airtime. Four years later, unionists in at least six cities (Memphis; Rochester, New York; Kenosha, Wisconsin; Topeka, Kansas; Philadelphia; and Baltimore) broadcast weekly programs at different points during the year. In addition to the occasional local program, the networks sometimes made time available for speeches by labor leaders, especially on Labor Day.[12]

The AFL leadership in the 1920s had little interest in challenging corporate America's power either in broadcasting or in the workplace. William Green, a former United Mine Workers official, had become president of the AFL in 1924 upon the death of Samuel Gompers. A decent, capable, and deeply religious man, he was also conservative and unimaginative. Under his leadership, the AFL responded to employers' aggressive anti-union drives by abandoning independent political action and militancy in favor of union-management cooperation. Green's interest in cooperating with corporate America extended to the broadcasting industry, and he gave little encouragement to unionists seeking to reform radio.[13]

On the whole, during the early years of radio, the AFL and most of its affiliates made relatively limited use of broadcasting and had a narrow view of how to use the medium. In particular, using the airwaves to organize had little appeal to Green or most AFL leaders. The goal of the craft unions that dominated the federation was to control craft labor markets, and the mechanisms they used typically were exclusive and restrictive. Many workers automatically became union members through apprenticeship or hiring halls; craft union leaders thus had little desire to engage in the mass-organizing campaigns that came to be associated with industrial unionism of the 1930s. In 1940, the AFL's publicity director, Phillip Pearl, asserted that the AFL was not interested in using radio to organize workers because radio appealed to the emotions, and "union membership was a practical life-time affair."[14]

Labor traditionalists primarily thought of radio as an educational vehicle, either for promoting the union label or improving the public image of organized labor as a respectable institution. In 1929 the AFL Executive Council anticipated that radio programs "would add to Labor's standing in the community [and] would get wider understanding of trade union ideals and purposes." The historians Michael Kazin and Steven Ross have suggested that labor speakers during the 1920s portrayed themselves as "representatives of the general public and defenders of the American way of life." Reflecting the AFL's defensive, craft-oriented posture, broadcasts avoided discussion of strikes or labor conflict, focusing instead on how skilled production makes possible the shorter workday, the link between high wages and efficiency, and organized labor's contribution to the economic, spiritual, and intellectual growth of the nation.[15]

"Labor Speaks for Itself," a series of network programs developed by the AFL and its education arm, the Workers Education Bureau, reflected the federation's view of radio as primarily educational. In 1932 and again in 1934, CBS donated airtime for a series of ten half-hour labor addresses. Prominent labor leaders presented the story of the growth and development of the AFL and explained the federation's position on major social and economic issues, including the closed shop, technological unemployment, collective bargaining, and the relationship between unions and minorities. CBS again donated time in the fall of 1935 for ten educational Friday-evening broadcasts. Each program consisted of a dialogue between a labor leader and a man in overalls to give the rank-and-file point of view on topics such as labor standards, economic security, the role of the AFL, and dictatorship and democracy. Between 1938 and 1940, the Workers Education Bureau broadcast on CBS a weekly series entitled "Americans at Work," which sought to present in a vivid manner the "dignity of labor" and the continuing importance of skill in industrial work. Originating from the job site, each program described one occupation, ranging from sandhog (tunnel worker) to longshoreman to beautician. An announcer interviewed a worker or groups of workers with the sounds of the workplace in the background. The Workers Education Bureau boasted that millions listened each week and that "Americans at Work" was one of the most popular educational programs in the nation.[16]

A few local trade unionists and independent radicals had a more ambitious vision for the future of labor and radio than that of the AFL. Not content to rely on the small bits of airtime made available by the networks and local commercial stations, they proposed to challenge the emerging corporate-dominated broadcasting system. Labor, progressive, and radical leaders in Chicago and New York established their own stations. In 1926, the Chicago Federation of Labor founded WCFL as a "non-profit, listener-supported station, dedicated to serving the interests of workers and their communities." For most if its fifty years on the air, it was the only labor-owned station in the nation. Under the leadership of CFL secretary Edward Nockels, WCFL joined the battle to save broadcasting from monopolistic control. It challenged the Federal Radio Commission's 1927 decision that large commercial stations, rather than the more numerous smaller stations operated by nonprofit religious, labor, educational, or community groups, best served the public interest.

Even before taking on the FRC, Nockels had a reputation as a radical reformer. An electrical worker by trade, he became the CFL secretary in 1903. With CFL president John Fitzpatrick, he challenged the top-down, craft orientation of the AFL by aggressively seeking to organize unskilled workers, empower local union organizations, and promote independent political action. Living in a city with some of the most rabidly antilabor newspapers in the nation, CFL leaders understood the importance of the press in shaping public attitudes. During World War I, Nockels and Fitzpatrick began crafting a media strategy to offset the pro-business propaganda of the Chicago press. In 1919 they began publishing the *New Majority* and helped form the Federated Press, a labor news service.

Nockels fought the FRC in the courts and in Congress not only because WCFL's broadcasting hours and power were restricted by the 1927 decision but because he believed it would result in an increasingly undemocratic broadcasting system. Nockels received minimal assistance from the AFL in this battle. Seeking to win acceptance from business as a responsible institution, the federation refused to actively support WCFL's campaign for broadcast reform for fear of offending commercial broadcasters, who donated time for labor speeches and programs such as "Labor Speaks for Itself" and "Americans at Work."[17]

Severe financial pressures complicated WCFL's struggle for survival in a hostile political climate. Initially, WCFL operated as a noncommercial, listener-supported station. Seeking to attract working-class audiences, the station regularly integrated labor messages into entertainment shows such as musical programs, vaudeville, and sports and foreign language programs.

In its early years, however, the station's primary commitment was to serving labor. It provided open access to WCFL's facilities to the entire labor movement as well as to groups advancing progressive issues. During times of labor conflict, such as strikes, boycotts, and lockouts, the station gave unions free airtime to communicate with workers. In March 1928, for instance, WCFL broadcast a major benefit to aid striking coal miners that featured music, dramatic sketches, and a talk by John Fitzpatrick. Three years later, the station provided critical support to the Moving Picture Operators' Union strike against Chicago theaters. Irate theater owners threatened to seek an injunction to stop WCFL attacks on scab operators. During non-crisis periods, most of WCFL's labor programs focused on educating the public and non-union workers on the functions and benefits of the labor movement; this programming mainly consisted of talks by local labor leaders. While most of the time was provided free of charge, increasingly the station encouraged unions to sponsor entertainment programs, with commercials promoting organized labor. In the late 1920s, about 8 percent of the station's airtime went to labor, agricultural, civic, and educational programs. Though a small portion of the total airtime, as WCFL's historian Nathan Godfried has observed, "this programming served a vital function within Chicago's progressive and working-class communities."[18]

Despite its vital contribution to the Chicago labor movement, local unions were apathetic toward WCFL, rarely making use of its services and providing little financial support. As a result, the station's financial situation was always precarious. Within a decade of its founding, it had become commercialized, dependent upon advertising, and linked to a major network (first NBC and later ABC). Subsequent years saw increasing tension between labor progressives, who wanted WCFL to serve as an oppositional voice promoting working-class consciousness, and business unionists, who had a much more limited vision of labor radio.[19]

In 1927, WEVD went on the air in New York City. The Socialist party erected the station as a "living memorial to Eugene V. Debs," the Socialist leader who had recently died. The desire to offer a forum for liberal, progressive, and labor groups as well as the refusal of several stations to broadcast speeches by Norman Thomas, the new Socialist party leader, led the party to apply for a station license. While labor had no institutional connection to WEVD, garment unions, especially the ILGWU, provided critical financial support. Prominent trade unionists, including Sidney Hillman, James H. Maurer, Max S. Hayes, and A. Phillip Randolph, served on the station's Board of Trustees. Like WCFL, WEVD suffered from severe financial problems and poor power, frequency, and time allotments. It had only a few of the most desirable evening hours, since it was forced to share its wavelength and broadcast time with several other small stations. In 1931, with its license in jeopardy, WEVD turned to the *Jewish Daily Forward* for assistance. The Yiddish newspaper provided the necessary infusion of financial resources to ensure the station's survival and assumed management of station operations.[20]

WEVD was committed to enabling "representatives of the dissident minority viewpoints to broadcast their messages of Hope and Progress." Its programming emphasized diversity, advocating the interests of labor and social reform and promoting the Socialist message. In the 1920s, programs included a "Jewish Hour," a "Negro Art Group" program, and a weekly "Pullman Porter's Hour" featuring "Negro singers and musicians" and talks on the union's "fight for the living wage." WEVD's program "Labor Looks at the Week," featuring the well-known labor journalist McAlister Coleman, offered talks on labor conditions and eyewitness accounts of the 1928 Colorado coal strike. The station championed the strikers' cause by urging listeners to provide financial support to the miners. The Federated Press sponsored a weekly news show in 1929. To promote workers' education, the station offered a series of evening educational courses on economic problems hosted by A. J. Muste and a weekly program produced by the Rand School, an adult education institution founded by the Socialist party.[21]

Unionists in the late 1920s were only beginning to explore the "promise of labor radio." During the Depression decade, the labor movement, the business community, and other elements of American society came to appreciate the power of radio to shape political ideas and invigorate emerging social movements. Most notably, as Lawrence W. Levine observes, Franklin Roosevelt, Father Charles Coughlin, and the fiery Louisiana politician Huey Long used radio to promote their political agendas and "to build communities of followers." Radio provided these speakers direct access to a national audience. Roosevelt used radio more effectively than any previous politician, speaking directly to American citizens in their own homes to build support for the New Deal. Similarly, radio helped Roosevelt's critics such as Coughlin and Long to create their own personality cults and to publicize their plans for reforming the American economy. Coughlin had one of the largest radio audiences in the 1930s, and Long's broadcasts often drew more than a hundred thousand letters of support. By late 1935, broadcasting had enabled Coughlin

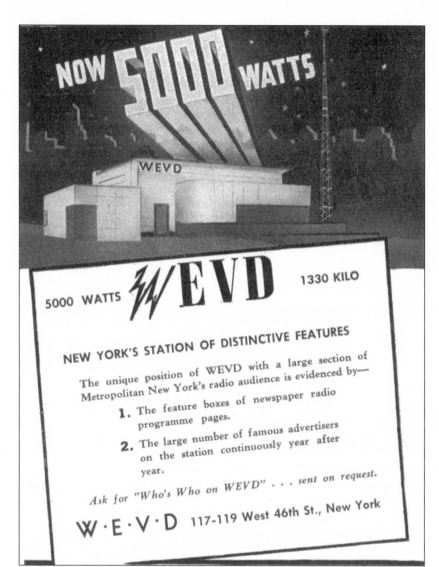

WEVD served as a forum for liberal, progressive, and labor groups in New York City. Reprinted from *Broadcasting Magazine*.

and Long to gain so much national popularity that for a brief period they seemed capable of jeopardizing Roosevelt's reelection in 1936.[22]

Taking their cue from Roosevelt, Coughlin, and Long, business leaders recognized that they too could use radio to sell not only their products but also their ideology and their company's image. They had long been aware of the importance of projecting a positive image to the public. During the early part of the twentieth century, in the face of growing hostility toward business and demands for greater state regulation, firms turned to public relations to improve their reputation. They began hiring press agents and engaged in a host of image-building initiatives, from welfare capitalism and institutional advertising to factory tours and elaborate exhibits at World's Fairs and exhibitions. These campaigns often had multiple goals. Many targeted employees as well as the public, seeking not only to shape political opinion but also to promote good morale within the company. By the end of World War I, companies such as AT&T, Swift, Bethlehem Steel, and Du Pont and business organizations such as the National Association of Manufacturers (NAM) had established public relations programs. Their efforts not only deflected Progressive-era attacks against corporations, they enhanced public esteem for business enterprise in the prosperous 1920s. By the end of that decade, the executives of many large national firms believed that they had achieved for business the status of a respected "national institution."[23]

The economic collapse of the 1930s, however, shook the nation's faith in corporate America. As Eric Foner observes, the Depression "discredited the idea that social progress rested on the unrestrained pursuit of wealth." Massive unemployment, strikes, violence, and open class conflict, combined with the failure of the nation's financial and banking systems, sparked demands for far-reaching economic and social change. American workers turned away from their employers and looked to the state and organized labor to provide for their welfare. While Roosevelt's New Deal placed new and, to many employers, alarming constraints on business, millions of workers flooded into unions. Particularly appealing were the calls from the newly formed Congress of Industrial Organizations for industrial democracy and economic security for the working class.[24]

This invigorated working class threatened business dominance not only in politics and the workplace but also within the realm of culture. In the 1930s, working-class Americans had increasing influence on mass culture and the arts. This new plebeian sensibility infused proletarian literature, the New Deal arts programs, blues and folk music, popular musical theater, and even Hollywood films. Movies increasingly cast businessmen as villains, and the common people triumphed over the rich and powerful. Individualism often resulted in economic chaos, not progress. Comics in the early 1930s, such as the Marx Brothers, Will Rogers, and W. C. Fields, "humorously attacked the pretensions of the rich and status symbols" and subtly questioned the new consumer culture that was celebrated by business in the 1920s.[25]

Faced with these threats to corporate power, public relations advocates advised businesses that they must "sell the American way of life to the American people." Business needed to restore public faith in its leadership and promote the corporate vision of the American way, which emphasized freedom, individualism, and harmony between employer and employee. As the renowned advertising expert Bruce Barton put it in a 1935 speech before the NAM, it was imperative for industry to "'regain its rightful position of social and political leadership lost to the New Deal.'" Companies began to pour resources into aggressively carrying their message to the American people. They revitalized employee magazines, conducted institutional advertising campaigns, produced films, and staged fairs and industrial exhibitions designed to foster "the confidence, respect, and goodwill of the public." As Roland Marchand observed, "[N]ever before had big business reached out so ardently to the common man and invited him into its confidence."[26]

Reaching out to the common man increasingly involved the use of a new medium, radio. As the Depression deepened and public hostility toward business intensified, networks encouraged companies to use radio as a public relations tool. Exploiting fears about the future of the free enterprise system, NBC urged industry to "'campaign for public favor as never before.'" It advised, "'Get your story across through the greatest force the world has ever known for influencing lives and thoughts—Radio.'" According to the networks, radio had special advantages over the printed word. David Sarnoff, the head of RCA, argued that radio is "'personalized and intimate, man-to-man, friend-to-friend, as no message through any other channel except personal communication can be.'"[27] Opinion polls of the late 1930s reinforced the networks' sales pitch. A *Fortune* magazine survey found that radio had higher credibility among Americans than the press. Radio commentators such as H. V. Kaltenborn, Boake Carter, Lowell Thomas, and Elmer Davis were more respected than newspaper editors and columnists. Paul Lazarfeld's study of the media preferences of more than five thousand Americans concluded that radio provided a "'feeling of personal touch with the world'" and that listeners felt that radio personalities "'spoke directly to them.'"[28]

A number of major firms began sponsoring nationally broadcast programs with institutional rather than commercial messages. General Motors,

Ford, Chase National Bank, Armco, Du Pont, Texaco, and Firestone underwrote prestigious classical music programs and serious dramas. Employers believed that this type of programming provided the dignified atmosphere necessary to accompany institutional messages. Alternatively, Wheeling Steel's show, aimed at both the company's workers and the general public, featured the amateur talent of the company's ten thousand employees and their families.[29]

Institutional advertising aimed to create a positive corporate image, while advocacy advertising attempted to shape public policy. Assuming that public hostility toward industry was based on a lack of knowledge, companies used their programs to present information about their labor policies, safety record, and support for charities. In an "informative and confidential fashion," General Motors spokesmen mixed discussion of the technical problems of automobile construction and driving safety with occasional remarks on wage levels and the benefits of the American economic system. Wheeling Steel's folksy "Musical Steelmakers" began each program with Old Timer, the master of ceremonies, telling "authentic stories on the daily drama of making steel." In an industry beset with labor troubles, the primary goal of advertising manager J. L. Grimes was to convince people "from coast to coast that here is a large corporation that is human."[30]

Du Pont had special reasons for sponsoring "Cavalcade of America," which began in 1935. It had been tagged with a "merchant of death image" when the Senate investigated munitions profits in the early 1930s. The Du Pont family also worried about the influence of the "many strange and bewildering doctrines" that were gaining public support during the Depression. They believed that the New Deal and the increasingly militant labor movement were destroying the freedoms associated with the American economic system. Through its historical drama series, the Du Pont company sought to refurbish its image while taking subtle shots at the New Deal. The radio program reminded the public of the "origins of our unique freedom through dramatic stories of the men and women who won it, of those who fought to hold it." Designed to be inspirational, it focused on the lives of such prominent Americans as Thomas Jefferson, Daniel Boone, Robert E. Lee, Tom Paine, and Roger Williams. The show's commercials emphasized the contributions of the company's products to American society. Each episode concluded with the slogan, "Better Things for Better Living through Chemistry."[31]

The company carefully crafted the program to enhance its legitimacy. Generously financed, "Cavalcade" attracted well-known actors and such talented writers as Arthur Miller. To ensure historical accuracy, Du Pont enlisted the Yale historian Frank Monaghan to review the scripts. The company vigorously promoted the program among educators and other opinion leaders, distributing tens of thousands of promotional pamphlets to teachers and hosting dinners for state superintendents of education.[32]

Like the Du Ponts, Henry Ford was appalled at the economic reforms of the New Deal. Ford battled with the Roosevelt administration over the efforts of the National Recovery Administration (NRA) to regulate the auto industry and later ignored the provisions of the National Labor Relations Act. His company's violent reaction to workers' efforts to organize prevented the unionization of the Ford plants until 1941.[33] The "Ford Sunday Evening Hour" began broadcasting in October 1934 over the CBS radio network. At a cost of more than a million dollars a year, it gave Henry Ford a public platform from which to defend his firm and share his economic philosophy with the American public. The program offered classical music with ten-minute intermission talks by William J. Cameron, Ford's director of public relations. Although not a top-ranked show in its time slot, it was among the most popular concert programs of the 1930s, with an audience of more than ten million. Tens of thousands of Americans wrote the company asking for copies of Cameron's speeches, and forty-five million were distributed over the years. To one listener, Nora Huey, the talks were the "warp and woof of American life." She believed that they served as "a steadying influence amidst the clamor of shortsighted demagoguery."[34]

Cameron's talks were never strident. He assured his audience that the Ford Company had "no political axe to grind" and "no theories to propagate." Striving to be the voice of "sweet reasonableness," he charmed his listeners with regular tributes to America, its institutions, its history, and its holidays. The virtues of Mother's Day, for instance, were rarely overlooked. Cameron's primary goal was to create a favorable impression of the company and its founder. His talks were filled with stories about Henry Ford's ingenuity, compassion, and good business sense. Cameron described how much Ford cares for his employees, pointing to the hiring of disabled and older workers and emphasizing Ford's commitment to boosting wages.[35] Dismissing "alluring schemes" for "sharing the wealth," Cameron ardently defended free enterprise and the existing distribution of wealth. He argued that business, not government, was the key to recovery and criticized the NRA, relief programs, unemployment insurance, and increased taxation.[36] On December 30, 1934, as Federal Emergency Relief Administration checks helped millions of Americans escape starvation, Cameron warned listeners that "the more heavily we lean on government for support, the more heavily government must lean on us." Ford's spokesman never explicitly attacked the autoworkers' union or its leader, but he condemned strikes and asserted that employers are the true labor leaders. According to Cameron, history shows that "every improvement in industrial conditions, every advance in industrial justice," originates with management.[37]

While Ford and Du Pont may have contended that they were simply seeking goodwill for their firms, other business programming was overtly political. From 1934 to 1936, the Crusaders, an organization of conservative business leaders that opposed "all forces destructive to sound government," went on the air with a weekly program broadcast over seventy-nine CBS stations. With financial backing from executives of General Foods, Du Pont, General Motors, Nabisco, Heinz, Sun Oil, Weirton Steel, and Standard Oil of Indiana, "The Radio Voice of the Crusaders" defended American industry and excoriated the New Deal and its regulatory agencies.[38] The entertainment-industry journal *Variety* described the Crusaders program as "sugary propaganda" that asked listeners to "rebel against a dictatorship in the U.S." The Crusaders' national commander, Fred G. Clark, dismissed the problem of unemployment as simply "a state of mind." To solve the nation's problems, he called for his audience to participate in a spiritual revival and to fight for constitutional liberty, individualism, patriotism, and limited government.[39]

The NAM's radio series, "The American Family Robinson," fought the New Deal and organized labor in a more subtle fashion. The NAM generally used this program, which first aired in the fall of 1934, to teach economic lessons and to argue that Roosevelt's social policies were utopian and disruptive. Within six months, "The American Family Robinson" was being broadcast on 207 stations. By the late 1930s, almost three hundred non-network stations carried the program. The NAM paid production costs, and either local employers bought airtime or stations provided it for free.[40] The most expensive item in its public relations budget, the program was an important element of the NAM's campaign to restore America's faith in business—not government—leadership. According to the NAM's public relations director, James P. Selvage, the program was "industry's effective answer to the Utopian promises of theorists and demagogues at present reaching such vast audiences via the radio."[41]

The fifteen-minute program focused on the trials and tribulations of the Robinson family in the small manufacturing city of Centerville. Like the rest of America, Centerville felt the impact of the Depression: its citizens suffer from unemployment, labor unrest is rampant, workers blame their employers for wrecking the economy, and ideologues peddle economic panaceas that

Meet . . .

THE AMERICAN FAMILY ROBINSON

Luke and Myra Robinson (center) chat with neighbors

and introduce them to
YOUR AUDIENCE

- The oldest transcribed show on the air.
- Heard over more than 250 stations.
- Two 15 minute spots weekly.

Emphasizing
The Fundamentals of
THE AMERICAN WAY OF LIFE

Between 1934 and 1939, the National Association of Manufacturers sponsored the radio series "American Family Robinson," which was broadcast over three hundred stations. Courtesy of Hagley Museum and Library.

promise government-guaranteed security. In the first series of episodes, Luke Robinson, the "philosophical and kindly" editor of the *Centerville Herald,* defends his friend Dave Markham, whose local furniture factory is on the verge of closing because of exaggerated charges of unsafe conditions and ex- ploitation of workers. Meanwhile, Luke's daughter Betty finds her romance with a reporter, Bob Collins, jeopardized by his support for the "Friends of the Downtrodden." This radical group of agitators has been creating dis- sension among Markham's workers in an effort to organize Centerville's industry on "a communal basis." Through several episodes, the audience was left in suspense over the future of capitalism in Centerville and over the future of Betty's relationship with Bob. Luke Robinson defends Markham by demonstrating that the plant had been running for three years at a loss and that conditions had deteriorated when a government agency, presumably the NRA, forced him to increase pay and shorten hours. He also reminds the workers of Markham's many contributions to the welfare of the commu- nity. By the end of the first series of episodes, the ringleader of the Friends, a Mr. Margolies, flees after being unmasked as a professional "trouble-mak- ing agitator" from Buffalo who is wanted by the police. Harmony restored, Centerville's workers and Bob Collins regain confidence in the community's business leaders. Moreover, they learn that the "welfare of the town—the nation too—is tied up with the success of private enterprise." Just as things return to normal, however, another "mysterious stranger" arrives in town to threaten the industrial security of Centerville.[42]

In addition to creating their own dramatic or musical programs, the NAM and a number of individual firms also attempted to influence public opinion through the sponsorship of radio commentators. Radio news commentary became popular during the 1930s and expanded even further during World War II. Commentators were hired by the networks, local stations, or com- mercial sponsors. While many firms shied away from controversial commen- tators for fear of offending potential customers, businesses sponsored some of the most conservative commentators of the era, including Boake Carter, George E. Sokolsky, Fulton Lewis Jr., Upton Close, and H. V. Kaltenborn.[43]

In 1933, the newspaper writer Boake Carter signed a contract with Philco to broadcast a daily news commentary over CBS. This was one of the earliest commercially sponsored news broadcasts. Sporting an English accent and a pretentious manner, Carter's newscasts were "a mix of fact, opinion, fancy, and purple prose," but he fascinated Americans. With an audience of over five million, he was one of the most popular commentators of the era. Car- ter became a powerful critic of the Roosevelt administration and organized labor. In his broadcasts and daily newspaper columns, Carter attacked the CIO relentlessly, calling John L. Lewis a dictator and comparing strikes in the auto and steel industries to the strikes in Italy that led to the rise of Mussolini. In June 1937, for instance, he asserted that under Lewis's leadership the CIO had instituted a "reign of terror" against law-abiding American citizens and that the federal government refused to intervene against the sit-down strikers because the United Mine Workers had donated fifty thousand dollars to the Democratic party.[44]

During the latter part of the decade, other commentators joined Carter in the assault on labor and the New Deal. The author, lecturer, and industrial consultant George Sokolsky was described by *Time* magazine as a "one-man intellectual front for conservative capital." Sponsored by the NAM but also on the payroll of the American Iron and Steel Institute, Sokolsky charged in his weekly broadcasts that the unions were dominated by racketeers. He played a major role in the steel industry's multifaceted campaign to derail unionization following the formation of the Steelworkers Organizing Committee (SWOC) in June 1936.[45] In 1937, Fulton Lewis Jr. began a more than two-decade run on radio, delivering his commentary five times a week in the early evening over the Mutual Network. Lewis came from an upper-class Washington, D.C., family and worked for a Hearst newspaper before breaking into radio. The NAM paid for some of his earlier broadcasts, but during most of his years on the air Lewis was sponsored by a variety of local businesses. Although technically independent of the NAM, his commentary closely meshed with that organization's conservative, anti-union ideology. He quickly gained a reputation as the "blabber-mouthed mouthpiece of un-bridled Big Business" and the "worst anti-labor hate-peddler alive." Lewis regularly defended individual enterprise as the "most important, the most vital freedom of all" and attacked almost any kind of government intervention as "dangerous, un-American state control." By 1943, Lewis ranked fourth in a poll ranking the public's favorite radio commentators.[46]

What was the impact of business-sponsored programming on its audience? Ratings give some indication of the size of the audience. Business's institutional programs could never effectively compete with comedy and variety programs, such as those featuring Abbott and Costello, Burns and Allen, or Bob Hope. In 1938, for instance, national Hooper ratings indicate that Ford Motor Company's "Sunday Evening Hour" had the highest ratings of the concert music programs, drawing 8.3 percent of the audience. But its popularity paled in comparison with Ford's direct competitor, the popular Charlie McCarthy show, which attracted 40 percent of Sunday-evening listeners. Still, significant numbers of Americans listened. *The Pulse of New York's* 1942 ratings list Du Pont's "Cavalcade of America" with a respectable 19 percent of the Monday night audience, second in its time slot behind "Vox Pop," with 40 percent. Some business-backed commentators drew better than the institutional programs. According to 1936 Hooper ratings, Boake Carter, broadcasting five times a week at the prime evening hour of 7:45, attracted more listeners than any other commentator.[47]

The companies were concerned about the effectiveness of their radio programs. Du Pont and Ford Motor Company used fan mail and surveys to help determine their programs' influence on public attitudes. During the 1938–39 season, Ford conducted five thousand personal interviews with listeners, and it concluded that "[t]he Ford Sunday Evening Hour has made friends for the Ford Motor Company." In terms of improving the image of the firm, in the late 1930s Du Pont found encouragement from letters, like one from a Seattle listener who wrote, "You have provided me with an entirely different perspective of the aims and purposes of the du Pont Company." "Cavalcade" fan mail included comments such as, "It's a very good company, and they do a lot for society," and, "Du Pont is always looking in the future for your benefit and mine." Over the years, Du Pont conducted increasingly sophisticated surveys of "Cavalcade" listeners to determine the extent of audience absorption of its message.[48]

Business leaders acknowledged that the impact of their radio programs was difficult to measure. In 1940, the Ford Motor Company executive A. R. Barbier admitted that the "results of such a program ["Ford Sunday Evening Hour"] are quite intangible, but the fact that we are nearing the end of the sixth season is evidence that we have faith in its efficacy. I must say frankly, however, that this faith is based as much upon logic as it is fact." It was clear that "a program such as ours can be supported only by the reasoning that if you provide people with worthwhile entertainment, you will cultivate their friendship and good will, and if you reach enough people, the effort will be worth the expense."[49] Similarly, Du Pont president Walter S. Carpenter conceded that "like most advertising expenditures it is pretty difficult to identify the earnings resulting" from the "Cavalcade" program. Like Barbier, Carpenter believed that "the long run advantages . . . make it worthwhile." If company officials were often uncertain about the specific impact of their radio programs, the advertising executive Bruce Barton had no doubts about the positive effects of institutional advertising. Barton's public relations firm, Batten, Barton, Durstine, and Osborn, had originally conceived of "Cavalcade," and in 1956 he argued that it was a "measurable factor" in helping to transform the public attitude toward Du Pont, influencing "not only the adult audience but the vast audience of young people, and even children, who are now mature citizens and voters."[50]

Commercial radio observers generally praised business-sponsored classical music and serious drama programs, such as Texaco's "Metropolitan Opera" and U.S. Steel's "Theatre Guild," with their minimal institutional messages. While initially dismissing Du Pont's "Cavalcade of America" as "sombre and dubious" entertainment, over the years *Variety* became increasingly respectful of the program, which won a steady stream of awards and endorsements from educational groups.[51] The content and presentation of some of the business-sponsored programs, however, may have limited the effectiveness of the corporate message. *Variety* often had little patience for overtly conservative, propaganda-laden programming. In 1936, it asserted that "The American Family Robinson" represented a "thinly veiled attack on the policies of the Roosevelt administration" and was likely to provoke resentment, even tuning out. While praising programs hosted by the more moderate postwar Chamber of Commerce, it characterized most of the NAM's shows as dull and as "unadulterated propaganda." *Variety* also condemned business-sponsored conservative commentators. The NAM's George Sokolsky delivered "pro-business propaganda" that would appeal only to that "segment of listeners tabbed 'conservative' and considered critical of the New Deal." The show-business paper had harsher words for conservatives such as Upton Close and Samuel Pettengill, describing Close as full of "hogwash" and Pettengill as "a disgrace to radio."[52]

Variety might easily dismiss this kind of business programming, but other detractors were not so complacent about its effect on audiences. The re-emergent labor movement in particular was concerned about the impact of a hostile press and business-sponsored radio programs. In the early 1930s, encouraged by section 7(a) of the National Industrial Recovery Act, which declared that workers have the right to organize and bargain collectively, millions of discontented workers surged into the AFL. Many of them toiled in semiskilled or unskilled jobs in new mass-production industries such as auto, steel, and rubber. They were greeted with mixed emotions by the conservative, craft-dominated leadership of the AFL, which for decades had exhibited disdain for the mass of unskilled workers comprised largely of first- or second-generation immigrants. By the summer of 1935, fierce employer resistance and ineffective AFL leadership had helped drive half a million of these new recruits out of the labor movement. A small corps of AFL union-ists, however, believed that the future of the labor movement lay in organiz-ing mass-production workers into strong industrial unions. In November 1935, eight unions, led by John L. Lewis, the flamboyant and eloquent leader of the United Mine Workers, defied the policies and formed the CIO. Call-ing upon workers to demand their democratic rights at the workplace and employing innovative tactics such as the sit-down strike, the CIO achieved impressive breakthroughs in the auto, steel, rubber, meatpacking, and electri-cal industries. Recalcitrant employers as well as conservative unions fought back against the rising tide of industrial unionism. The AFL expelled the CIO unions, but business was even more aggressive. While their public relations campaigns sought to undercut labor's ideological appeal, businesses armed and organized themselves. In the summer of 1937, the Little Steel companies, under the leadership of Republic Steel, unleashed "a bitter and violent cam-paign of opposition," handing the CIO its first major defeat.[53]

The CIO blamed the failed Little Steel strike, in part, on one of the "most extensive and highly-financed propaganda campaigns ever launched in peace times." It charged that big corporations were spending millions of dollars to discredit labor, especially the new industrial unions. According to the CIO, "every newspaper reader and radio listener felt the effects of this campaign," as "reactionary papers became hysterical in their denunciations" of unions, while radio commentators such as Boake Carter and George Sokolsky "spread the anti-labor catchwords far and wide." The findings of the La Follette Civil Liberties Committee seemed to provide proof that business was conducting a high-powered propaganda campaign to destroy the infant CIO. Unions publicized the committee's discovery that the NAM sponsored Sokolsky and that the organization also produced "The American Family Robinson," which was often broadcast without identifying its business-backed sponsors.[54]

The CIO and some local unions across the country denounced "The American Family Robinson" as "antilabor propaganda." They sent protests to the local stations broadcasting the program and to the Federal Commu-nications Commission. For example, a Baltimore unionist, W. M. Hayman, complained to FCC chairman Anning S. Prall that one character on the pro-gram argued that "our problem is that of proving to the American people that their best interests lie in the security of Business to remain in private hands." The biggest threat to the security of business and, implicitly, the security of the nation was organized labor, which sought "to take the prop-erty from the rightful owners." To Hayman, the program's dramatic skits were not "mere entertainment"; they were a "definite attempt to discredit" unions, which had "no opportunity to defend themselves."[55]

As the United Automobile Workers struggled to organize the Ford Motor Company, the union warned autoworkers that the "Ford Sunday Evening Hour" was part of a coordinated company campaign to combat unionization. The *West Side Conveyor* charged that the Ford offensive combined strongarm tactics with propaganda. The beatings and kidnapings of UAW organizers were designed to intimidate workers, while Henry Ford used his radio symphony intermissions to convince the public that he was a philanthropist who cared deeply about his employees.[56] The *United Automobile Worker* regularly debunked "all the lies about Ford's labor polices that Stooge Cameron croaks into the mike in the Sunday evening intermissions." One editorial fantasized that if the radio announcer for the "Ford Sunday Evening Hour" were to forget himself sometime and tell the truth, he might croon into the microphone, "I want you to bear with me for a few minutes while I explain to you that the Ford Motor Co. has an unreasonable hatred of unions. Our cars are good, but our labor policy stinks." The mythical Ford announcer concludes by urging autoworkers to boycott his company's products "until we come to our senses."[57] The union also lampooned the Ford program in a poem in which a listener muses about a wonderful Sunday-evening radio program with music "so soft and sweet." The poet continues:

> But in spite of the wonderful music
> And in spite of the soft-spoken lies,
> I know they are plotting and planning
> To take me by surprise.
>
> They fairly engulf me with music,
> My senses they try to o'erpower,
> And they try and ruin my judgment—
> With their wonderful symphony hour.
>
> Then a sudden hush of the music
> And life seems full and complete—
> Then Cameron steps up to the mouthpiece
> And over the air he bleats.
>
> He condemns the unions and labor,
> And when he rants no more,
> A beautiful symphony concert
> Has been spoiled by an arrogant bore.

Do you think, Henry Ford, you exploiter,
You can buy with this kind of stuff
The thanks and good will of thousands
Who haven't nearly enough?

So you might as well keep your music
And shut old Cameron's yap,
For while we enjoy your music
We haven't time for your crap.

And although I hear your good music
I remember that day long ago,
So keep all your love and your music
Just give us the CIO.[58]

Industrial unionists went beyond ridicule to help silence one hostile radio voice. In 1938, working-class economic power combined with political pressure to drive the commentator Boake Carter off the air. Carter's inflammatory comments about the New Deal and his railings against unions had aroused the wrath of the Roosevelt administration and labor. To muzzle him, industrial unionists turned to the boycott, a traditional craft-labor weapon that allowed workers to use their power as consumers to help shape the content of programming. Labor had already used boycotts in attempts to influence the representation of labor in film. In the 1910s, Chicago Socialists and Washington, D.C., unionists urged workers to boycott movie theaters that displayed antilabor films.[59]

Carter's sponsor, Philco—which produced radios, a popular consumer item—was in a vulnerable position. In late 1936 the first calls for a boycott of Philco radios came from the West Coast after Carter made scurrilous charges against the maritime unions. He had asserted, for instance, that longshoremen wearing American Legion buttons were being turned away from union hiring halls and urged Legionaires and members of other patriotic organizations to do "something about it." To Eleanor Fowler, labor secretary of the International League for Peace and Freedom, such inflammatory language was a virtual invitation to violence.[60]

In the summer of 1937, union anger flared again as Carter's attacks against the CIO intensified. Protests from trade unionists and their supporters flooded Philco offices for weeks. Anita Brophy, the wife of CIO vice president John Brophy, was appalled by Carter's "vituperation and vilification" and warned, "If I thought his utterances expounded the attitudes of the Philco Radio Company, I'd throw the Philco which I purchased just a few weeks ago right out the window and ask my friends to do likewise." The *Union Labor Record* of Philadelphia condemned Carter for using the "powerful instrument of radio" to laud vigilantism, encourage strikebreaking, and condone police brutality. It urged workers to strike back at Carter "where it hurts the most—in the pocketbooks." The Philadelphia Industrial Union Council then declared a boycott of Philco, which was based in their city, and WCAU, the Philadelphia station from which Carter broadcast his commentary. Viewing Carter as a "menace to their jobs," Philco's own unionists appealed to the company to replace him with a "genuine, honest news reporter."[61]

Philco, dependent on the sale of low-cost radios to workers, dropped Carter by December 1937. Although Carter and WCAU president Leon Levy met with several Philadelphia union leaders and promised to refrain from discussing controversial labor issues, the Philadelphia Industrial Union Council refused to lift the boycott. General Foods, whose chairman was an active NAM member, eagerly picked up sponsorship, but much to its chagrin, unions began to boycott this company as well. At the same time, the Roosevelt administration pressured General Foods to encourage Carter to moderate his commentary. The company and CBS began monitoring the show to prevent the "repetition of unpleasant incidents with labor." Finally, in August 1938, General Foods allowed its contract with Carter to expire.[62]

The successful boycott of Carter was an example of labor effectively exercising its consumer power to influence the radio industry. Despite this union victory, business voices remained strong on the airwaves, as companies continued to sponsor programming designed to promote the corporate agenda. Over the course of the 1930s, however, business began to face new competition from organized labor not only on the factory floor, where militant workers fought to form unions, but also on the air. Important elements of the labor movement, particularly unionists associated with the CIO, had recognized radio's exceptional ability to reach workers and the broader public and embraced the medium as an important economic and political weapon.

(())

2   Labor Radio: A Catalyst for Social Change
in Depression-Era America

THE STRONG REACTION to Boake Carter's radio commentary reflected the
growing appreciation within the labor movement of radio's ability to shape
public attitudes and influence political and economic policy. While a few
AFL unionists in the 1920s had recognized radio's tremendous potential for
contesting business dominance of political discourse, only in the late 1930s
did a revitalized and reinvigorated labor movement led by the Congress of
Industrial Organizations begin to more fully utilize radio. These unionists,
who were committed to militant organizing in the mass-production industries, had begun to understand that radio could serve as a unique tool for
organizing and union building and as a means of constructing an oppositional community for a working-class audience. By penetrating into the private sphere of workers' homes, radio enabled unions to reach workers who
were too frightened by their repressive employers to even accept a union
leaflet at the plant gate.

Having recognized radio's power, in the 1930s unions sought to use broadcasting to reach workers and the public. This would be no easy task, largely
because most broadcasters had little interest in giving organized labor (or,
for that matter, minorities, radicals, or any group challenging the status quo)
access to the airwaves. Fearful of offending advertisers, many commercial
broadcasters avoided airing what they considered to be controversial issues.
NBC and CBS refused to sell time to unions for national broadcasts, but the
networks could not keep labor completely off the air. The radio industry was
regulated by the government, and it operated under a mandate to serve the
public interest, which meant presenting a balanced, well-rounded schedule of

programming representing a variety of political viewpoints and public issues. To fulfill this mandate, broadcasters provided organizations with a limited amount of time without charge for public affairs programming. Occasional broadcasts of speeches by union leaders fell into this category. Many local stations adhered to the network's broadcasting guidelines, but some stations, especially those independent of the networks, were so eager for revenue that they were willing to sell time to unions for regular labor programs or single broadcasts. Still, organized labor was never able to get as much access to radio as it desired. This chapter explores what labor did with its available airtime in the 1930s, and the following chapter focuses on the barriers that prevented unions from fully taking advantage of broadcasting.

The labor leaders who embraced radio mostly represented emerging industrial unions. Many of the leaders of these new unions were young and comfortable with this new medium of communication. Like business leaders, they were well aware of Roosevelt's effective use of radio to win public support for the New Deal. For a few it almost seemed like a panacea, a powerful means to counteract business propaganda and organize vast numbers of industrial workers. In July 1936, for instance, UAW president Homer Martin boasted to the CIO Executive Board that "by use of radio alone, we could whip any auto company." Richard Frankensteen, director of the Ford organizing campaign, proposed emulating the UAW's corporate adversary. In the famous 1937 photographs of the "Battle of the Overpass," he was the husky, young, and confident figure who, along with Walter Reuther, was severely beaten by Ford security men. Frankensteen wanted the union to sponsor a series of performances by the Detroit Symphony Orchestra on Wednesday nights over network radio. While expensive—eighty-six thousand dollars for thirteen weeks—Frankensteen asserted that the music would attract Ford workers and enable labor leaders such as John L. Lewis, Philip Murray, and Sidney Hillman to directly refute William J. Cameron's statements on the Sunday-night program.[1]

CIO president John L. Lewis also believed in radio's power to sway public opinion and took advantage of every opportunity to address the American public on network radio. He asserted that he spoke for the millions of men and women "'heretofore unorganized, economically exploited, and inarticulate.'" Over the next two decades, his distinctive voice would become familiar to millions of listeners. At times, Lewis almost seemed convinced that through the radio he could shape the course of a particular labor conflict. At one point during the 1936 Goodyear strike in Akron, Ohio, workers refused a settlement offer, and the company threatened to send in scabs and armed guards. Lewis warned that if this happened, he would address the nation over network radio and "'accuse Goodyear officials of outright repression.'" According to Lewis, the likely result would be a "'general strike in Akron and a consumer boycott of Goodyear products and Chrysler cars that used Goodyear tires.'" At the end of that year, Lewis spoke to a nationwide audience on NBC on behalf of the sit-down strikers in the auto industry. He reassured the autoworkers of the CIO's commitment to their cause and reminded the Democrats and Roosevelt of their debt to organized labor for its support during the recent presidential election. Lewis declared over the airwaves that labor expected "'the protection of the Federal Government in the pursuit of its lawful objectives.'"[2]

As interest in using radio during organizing drives intensified in the mid-1930s, several national unions and one city central body sought to emulate WCFL by establishing their own radio stations. In 1935, the ILGWU applied to the FCC for a license for a New York City station, the International Typographical Union (ITU) applied for a license in Indiana, the Los Angeles Central Labor Council sought approval to erect a new station in East Los Angeles, and the United Electrical Workers (UE) began seriously investigating the possibility of buying a station in Philadelphia. The Los Angeles unionists asserted that ownership of a radio outlet meant "life or death" for the labor movement in California, and the American Civil Liberties Union (ACLU) supported their petition for a license, noting that organized labor was "poorly served by the existing assignments of radio licenses." Networks and individual stations "from time to time extended courtesy programs to labor leaders and groups," the ACLU observed, but there was "no guarantee at present that their viewpoint will have adequate representation on the air."[3]

The infant CIO gave a good deal of consideration to how they might best utilize radio. Among CIO leaders, James Carey, president of the UE, was probably the most intrigued with radio's potential. In 1937, at twenty-six years old, he was considered the "boy wonder" of the labor movement. A Philadelphia native, he gained his start in the union movement by organizing Philco during the union upsurge following the passage of the National Industrial Recovery Act. Carey was active in the Boake Carter boycott and led the UE's effort to obtain a station in Philadelphia, consulting frequently with WCFL's management about their experience with labor radio. At every opportunity, Carey stressed the importance of gaining access to radio and urged the CIO to explore the possibility of establishing a chain of labor stations throughout the country. At times he was frustrated that key individuals did not share his vision. In November 1936 he proposed the idea to the CIO Executive Board and was encouraged when Lewis and Thomas Kennedy of the United Mine Workers, Sidney Hillman of the Amalgamated Clothing Workers of America (ACWA), Charles Howard of the ITU, and David Dubinsky of the ILGWU entered into a "spirited discussion and indicated a keen interest." There was enough apparent enthusiasm for radio among the CIO leadership that over the next year rumors swept the broadcasting industry that the CIO was on the verge of launching a major national radio campaign.[4]

The chain of labor stations never materialized in the 1930s. Nor did the central office of the CIO conduct a national organizing drive through network radio. John L. Lewis respected the power of radio but doubted that a labor organization could compete with commercial broadcasting companies in operating multiple stations. Moreover, with limited financial assets, the national office of the CIO concluded that targeted radio campaigns aimed at particular industries would be a better use of resources. In addition, there was little likelihood that the networks, which generally shied away from controversy, would have even opened their facilities for broadcasts aimed at organizing workers. Finally, any hopes for a labor chain disappeared when the FCC, which had shown little sympathy for WCFL's demands for a clear channel and increased power, turned down all three union requests for licenses. Congressman Byron N. Scott of California protested the decisions, arguing that labor groups were the victims of discrimination. Infuriated at the FCC's treatment of labor, the CIO adopted a resolution at its 1937 convention condemning the FCC and urging a congressional investigation of the regulatory body.[5]

❖ ❖ ❖

Despite these setbacks, labor's voice was heard on radio during the 1930s more often and more widely than ever before. Bent on the mass mobilization of workers and understanding the importance of gaining public support, CIO national unions and organizing committees eagerly took to the airwaves. Given Carey's interest in radio, it is not surprising that in 1936 the UE arranged a series of broadcasts featuring speeches by union officers over WEVD in New York City and WBIG in Glenside, Pennsylvania. On the West Coast, the International Longshoremen and Warehousemen's Union sponsored a news program, "Labor on the March," which was broadcast five nights a week over a San Francisco station.[6]

Denied access to larger network stations, organizers in the steel and textile industries hooked up several small independent stations in areas where they were conducting organizing drives. In May 1937 the Textile Workers Or- ganizing Committee (TWOC) kicked off its New England campaign with a broadcast of a mass meeting in Lawrence, Massachusetts, over one of these improvised networks. Speeches by John L. Lewis and Sidney Hillman reached workers through five stations in Massachusetts and Rhode Island. In an ef- fort to communicate with an ethnically diverse workforce, WCOP in Boston carried four TWOC programs in English, Polish, Italian, and French.[7]

In the summer of 1937, stations in Baltimore as well as Allentown, John- stown, and Harrisburg, Pennsylvania, broadcast three Steelworker Organizing Committee programs each week as part of the Bethlehem Steel campaign. Emphasizing the union's Americanism, each program began and ended with John Phillip Sousa's march "Stars and Stripes Forever." The programs in- cluded labor news, recorded talks by labor leaders or sympathetic politicians like Senator Robert Wagner and Representative Maury Maverick, and live talks by local union leaders and mill workers who discussed current "out- rages and abuses" occurring at their plants. Unions publicized their broad- casts with sandwichmen parading outside the mill gates, the distribution of leaflets, and ads in local labor papers. In September 1937, the CIO expanded its radio operation to organize workers in the silk mills in Allentown, Ha- zelton, and Scranton, Pennsylvania.[8]

Most of these radio campaigns owed their existence to Morris S. Novik, the program director for WEVD and chief media advisor to the CIO. He set up the station hookups, provided technical assistance, and furnished the recordings of the speeches and labor songs, most of which were originally delivered over WEVD. Novik was one of the most impassioned advocates of union broadcasting. Born in Russia in 1903, as a youngster he came with his family to the United States, settling in the heavily immigrant Lower East Side of New York City. Drawn to leftist politics, he wrote for Socialist newspapers and magazines and became active in the Young People's Socialist League. Early on, Novik demonstrated the promotional and organizational skills that would serve him well in the broadcasting industry. A self-starter with tremendous energy, charm, and creativity, he was characterized by Gus Tyler of the ILGWU as a "first class entrepreneur with a social conscience." During the 1920s, Novik organized public lectures and debates for the Discussion Guild and served as social director of Unity House, the ILGWU's summer resort that provided education, culture, and entertainment for members and their families. This experience taught him the effectiveness of "combining new and old forms of education and entertainment to advance cultural and

Morris Novik was the
foremost promoter of
labor radio in the nation.
Courtesy of the George
Meany Memorial Archives,
Silver Spring, Md.

political struggles." In 1932, he began his lifelong association with broadcasting, becoming program director for WEVD. His goal was to make the
Socialist station a "significant instrument for labor and the general liberal
. . . and progressive movements of New York City." His success there caught
the attention of the mayor of New York, Fiorello La Guardia, and in 1938 he
became director of the city's municipal station, WNYC, which he soon revitalized. In the 1930s, Novik developed close relations with both major factions of the labor movement, and in 1946, when he became a private radio
consultant, he continued to work closely with the AFL and CIO on broadcasting issues.[9]

While Novik was promoting labor radio on the East Coast, the UAW made
intensive and innovative use of radio in the Midwest. During the summer of
1936, the union began broadcasting three times a week, with one program
on WCFL in Chicago and two others emanating from Detroit. Later in the
summer, the UAW offered a third Detroit broadcast over the Polish language
station WEXL, purchasing fifteen minutes for talks by the Polish organizer
Stanley Nowak each Thursday during Waclaw Golanski's popular radio pro-

gram. Groups of workers reportedly gathered in stores and barber shops in the Polish sections of Detroit to listen to these broadcasts. UAW organizers also gave short series of radio speeches in other centers of auto production, including Lansing, Michigan, and St. Louis. During January 1937, as the autoworkers battled General Motors in Flint, the UAW went on the radio in Detroit for fifteen minutes each evening to sell its cause to the public. Regular radio addresses also helped rally auto strikers in Cleveland and St. Louis.[10]

In the wake of the successful Flint sit-down strike, the UAW formed a Radio Department and broadcast a daily program that could be heard by workers in parts of Indiana, Ohio, and Michigan over the Detroit independent station WJBK. This program, part of the UAW effort to organize Ford Motor Company employees, included speeches and roundtable discussions, dramatizations of labor history and current labor news, dramatic skits, and an amateur night. On Saturday nights, children could listen to another Radio Department production, "Auto Kids' Union of the Air," a series of skits depicting the "trials and joys and problems" of an autoworker's family. In addition to promoting broadcasting in Detroit, the Radio Department assisted UAW locals in Lansing and Muskegon with their weekly programs.[11]

The recession of 1938 and factionalism within the UAW took a toll on the union's radio campaign. In May, with fewer resources available and the Ford organizing drive mired in internal conflict, the union dissolved its Radio Department and temporarily scaled back its broadcasts. With a few exceptions, the UAW's more innovative programs disappeared. Through the spring of 1939, much of the union's broadcasting was devoted to internecine struggle, as the two factions took their cases to the public and a dwindling membership through impassioned speeches over the radio.[12]

When unity was finally restored, the UAW focused on rebuilding its ranks. In late September, intensive radio campaigns helped it win a National Labor Relations Board (NLRB) election against the breakaway AFL-backed union at Chrysler plants in Detroit. The week before the election, union leaders were on the air every night. A series of three broadcasts presented in play form told the history of autoworker unionism, focusing particularly on AFL duplicity. Members played the roles of John L. Lewis, William Green, William S. Knudsen of General Motors, Michigan Governor Frank Murphy, and R. J. Thomas, president of the newly unified UAW. Radio also offered critical support during a forty-five-day strike that followed the NLRB election. The union broadcast as many as twelve programs each week on behalf of the Chrysler workers to counter "radio haranguing" by anti-union broadcasters, full-page newspaper ads, and front-page pro-corporate editorials.[13]

In the summer of 1940, UAW broadcasting moved into higher gear as the union mobilized for one final push to organize Ford. It inaugurated a program of daily talks on WJBK and scheduled even more broadcasts on other stations as the drive reached its crescendo. By the following spring, with Ford workers striking, the UAW was making two regular nightly broadcasts. There was a virtual barrage of union broadcasts during the six days leading up to the NLRB election in May 1941, including thirty-four special programs in nine languages: Italian, Polish, Ukranian, Czech, Hungarian, Croatian, Rumanian, Finnish, and Arabic. On WJBK alone, there were six labor programs a day. To help workers keep track, the River Rouge local paper, *Ford Facts*, urged workers to clip out the UAW broadcast schedule and paste it close to the dial of their sets.[14]

A number of radio programs sponsored by local unions were also initiated in the 1930s. In New York City, Morris Novik, WEVD's program director, encouraged locals to make fuller use of radio. He hoped to expand and improve the station's programming, especially its labor offerings. Novik had been disappointed in the labor movement's initial failure to grasp the possibilities of radio.[15] He argued that a union-sponsored radio program was "cheaper and more effective than any other medium" in arousing the attention and interest of most workers. In March 1934, Novik declared to Charles Zimmerman, the manager of Dressmakers Union Local 22 of the ILGWU, that he was personally "sold on the idea of converting radio, and our station in particular, into a lively medium of union education and propaganda."[16]

Novik and WEVD perhaps had the most success with locals of the ILGWU. In the spring of 1934, with Novik's encouragement, the national union set an example for its locals by sponsoring a ten-week series, "The International Hour." It originated from WEVD but through a hookup with other stations it also reached audiences in New Jersey, Connecticut, Washington, D.C., and Pennsylvania. The series, broadcast on Friday nights, included brief talks by union officials, politicians, and reformers such as Rose Schneiderman, the president of the Women's Trade Union League, musical pieces performed by "famous" chamber music ensembles and prominent stage and concert stars, and short sketches. During the show's first broadcast, David Dubinsky, president of the ILGWU, explained, "We wish to make this an open forum, a great labor meeting on the air." He hoped to obtain the audience's "reactions to the great problems that confront all of us and to make our leadership as sensitive and responsive as possible to the will of the membership."[17]

With the conclusion of the national union series, Novik urged ILGWU Italian Dressmakers Local 89 to begin its own regular Saturday-morning

Flyer publicizing a local ILGWU program in 1938. ILGWU Papers, Kheel Labor Management Documentation Center, Cornell University; courtesy of UNITE HERE.

Italian-language program on WEVD. "The Voice of Local 89" became an institution of labor broadcasting that was still on the air twenty years after its inception in 1934. Coordinated for years by Novik, it followed the format of "The International Hour," combining entertainment with education.[18] In subsequent years, other New York City ILGWU locals joined the radio broadcasters' parade, including Dressmakers Local 22, Infant's and Children's Wear Local 91, and White Goods Workers' Local 62. WEVD also offered a "Labor Hour" sponsored by various local unions that included labor news, labor jokes, human interest stories, trade-union amateur artists, music, and short talks by local labor leaders. In early 1937, *Variety* observed that WEVD had "gradually grooved in" as a station chiefly championing labor and trade unionism. According to the trade paper, in a city "where militant trade unions abound like peanuts in Virginia," WEVD had managed to get unions into the habit of buying time on the radio.[19]

Local unions also went on the air elsewhere. In Philadelphia in 1934, William Leader, the president of Local 706 of the Full Fashioned Hosiery Workers, began a series of weekly talks on the station WIP. Three years later, the Philadelphia Industrial Union Council joined Leader on the air to counteract anti-union, anti-CIO publicity campaigns with a twice-weekly program on the same station. In March 1935, six Kansas City, Missouri, unions sponsored their city's version of "Labor Hour." One autoworker, William Dowell, reported that the reaction to the first program "was quite favorable, everyone in the shop thought it was wonderful and thought it should be continued." Similarly, L. H. Turner, the chairman of the Transportation Brotherhoods, reported that his members had become "enthusiastic listeners, to what we estimate to be the most beneficial program ever broadcast from any Radio Station in the central states."[20] Steelworker locals in Portsmouth, Ohio, went on the air over WPAY on "The Amalgamated Hour," which aired for two years on Sunday afternoons. The program had a folksy quality, featuring talks and music by local union leaders and musicians. In some cases they were one and the same; one regular speaker, Richard Evans, president of the Amalgamated Golden Rule Lodge and later district supervisor for the SWOC, was described by the local labor paper as a "silver tongue orator" who occasionally added "color and spice" to the program by playing various musical instruments, including the harmonica and organ.[21]

In the last two years of the decade, UE Local 1002 of Evansville, Indiana, UAW Local 248 representing Milwaukee Allis-Chalmers Company workers, the Akron Industrial Union Council, the San Francisco Industrial Union Council, and the Chicago Packinghouse Organizing Committee, among others, inaugurated radio programs. After six months on the air, the San Francisco Industrial Union Council reported that letters from listeners had poured in from all parts of the West and as far north as British Columbia as well as from ships at sea. It estimated that the audience for "Labor on the Air," a weeknight news show that focused on working-class issues, was between three and four hundred thousand, the largest of any program in the state. By 1940 the union reported that the show's fan mail frequently exceeded a thousand letters a day.[22] Of course, the Chicago Federation of Labor's station, WCFL, continued to serve as an outlet for labor programming throughout the 1920s. The station mostly broadcast music and musical variety shows, but it regularly gave time to local unions, particularly those associated with the AFL, supporting their strikes and organizing efforts.[23]

❖ ❖ ❖

Labor's programs had overlapping and intertwined purposes. Unions used radio as a tool for organizing, as a weapon during strikes, as an aid to building union community and identity, and as a vehicle for education, public relations, and political action.[24] While some broadcasts were aimed at the general public, others targeted current or potential union members. A significant portion of labor's broadcasts simply extended traditional types of union communication. The messages conveyed over the radio during organizing campaigns and strikes were often similar to what workers might have read in the labor press or heard at a union meeting or rally. These programs discussed issues of direct concern to workers, including wages, working conditions, arbitrary treatment of employees, job security, and the limitations of company unionism.

Radio also provided labor with a new tool to break through the veil of fear and intimidation that still surrounded many workplaces in the 1930s. Most unionists recognized that personal contact made on the job, during home visits, or at meetings, supplemented by union publications such as newspapers and leaflets, was the best way to recruit members. However, as Robert Zieger asserts, joining a union or even talking to an organizer in the 1930s "was a risky business." As a result, despite the passage of the Wagner Act and the well-publicized union victories in Akron and Flint, union campaigns often had trouble recruiting workers. Many of these workers, Philip Murray noted in a 1936 report to the SWOC, were "shot through with fear—fear of the boss" and of losing their jobs. Similarly, William L. Munger, research director of the UAW, observed, "[O]wing to the almost universal practice by the automobile companies of employing spies, stool pigeons . . .

to report any conversation or activities faintly hinting at Unions," workers were "under a constant fear of being watched and do not dare to speak to one another in the plant concerning unions."[25] Worried about the spies in their ranks, some workers refused to attend union rallies or take the leaflets distributed by organizers outside the plant gates. In communities politically dominated by employers, it was difficult to rent halls for meetings, and local ordinances made it impossible for organizers to distribute leaflets or engage in picketing without risking arrest or worse. Mayor Frank Hague of Jersey City, for instance, would tolerate no CIO activities in his town. Ordinances prohibited meetings and sound trucks, and police escorted CIO organizers, often in a none-too-gentle manner, out of the city. Elsewhere, beatings, such as the widely publicized 1937 assault on Walter Reuther and Richard Frankensteen as they attempted to distribute leaflets at Ford's River Rouge plant, arrests, and killings reinforced workers' fear of supporting unions.[26]

Radio enabled labor to bypass these barriers and communicate directly with workers and their families in the safety of their homes. For example, barred from the city streets and halls of Jersey City, CIO organizers used WEVD to broadcast the union message across the river to New Jersey workers. During the Ford campaign, UAW organizers and officers spoke to workers every night via the radio. Local union leaders from companies that had already been organized, such as Briggs and Chrysler, testified about how much the union had improved their members' lives. They assured employees that they could join the ranks of organized labor "safely—with the protection of the union and the United States Government." Broadcasts encouraged workers with questions to call the UAW or come to the local union office for a membership application. A worker could join the union by mail or have his wife drop off his application "while she's doing her shopping." The announcer reassured the audience that "everything will be kept confidential." John Ringwald, an organizer, found that the radio broadcasts made his job easier. He explained that although the union held meetings, printed a special newspaper, and distributed leaflets, "[W]e need the radio to reach the Ford workers, and it is doing the job." When he contacted Ford employees, he found "quite often that it's easier to get down to business because they have listened to our radio talks." According to Ringwald, they felt that what they read in the papers had been "doctored by the editors and the business office, but what they hear from our own speakers over the radio comes direct from the union without any poisoning or twisting."[27]

Programs targeted specific groups of workers who were considered especially difficult to reach by traditional methods. Thus, the UAW sponsored foreign-language broadcasts, such as Stanley Nowak's talks in Polish, and special programs for African Americans. The 1937–38 Ford organizing drive included "Negro radio broadcasts" and a symposium comparing the company's policies towards African Americans to the union's as well as a radio drama focusing on black history. During the successful 1940–41 drive, the UAW again aimed radio broadcasts at African Americans. Black community leaders, local officers, and rank-and-file workers spoke regularly on the daily Ford show, stressing the importance of racial solidarity. One Ford worker, Veal Clough, who had been fired twice for union activity, promised that the UAW would address wage inequality, and Luke Fennell, vice president of a Budd local, suggested that listeners look at a picture in the union paper of black and white workers together, each waving a vacation bonus check, compliments of the union contract. Prior to the union, he argued, companies didn't pass out bonuses, "especially not among us colored workers."[28]

Some unions developed innovative ways to use radio broadcasts to boost organizing drives. The Los Angeles Industrial Union Council's nightly program, "Our Daily Bread," featured a surprise guest, an employee from a plant engaged in an organizing drive. Each guest gave a special message to fellow employees and invited them to attend a mass rally the next night. To ensure a large and interested audience, organizers informed workers through a special leaflet distribution that a fellow worker was to participate in the program. Keeping the worker's name secret helped stimulate curiosity about the broadcast. According to the CIO News, "[T]he men were as much interested to find out who the speaker will be as they are to hear his message. Then when he comes to work the next morning and the boss doesn't fire him, confidence grows—and so does the CIO."[29]

Popular shows could yield tangible increases in membership. The SWOC captured the attention of steelworkers in southeast Ohio with a labor chautauqua broadcast from the town of Portsmouth over five consecutive nights in December 1936 on the station WPAY. The widely publicized broadcasts, staged in Radioland Hall before large audiences of workers, were picked up by several other radio stations and reached listeners in three states. In some towns, workers gathered in halls to listen to the event. The first night began outside Radioland with a parade featuring the SWOC brass band, followed inside by musical entertainment and a speech by CIO director John Brophy. Brophy spoke not only to the steelworkers but to every working-class listener, urging every man and woman who worked for wages to become "a part of our great movement that is seeking a better life for all. On our shoulders rests the task of ending unemployment and poverty and fear of poverty." Millions of workers, he contended, wanted unionism and were "stirred to new hope by the activities of the CIO." Ensuing evenings combined musical performances with speeches by national labor leaders. The local SWOC declared the chautauqua a success, reporting, "Our invisible radio audience is sending congratulatory messages on the splendid reception of our entire program. Everywhere workers are talking organization, several new groups want organization as a direct result of the chautauqua." Within a week of the broadcast, the SWOC gained eighteen hundred new members in Portsmouth and the surrounding steel towns. The labor journalist Mary Heaton Vorse concluded that the labor chautauqua "resulted in Portsmouth becoming a CIO town."[30]

Radio invigorated the ILGWU drive to organize the largest cotton dress plant in the United States in 1941. When the campaign to unionize the Har-

This cartoon symbolizes the important role of radio as an organizing tool for the ILGWU in the 1930s. *Justice,* Mar. 15, 1936; courtesy of UNITE HERE.

Lee Manufacturing Company of Fall River, Massachusetts, lost steam, the ILGWU cast plant workers in a soap opera, "Rita Quill, Union Member." The show aired three days a week in the month before the NLRB election. The scripts mixed the labor problems of Rita and her girlfriends at the "Tip Top" plant with "emotional fusses, boyfriend troubles," and other soap opera conventions. In one typical episode, Rita attends a union meeting where the organizer assures the workers involved in the organizing drive of the democratic nature of the union, declaring: "YOU WILL CALL THE STRIKE IF YOUR DEMANDS AREN'T SATISFIED. . . . That's called democracy, and that's what we believe in. . . . YOU decide, YOU vote, YOU fight—YOU win. . . . Ketch? And the Union backs you up . . . 100 percent, the limit." Following the meeting, Rita meets her boyfriend, Mickey, who is suspicious of the ILGWU. He insists that she quit her union activity, but when Rita explains that the union gives her a sense of empowerment, Mickey agrees to reconsider his stance. The episode ends with the announcer reminding the audience to tune in for the next exciting installment of the story, when it will be revealed if the girls vote to strike, or if the Tip Top bosses agree to a conference with the shop committee. According to the liberal paper *PM*, within two weeks "the whole town was listening and talking Tip Top." Reporting just prior to the NLRB election, the paper predicted that the winner, "unless the power of radio has been greatly oversold," would be Rita's ILGWU. The union did win the election, with 80 percent of the ballots cast in its favor.[31]

❖ ❖ ❖

Radio became an important weapon in contract negotiations and strikes during the 1930s, as unions increasingly exploited its ability to mobilize and forge a sense of solidarity among workers. Radio was particularly significant in conflicts involving industries with large, scattered workforces, such as the garment and textile industries. In September 1935, New York City ILGWU Local 91 began contract negotiations with employers and anticipated a strike. Its first action in preparation for the struggle was to inaugurate a radio program over WEVD to "inspire and instruct the huge army of workers" who made up the membership of the local. The local hoped to heighten solidarity by keeping the thousands of members, who were dispersed throughout the metropolitan area, abreast of the status of negotiations and prepared for action. Through the "Message of 91," workers heard their union "speaking, arguing, fighting, and expressing its inflexible will to win its just demands."[32] In the South, radio also helped workers find their voice. A sociological study of southern textile worker insurgency during the early 1930s found that strikes were more likely to occur in mill towns with a radio station. During the great uprising of 1934, radio helped the United Textile Workers reach formerly isolated mill workers, providing them with a "larger sense of place and community." Words spoken by union leaders and music, especially mill and strike songs, were equally important in helping to forge a collective oppositional consciousness.[33]

During some strikes, the airways became an arena of conflict, as both sides jockeyed for the support of workers and the public. In September 1938, a local citizens' committee in San Francisco sponsored a two-hour broadcast presenting the workers' side of a department-store strike. Concerned about the effect of that broadcast, several days later the Retailers' Council bought time three evenings in a row to argue the owner's case. The Retail Department Store Employees Union, which had called the walkout, jabbed back with a program the following week to answer the owners' broadcast. During the Goodyear sit-down strike in the spring of 1936, both sides fought what the United Rubber Workers Union later characterized as a "mighty battle of the air." Two local stations carried hours of programs from the union and the company. In one typical anti-union speech, the company president, Paul Litchfield, charged that a relatively small group of employees had forced thousands of satisfied workers off the job. He asserted that "this was not accomplished by peaceful persuasion, or acts within the law, but by intimidation and force." These strikers were depriving "non-striking employees of their rights" and keeping "the civic forces from maintaining law and order." Litchfield contended that Goodyear was making a genuine effort to identify and correct the workers' grievances. The best solution to the conflict was to reopen the factory and continue negotiations through the company union. In rebuttal, a union spokesman asserted that if the people of Akron wanted to end the strike, "they should demand that Mr. Litchfield tell why he stubbornly refuses to do what thousands of other employers throughout the United States have done, namely to meet the representatives of organized labor and work out a relationship that will be mutually satisfactory."[34]

Newspapers in Akron provided balanced coverage of the strike. Elsewhere, however, the press tended to favor employers. Radio enabled organized labor to respond quickly to company propaganda whether it appeared in local papers as news articles or as advertisements. Richard Frankensteen dedicated his radio program in the summer of 1936 to repudiating the "many malicious and false statements" that appeared in the press. During the Wheeling Steel strike in Portsmouth, Ohio, which ultimately ended with the union winning a contract, the company published a full-page advertisement charging the

CIO with complicity in the murder of a strikebreaker. The Steelworkers radio show, the "Amalgamated Hour," enabled the union to effectively refute the charges and maintain public support.[35]

In an era when relatively few workers had telephones, union leaders also learned that radio could serve as a conduit of information vital to the functioning of the union. During organizing campaigns and strikes, short spot radio announcements enabled them to call workers to rallies and other union events. In June 1937, for instance, after their victory earlier in the year during the sit-down strike, Flint autoworkers faced an employer counteroffensive and a hostile political climate. Local courts issued a barrage of injunctions restraining picketing, and Victor Reuther was to be tried for charges stemming from his union activity during the strike. Determined to demonstrate labor's solidarity and strength, Flint unionists planned four days of protests, beginning on Thursday, June 3, with a rally for Chevrolet workers on the site of the "Battle of Bulls Run" and culminating on Sunday, June 6, with a massive gathering at Kearsely Park for speeches by union leaders, including Homer Martin, the Reuther brothers, and Bob Travis. Radio announcements every two hours publicized the various demonstrations. On Sunday, Kearsely Park was packed with workers. Immediately after the speeches, the unionists joined in a torchlight parade, complete with floats, bands, sound cars, and banners, marching prominently down the main street past the City Hall and the court house. In addition to these special broadcasts, regularly scheduled union programs kept members abreast of developments in organizing campaigns or the state of contract or strike negotiations.[36]

This communication function was especially important when union leaders used the airwaves to counteract rumors and coordinate action during strikes. In the spring of 1941, for instance, frustrated Bethlehem Steel workers walked out to force the company to recognize the SWOC. The company attempted to convince the workers that the strike had failed by pretending that production was continuing unhindered. Foremen moved red ingots around the plant, burned tar paper in the stacks, and clanged bells and blew whistles to give the illusion that the steel company was in full operation. The SWOC's John Ramsay took to the air to expose the company's charade and reassure workers of the strike's effectiveness.[37]

Communication via the radio was vital to the success of the Goodyear sit-down strike. At one point, negotiations broke down, and the leader of the newly formed, company-funded Law and Order League, the former mayor C. Nelson Sparks, gave two inflammatory radio broadcasts. He called upon law-abiding citizens to help get rid of union leaders, whom he characterized as "radicals, communists, Red orators, flocking in here from all over the country like jackals around a carcass." Union leaders anticipated that an attack on the picket line would take place during the night or early morning hours of March 17 and needed a way to bring large numbers of workers to the plant on short notice to reinforce the picketers. Frank Grillo, the United Rubber Workers' secretary, hired the facilities of a local radio station for an all-night broadcast that lasted from 11 P.M. to 8:30 A.M.. At eleven, Grillo stepped to the microphone, declaring, "Attention! All union men and women! Attention! All United Rubber Worker members! Attention!" He explained the threat to the union and asked every listener to stay tuned to their radios throughout the night. "At the slightest sign of trouble," he continued, "you will have an instant report." Grillo and the CIO organizers improvised a program in the studio, giving impromptu talks on the need for unions and reading from Edward Levinson's "I Break Strikes." The labor journalist McAlister Coleman turned out copy—news, skits, and talks—as fast as he could type. They played recorded songs requested by listeners, and union members gave live performances of hillbilly and cowboy songs, many of them paraphrased to deal with strike issues. One request for "The Old Oaken Bucket" came from a woman with six men, two of them her sons, listening in her living room, poised for action. The Law and Order League attack never materialized, and at 8:30 the union went off the air. Grillo thanked the thousands who stayed up all night listening. "Your vigilance," he proclaimed, "prevented a violent attack on the Goodyear picket lines by Mr. Sparks and his hoodlums."[38]

❖ ❖ ❖

Participation in events such as the United Rubber Workers' all-night broadcast encouraged workers new to unionization to identify with the union. Having successfully weathered a strike and recruited members, some industrial unions understood that their next important challenge was to retain the newly organized workers' enthusiasm and loyalty. These CIO leaders realized that they needed to develop a sense of shared objectives and camaraderie among members. They sponsored social, recreational, and educational initiatives to nurture a "culture of unity" among industrial workers of varied ethnic backgrounds who often had little contact on or off the job. CIO unions fostered a union-centered culture by sponsoring dances, picnics, sports leagues, labor theater, and an array of classes. Such activities helped create a sense of cohesiveness among workers that enabled them to more effectively advance their economic goals. As the UAW educational director, Richard Deverall, observed, if labor could build "a union which is a way of life ... nobody [would] be able to destroy that union."[39]

Radio contributed to the development of this movement culture. Scholars drawing on the work of Benedict Anderson have suggested that listening to radio in the 1930s created among audiences the "sense of belonging to communities of the airwaves." Listeners "constructed new types of communities" and even new identities based on radio programs. While advertisers sought to use radio to enhance listeners' identity as consumers, some CIO unions began experimenting with radio as a tool for building union consciousness and community among listeners. That was the primary goal of the ILGWU's program, "The Voice of Local 89." Luigi Antonini, the general secretary of Local 89 who spoke weekly on the program, regarded it as a "powerful influence in maintaining solidarity" among the forty thousand members of the Italian-language local. Antonini understood that as the union expanded, radio provided a unique tool with which "to teach new members the history [and] general objective of labor." Drama offered a way to make "labor education entertaining as well as informative," and the ILGWU went so far as to create its own Drama Department. In July 1935, it began a six-week series of radio plays over WEVD that dramatized the history of the union. Recordings were made of the production, to be replayed in garment centers throughout the nation. As described by one union critic, the *The Story of the ILGWU* was a "stirring narrative of fearless and courageous leaders and of moving self-sacrifice of thousands."[40]

The autoworkers also experimented with drama as an element of their radio campaign to build union identity among listeners. The UAW Radio Department, which operated from 1937 to 1938, formed the UAW Radio Players to perform skits and more formal productions on the air. One such production was a dramatization of *The Flivver King,* Upton Sinclair's exposé of the Ford Motor Company. By focusing on the impact of Henry Ford's labor policies on the lives of three generations of a working-class family, the play personalized the drive to organize the company. To reach the ethnically diverse Ford workforce, its thirteen installments were broadcast in English and Polish. The Radio Department worked hard to get members involved in the daily radio program. Like the ILGWU, the UAW encouraged locals to form dramatic clubs to put on plays for the membership and appear on the union radio show. Amateur playwrights from among the membership were encouraged to submit their scripts for possible production on the air. A Saturday-night show featured UAW amateur performers. The *United Au-*

tomobile Worker reported that "hundreds of enthusiastic amateurs have been crowding the UAW radio office to get a chance to appear."[41]

Incorporating families into the union was an important element of the CIO's culture of unity, and radio gave unions direct access to the home. Broadcasts often spoke directly to workers' wives, who influenced their husbands' decisions to join the union and provided critical support during strikes. In November 1936, Norman Smith, an organizer for St. Louis General Motors Local 25, asked autoworkers' wives to compare the insecurity of their husbands with security of those employed by unionized firms. Two months later, St. Louis GM workers were striking for recognition of their union, and management was pressuring them to sign back-to-work petitions. Local 25's secretary, John Kociscak, warned wives to "beware of a visitor in the night who may be attempting to dissuade your husband from taking his rightful stand with the Union." Don't forget, he advised, that the wife and family of strikebreakers are "shamed and shunned along with the worker himself." During the Chrysler strike in November 1939, female auxiliary members participated in a radio skit designed to strengthen wives' resolve. In the skit, six women discuss the family response to the strike. They conclude that wives who had worked in union shops before marriage know that it is "the union that makes the boss play fair." The difficulty is with women who have no factory experience. "Their husbands know all right what the union does for them. The trouble is the women don't." Uppermost on these women's minds is their husbands' failure to bring home a paycheck. One of the women in the skit observes that her neighbor, whose husband works at Plymouth, is "a holy terror" who "scolds against the union every time I see her. She blames the union for everything." The auxiliary woman set her neighbor straight by reading a statement from the archbishop condemning the way the newspapers misrepresent the conflict. At the end of the skit, the women conclude that they must keep working and talking "until all the women of the Chrysler workers" are 100 percent union. The union worker Ann Petrosky made a similar appeal in a broadcast aimed at steelworker wives, declaring, "[W]hen a union man has a sympathetic, understanding woman behind him he will go far in the fight" against the "greedy, grasping" forces of industry.[42]

Radio also enabled children to develop a special relationship with the union. One of the UAW Radio Department's regular offerings was "Auto Kids' Union of the Air," designed primarily to help the children of autoworkers become part of a union community. It consisted of a series of radio skits focusing on the "trials and jobs and problems" of an American autoworker's family. Contests helped maintain interest in the program. The UAW urged all its members to involve their children in the union through listening to "Auto Kids' Union of the Air." To create an even stronger connection, it encouraged locals in conjunction with their women's auxiliaries to organize actual Auto Kids' Unions. "Help the children to become union conscious," advised the *United Automobile Worker*. "If you want a strong union tomorrow," then "you must begin to interest your children today." Let that interest, it continued, "make union ideals and union principles an integral part of your children's lives."[43]

❖ ❖ ❖

Radio significantly enhanced labor's ability to communicate with the working class. Equally important, this new medium brought organized labor into more direct contact with the general public. Labor, like business, understood the necessity of generating favorable public opinion. According to the UAW's secretary-treasurer, George Addes, the public "is the most important element with which the union has to deal. If the people understand and approve what the union is doing, we auto workers will have little trouble with the corporations."[44] Before radio, the union message was filtered through an often hostile media. Radio provided union leaders the same opportunity it gave President Roosevelt and other politicians to circumvent the press and speak directly to listeners. Like Roosevelt, union speakers tried to create a personal connection with the audience. They greeted listeners with a "howdy, folks," or with the salutation, "My friends." When the steelworker B. J. Damich went on the air in Cleveland in July 1937 to explain to the public the union perspective on the strike against Republic Steel plants, he began with, "My dear Friends and Fellow Citizens," and in the course of his address he spoke repeatedly to "my radio friends."[45]

Broadcasts aimed at the public sought to demystify and legitimize organized labor. One of the first items on John L. Lewis's agenda after the founding of the CIO was to speak to the nation over the CBS network to explain the reasons for the formation of a new labor organization. He stressed the limitations of craft unionism and asserted that the millions of workers in mass-production industries are "entitled to a place in the American economic sunlight." Other CIO national and local union leaders repeatedly and patiently explained to the American public the nature of industrial unionism and the aims and achievements of organized labor. The UAW organizer Harry Elder began his broadcast in October 1937 in Memphis with the assurance that "there is nothing mysterious in the symbol, CIO. It is simply the alphabetical abbreviation for the Committee for Industrial Organization." Seeking to counteract the fear and suspicion of organized labor, SWOC Local 1123 of Canton, Ohio, broadcast an entire lodge meeting during which new officers were elected and the lodge president, I. W. Abel, gave a detailed report of the local's activities. The purpose of the broadcast was to give the public an opportunity to hear firsthand how a union operates. Abel explained to listeners, "We want you to hear and be convinced that the main purpose of a union is not to call strikes nor to extort unreasonable demands from employers." Strikes, he argued, "were unusual and unwanted things in the life of the average union."[46]

In seeking to legitimize the CIO, labor leaders emphasized the responsible nature of organized labor and its desire for harmony between capital and labor. Richard Evans, the president of a steelworkers lodge, declared to the city of Portsmouth, "We are going to show you, better than we can tell you, that the Amalgamated, as an instrument of peace and progress, is the best friend you've got!" In December 1936, the UAW organizer A. J. Pickett assured the citizens of St. Louis that the workers seeking to organize General Motors "certainly do not desire to run the business of the Company, as is so often charged." Unions wanted the public to understand that business, not labor, is primarily responsible for most strikes and violence. In his Labor Day radio speeches, John Brophy argued that strikes are caused by the "stubborn refusal" of corporations to obey the laws of the United States and bargain collectively and that employers have invariably provoked the violence associated with strikes. According to Brophy, for the enemies of labor to level the charge of violence against the CIO "is like a thief trying to make his get-away by starting a cry of 'stop thief' against the very man whom he has robbed." The CIO, he declared, "is not only a non-violent movement, but it is most strongly opposed to violence in labor disputes, knowing that the workers are always the worst sufferers when violence occurs."[47]

Unionists in their radio talks appealed for public support by emphasizing that organized labor is committed to building a better America for everyone. Drawing on a Keynesian interpretation of the economy, they regularly argued that the government-sanctioned organization of workers through collective bargaining would boost wages and thus increase the purchasing power of the masses, which was crucial to permanent recovery from the Depression. Job security, another key goal of organized labor, also increased the consumption of goods. As the UAW organizer Norman Smith explained to the people of Memphis, the benefits of organized labor are not restricted to workers alone; the entire community, and particularly small business, gains from a successful labor movement. In a similar vein, the UAW secretary-treasurer George Addes asserted in a Detroit broadcast that strong, responsible unionism means prosperity and stability for the entire community: "the auto worker comes home with more money to spend at the grocery and meat market, and with his dentist and doctor, and with the movie houses and the clothing and department stores." The bottom line is that more money is spent "where the auto workers live and work and less money is drained off to Wall Street."[48]

Radio enabled labor to share with the American public its democratic vision of a workplace free of industrial autocracy. Through radio, the CIO transmitted the concept of industrial democracy from union halls and shop floors into homes across the nation. Labor's broadcasts consistently wrapped the CIO within the mantle of American political democracy. John Brophy explained to listeners in his 1937 Labor Day broadcast that the ultimate aim of the CIO is to "extend democratic rights, such as all Americans are supposed to enjoy politically, into the realm to industry." As Brophy saw it, labor deserved the support of the American public not only because it was more moral than industry and committed to defending human rights above property rights but because unionism epitomized Americanism. In that same Labor Day address, Brophy proclaimed that organized labor had made a "greater contribution to true Americanism" than almost any other voluntary organization of the American people.[49]

❖ ❖ ❖

What difference did radio make to organized labor in the 1930s? Unlike business, unions had no regular network programs, so there are no ratings available to judge the size of audiences. We do know that radio gave labor unprecedented direct access to the public. Because networks and local stations had to fulfill the mandate to serve "in the public interest, convenience, and necessity," broadcasters did open their microphones to representatives of the working class. Not only did union leaders such as John L. Lewis, John Brophy, and William Green gain a national audience through radio speeches, but other oppositional voices, such as the Socialist leader Norman Thomas, spoke to the American public as well. Numerous times between 1935 and 1938, Thomas brought the plight of southern sharecroppers to the nation's attention, and he rarely minced words in describing the conditions they endured and the brutal response to their attempts to organize. His prime-time speech over the NBC network on April 3, 1935, began, "There is a reign of terror in the cotton country of eastern Arkansas. It will end either in the establishment of complete and slavish submission to the vilest exploitation in America or in bloodshed." Recognizing the power of radio as a political force, Thomas appealed "for the sake of peace, liberty, and common human decency . . . to you who listen to my voice to bring immediate pressure upon the federal government to act."[50]

Although it is clear that people were listening, it is difficult to determine the impact of media on behavior and attitudes. Certainly business was listening closely. In the midst of the 1937 Flint sit-down strikes, the *Journal of Commerce* warned the business community that the CIO had launched a publicity campaign, of which radio was a central component. Later that year, U.S. Steel hired a firm to monitor every labor speech on every radio station in the nation.[51] In Memphis, though violence against union organizers occurred routinely, it is of some significance that the UAW organizer Norman Smith was brutally attacked by six men while on his way to broadcast a speech on a local radio station in 1937. The night before, Smith had spoken to the people of Memphis about the benefits of industrial unionism. The assailants, however, failed to silence the autoworkers. Smith's companion, Harry Elder, beaten less severely, managed to reach the radio station, where he delivered the talk Smith had intended to make.[52]

While Smith's story is inspiring, it does suggest the limitations of radio as a motivational force. Harry Elder and Norman Smith, when he had recovered from the assault, spoke for over two months almost nightly to the citizens of Memphis. But radio alone was not powerful enough to overcome the climate of fear inculcated by employers and civil authorities. In the end, the UAW withdrew its organizers, and it took federal intervention during World War II to bring industrial unionism to this antilabor citadel.[53]

Rose Pesotta, a veteran ILGWU organizer, was struck by another kind of limitation. In 1935, the union sent her to Buffalo, regarded as New York's open-shop center. In addition to the usual organizational activities, she bought radio time, broadcasting Friday evenings in English and Polish. The program began and ended with labor songs and included news commentary. Pesotta learned that the young women, who made up the bulk of the garment industry workforce, enjoyed listening to the broadcast. But when she asked them when they planned to sign up with the union, she later recalled, "they looked at me in astonishment." It never occurred to them that "just because they enjoyed our literature and listened to our radio programs they ought to join the union." The mass media was unable to motivate them to change their lives by joining the union, and neither the union message nor advertisers' messages seem to have much impact. Pesotta observed that although the young women listened to many radio programs, "none of them bought Chase & Sanborn coffee, nor smoked Chesterfield cigarettes, nor used Sweetheart soap, or Pepsodent toothpaste, though some did buy Jello because it 'took no time to make.'"[54]

Yet it is perhaps premature to dismiss the significance of radio's contribution to the revitalization of organized labor in the 1930s. Like the worker-made films of the 1910s and 1920s, radio helped labor gain a new voice and possibly a new legitimacy within the public sphere. In addition, it provided a mechanism to speak directly to workers, enabling unions to reach them across the barriers of fear that had been forged by employers. One southern textile worker recalled that he did not belong to a union until "'one time I heard a man speaking on the radio and he said, "Suppose you go into the mill tomorrow to do your job, and they's to tell you they didn't need you anymore? Who'd you turn to?" So I got to thinking about that. The next morning I asked one of the members for a card, and I signed that card, I went in.'"[55]

Finally, radio helped at least some working-class listeners to reformulate their identities. These listeners first joined imagined oppositional communities of organized labor through the airwaves. Emboldened by a connection created through the radio and often reinforced by the rising militancy of the era, many working-class listeners then took concrete steps to join union ranks. In Detroit, for instance, radio helped forge a vital connection between Polish female cigar makers and the labor movement. For over six months these women listened in as the UAW organizer Stanley Nowak spoke weekly to Polish autoworkers. In early 1937, in the midst of the sit-down strikes in the auto industry, twenty-five women were arbitrarily fired from a cigar shop. The women struck and immediately sent a delegation to the UAW's central office asking for Stanley Nowak's help. The UAW secretary-treasurer George Addes asked, "Why Nowak?" The cigar workers replied that they listened to Nowak on the UAW Polish radio program and wanted him to help guide their struggle. In the absence of a concrete union presence in the cigar shops, Stanley Nowak had created a personal contact between these workers and the labor movement. Nowak's radio voice became the vehicle for helping cigar workers act collectively. With radio's help, they moved from being members of an imaginary oppositional community to a real community, a union affiliated with the CIO.[56]

In the 1930s, unions were still experimenting with radio, exploring its potential for organizing and community building. By the end of the decade, they were prepared to make a larger commitment. In 1939, the CIO's Committee on Press and Publicity urged its affiliates to make broader use of radio, asserting that it was one of labor's "most effective means of reaching its own members and the public."[57] But even during the 1930s there had been significant impediments to labor's free access to radio. By the end of the decade, the broadcasting industry constructed an even stronger barrier to broadcasting unionism.

((O))

3   Codes of Silence: Censoring Labor
     on the Airwaves

JUST AS UNION INTEREST in radio was expanding, labor found its access to
the air sharply curtailed. Hoping to silence growing criticism of the industry and to prevent threatened federal regulation, the National Association of
Broadcasters, radio's trade organization, adopted a new voluntary code of
ethics in mid 1939. The code barred member stations from selling time for
the discussion of controversial issues, with the exception of political broadcasts. Instead, as part of their public duty, broadcasters were to provide free
time to representative spokesmen of opposing points of view. According to
the NAB, the goal was not to censor but to promote balanced discussion
of public issues and to prevent those with the most economic power from
monopolizing the airwaves. The broadcasters' association ruled that labor
issues are inherently controversial and instructed its members to refuse to
sell radio time to labor unions. In the months after its adoption, the code
virtually knocked labor off the air in some locales.[1]

Unions often struggled for access to the airwaves even prior to the adoption of the NAB code. Indeed, the code was modeled after existing network
standards and policies, which limited labor's airtime. Controversial issues,
from politics to religion to social and economic questions, were technically
confined to the unsponsored time slots that the networks designated for the
discussion of issues of public importance. Consistent with this policy, the
networks had never sold time to unions. Instead, several times a year, they
allotted free time for speeches by prominent labor leaders. In contrast to the
networks, the microphones of local stations were more likely to be open to
organized labor. Still, even local stations routinely rejected union program-

ming as too controversial.[2] Broadcasters at the network and local levels, however, found little that was controversial about business, which provided the bulk of advertising revenues. While they avoided selling airtime for some of the most partisan business programs, they welcomed such institutional programs as "Cavalcade of America" and "The Ford Sunday Evening Hour" and often ignored the antilabor diatribes of business-sponsored commentators. Essentially, the NAB code brought more local stations into line with network policy towards unions, making it even more difficult to reach the public with labor's message after 1939. To the CIO, it was clear that labor had become the victim of a business-orchestrated "conspiracy of silence."[3]

❖ ❖ ❖

During much of the twentieth century, workers struggled to gain access to the mass media. In the 1910s and 1920s, state and local censors often banned worker films that depicted strikes and union organizing, charging that they "incited class antagonisms." Hollywood's Production Code Authority (PCA), the self-censoring body that ruled from 1934 until the 1960s, discouraged the production of films dealing with class conflict. Pressure from the PCA and state censors ensured that the few films that did touch on organized labor or workers promoted conservative political messages.[4]

As the historian Daniel Czitrom observes, "[P]olitical censorship, both flagrant and subtle, also characterized commercial radio from the beginning." With the acquiescence of the federal government, commercial broadcasters had seized control of radio in the 1920s. Owned by large corporations, broadcasters tended to promote the status quo and ignore or censor nonmainstream political opinions. The commentator H. V. Kaltenborn observed that only occasionally, in an effort to deflect public criticism, did the networks allow on the air "a well-behaved liberal or radical speaker." During the late 1920s and early 1930s, concerned that these private broadcasters had little interest in protecting diversity of opinion, civic, educational, religious, farm, and labor groups fought for public control of radio. They argued that radio should serve the public interest and that "commercial broadcasting was inimical to the communications needs of a democratic society." The journalist James Rorty, for instance, contended that corporate control of broadcasting protected business from meaningful criticism. According to reformers, radio was too powerful a medium to be controlled by companies driven solely by the profit motive.[5]

The struggle for noncommercial broadcasting ended unsuccessfully with the passage of the Communications Act of 1934, which established the Federal

Communications Commission. Commercial broadcasters retained control of radio, though the industry was regulated by the government and required to operate under a mandate to serve "in the public interest, convenience, and necessity." The FCC issued stations short-term licenses and could deny renewal if there was evidence of violation of federal regulations. Stations were required to present a balanced, well-rounded schedule of programming, representing a variety of political viewpoints.[6]

Through much of the 1930s, the FCC wielded its authority with considerable restraint. The commission rejected few license renewals and maintained cordial relations with the broadcasters. Still, the "threat of government mischief haunted the industry," particularly the networks, NBC and CBS.[7] While not under the immediate jurisdiction of the FCC, the networks owned outright some of the most powerful local stations, and most of the other high power stations were affiliated with them. In some ways, the networks were even more politically vulnerable than local stations. Broadcast reformers' charges that the networks had gained monopoly control of the industry raised the specter of antitrust and other kinds of regulation. Industry fears were not completely unwarranted. In 1938, in response to congressional pressure, the FCC began an investigation into chain broadcasting, and in 1941 it launched an inquiry into newspaper ownership of broadcast stations. Given this pressure, broadcasters sought "to foster a spirit of accommodation with the administration."[8]

To reduce the possibility of further federal regulation, the networks generally discouraged criticism of government policy and shied away from selling time for programs on subjects that they deemed controversial. Moreover, they attempted to maintain at least a public facade of political neutrality. In July 1936, NBC reminded stations managers that "'none of our news broadcasts, commercial or sustaining, must in any way reflect political opinions or take partisan views on any issue.'" The networks sold time for political broadcasts only during election campaigns, as prescribed by the Communications Act. Broadcasters met the mandate that they operate in the public interest and that they offer a balanced schedule by sponsoring public-service programming. This included talks on current political, economic, and social questions by government officials, representatives of organized social groups, and other public figures. Broadcasters, of course, determined which subjects were of public interest and who were legitimate representatives of particular issues. When controversial matters were discussed, equal time was to be offered to both sides. In 1935 only 5 percent of NBC network time was given over to this kind of programming, and only a small proportion of these shows addressed issues of a controversial character. To varying degrees, local stations followed the network policies on controversial issues. As a result, unable to buy time and with little free time available, advocates of dissident political or social views, such as Socialists, pacifists, Communists, or promoters of birth control or racial equality, were often denied access the airwaves.[9]

Beyond fear of government interference, radio stations also worried about maintaining public goodwill. The desire to maximize their audiences and thus increase advertising revenues made broadcasters leery of airing programs that might alienate potential listeners. To prevent this from happening, stations and the networks censored scripts to eliminate not only controversial issues but anything that might be considered in poor taste or offensive. John F. Royal, the NBC network's vice president for programming, established a network policy of "giving offense to no one." Royal had made his reputation in vaudeville, working as a press agent for Harry Houdini and then serving as a regional manager for the Keith-Albee theaters. The big-time Keith vaudeville theaters had attracted large audiences by offering centrally controlled, inoffensive, family-oriented entertainment. After the collapse of the Keith chain in 1930, Royal became manager of the NBC Cleveland affiliate. Impressed with his managerial skills and showmanship, NBC president Merlin H. Aylesworth brought him to New York as vice president in 1931. At NBC, Royal applied the lessons he had learned during his years in vaudeville, particularly the importance of avoiding offending any part of the audience. In 1933, reflecting this commitment, Royal vowed, "[W]ithout being arbitrary, we must take a firm stand and despite income or expediency, protect our institution. It was built on clean, wholesome material, that's the way we are going to stay, or we're lost."[10]

❖ ❖ ❖

Labor was one of the victims of the broadcasters' restriction on freedom of speech. With only two small radio stations committed to broadcasting labor issues—WCFL in Chicago and WEVD in New York—unions had to rely for airtime on commercial stations, many of whom were hesitant to serve as a platform for organized labor. Broadcasters tended to relegate labor to the controversial category. As early as 1926, the leader of the Socialist party, Norman Thomas, observed that labor and liberal groups "'have rarely been able to get hearings over established stations,'" partly because of the cost but also because of "'direct censorship.'"[11]

Some stations shied away from any discussion of labor issues altogether. In late May 1935, WLW in Cincinnati, the most powerful station in the Midwest, issued an order that "no reference to strikes is to be made on any news broadcasts over this station." A few days later another message further clarified station policy: "Our news broadcasts, as you have already been told, and which has been our practice for some time, will not include mention of any strikes. This also includes student strikes and school walkouts." Norman Corwin, a writer who had only recently joined the station as a newscaster, questioned the policy and was promptly fired. After leaving the station, he sent copies of the memos to the American Civil Liberties Union, which was investigating radio censorship. In August, with evidence in hand, the ACLU publicly accused WLW and its owner, the wealthy manufacturer Powell Crosley, of practicing censorship. Given WLW's prominence, the ACLU's charges gained national attention. Unaware that the ACLU had copies of the memos, the station manager, John L. Clark, issued an indignant denial of the charge that his station suppressed strike information. "Apparently," he wrote, "you have been terribly misinformed on this situation and have done this station a tremendous damage by releasing erroneous information." When the ACLU produced copies of the orders, WLW abruptly announced that the matter was a "closed incident."[12]

The following spring, William Papier published an article that provided further evidence of the station's anti-union bias. Between 1934 and 1935, Papier was the "Modern Problems Instructor" of "The Ohio School of the Air," which was broadcast each weekday over WLW to an estimated audience of half a million. Teachers ranked "Modern Problems" the highest of all the segments offered on the educational show. WLW required that all of the instructors' scripts be approved by the station's education director. Papier quickly learned that there were boundaries that he could not cross. For instance, during the program's first year, the station prevented the educator from delivering a talk on anti-union employers. The following year, Papier announced that he planned to present four or five talks on the "functional aspects of unionism." Despite his high ratings, the station abruptly canceled his program and replaced it with a series entitled "Modern Problems of Seniors."[13]

Unions faced several barriers when they tried to reach the public via radio. Stations might refuse outright to sell airtime. In the mid 1930s, an ACLU survey of radio censorship found an unwritten law among many radio station owners that forbade labor use of the air. It also discovered that larger stations affiliated with the networks tended to be the most rigid enforcers of this policy.[14] Often, stations initially agreed to labor broadcasts and then backed out under pressure from employers. In November 1934, for instance, the Newspaper Guild in San Francisco, which was engaged in a controversy with the *Oakland Tribune* over the firing of three employees, corresponded with seven stations, seeking to buy time for a fifteen-minute broadcast to explain the union's side of the dispute. The Guild informed the stations that it planned to encourage listeners to cancel their *Tribune* subscriptions. Six of the stations, including two large stations owned by NBC and one owned by CBS, either ignored the Guild's request or refused to sell the union broadcast time. Finally, KJBS, a locally owned, low-powered station, agreed to give the Guild fifteen minutes gratis, with the provision that the newspaper would have a chance to reply. Shortly before the broadcast, however, the station backed out of the arrangement because the *Tribune* publisher threatened KJBS with a libel suit "if one word of the Guild's story went on the air." Similar pressure silenced the Lumber and Sawmill Workers Union in Eureka, California. In June 1935 the union was on strike, and eighty of its members had been charged with inciting a riot. The union contracted with KIEM in Eureka for a series of nine fifteen-minute broadcasts to take its case to the public. Two hours before the first program, the series was canceled. The station asserted that the contract gave it the right to preempt programs "in case of emergency or unusual event." The only emergency in Eureka in the summer of 1935 was the lumber strike. About the same time, on the East Coast, the American Federation of Hosiery Workers in Philadelphia charged that the station KYW had canceled a contracted union speech on the collapse of the National Recovery Administration because it urged "militant strike action against chiseling by manufacturers."[15]

As the CIO organizing drive intensified in 1936 and 1937 and more unions sought access to radio, denial of airtime became even more of a problem. While the UAW could broadcast from Detroit over WJBK, neither the Flint sit-down strikers nor striking steelworkers in Youngstown could buy airtime at local radio stations.[16] Stations used a variety of excuses to refuse union broadcast requests. In December 1936, the United Electrical Workers Union was conducting an organizing campaign at the General Electric plant in Schenectady, New York. Just prior to the representation election, the union sought to present its case to the community over the station WGY, an outlet owned by General Electric and affiliated with NBC. The station denied the request on "the grounds that the controversy was only of 'local interest' and therefore not suitable for a network station."[17]

Other radio stations simply claimed that labor broadcasts were too controversial. Both stations in Dayton denied their facilities to UE Local 801. Ernest De Maio, an organizer, reported that "they say we are controversial, whatever that may mean, and therefore, refuse to sell us any time whatsoever." This was particularly frustrating because the union had also been unable to hire any of the larger halls for meetings.[18] In January 1937, ILGWU Dallas dressmakers locals had hoped to boost union-label products and publicize its organizing drive through a radio advertising campaign that consisted of a series of brief announcements. The first one asked "the cooperation of every man and woman in our city and state in the fight to wipe out sweatshops and obtain living wages and decent hours and working conditions." It urged listeners to "do your share by insisting on the Union Label in the dresses you buy." Although the station KRLD had initially agreed to a series of fifty-two announcements, upon reviewing the scripts, the station manager canceled them as "unacceptable because they were 'controversial.'" Samuel S. White of the dressmakers' local observed bitterly: "[I]f the station is permitted to brand any matter as 'controversial,' we might as well not attempt to go on the air. Everything is 'controversial' when it comes to labor."[19] Turned down in Milwaukee because its broadcasts were too controversial, the Federated Trades Council aired its programs from Chicago via the labor station WCFL. A grateful Herman Seide, secretary of the council, observed that without WCFL, "labor would not be able to get its story before the public at all, as most of the other stations and newspapers are under control of the business interests. So more power to you in your efforts to protect labor's only real uncensored contact with the public."[20]

Anti-union radio owners or station managers often needed little or no excuse for denying airtime to labor. In the spring of 1937, garbage collectors in Bridgeport, Connecticut, organized in the CIO Municipal Workers Industrial Union, went on strike. Mayor Jasper McLevy refused to negotiate with the union, and in mid-May he received fifteen minutes, free of charge, to explain the city's position over the station WICC, which was owned by the Yankee Network, a regional New England chain of stations. Upon learning of the mayor's intention to broadcast, the Municipal Workers asked for and initially received the station manager's promise of equal time to make their case. At the last moment, the station manager canceled the union broadcast, explaining that the owner of the Yankee Network, John Shepard, "is opposed to the sit-down strike." Shepard was an aggressive, innovative businessman who in 1922 opened a radio station in Boston to promote his department stores. In 1930, he founded the Yankee Network to provide programs of region-wide interest. Shepard was angry at the CIO because workers in his Providence department store had just used a sit-down strike to win higher wages and shorter hours. He later exhibited his reputation for being abrasive when he brushed aside an ACLU inquiry into his "apparently discriminatory and unfair act," asserting that he did not consider the labor broadcast to be of "public interest."[21]

Getting on the air was no guarantee that the union message would get through uncensored. If a station agreed to broadcast a union program, the manager often requested advance copies of scripts and might demand changes prior to airtime. Station managers commonly cut material that they considered inflammatory or controversial from union scripts. The UAW found that even "reasonable and factual criticism of some of the larger corporations" was taboo on the air. If the talk was extemporaneous, which was seldom allowed, or the unionist deviated from the script into objectionable territory, the station manager could turn off the connection and leave the speaker talking into a dead microphone. One early example of this occurred in the spring of 1928 in Paterson, New Jersey. Henry Berger of the Typographical Union was speaking over WODA, questioning those who spoke of Coolidge prosperity when Paterson workers suffered from low wages and unemployment. In the middle of the speech, the station owner, Richard O'Dea, suddenly pulled the switch, complaining of the "communistic" tone of the address.[22]

In the late 1930s, as the CIO sought to make more aggressive use of radio, conflicts over censorship as well as struggles over access intensified. During the 1937 GM strike, WHK in Cleveland repeatedly censored UAW Fisher Body Local 45's regular addresses. For example, it cut references to the company's purchase and use of arms, ammunition, and tear gas and censored descriptions of the battles between supporters of the sit-down strikers and police in Flint. The local discovered that even if its speaker adhered to the script, their radio audience might suddenly disappear. On January 25, 1937, as the president of Local 45, Louis F. Spisak, delivered a speech that had already been edited and approved by the management, the station "abruptly and without warning" cut him off the air. The station then terminated the union's contract and refused further access to its facilities. The union's secretary, Steve Jenso, angrily charged WHK with violating freedom of speech and "overtly and deliberately aiding General Motors" by censoring and then suppressing the broadcasts.[23]

Even without censorship, station owners could undermine the union message. The Textile Workers Organizing Committee had intended to kick off its New England organizing drive with a one-hour broadcast of a mass meeting in Lawrence, Massachusetts, featuring speeches by John L. Lewis and Sidney Hillman. The CIO succeeded in buying time over the Colonial

Network, another New England chain owned by John Shepard. While reviewing the arrangements, Lewis discovered that Shepard intended to make a personal disclaimer on the air repudiating the CIO. Shepard planned on stating immediately before and after the union broadcast that the "following (or preceding) speeches are the opinion of the speakers and the Textile Workers Organizing Committee (TWOC) and do not reflect the opinion of the network, the management of which is definitely opposed to certain principles of the CIO, notably the sit-down strike." Despite Lewis's objections, the station refused to delete the editorial announcement. Characterizing the statement as "a violation of the rights of free speech and fair play and a deliberate distortion of the principles of the CIO," the TWOC canceled its contract with the Colonial Network and engaged several other independent radio stations to carry the speeches. Annoyed at Shepard's actions, Lewis declared that "the radio companies do not yet own the air" and warned that it "is this sort of thing that will result in legislation."[24]

Aware of the vulnerability of their licenses and fearful of federal interference, few broadcasters displayed their antilabor sentiments as overtly as John Shepard. One network official condemned Shepard's "fight 'em to the last drop" stance towards unions as "'heroic but unrealistic,'" while a prominent advertising agency partner declared: "There's a right way and a wrong way to handle social pressure."[25] The networks set the example for the broadcasting industry on the right way to handle pressure for access from organized labor. NBC and CBS consistently asserted that they sold time only for the advertising of goods and services and never for propaganda or controversial public issues. In 1937, William S. Paley, president of CBS, defined propaganda as "any attempt to influence legislation, regulation, taxation, and the like." The networks viewed unions as agents of propaganda and thus classified them as inherently controversial. Therefore, organized labor was ineligible to buy network time.[26]

NBC adhered so strictly to this rule that it initially banned the ILGWU's acclaimed Broadway musical, *Pins and Needles,* from network broadcast, arguing that the show's songs were full of controversial subjects. It finally agreed to schedule the show once numbers like "Doing the Reactionary" and "Sing Me a Song of Social Significance" were cut. The executive John Royal allowed the song "Sunday" to be included after he was convinced that it was strictly a romantic tune that contained nothing critical of the economic system. After the show's songwriter, Harold J. Rome, revised the lyrics of "One Big Union for Two," deleting references to court injunctions, closed shops, scabs, and lockouts, NBC allowed the song to be broadcast.

Finally, the network insisted that the last line of the song be changed from "fifty million union members can't be wrong" to the more innocuous "fifty million happy couples can't be wrong."[27]

❖ ❖ ❖

The networks claimed that as part of their public service mission, they provided ample free time for the discussion of controversial issues, including labor. Each year NBC and CBS broadcast parts of the AFL and later CIO conventions and Labor Day speeches by prominent union leaders. They also provided airtime for union speeches at several other times during the year. In 1936, for instance, in addition to his Labor Day address, John L. Lewis spoke over the networks on July 6 and December 31.[28] During the 1930s, the networks publicly demonstrated their commitment to representing all political and economic viewpoints by giving time for speeches by Norman Thomas, leader of the Socialist party, and occasionally even by the Communist party leader Earl Browder. Thomas, who often spoke about labor issues, admitted that he served as NBC's "'pet radical.'" As he wryly put it, he was valuable to NBC "'as proof of [its] liberalism.'"[29]

In reality, relatively little network time went to labor in the 1930s. Barred from buying time, labor was essentially dependent on the network's charity. Free airtime was available only for issues that the networks deemed of sufficient public interest. NBC denied Norman Thomas's request for time to discuss Mayor Frank Hague's attack on workers seeking to organize Jersey City, arguing that it was not a public issue. The NBC executive John F. Royal contended that the meaning of "'public issue' . . . is a matter of opinion." He explained that NBC did not "permit free *speech* on the air. We *do* permit free discussion, under radio's editorial judgment." NBC editorial judgment often meant little airtime for unions. As Royal admitted in a December 1939 internal memo, the network had "never given much time to labor as labor— there have been occasional talks by the A F of L and the CIO."[30]

Even when the networks scheduled a labor speaker, rarely did all its affiliated stations carry the broadcast. Networks required affiliates to carry sponsored programs, such as "Fibber McGee and Molly" or "The Jack Benny Show," but allowed them to take or reject unsponsored or sustaining programs. Thus, as the ACLU secretary Hazel L. Rice observed, "every station on a network must have the Ford hour, with Mr. Cameron's little talk in the middle of the hour, [but] should Mr. Lewis follow him (and the only way he could do it would be to have the time given to him) all the affiliated stations could cut him off if they chose to." Local affiliates did indeed often refuse to carry network labor speeches. David Dubinsky, president of the ILGWU, for instance, spoke over NBC at 6:15 P.M. on April 14, 1938. Workers in Los Angeles, Montreal, and Fall River, Massachusetts, many of whom had gathered at their union headquarters, were disappointed when their local stations failed to pick up NBC's coast-to-coast broadcast. Aware of this problem, prior to John L. Lewis's speeches, CIO headquarters sent letters to all affiliated national unions asking them to publicize the broadcasts and to urge local network affiliates to transmit the program.[31]

While networks were stingy about airtime for labor, they welcomed such business institutional programming as "Cavalcade of America" and "The Ford Sunday Evening Hour." But, fearful of government intervention, they refused to allow corporations carte blanche. In the mid 1930s, for instance, NBC's vice president John F. Royal worried about associating NBC too closely with anti-administration business organizations, and he refused to sell time to the Crusaders, an anti–New Deal, business-backed organization.[32] NBC also rejected the NAM's "American Family Robinson," characterizing it as "decided propaganda." According to Royal, some members of the NAM believed that NBC was going to "give them unlimited time." But, he argued, although "they are our biggest clients, there is a much bigger question facing [us]. That is the very question of our existence for 'public interest,' convenience, and necessity."[33]

Network principles on controversial programming placed impediments to business self-promotion but certainly not insurmountable barriers. Network polices could be remarkably inconsistent. CBS, for example, did sell time to the Crusaders, and during the 1936 election, NBC sold time to the American Liberty League, another anti–New Deal business organization. CBS, of course, carried Ford's "Sunday Evening Hour," which featured the anti–New Deal and antilabor commentary of William J. Cameron. However, it repeatedly urged Cameron to moderate his commentary. Cameron's talks plagued CBS, for it wanted to offend neither the Ford Motor Company nor the Roosevelt administration.[34]

NBC normally refused to allow discussion of controversial issues, such as strikes, on commercial programs. Even comedy dealing with strikes was taboo. At the April 1938 meeting of the NBC's National Advisory Council, the network president Lenox Lohr asserted, "If a motor company were having a strike and should attempt to use their time to influence public opinion on the subject, we would stop them from presenting such a case in time sold for advertising a product." But in early 1937, NBC permitted General Motors to use the intermission of its "Concert Hour" to make a subtle attack against the Flint sit-down strikers, who had forced the closing of several of the corporation's plants. The GM announcer never specifically mentioned the strike but instead defended the "age-old principle of the right to work." He contended that "whether one shall work—how one shall work—when one shall work—has from the earliest days of our national existence been the acknowledged right of each one of us to decide for himself, with no man's interference." The appeal was "so cleverly done" that John Royal felt confident in taking "a chance on it."[35]

Networks were also much more likely to give time to business than to organized labor. During April 1935, for instance, NBC broadcast speeches by fifteen business leaders representing some of the most powerful corporations in the nation, including Lammot Du Pont, William B. Ball, president of American Cynanamid Company, Alfred P. Sloan, president of GM, and T. K. Quinn, vice president of General Electric. The only labor speaker to grace NBC's microphone during that period was David Dubinsky, reporting for fifteen minutes on an international labor conference in Geneva, Switzerland.[36]

When networks did refuse to air business programming deemed overtly propagandistic, organizations like the NAM could always turn to the hundreds of small, independent stations, which willingly sold or gave time to business. In 1940, praising the "friendly and constant cooperation" it had received from stations all over the nation, the NAM reported that the radio industry had provided the association with 7,960 free radio hours for "American Family Robinson" and for commentary by George E. Sokolsky on government, economics, and business. Hungry for programming and often less fearful of public criticism than the networks, some non-network stations readily accepted all kinds of business offerings. Most had little fear of regulatory repercussions, for despite FCC threats, few station licenses were ever revoked. These stations, some of whom also sold time to unions, provided a much smaller audience than the powerful network-affiliated outlets, but by avoiding the networks, business groups were freer to say whatever they pleased on the air.[37]

If the networks trod lightly when it came to labor conflict, some local stations readily enlisted on the employer's side. This is not surprising, since stations recognized their dependence on employers for advertising revenues. Moreover, many stations were owned by companies whose owners held an anti-union perspective. William Randolph Hearst, for instance, was notoriously hostile to organized labor. During the Remington Rand strike, his New York station WINS allowed Remington's vice president to take time from the "News Comes to Life" program to make a speech applauding his firm's labor policy.[38]

In some cases, stations had intimate ties to the employers fighting organized labor. During the 1934 Minneapolis Teamsters strike, WCCO, which had close ties to General Mills president Donald Davis, actively backed the Minneapolis Citizens Alliance of which Davis was a member. Daily radio broadcasts charged that the Teamsters union was Communist-dominated. In a typical broadcast, Joseph Cochran, director of the Citizens Alliance, warned that the "Communists hope that this strike is the beginning of a revolution that will overthrow all existing government." The broadcasts seemed to have an immediate impact. One observer wrote to the Minnesota governor that "the radio talks of the Employers' Association are turning sentiment against the strikers by using the charge of Communism." After the strike was broken, to help prevent any further labor uprising, WCCO allowed the Law and Order League to broadcast sixteen additional weekly radio programs.[39]

❖ ❖ ❖

The CIO chafed at the restrictions and inequities that labor faced in broadcasting. R. J. Thomas, president of the UAW, pointed out that radio stations gave "free rein to notorious demagogues and unscrupulous foes of our union and the CIO," while the autoworkers often had "difficulty in purchasing an adequate amount of time from the large stations." In January 1937, Samuel S. White of the Dallas Dressmakers asked why the station KRLD banned his union's ads, while on the previous Sunday it had broadcast General Motors' talk on "the right to work." Similarly, the union-backed Seattle People's Radio Guild wondered why KIPO considered its labor program inappropriate but carried CBS's Boake Carter, who attacked "John L. Lewis, the administration, and the Maritime Federation of the Pacific without any sort of restraint." Moreover, the guild complained that KIPO also carried Ford's "Sunday Evening Hour," during which "Mr. Cameron has time and again declared that Ford's way is the American Way, implying that the policy of the Administration and the policy of Organized Labor is not American."[40]

The ACLU and the radio critic Ruth Brindze joined the chorus of protests. Hazel Rice, secretary of the ACLU, pointed out that while no labor union could buy time on the air, advertisers such as Philco and Ford "put people like Boake Carter and Cameron on the air who, under the guise of institutional advertising, get away with social propaganda." Brindze devoted much of her 1937 exposé on broadcasting, *Not to Be Broadcast*, to documenting the influence of big business over the medium. She claimed that one of the great American myths was that "the operation of radio broadcasting for private profit assures the freedom of the air waves from political interference." Brindze juxtaposed examples of labor censorship with examples of business's ability to use radio to disseminate its propaganda. She devoted an entire chapter to Ford's "Sunday Evening Hour," asserting that "there is not even a rumor that the Columbia Broadcasting System has been troubled by the demagogic nature of the Ford talks."[41]

In the late 1930s, some CIO unions began taking their complaints about unfair treatment to the FCC. The most vigorous protest came from San Francisco, when the station KGCC refused to renew the contract for the International Longshoremen and Warehousemen's Union's daily program "Labor on the March." More than thirty local unions wrote to the FCC condemning the station's action and urging that the commission refuse to renew KGCC's broadcasting license.[42] Oriented towards the broadcasters' interests, the FCC generally assumed a "hands-off" policy in dealing with these kinds of complaints. It usually asked stations for an explanation but went no further. Accordingly, it responded to the West Coast unionists by claiming that the law prevented the FCC from intervening in specific programming decisions.[43]

Unionists found this kind of response frustrating. Bridgeport municipal workers, for instance, were incensed when the chairman of the FCC, Anning S. Prall, answered their protest over John Shepard's refusal for airtime with a "senseless wire."[44] Angry CIO members adopted a resolution at the 1937 CIO convention, urging Congress to make a thorough probe of radio, and in October 1938 the CIO asked to participate in the FCC's chain-monopoly investigation. By giving testimony that documented the broadcasting industry's discriminatory treatment of organized labor at this high-profile hearing, the CIO hoped to pressure more radio stations to open their facilities to unions.[45]

Relations between the broadcasters and the regulatory agency, however, became chilly toward the end of the 1930s. Under the chairmanship of Frank McNinch, the commission seemed to be moving toward exercising more control over broadcasting. Several times during 1937 and 1938, the FCC rapped the networks' knuckles for inappropriate behavior. Most notably, the commission reacted strongly to the infamous Mae West episode with its sexually suggestive dialogue, to the inclusion of such expressions as "hell," "damnation," and "for God's sake" in the broadcast of Eugene O'Neill's play *Beyond the Horizon,* and to Orson Welles's *War of the Worlds* broadcast, which created anxiety across the nation. There was also increasing concern over the far-right broadcasts of Father Charles Coughlin. Deemed controversial, he was unable to buy time over NBC or CBS, but the priest had cobbled together a large chain of stations to carry his speeches. By 1938, Coughlin's inflammatory radio talks had become a major embarrassment to the broadcasting industry. Adding to the industry's unease was pressure from Congress for an investigation of network domination of the airwaves. In the spring of 1938, the FCC responded to congressional antitrust sentiment by authorizing an investigation into the allegations of monopoly in broadcasting.[46]

❖ ❖ ❖

In the hope of derailing the drive for increased government regulation, broadcasters proposed that the industry adopt a strong voluntary code of ethics modeled after the motion picture industry's code, which had been enacted in 1930 to avert government regulation and to undercut the protests of religious and civic groups. The Motion Picture Producers and Distributors of America agreed to abide by a voluntary code, establishing standards for the representation of sex, crime, and violence.[47] Testifying on the opening day of the FCC's chain-monopoly hearings, the president of RCA, David Sarnoff, called for a similar kind of industry self-regulation, which he described as the American answer to an American problem. The NAB moved quickly to implement Sarnoff's suggestion. Neville Miller, the president of the NAB, proposed strengthening radio's existing code of ethics, a nonbinding and rather vague statement of standards that had provided little concrete guidance to stations. Working closely with the networks in drafting a set of guidelines, the NAB adopted a new code at its July 1939 annual meeting.[48]

Ironically, the reform measures enacted by the broadcast industry in response to public and FCC pressure made it even more difficult for unions to gain access to the airwaves. Among other things, the new code addressed the question of controversial public issues. Seeking to discourage stations from "becoming mouthpieces of demagogues or subversives," the NAB followed the networks' lead in barring member stations from selling time for matters of controversy, with the exception of political broadcasts during election campaigns. Instead, as part of their duty to serve in the public interest, the NAB wanted broadcasters to provide free time to representative spokesmen of opposing points of view and expected news commentators to present information "free of bias" and to refrain from editorializing. The goal, according to the NAB, was not to censor but to promote more balanced discussion of public issues and to prevent those with the most economic power from monopolizing the airwaves.[49]

In drafting the code, the NAB gave consideration to the CIO's concerns about the broadcasting industry's treatment of labor. Ed Kirby, the NAB's public relations director, noted that this is a "tremendous and complex problem that should be receiving the attention of serious industry leaders." Unfortunately for unions, the NAB ultimately determined that labor issues are "almost always of a controversial nature." In line with existing network policy, it instructed its members to refuse to sell radio time to organized labor for any purpose. The broadcasting association "denied any bias" against labor unions. It also opposed selling time for the most blatant forms of business propaganda, such as the NAM's "American Family Robinson" series. But the new NAB *Code Manual* candidly reveals the organization's underlying reasoning for classifying labor as controversial. It bluntly acknowledged the power of business, which provided the bulk of advertising revenue, advising members that employers are inclined to "frown on those stations, especially in smaller communities, which open their facilities to labor unions." Not surprisingly, the NAB made no mention of business sponsorship of institutional programming.[50]

Observers of the broadcasting industry initially anticipated that the code would not only raise broadcasting standards but would also help level the playing field for groups such as organized labor. They were certain that the most vitriolic voices, like Coughlin's, would no longer be welcome on commercial time. They also predicted that some of the most fervent antilabor voices on radio would find their wings clipped. If broadcasters interpreted the section of the code dealing with controversial issues in a strict fashion, some analysts argued, the future would bring strong limitations on programs like "The Ford Sunday Evening Hour" and news commentators like Boake Carter, who had carried on a vendetta against the CIO. As one *New Republic* writer observed, "Henry Ford and W. J. Cameron have a right to hold antilabor views . . . but the place to express those views is in the open forum of radio and not in the midst of a richly upholstered Ford Symphony Hour such as no union could afford to sponsor in rebuttal."[51]

Not everyone welcomed the new code. Debate over it intensified during the fall of 1939, as the NAB moved to enforce the code's provisions. The most contentious part of the code was the controversial issues rule. Critics such as David Lawrence, editor of *U.S. News,* and Elliott Roosevelt, the president's son and owner of ten Texas radio stations, argued that the code limited freedom of speech. They denounced it as censorship imposed by an outside authority and asserted that it must be the responsibility of each station manager to decide what to broadcast. Lawrence pointed out that it was unfair that business could buy time to sell products, but citizens could not buy time for the spread of ideas. He found it odd that broadcasters were willing to accept money for the sale of everything from laxatives to cars but were unwilling to allow radio time to be bought for the education of the public on social and economic questions. The *U.S. News* editor further charged that "to deny Father Coughlin or anybody else the use of paid facilities is to deny freedom for the thought with which we differ. If Father Coughlin's ideas are bad, let the citizens who believe otherwise organize to answer him." Lawrence concluded that the cure "lies in expression rather than suppression." Elliott Roosevelt questioned the concept that controversial issues could be effectively presented on sustaining (free) time. The best broadcasting times, he insisted, would never be given away, especially by smaller stations that could ill afford the loss of revenue. John F. Patt, manager of the Cleveland station WGAR, joined in the fray, predicting that unless the code was modified, "we shall see an emasculation of private enterprise in broadcasting with a solar plexis blow to freedom in this country and an invitation to further government regulation."[52]

Urged on by network executives, who warned that any compromise would ruin the code, the NAB rallied its troops in defense of the new standards. Neville Miller, secretary of the NAB, visited radio stations throughout the nation to explain the benefits of the code. He also took to the airways, defending the code in speeches and forums. Miller argued that those who cried censorship did not really understand the code's intent or its provisions. Rather than barring those holding controversial viewpoints from the air, the NAB secretary asserted that the code recognizes "their right to speak, but provides that those holding other views *shall not be deprived of the right to present their views under similar conditions.*"[53]

The NAB publicized endorsements from numerous influential organizations and individuals, including the Federal Council of Churches, the Boys' Clubs of America, the General Federation of Women's Clubs, the National Education Association, W. Russell Bowie, director of Grace church of New York City, Henry S. Coffin, president of the Union Theological Seminary, and the new FCC chairman, Lawrence Fly. The broadcasters' association paid special attention to religious leaders and women. It circulated the Federal Council of Churches' secretary Samuel McCrea Cavert's pro-code speech to local ministerial associations throughout the country and sent copies of the code to the nation's Catholic bishops. The NAB also invited sixty-eight national and state leaders of the major women's organizations to a luncheon meeting at a Washington, D.C., hotel, and NAB representatives spent over four hours explaining the goals and operation of the code.[54]

The broadcasters' association attempted to insulate itself from charges of censorship by enlisting the support of the American Civil Liberties Union. While drafting the code, the NAB had consulted with the ACLU and secured its backing.[55] As the nation's self-designated guardian of free speech, the ACLU had a long-standing interest in radio. Victims of radio censorship, including unions, had regularly taken their complaints to the group. In the early 1930s, the ACLU joined with other advocates of nonprofit and educational broadcasting in calling for a restructuring of the industry. It condemned the commercial broadcasting system as "inherently incapable of presenting controversial programming and innately undemocratic." With hope for structural reform shattered after the passage of the Communication Act of 1934, the ACLU accepted the status quo and sought to develop a more congenial relationship with commercial broadcasters, especially the networks. It nevertheless pushed for legislation requiring stations to provide time for "non-commercial, uncensored discussion of social and political problems." There was little support in Congress for the ACLU's initiative, and by the end of the 1930s it was still seeking ways to protect free speech on the air.[56] ACLU leaders viewed the NAB's code as an important step in this direction, believing that it represented a sincere effort on the part of broadcasters to make radio a "more socially minded service." As debate intensified, the ACLU repeatedly came to the NAB's defense, arguing that the code was "wholly in the interest of free speech since it puts everybody on the basis of equality and puts people without money on the same footing as people with it."[57]

The AFL also chimed in with its blessing for the new broadcasting standards. Most AFL leaders professed their complete satisfaction with the operation of the existing broadcasting system. Indeed, with little interest in using radio for organizing, few AFL unions had clashed with local broadcasters over access. NBC in particular had long curried favor with the AFL, which it viewed as representing the most responsible element of the labor movement. It appointed AFL president William Green to the network's National Advisory Council and willingly gave the AFL leadership airtime for speeches. In 1936, NBC president M. H. Aylesworth sent Green a "gilt-edged pass" to the NBC Studios with the message that he hoped that Green would "use it often." Green, in turn, regularly praised the networks for their generosity to organized labor.[58]

Therefore, few were surprised when the AFL endorsed the code, which had strong network backing. In an October 6, 1939, speech over CBS, Matthew Woll, vice president of the AFL, praised the NAB's new initiative, asserting that it insured that radio "would continue to provide an open forum for the discussion of public issues." It further guaranteed that "no one side shall monopolize the airwaves when great public issues arise, but that all sides—majorities and minorities—rich and poor alike—shall have free access to the microphone to state their case."[59]

Neither the ACLU nor organized labor, however, was completely united on behalf of the code. One member of the ACLU Radio Committee, Henry Eckstein, had serious reservations about its operation. He worried that "however disinterestedly, sincerely, and altruistically" broadcasters might determine the topics and representatives of controversial subjects, they could not avoid criticism, because "the line between selectivity and censorship is too finely drawn." Eckstein also wanted to maintain some distance between the ACLU and the broadcasters to protect the civil liberties union from manipulation. He argued that there was no need to immediately respond to every request of the NAB "to help pull their chestnuts out of the fire" and warned against "too blindly accepting broadcasters' 'liaisons.'" He was convinced that the broadcasters' goals regarding freedom of the air differed significantly from the ACLU's.[60]

The ACLU's general counsel, Morris Ernst, also publicly denounced the code. Ernst was one of the most renowned civil liberties advocates in the nation, having litigated many of the important court cases attacking censorship, including the case over the publication of James Joyce's novel *Ulysses*, which the government had banned on the grounds of obscenity. Ernst wrote extensively in defense of freedom of speech, press, and assembly and was a staunch advocate of racial equality. A longtime member of the ACLU's Radio Committee, Ernst was well aware of the power of radio, depicting it as a "miracle" of communication. Like Elliott Roosevelt, Ernst argued that the code failed to safeguard the presentation of unpopular or minority interests. Few stations would willingly give away the most lucrative commercial evening hours, and he predicted that most broadcasters would refuse to air the most contentious issues at any time of the day. When questioned about dissenting from his organization's official position in support of the NAB's code, he noted that the ACLU believes in free speech for all, even for its counsel.[61]

Initially, the CIO had hoped that the code would improve labor's relationship with the mass media. In the fall of 1938, the NAB had professed interest in addressing union complaints about censorship and lack of access. While the code was being drafted, the CIO gave the NAB Labor Department the opportunity to settle complaints against member stations before sending grievances to the FCC. Assured that the new code would solve labor's problems, Lee Pressman, the CIO general counsel, even agreed to withdraw from his scheduled appearance before the FCC's chain monopoly hearings. Pressman warned the NAB, however, that if the code was not satisfactory or "proved to be unworkable," the CIO would demand new radio legislation from Congress.[62]

❖ ❖ ❖

The CIO's worst fears about the code quickly materialized. The NAB began enforcement in October 1939, and complaints over denial of airtime immediately escalated. Akron workers, who had so effectively used radio during their 1936 strike, were among the first to feel the impact of the new regulations. On October 23, WJW canceled the Akron Industrial Union Council's weekly program, "The Voice of Labor," which had been on the air for over two years. This was a popular program that, according to the president of the United Rubber Workers, S. H. Dalrymple, enabled labor "to present its message in a fair and honest manner" to the community.[63] Although the council's contract with the station was not due to expire until February, the station manager, Edythe Fern Melrose, explained that she had canceled the program in compliance with the ruling adopted by the NAB against controversial material on paid time. Union leaders asserted, however, that the management of WJW had been harassing the program with unreasonable censorship before the cancellation. According to H. R. Lloyd, president of the Akron Industrial Union Council, the station began prohibiting so many subjects that it "was almost impossible to talk about anything of general interest." Melrose replied that she had only deleted words like "lousy" and "rotten" and defended her actions as being in accordance with the FCC's regulation that all broadcasts must be in good taste.[64]

The cancellation evoked a storm of protest from organized labor. The Akron labor leader William Tate denounced the code as a "conspiracy between big business and the NAB," and Dalrymple filed a complaint with the FCC, condemning the cancellation as "an unwarranted and dictatorial invasion of our rights as citizens." Broadcasters were pleased when the FCC, which had given the code a nod of approval, dodged the issue, asserting that it had no control over a station's programming decisions.[65] Still concerned about the protests, the NAB's director of labor relations, Joseph Miller, went to Akron to attempt to settle the controversy. He proposed that WJW sponsor debates and forums with speakers representing the AFL, the CIO, and the Chamber of Commerce. While agreeing to offer labor forums, the station manager was unwilling to commit to any regularly scheduled programs and made clear that at times of "violent disagreement," labor "would not have any right to the air whatsoever."[66] Tate denounced the free forums as "soothing syrup to lull us while we are robbed of our basic rights." Lloyd asserted that occasional forums were not sufficient. Akron labor was "on the air for the same purpose as all radio advertisers—to build up an audience to let them know what we stand for and to sell our product—which is unionism." For that purpose, he continued, organized labor needed a regular program, not sporadic debates. Lloyd also questioned the NAB's argument that the sale of products was without controversy, pointing out that there was often a great deal of disagreement over the merits of a particular product. "If automobile companies and tire companies and breakfast food companies are given liberty to regularly advertise their products over the air," he argued, then "labor should be given the same consideration."[67]

After several weeks of protest, WJW temporarily rescinded the order canceling "The Voice of Labor." While initially intending to begin enforcing the code on October 1, the NAB found that numerous stations had been reluctant to break existing contracts. This was especially true of stations that broadcast Father Charles Coughlin, whose talks had been classified as controversial. On November 6, to avoid an immediate confrontation over the code, the NAB ruled that stations should honor existing contracts for controversial programs.[68] These contracts, of course, were not to be renewed upon expiration. Citing this loophole, WJW offered to restore the labor program. Aware that this was a temporary reprieve and angry over the station's earlier censorship of the program, the Akron Industrial Union Council voted not to return to WJW. In early December, the group found another station, WDAC, to broadcast its program. WDAC was not a member of the NAB and assured the council that it would have full freedom to discuss controversial issues. H. R. Lloyd triumphantly declared that the "attempt of the radio interests to keep labor off the air has been defeated."[69]

While Akron workers were able to find a station willing to defy the NAB code and broadcast a labor program, San Francisco unionists were not as fortunate. When the San Francisco Industrial Union's contract with KYA for "Labor on the Air," a daily labor news broadcast, expired in October 1940, the station canceled the show. Like WJW, KYA cited the NAB code as justification for the cancellation. Again there was a flood of protests, originating from all over the West Coast. Over seventy unions from cities across California and Washington joined CIO president John L. Lewis in protesting KYA's action to the FCC. Lewis argued that the ban on "Labor on the Air" threatened "to make radio communication inaccessible to organized labor for all practical purposes," while employers were still able to purchase all the time they wanted to attack unions. Again the FCC declined to take action. The San Francisco Industrial Union Council was unable to shift its program to another station. Although "Labor on the Air" had built one of the largest listening audiences in the state, no other San Francisco station was willing to pick up the show.[70]

Pointing to KYA's cancellation of "Labor on the Air" and the increasing difficulty of scheduling union programs, the CIO contended that stations were using the NAB code as an excuse to rid themselves of troublesome programs and to keep unions off the air. Stations invariably replied that they were simply complying with the code. Until the fall of 1941, unions had no concrete evidence for their allegations. A year after the cancellation of the San Francisco Industrial Union Council's program, however, information surfaced during FCC hearings that provided evidence that the NAB code was being deliberately used as a cover for silencing labor.

In March 1941, urged on by President Roosevelt, who was frustrated with newspaper opposition to the New Deal, the FCC ordered an investigation and hearings on newspaper ownership of radio stations. During the course of the investigation, FCC staff subpoenaed correspondence from the Hearst Company files on the relationship between its newspapers and its radio stations. The FCC was not seeking evidence of radio bias against organized labor, but it inadvertently uncovered letters that confirmed the CIO's suspicions. At least in San Francisco, there was more to the cancellation of "Labor on the Air" than simple compliance with the NAB code.[71]

The correspondence from the Hearst files, along with the testimony of the general manager of Hearst Radio, E. M. Stoer, revealed that in the late summer of 1939, the Hearst Company had become concerned that political broadcasts might be reducing radio and newspaper revenue. Stoer reported to John S. Brookes, then head of the Hearst holding company American Newspapers, Inc., that the "only dangerous program" on KYA, the Hearst station in San Francisco, was the CIO's "Labor on the Air" and that the station manager who had accepted the program had been fired. Brookes demanded that the show be terminated.[72] Pressure also came from the local Hearst newspapers, the *Examiner* and the *Call.* The CIO program embarrassed the papers, particularly in their dealings with the Chamber of Commerce and with advertisers. Clarence Lindner, publisher of the *San Francisco Examiner,* feared that his paper as well as KYA were becoming associated in the public mind with "leftist-CIO propaganda" from the Industrial Union Council's "one-sided" labor show.[73] Stoer wanted to get rid of the show but hesitated to because he was afraid of labor strength in San Francisco, anticipating that unions would react with "physical violence, boycott, or picketing." He believed that the government would side with the CIO, possibly leading to an FCC citation or even the cancellation of KYA's broadcasting license. In March 1940, Stoer wrote to KYA's station manager, Reiland Quinn: "I am quite willing to forego the revenue from this program if there is any way to get it off, even though I realize that the loss to the station would be felt very considerably . . . so if you have any scheme in mind that would enable us to dispense with this program without jeopardizing the station or its license, I would be very interested in hearing it."[74]

Fearing to cancel "Labor on the Air," the station sought to dilute the show's influence. Although KYA already carried the NAM's "American Family Robinson," it sought to develop another business program to counterbalance the CIO broadcast. After considerable effort on the station's part, a "forum" program was outlined for the NAM that Reiland Quinn admitted in a letter to Stoer "sounds very stupid." The AFL offered another way to offset the CIO program. In early June 1940, the AFL's Labor Council asked to purchase time for a program immediately following the CIO three times weekly. KYA anticipated that the AFL, which was in the midst of an internecine struggle with the CIO for the loyalty of San Francisco workers, would use its show to attack its competitor. Quinn believed "this would help in a measure inasmuch as it will show conflict in the labor movement, which would be a decided advantage."[75]

The AFL went on the air in early July, but in addition to engaging in dogfights with the CIO's Industrial Union Council, it also went after local businesses. Its program, however, was short-lived. In late September, angry at the station's severe censorship of its scripts, the AFL central body canceled its contract. With the AFL show out of the way, the newly appointed station manager, Harold Myer, proposed canceling the CIO show, whose contract was about to expire. Stoer affirmed that the CIO contract should not be renewed and wired Myer to make the refusal as "plausible as possible." He added, "good work on AFL. Delighted to hear the news." KYA then promptly canceled "Labor on the Air," citing the NAB code as justification. Stoer wrote to FCC chairman James Lawrence Fly that the station was simply trying "to conform its policy to that of the NAB code." Shortly after labor went off the air, Clarence Lindner reported to the San Francisco Chamber of Commerce that KYA had "'cleaned up,' and those programs which your people perhaps justly lacked appreciation for, are no longer on the station."[76]

The FCC investigation reaffirmed what the CIO had quickly come to suspect: the NAB code was simply a handy excuse for blocking labor's access to the air. Meeting in October 1939, shortly after radio stations began to enforce the code, the CIO convention expressed its concern about the impact of the NAB's new regulations. The unionists asserted that radio was one of labor's primary means of communicating with its members and the public. Although the ramifications of the code for labor were just beginning to become clear, the 1939 convention recognized that the NAB's new regulations posed "one of the most important problems that we will have to consider in the immediate future." The convention urged unions to challenge the code and demand the right to purchase time for the discussion of controversial issues. Over the next several years, the CIO's criticisms of the code became even stronger, especially as more and more unions were denied access.[77] In the early 1940s, as the nation edged towards war against fascism, the CIO began its own mobilization aimed at overturning the NAB code and asserting labor's rights to the airwaves.

PART 2

Broadcasting Reform

4   "The Air Belongs to the People":
     Breaking the NAB Code

ON AUGUST 29, 1942, the Media Division of the U.S. Office of War Information's Bureau of Intelligence issued a confidential report analyzing the editorial comments of leading radio network news commentators for the previous week. It found that 90 percent of the commentary on organized labor was unfavorable. H. V. Kaltenborn's remarks were typical. A top-ranked news commentator whose daily show drew over nine million listeners, Kaltenborn protested that an employer must "forfeit control of his business if he doesn't give the union what the government says the union ought to have" and pointed out that even a small percentage of total U.S. production lost in strikes and slowdowns "might make all of the difference between victory and defeat" in the struggle against the Axis powers.[1]

Labor leaders certainly would not have been surprised at the Office of War Information's findings. The media wars between labor and business continued to rage during World War II, though the conditions of battle altered significantly. During the war the mass media hammered organized labor, charging that wildcat strikes, absenteeism, and exorbitant wage demands undermined production. Unions responded that these attacks were part of a "huge and sinister propaganda drive" designed to rob labor of its "democratic rights and freedom and to deprive American workers of the great social gains" that had been won by organized labor through years of untiring effort.[2]

World War II dramatically changed the nation's labor-relations climate, as unions made important organizational, economic, and political gains. Between 1939 and 1941, mobilization for defense ended the Depression, while tight labor markets and renewed militancy helped organized labor break long-standing bastions of anti-unionism, including Ford Motor Company and Bethlehem Steel. Once the United States entered the war, government labor policy provided unions with organizational security, and the number of organized workers jumped from about ten million to almost fifteen million. Wartime economic conditions, including scarce labor, "cost plus" financing, and the necessity for continuous production, contributed not only to a surge in union membership but also to a loss of managerial authority. In factories across the nation, aggressive union representatives demanded and received a voice in shop-floor operations. At the same time, labor leadership gained increased prestige and influence in the political realm, as organized labor's relationship with the Democratic party blossomed into a full-blown alliance. Union leaders served as members of wartime government advisory boards, and the CIO's Political Action Committee (CIO-PAC) played a prominent role in the 1944 election.[3] Many employers were alarmed by the growth of organized labor and the vast wartime expansion of government. These changes threatened a further decline in corporate power, which had already been battered by the Depression.

Business quickly realized, however, that the war also provided the opportunity to regain the confidence of the American people. To help restore their moral legitimacy, corporations turned to public relations. Corporate publicists trumpeted the business contribution to the war effort and promoted the "fifth freedom," the freedom of enterprise.[4] They also fed the barrage of antilabor propaganda that inundated the American media during much of the war. Although labor leaders had signed a no-strike pledge, wildcat strikes and work stoppages left unions vulnerable to the charge that they were greedy and unpatriotic. Radio, the nation's primary communications medium, played a prominent role in business's wartime propaganda effort. Goodwill programs enhanced business prestige, while corporate-sponsored news commentators regularly fueled public hostility towards organized labor.

Organized labor had difficulty competing with the wartime corporate public relations campaign. In most cases, unions were unable to counteract biased newspapers; nor could they compete financially with business groups in purchasing extensive newspaper advertising. Moreover, the NAB code barred unions from buying radio time from the networks and most local radio stations. The AFL and CIO denounced media attacks on labor's patriotism, though until late in 1944 the AFL was relatively complacent about radio restrictions on labor. In contrast, the CIO was outraged and contentious. Arguing that "the air belongs to the people," it launched a multipronged campaign to open the airwaves to labor. The trade journal *Broadcasting* recognized the drive to "obliterate" the NAB code as the "greatest pressure campaign" in radio's "short but turbulent history."[5]

❖ ❖ ❖

World War II enabled the business community to regain at least some of its lost power. The wartime "miracle of production" brought renewed prestige as industry leaders demanded and received the largest voice in establishing policy concerning economic mobilization. Moreover, business leaders drew on their increased influence with government to encourage the more conservative wartime Congress to dismantle some of the New Deal.[6] To corporate leaders, war production symbolized one of the finest hours of the free enterprise system. In 1942, the leader of the National Association of Manufacturers, H. W. Prentis, asserted that it was "not government that has wrought the miracle that is being accomplished today in the production of war material but the initiative, ingenuity, and organizing genius of private enterprise."[7]

Business leaders took pains to ensure that this view held sway over competing explanations. Because much of the vast expansion of the economy took place within the context of centralized planning and government regulation, corporate leaders worried that these additional controls might become permanent fixtures of the postwar economy.[8] Public relations and advertising offered a means to teach the public that business, rather than government or organized labor, was key to the successful mobilization of the economy. With this goal in mind, the NAM expanded its public relations program. Radio programs, pamphlets, press releases, speakers, plant rallies, and an elaborate series of conferences with agriculture, education, and church leaders publicized American industry's vital contribution to the war effort. The NAM constantly linked production accomplishments to the free enterprise system, reminding Americans that they were fighting to preserve the "freedoms and liberties upon which the American way of life has been based."[9]

Individual corporations eagerly exploited the war to improve their image and to sell the free enterprise system. General Motors, for instance, sponsored an elaborate traveling theatrical and musical revue that touted the company's contribution to the war effort. Most companies, however, relied primarily on advertising. The high wartime excess-profits tax combined with the Treasury Department's decision to allow corporations to deduct advertising costs from taxable income encouraged companies to advertise. Even companies that had shifted entirely to war production engaged in institutional or goodwill advertising, which kept brand names before the public. Firms inundated popular weekly magazines and newspapers with advertisements identifying their products with victory. Innovative advertisers even made the case for chewing gum as an essential war material.[10]

Beyond boosting products, wartime institutional advertising sought to sell political and economic ideas. Ads characterized the war as a battle to preserve the American way, which was defined as freedom from governmental regimentation, protection of individual opportunity, and free enterprise. For instance, in a typical ad for Nash Kelvinator, published in full color, a young, lonesome soldier quietly reflects on what kind of country he yearns for when he returns from overseas: "I'm not playing for marbles. I'm fighting for freedom. I'm fighting for the things that made America the greatest place in the world to live in. . . . So don't anybody tell me I'll find America changed. . . . Don't anybody tell me there's a ceiling on my opportunity to make a million or be President." Numerous other employers also promoted the "Don't Change Anything" theme, implying that postwar America should be restored to the status quo of the 1920s, when private industry rather than government safeguarded the public interest.[11]

Radio played an important role in the campaign to sell American business and its ideology during World War II. Because of paper shortages, advertising in the print media decreased slightly during the war, while radio's advertising volume almost doubled. Networks and individual stations found sponsors for even the most unpopular time slots, which in the past had been filled by unsponsored or sustaining programming. The historian Gerd Horten suggests that radio was more effective than the print media in promoting the business message. By fusing advertising and entertainment, radio "provided the most powerful and persuasive medium for advertising before and during the war years."[12]

As part of its effort to win public goodwill, business enlarged its institutional programming. Corporate sponsorship of high culture featured prominently in their strategy. With no consumer products to sell, more American companies began to underwrite prestigious arts organizations, which in the past had struggled for sponsorship. Before the war, only five of the seventeen concert music programs had commercial sponsors; by the 1944 season, twenty out of twenty-two boasted major corporate sponsorship.[13] U.S. Rubber underwrote the New York Philharmonic, Allis Chalmers the Boston Symphony Orchestra, and Texaco the New York Metropolitan Opera. In assuming sponsorship of the newly created NBC Symphony Orchestra under Arturo Toscanini, General Motors sought to "tell the facts of its wartime production" to the public "in accompaniment of this great music." The program enabled the GM executive Charles Kettering to speak directly to the American people on a weekly basis. His stories of how the corporation's "technical and managerial genius" contributed to the war effort reinforced the auto company's extensive newspaper and magazine advertising campaign.[14]

Corporate sponsorship of radio news and commentary programs expanded as well. As early as 1939, more Americans were getting their daily news from radio than from newspapers. That year, 70 percent of respondents from one survey reported that they listened on a regular basis to news and commentary, and 68 percent of these listeners found commentators to be honest and fair. Many listeners placed more trust in what they heard on the radio than what they read in their local newspaper. The U.S. entrance into the war further heightened interest in the news, and the percentage of network and local radio time devoted to news and commentary increased significantly. By 1944, almost 20 percent of commercial network time was devoted to news, and news shows were second only to dramatic production in attracting advertising.[15]

There were about sixty commentators on the networks in 1943. Listeners religiously followed their favorite pundits, who took on the status of "heroes and celebrities," in Susan J. Douglas's words.[16] A number of them were progressives: Frank Kingdom, Robert St. John, John Vandercook, and Raymond Swing provided stanch support to Roosevelt and to organized labor. As during the 1930s, business sponsored some of the most popular and controversial commentators. Boake Carter and George E. Sokolsky, who had railed against the New Deal and organized labor during the Depression, were off the air when the war began, but Fulton Lewis Jr., Upton Close, H. V. Kaltenborn, and Henry J. Taylor easily filled their shoes. Lewis continued to wage war against the Roosevelt administration and unions. He carried on a vendetta against the Office of Price Administration. In one characteristic outburst he described the New Deal as "a flim-flam structure of specious flap-doodle and preposterous mumbo-jumbo, honeycombed by termites, and operated by radical CIO-PAC, Communist-backed pseudo economists." He ridiculed the president's Four Freedoms, especially the Freedom from Want and the Freedom from Fear, which he considered socialistic. He reminded his listeners, "Joe Louis didn't become the most famous and most powerful fighter in the world or in world history by lying in bed twenty-four hours a day and having a government of college economists in Washington serve him his meals on a tray." Instead, Lewis advocated a fifth freedom, the "freedom of individual enterprise."[17]

Upton Close and H. V. Kaltenborn also gained notice during World War II by attacking Roosevelt's foreign and domestic policies. In September 1942, Shaeffer Pen Company hired Upton Close to provide a Sunday-afternoon political commentary over NBC. Close had appeared sporadically on NBC news programs from 1934 to 1941, but with corporate sponsorship he felt freer to express his opinions. He attracted a large audience during the first years of the war, when his bitter denunciations of the Roosevelt administration, American labor, the Soviet Union, and Great Britain "seemed to express the pent-up feelings of a sizable group of listeners."[18] For much of the 1930s, H. V. Kaltenborn was an obscure CBS news analyst whose unsponsored newscast was carried by the network at a variety of unpopular times. In September 1938, however, he rose to national prominence as he provided an anxious American public with almost continuous coverage of the Nazi takeover of Czechoslovakia. In the aftermath of this exposure, General Mills briefly became Kaltenborn's sponsor. The company already sponsored a variety of radio programs, including "Jack Armstrong" and three soap operas.[19] It viewed the Kaltenborn program as institutional advertising, "differing materially from product advertising in that its primary function is to create goodwill," and hoped that Kaltenborn would help create "a better understanding of American institutions and principles." General Mills promised Kaltenborn complete "freedom of selection and expression." But after only thirteen weeks, the firm backed out of the relationship when Catholics, angry at Kaltenborn's views on the Spanish Civil War, threatened to boycott General Mills products. Kaltenborn found a more supportive sponsor in Pure Oil, which picked up his program in the spring of 1939 and shifted it to NBC. Broadcast five times a week during prime evening hours, Kaltenborn's show became one of the top-ranked news programs.[20]

Kaltenborn was highly critical of the administration's management of the wartime economy. He argued that government policies hindered war production, and he carried on a virtual crusade against the labor movement. Day after day, Kaltenborn attacked labor, contending that "labor union practices are injuring and destroying America's war effort."[21] He opposed wage increases for workers and lashed out bitterly against wartime strikes. In covering strikes, he frequently aired partisan statements from company officials and ignored the union response. For instance, in October 1942, he reported only on the company side of a dispute at a Chrysler plant, quoting a management spokesman who described a walkout as "definite sabotage against the nation's war effort." Kaltenborn blamed strikes on "a pro-labor Administration," complaining that for ten years, "we have pampered the

Newspaper advertisement promoting H. V. Kaltenborn's NBC news commentary program, ca. 1943. H. V. Kaltenborn Papers; courtesy of the State Historical Society of Wisconsin.

labor unions to the point that they act like spoiled children whenever they don't get what they want." Business groups were so pleased with Kaltenborn's broadcasts that they asked NBC if they could buy recordings. One Dallas employers' association wanted to rebroadcast them to the local community over a sound truck.[22]

Late in the war, General Motors assumed sponsorship of another prominent critic of labor, the wealthy retired advertising executive Henry J. Taylor, who had broadcast an unsponsored show on NBC since 1943. Taylor attacked unions with a zeal developed during his years as a corporate executive. The National Maritime Union was a favorite target. Attempting to stir up public anger, the commentator repeatedly charged that merchant seamen were exploiting the wartime emergency to make incredibly high wages. During the 1944 presidential campaign, Taylor gained notoriety through his blistering assaults on the CIO, accusing Sidney Hillman, head of the newly formed CIO-PAC, of subverting the political process and asserting that he was the virtual ruler of America. He warned in one broadcast that "PAC leaders already have more cash in their treasury than the Republican and Democratic Parties combined." NBC dropped Taylor's program in 1945, but General Motors picked it up, shifting his commentary to the Mutual Network. For the next ten years on Monday nights, Taylor railed against the expansion of the welfare state (which he equated with socialism), increased taxes, and the growing power of unions.[23]

Like the corporations, the NAM also focused on wartime themes in its expanded radio efforts. The organization canceled the nonnetwork shows "American Family Robinson" and George Sokolsky's radio commentary to concentrate its resources on network broadcasting. In the spring of 1941, Mutual and NBC agreed to provide time to the manufacturers' association.[24] Mutual aired the NAM's "Your Defense Reporter" on Thursday nights in 1941, and NBC broadcast "Defense for America" on Saturday nights. Later during the war, NBC carried the NAM's "This Nation at War." These programs highlighted industry's contribution to the war effort. NAM reporters, including Fulton Lewis Jr., visited key centers of defense production, describing the production process and interviewing workers at their factory benches, plant superintendents, government officials, and business leaders. Visiting Weirton Steel Company in June 1941, the NAM found evidence of the "American spirit of free enterprise," as a "great American symphony of men, machines, and management, working in perfect harmony," prepared "our nation for any emergency." "Defense for America" regularly reminded listeners that managers and workers were "girding to defend the American way of life, a way of life that rests on a base of three inter-dependent free-doms . . . representative democracy, civil and religious liberties, and free enterprise." The general manager of station WKPT of Kingsport, Tennessee, lauded the program as "without a doubt the most inspiring [program] on the air." He predicted that it would "surely do more toward promoting real honest to God Americanism than anything that has been done so far."[25]

Two years into the war, the NAM took comfort in the belief that the "magnificent war record of American industry" had "restored the *symbol,* at least, of free enterprise to public favor." Yet more work needed to be done, its leaders noted. Although Americans believed in the basic philosophy of free enterprise, they still recalled the hardships that followed 1929 and leaned towards government-guaranteed security. Beginning in 1943, to help shape public thinking about postwar planning, the NAM began distributing a re-corded series of weekly talks, "Businessmen Look to the Future," which were broadcast by 302 local stations across the nation. The program, which aired for two years, presented the point of view of business leaders about reconversion and the postwar economy through informal roundtable discussions.[26] Employers from the Glen L. Martin Company, Standard Oil, Nash-Kelvina-tor, Du Pont, and other companies discussed the future of their industries, including new products and job opportunities, particularly for veterans. The November 9, 1944, show, with William Lydgate of the American Institute of Public Opinion and Cloud Wampler of the Carrier Corporation as panelists, addressed one of the nation's central concerns about reconversion, the pos-sibility that the unemployment of the 1930s would return. Wampler warned that "an awful lot of loose thinking is being done about giving people jobs and doing it in a way that requires a loss of freedom." The panelists agreed that high levels of employment were necessary but absolutely opposed gov-ernment-guaranteed jobs or any expansion of government control over the economy. "We must have freedom," declared Wampler.[27]

The AFL and CIO were incensed by the propagandistic discourse emanating from business-sponsored programming. They argued that the press and radio gave a lopsided picture of the relative contributions of labor and industry to the war effort. According to the CIO, corporate goodwill programs and institutional advertising constantly drove home the war achievements of business and glorified free enterprise without giving credit to unions or the workers who made the production records possible. Union leaders blamed radio commentators as well as the daily press for the growing public hostility

towards labor during the war, pointing in particular to stories exaggerating
the numbers of strikes and the extent of absenteeism. They attributed the
quick passage of the Smith-Connally antistrike bill to "the barrage of misinformation thrust into the air by radio commentators."[28]

To combat the business campaign, labor lodged a steady stream of protests with the networks, local stations, sponsors, and the FCC. Kaltenborn's
crusade against organized labor in particular generated widespread opposition. In April 1942, *Time* magazine found his broadcasts on labor "tenden-
tious" and "shallow in perspective" and warned that "from his treatment of
isolated cases of bumptiousness in labor, listeners might easily have become
inflamed against labor in general." Unionists across the country demanded that NBC bar Kaltenborn from the air. The Duluth local of the Textile
Workers Union advised NBC in March 1942 that "labor is fed-up with Mr.
Kaltenborn's false charges," which were "hindering war production."[29] William Kahn of Labor's Non Partisan League of Connecticut took similar objections to the FCC, observing that the "working people of Connecticut do
not object to fair criticism . . . but repeated public incitations against labor,
based on prejudice and little else, merely serves today to cause disunity and
strife where maximum unity and cooperation is so direly needed."[30] The
AFL complained to NBC after Kaltenborn asserted in a March 1942 broadcast that "no man can produce war material in any of the major war plants
of the United States without first paying tribute to a labor union." Philip
Pearl, publicity director for the AFL, condemned the statement as "vicious
labor-baiting" and asked the network, "[W]here does Kaltenborn get the
gall to spread over the radio" such "malicious anti-labor propaganda?" Such
assertions, he continued, "have been, for many years, the last refuge of chiseling, labor-hating employers, the scum of industry." The following year, a
disgusted federation turned to the FCC after Kaltenborn declared that non-
union aircraft plants had a better production record than unionized plants.
When Kaltenborn refused either to produce evidence for his assertion or
broadcast a retraction, AFL president William Green demanded from NBC
and the FCC "summary and remedial action" against this "flagrant abuse
of the right of free speech."[31]

Emulating the boycott campaign that had driven Boake Carter off the air,
unions representing hundreds of thousands of workers launched boycotts
against Kaltenborn's sponsor, Pure Oil. By late spring 1942, Pure Oil dealers
were already feeling the impact of the boycott. The local Pure Oil agent in
Duluth asked the company to discontinue the program immediately, and in
1943 the West Virginia agent complained that "business is too damm hard

to get at this time to pay somebody to drive business away from you." F. H. Marling, the company's advertising director, advised Kaltenborn that "if this sentiment from our field sales organizations spreads, we will be up against serious trouble."[32]

Despite the economic pressure, the president of Pure Oil, Henry May Dawes, stood by Kaltenborn. In the midst of labor's fiercest attacks against the commentator, the company expanded his broadcast schedule from three to five times a week. The company contended publicly that it had no control over Kaltenborn's broadcasts; privately, Dawes urged him to moderate his commentary. In an effort to reduce tension, Kaltenborn met with AFL officials in December 1943 and promised to "do his utmost" to emphasize more frequently "labor's constructive achievements." But Dawes never asked Kaltenborn to make significant changes. He confided to Marling that Kaltenborn's broadcasts "appealed powerfully to all of my personal feelings and instincts. They are the forcible, effective utterances of a patriotic and courageous person, and they are timely." He continued: "[O]ur stockholders would certainly be willing to take any losses" as a result of the controversy. Appreciative that Pure Oil Company was "sufficiently courageous" in the face of the labor movement's "very vigorous and widespread criticism," Kaltenborn continued throughout the war to speak the "unpleasant truths" about unions.[33]

Although Kaltenborn often created a storm of public controversy and caused discomfort within the networks, CBS and then NBC regularly renewed his contract. In June 1940, after he "gave labor hell for striking" at a New Jersey shipyard, NBC's news director, A. A. Schechter, complained to the network president, Niles Trammell, that the commentator had violated "one of the fundamentals of the news business" by getting "into strikes of labor." According to Schechter, strikes, "along with religion or politics," were "dynamite!" He worried that "we are now treading on dangerous ground" and suggested putting "this fellow in a corner" and talking "sense to him." The network, however, never cracked down on Kaltenborn, for "as long as Pure was happy, so was NBC."[34]

Many business-sponsored broadcasts routinely violated the NAB code, which prohibited stations from selling time for the discussion of controversial issues. If business's institutional programming was at times controversial, its commentators posed an even greater problem to broadcasters who claimed to have endorsed the code. Moreover, the networks also had policies forbidding editorializing on the air. In the case of commentators, the code and network guidelines were almost completely ignored. In September 1941, the

ACLU observed that "there can be no doubt that every news commentator violates the letter if not the spirit of the code every time he speaks." News commentary, however, was a lucrative business. As long as the commentator did not offend the sponsor, there were generally few repercussions.[35]

Upton Close, the Shaeffer Pen commentator, was a prominent exception. Between 1942 and 1944, Close's extreme criticism of the Democrats and the Roosevelt administration gave NBC "many embarrassing moments." The network sought to keep him from going "off the deep end as he has occasionally tried to do." Finally, in December 1944, NBC dropped Close from its broadcasting schedule. Close and his supporters charged the network with censorship, and hundreds of listeners signed petitions protesting the cancellation of his show. Close was picked up briefly by Mutual, which had a reputation for permitting strong partisanship from its commentators. About the same time, NBC also dropped Henry J. Taylor, whose program was unsponsored and thus particularly vulnerable.[36]

When it came to union-sponsored programming, most broadcasters adhered rigidly to the code. As a result, labor was denied access to the air during most of the war years. Subjects deemed appropriate when proposed by business were judged controversial when presented by labor. Business, for instance, had no difficulty obtaining airtime to boast about its wartime achievements. In contrast, WNVA of Martinsburg, West Virginia, refused to sell the Amalgamated Clothing Workers of America time for a broadcast on the clothing workers' contribution to the war effort.[37] Similarly, the networks welcomed corporate sponsorship of commentators, but when the CIO considered sponsoring a commentator, the networks made clear that they would frown on any such program.[38]

Even union programs that had nothing to do with labor were taboo. In the summer of 1943, the UAW sought to buy time for a series of short recorded spot announcements dramatizing the necessity for reducing the cost of living and urging voters to demand congressional action. The NAB sent out a special information bulletin advising its member stations to reject the broadcasts. Not only were they controversial, but the recordings employed dramatic techniques. Under the code, it was improper to dramatize or "play upon the emotions" in broadcasts involving public questions. The NAB tossed the UAW a bone, noting that if stations considered the rising cost of living to be of sufficient public interest, they could schedule a public forum broadcast on the issue. None of the stations that refused the UAW broadcasts, however, scheduled forums or offered to provide free airtime as a public service.[39]

That the stations failed to allocate time for discussion of price rollbacks was of little surprise to the UAW. Although the NAB code stipulated that broadcasters were to provide free time for the discussion of controversial issues, they often denied labor's requests. With advertising essentially subsidized by the government through corporate tax deductions for advertising expenses, there was little unsold time available for public service offerings. The squeeze on public service programs was especially tight during the prime-time evening hours, when the largest audiences were available. As a result, the free time that stations did grant to labor was generally infrequent, irregular, and often late at night when few were listening. To the *New Republic*, it was "inconceivable that organized labor, the second largest organized group in the country, second only to churches, couldn't get time, even when it offered to pay for it, while employer associations were given millions of dollars' worth of free time to present their views and policies."[40]

In April 1943, the NAB tightened the code, making it even more difficult for labor to buy airtime, especially during organizing campaigns. The NAB convention added a new clause, decreeing that time should neither be "given nor sold" for programs involving solicitations of memberships in organizations, except "where such memberships are incidental to the rendering of commercial services such as an insurance plan" or for membership in charitable groups. The code now clearly prohibited unions from using radio to organize. The CIO immediately condemned this further restriction by "our radio dictators" on "labor's free speech." It asked, "[H]ow much longer can we tolerate such denials of free speech by business dictators, who want to control the air for their private interest without regard to the rights of America's working population?" *Variety* also attacked the broadcasters' decision, observing that the implications were "ominous": the "masterminds of the NAB have . . . served notice on the American people that our broadcasting system is no longer open to any form of commercial solicitation unless it involves something like the transfer of a can of soup or a cake of soap across the counter." *Variety* recognized that the new clause stifled the voices of organizations such as unions, which had "become the basic fabric of the economic and social life of the American community."[41]

The union voice was not entirely silent during the war years. A number of independent local stations, most of which were not members of the NAB, ignored the code and sold time to unions. Many of the programs showcased labor's contribution to the war effort and were generally uncontroversial. In

1942, for instance, the AFL dockworkers locals in San Francisco sponsored "Jobs for Victory," while in New York City the Industrial Union Council's "Win the War" dramatized how CIO members were working, fighting, and giving for victory. Commercials on the Utah State Federation of Labor's ten-minute daily news show, which began in November 1943 and was broadcast by six stations in Utah, promoted the wartime activities of not only AFL workers but also industries and businesses in the state.[42]

In a few localities, labor succeeded in airing harder-hitting programs. The Los Angeles Industrial Union Council initially launched "Our Daily Bread: Labor's Newspaper of the Air" in 1940 to aid the UAW's organizing drive in the aircraft industry. Broadcast throughout the war five times a week on an independent station, it sought to serve as an "antidote for the lies and poisons which nightly are drummed into the ears and minds of the average radio listener." Thursday was Political Action night, and the program battled employer-backed antilabor initiatives, such as one banning secondary boycotts. In addition to promoting labor's political objectives, the show aggressively supported contract negotiations and organizing campaigns. The "Workers Service Radio Program," broadcast by an AFL and CIO coalition in Madison, Wisconsin, explained to new workers the aims and objectives of the labor movement and publicized the union perspective on issues such as overtime pay, war profits, safety, and postwar conversion. In one program, Leo Leary of the Madison Federation of Labor contended that unions improve economic conditions, insure long-term security, and defend workers' freedom. In another program, Russell Hendrickson, secretary-treasurer of Steelworkers Local 1404, disputed commentators' charges that war workers were overpaid, pointing out that his local had waived double time for overtime work to enable the company to operate on a seven-day week.[43] In addition to this local programming, the networks continued to occasionally broadcast speeches by national union leaders, and representatives of the AFL and CIO also regularly participated in public service programs such as "American Forum on the Air."[44]

In 1941, after Mutual and NBC had given time to the NAM and the Chamber of Commerce for business-defense programs, the AFL and CIO began lobbying the networks for their own regularly scheduled defense shows. Initially, all the networks resisted. Then, in the spring of 1942, as a "public service," NBC granted labor a fifteen-minute weekly sustaining (or free) program, "Labor for Victory," with the AFL and CIO broadcasting on alternate weeks. Peter Lyon, a scriptwriter, recalled, "NBC was very nervous. They were afraid of the CIO's people and expected them to have long hair and bombs in their pockets."[45]

Ostensibly, the program's primary purpose was to acknowledge labor's participation in the war effort. By giving labor a regular forum, NBC also sought to mute the flood of unionists' complaints over H. V. Kaltenborn's attacks on organized labor. After launching the labor program, the network was able to advise Kaltenborn's critics that unions now had their own program, albeit one that was supposed to be noncontroversial and focus only on labor's contribution to the war effort. NBC also used "Labor for Victory" as a justification for denying unions any additional airtime over the network. In December 1942, American Small Business Organizations, Inc., condemned unions on the air for striking during wartime and recommended that strikers be shot. An NBC assistant manager responded to labor's demands for time to answer the attack with the statement that he saw "no reason why labor should have time on the air" because unions already had a weekly program.[46]

"Labor for Victory" was a milestone, theoretically providing organized labor with a national platform. To guarantee that labor's message reached the largest possible audience, the AFL and CIO urged their affiliates to ensure that their local stations offered the program. They had little success: "Labor for Victory" was broadcast at an unpopular time (first late Saturday evening, and then Sunday afternoon) on only forty-four of the 150 NBC affiliates, less than a third of the network. The AFL and CIO appreciated NBC's providing regular access to network radio, but the CIO recognized that a single weekly fifteen-minute period on one network, at a time when the audience was small, did not "in any way compare in frequency, regularity, or good timing with the time afforded to business and employer interests."[47]

NBC envisioned "Labor for Victory" as nonpartisan and uncontroversial. The network executive William Burke Miller made clear that the network never intended the program to serve as an "open forum for labor."[48] The AFL, led by William Green, who continued to have a close relationship with NBC, was grateful to the network for the airtime and had little problem with these restrictions. It used its segments to inform the American people what labor was doing to win the war, showcasing the role of individual unions in boosting production, and stressing labor's good relationship with management. Most of the AFL programs consisted of talks by labor leaders, interviews with government officials and industry leaders, and roundtables, all of which the scriptwriter Peter Lyon characterized as "very boring." In November 1942, for instance, the navy, represented by assistant secretary Ralph A. Bard, and

AFL president William Green, exchanged reciprocal pledges of unqualified cooperation to win the war. In another typical segment, broadcast in 1943, the AFL's press chief, Philip Pearl, interviewed two former labor officials serving with the War Production Board.[49]

The CIO emphasized some of the same themes as the AFL, but many of its programs addressed more politically charged issues, such as taxation, rationing, absenteeism, inflation, economic reconversion, and racial discrimination. In terms of broadcasting techniques, the CIO segments tended to be more imaginative than those of the AFL. The industrial unionists tried to limit speeches to a minimum, using instead dramatizations and musical entertainment. For the first time, the CIO enlisted the assistance of professional artists, including scriptwriters such as Peter Lyon, actors, and singers, in an effort to produce more entertaining and powerful programming that would attract a larger audience.[50]

One typical episode of the CIO's "Labor for Victory" promoted the struggle for racial equality by dramatizing a story of the mighty black worker John Henry seeking to swing his hammer on behalf of the war effort but being turned away from a non-union plant because of discriminatory employment policies. Hired finally in a CIO plant that enforced the president's Fair Employment Practices Order, Henry, played by the renowned actor and singer Paul Robeson, learns that the CIO stood for "the whites and the Negroes working together." At the end of the play, Robeson stepped out of character and spoke directly to the audience, declaring, "Jim Crow has got to go . . . every form of discrimination against an American on the basis of color, race, creed, or national origin—whether it is discrimination, political, or economic—has got to go . . . if we are going to win this war."[51] The CIO reported that letters reflected a wide range of listeners outside the ranks of organized labor who were seeking an alternative to the "dreary soap operas poured out in endless torrents." They appreciated programs that "cut through the lies and distortions of a Hans von Kaltenborn or others among the shoals of anti-labor, and anti-victory commentators."[52]

NBC repeatedly and increasingly censored the CIO's segment of "Labor for Victory" on the grounds that it was too contentious. The network also argued that the program routinely violated network policy against the dramatization of controversial issues. CIO president Philip Murray responded that since radio companies refused to sell time to labor because of the NAB code, there should be no restriction during the free time, which was supposed to be dedicated to controversial questions. He also argued that programs that made good use of the dramatic arts and music won more listeners than the average straight speech. In the spring before the 1944 elections, tensions between NBC and the CIO escalated, coming to a head over a drama encouraging listeners to register and vote, which the network viewed as controversial. The network finally pulled the program, citing a concern about political partisanship. Skeptics questioned the network's justification, suggesting that NBC considered any CIO program, even on a nonpartisan theme, controversial, since it might help win Roosevelt's reelection.[53]

❖ ❖ ❖

While the AFL remained complacent about the radio restrictions until 1944, the CIO grew increasingly outraged. In 1943, the AFL's publicity director, Philip Pearl, testified before a congressional committee that the AFL had no interest in buying airtime and had no difficulty in obtaining free time from the networks, though he did express concern about the code clause banning solicitations for membership. In contrast, the CIO fumed that labor did not get a fair break over the air, which was "monopolized by big business interests." Moreover, the "sum total of radio propaganda" was "one-sided, reactionary and anti-labor."[54]

For industrial unionists, access to radio was critical because the "thinking of the American people on labor, social, and political issues is influenced more than almost anything else by what they read in the papers or hear on the air."[55] The CIO argued that under the Federal Communications Act of 1934, stations were licensed to serve in the public interest. It declared that the air "belongs to the people . . . the people have the right to have their viewpoints expressed." It also asserted that the FCC requirement that stations be neutral and present both sides of public issues was a travesty, since under the code, business was still on the air, while labor faced severe censorship. The CIO pointed out that the networks and individual stations generously provided free time to the NAM and allowed companies such as General Motors to continue sponsoring commentators such as Henry J. Taylor, Upton Close, and Fulton Lewis Jr.[56] The CIO also charged that business-sponsored programming promoted corporate ideology in more subtle ways. Len De Caux, publicity director of the CIO, asserted that as commercial enterprises owned by corporations, networks and stations are invariably biased in their handling of labor and social questions. Moreover, the networks and stations obtained most of their revenue from big business sponsors and advertisers. It was little wonder that so many radio programs reflected a pro-business slant.[57]

The CIO launched a multipronged assault on the NAB code, which it viewed as one of the main barriers to labor's access to radio. It urged unions to "assert labor's right to the air" by demanding free time and purchased time.[58] The CIO's Publicity Department assisted affiliates in challenging the code by protesting to the NAB Code Compliance Committee on behalf of unions that were refused time.[59] While the NAB stood by the code's provision against the sale of time for discussion of controversial issues, it encouraged offending stations to offer free time spots. This, the NAB asserted, would ensure that labor was given a fair hearing. According to De Caux, time was sometimes granted but more often denied. Moreover, De Caux argued that occasional free time or a spot on a forum program was an inadequate substitute for a regularly scheduled program.[60]

Publicly, the NAB brushed aside the CIO's complaints, contending that unions received generous exposure, especially on the networks. In May 1942, while acknowledging that some local stations were reluctant to give airtime to union leaders, the broadcasters asserted that the "great majority" of stations gave labor a fair shake. Any difficulties were dismissed as an isolated "local problem."[61] In fact, the NAB blamed unions for the tensions between labor and broadcasters, contending that they were asking for unreasonable amounts of time or that the labor shows were "plainly libelous." Even worse, according to the broadcasters, was the fact that labor shows often failed to meet station standards. They charged that union programs were boring and potentially could weaken the listening base. According to the NAB, many stations offered plenty of time to labor, but unions preferred to "yell about being discriminated against rather than using what is available to them." Privately, however, Joseph L. Miller, the NAB's director of labor relations, admitted that "too many stations have used the Code to keep labor off the air" and advised the Code Committee that "labor must be given a better break under the Code, or we are in for continued trouble."[62] Miller's warning had little effect on NAB policy; for many broadcasters, the code was a convenient means for blocking labor programs, which they viewed as being of limited interest to audiences. Moreover, according to the president of the NAB, Neville Miller, union shows tended to offend advertisers and thus could potentially reduce revenues.[63]

The ACLU joined the CIO in raising questions about the operation of the NAB code. The ACLU's Radio Committee had participated in the development of the code, believing that by taking off the air "all *paid* discussion of public controversial issues" and giving equal facilities to both sides, it put "the poor man on a basis of equality with the well-to-do."[64] During early 1940, as complaints escalated, it conducted an investigation of the code's initial performance, particularly in relation to coverage of controversial issues, and concluded that overall it was "working very smoothly."[65] Still, Roger Baldwin, director of the ACLU, admitted that news commentators and labor's treatment under the code were problems that remained "yet to be solved." In November 1940, a little over a year after the code's inauguration, he was confident that "satisfactory solutions would be achieved" but promised that the ACLU stood ready to "make a loud noise if any labor organization is denied time to state its case on the air whenever it has any matter of public interest to voice."[66]

The ACLU discovered that there was no easy solution to the discrimination labor faced on radio. The Radio Committee was sharply divided over this issue, with one faction calling for the abolition of the code and a second, larger faction urging only its modification. Morris Ernst and Morris Novik were the code's sharpest critics on the committee. Ernst, the ACLU's legal counsel and a longtime critic of the increasing monopolization of the media, favored selling time to labor without restriction. He was supported by Novik, who in the 1930s had begun helping both AFL and CIO affiliates produce radio shows. In an interview with an ACLU investigator, Novik explained that he opposed the code because "it interfered with organizing labor unions over the radio."[67] The radio researcher and ACLU Radio Committee member Paul Lazarsfeld characterized the "situation of labor over the air [as] deplorable." He urged unions to document media bias through a scientific analysis of the scripts of news commentators. Lazarsfeld was even more concerned about the invisibility of unions on commercial entertainment programs, the shows with the largest audiences. He complained to Roger Baldwin that not one of the many commercial programs he had studied "takes up the problems of a labor organizer and dramatizes it in a favorable light."[68]

On the other side, Baldwin and Thomas Carskadon, head of the Century Fund's Education Department and the Radio Committee's chair, agreed with the philosophy underpinning the code and called only for minor adjustments that would increase labor's representation on the air.[69] Robert J. Landry, a member of the ACLU Radio Committee, director of program writing for CBS, and formerly the radio editor of *Variety,* saw no need for any change in the code or its application and was absolutely opposed to Lazarsfeld's idea of injecting entertainment programs with progressive social ideas. Broadcasters, he asserted, should not "recede from the sound position that controversy should be confined to properly captioned segments of unpaid time and that radio's entertainment features should not be infused or confused with capital-labor combative elements." The Socialist Norman Thomas took a middle position; while he opposed a private code and believed that "unof-

ficial censorship" operated in most radio stations, he asserted that controversial issues should only be discussed on sustaining time. Any other policy,
he warned, would "play into the hands of those with the longest purses."[70]

For five years, the ACLU wrestled with the problem of achieving fair and
equitable treatment of labor on the air. The Radio Committee repeatedly
addressed the question and met on a number of occasions with representatives of the NAB. In January 1944 it brought together the NAB's Program
Managers Committee and officials from the AFL, the CIO, the Amalgamated
Clothing Workers, the ILGWU, and the UAW in an attempt to find common
ground.[71] The ACLU was so persistent that some in the NAB grew tired of
dealing with the issue. After one meeting between the two groups, a member
of the NAB Code Committee privately suggested that the NAB "should have
been franker and ended the question once and for all by stating that labor
union programs would never be on the air."[72]

Although they acknowledged that the code had done little to ameliorate
the antilabor and pro-business bias in broadcasting, the majority of the ACLU
Radio Committee remained committed to it.[73] Like the broadcasters, they
tended to blame the victim. According to Baldwin, if labor was underrepre-
sented on the air, it was due to "a lack of organized demand for radio time."
Unions needed to be educated about "their present rights and opportunities
on the air." The CBS executive Robert Landry agreed that "labor leadership
has notoriously failed to take advantage of radio's willingness to provide it
with free time for discussions."[74] Pushed by Novik and Ernst, however, the
Radio Committee continued to try to find ways to increase labor's airtime
within the context of the code. In 1943, the Radio Committee asked the NAB to
modify the code to allow unions the same right as business to act as sponsors
of institutional prestige and goodwill entertainment programs or to buy time
for features promoting membership by publicizing their services and benefits.
The ACLU also responded to labor's complaints about hostile commentators
by recommending that stations permit replies to one-sided presentations of
industrial conflict. It urged the industry to make a voluntary commitment
to "exercise judgment, taste, and accuracy in the treatment of news" and to
adhere to the principle of fairness and balance in total programming.[75]

The NAB agreed that unions could technically buy time for noncontroversial programs, but it refused to budge on the issue of membership solicitation. Both sides agreed that individual stations should remain the arbiters
of what constitutes controversy. In the end, the broadcasters had made a
rather empty concession. They understood that it was unlikely that any union
would ever buy an institutional program that carried only a brief mention

of labor sponsorship because it "would not be worth the money charged." According to the NAB, what unions really wanted was a commercial show "picturing the life of an average family glorifying labor." Such a program, of course, would be classified as controversial and banned from labor sponsorship. In private, NAB officials were convinced that most stations would turn down any program submitted by labor. They agreed that the best strategy in the face of labor complaints and ACLU pressure was to "keep the door open and turn the programs down as they come up."[76]

❖ ❖ ❖

While the NAB and the ACLU negotiated, unions continued to take their complaints to the FCC. In November 1941, for example, striking department-store workers in San Francisco complained that the city's radio stations refused to sell time to their union to present labor's side of the conflict. The union's secretary-treasurer, Larry Vail, asked the commission, "[I]f stations sell time to the Employers are they obliged to do the same for us?" The FCC refused to intervene, giving its typical response that while stations were obliged to present "well-rounded, rather than one-sided, discussion of public controversial questions," the selection of programming was the individual station's responsibility. The commission often advised, however, that when stations came up for relicensing, unions could challenge their right to hold a license on the grounds that they failed to provide "a balanced, diversified program service."[77]

Seeking to bring public attention to the restrictions on labor's radio rights, CIO officials testified at a series of hearings on broadcasting issues conducted by the FCC and the Senate Committee on Interstate Commerce in 1941 and 1942. At the 1941 hearings on newspaper control of radio stations, the organizing director of the CIO, Allan S. Haywood, testified that since "most of the daily press is biased against labor," unions turned to radio "as a medium through which it might find fairer treatment and greater opportunity for expression." But publishers, who owned one-third of the stations, blocked labor from using radio to offset the "misleading propaganda" that filled the press. Haywood contended that "some of the most glaring instances of discrimination against labor unions have been committed by newspaper-owned stations."[78]

In 1943, Len De Caux, the CIO's publicity director and a fierce defender of labor's rights on the air, testified before the Senate Interstate Commerce Committee on a bill to reorganize the FCC. A native of New Zealand, in 1921 De Caux immigrated to the United States, where he became involved in radio politics and gained experience as an editor and correspondent for the labor press. He became editor of *CIO News* in 1937. From its pages, he regularly attacked business antilabor propaganda and encouraged unions to get out the truth about organized labor through their own press and radio programs. At the Senate hearings, De Caux recounted numerous instances of denial of airtime or censorship of labor programs and charged that not only radio but the entire mass media were controlled by wealthy and employing interests. He characterized labor as the victim of a "conspiracy of silence."[79]

The president of the UAW, R. J. Thomas, also testified at the 1943 hearing. He bristled at Fulton Lewis Jr.'s attacks on organized labor, charging that he posed "on the air as impartial while he knifes labor every day in the week and labor cannot buy or borrow a chance to answer him." He contended that the preservation of democracy in America required that the NAB code be abolished and that labor be guaranteed access to radio by legislation if necessary. According to Thomas, if the voice of labor and other progressive groups could be throttled by a private association of broadcasters, then "radio has become the weapon of one group in society, the moneyed, reactionary group, and we are on the high road to Fascism."[80]

Important elements of the FCC were sympathetic to labor's plight. In fact, during the early 1940s, relations between the FCC and broadcasters were chilly, as the commission battled owners over monopoly control of the industry. It represented one of the last bastions of reform in a government that was increasingly devoted to winning the war, not promoting social justice.[81] Clifford Durr was one of the most outspoken reformers on the commission. An Alabama attorney, in 1933 Durr joined the New Deal, working for the Reconstruction Finance Corporation. Although he had no experience in radio, in 1941 President Roosevelt appointed him to the FCC, and he quickly gained a reputation as a "high-principled, courageous fighter" on behalf of the public interest. He found prejudice inherent in a code in which anything about labor is defined as controversial, but a manufacturing firm, in the midst of being sued for violating the antitrust laws, could set "his listeners right" by explaining the "benefits" of international cartel arrangements.[82]

James Lawrence Fly, chairman of the FCC and also an ardent New Dealer, was determined that control of broadcasting should not gravitate into the hands of a small segment of society. Fly had studied at Harvard Law School with Felix Frankfurter and shared his mentor's suspicion of business monopolies, believing that they increase economic inequality and undermine democracy. In 1934, Fly became head of the Tennessee Valley Authority's legal department and defended the agency against attacks by private power companies. Five years later, Roosevelt appointed him to preside over the FCC. Fly sought to increase competition and democracy within the media and was roundly disliked by the broadcasting industry leaders, who at one point labeled him "public enemy number one."[83] While he believed that stations, once licensed, should have utmost freedom in their broadcasting decisions, he felt that the FCC through its licensing function should promote competition in ideas as well as ownership. According to Fly, the airwaves must be kept free as a guarantee of liberty and democracy. He added an additional freedom to Roosevelt's Four Freedoms, the freedom to listen. "Complete freedom to listen," Fly declared, "demands that divergent views must be aired."[84] Fly had initially endorsed the NAB's attempt at self-regulation, hoping that the code would prevent radio from being dominated by groups with the most economic power, but he became increasingly troubled by the operation of the code.[85]

By 1943, the inadequacies of the NAB code had become clear to the head of the FCC. Fly argued that it is the duty of the broadcasting industry to ensure fair and honest news broadcasts as well as to air both sides of any controversial issue. The code was failing in both areas. Some news programs tended to focus less on the news of the day and more on the philosophy of the sponsor. By careful listening, Fly advised reporters during a September 1943 news conference, "you discover that he is not giving you news or comment on the world news, but is peddling ideas to you from the company headquarters." Advocates of particular ideologies should be identified and their arguments counterbalanced, he contended.[86] The NAB's code, which banned the sale of time for controversial discussion, suppressed the marketplace of ideas and prevented important elements of society from gaining access to a nationwide audience. Fly agreed with unionists that the NAB's provision of free time for controversy was an inadequate substitute for a sponsored program. He pointed out to broadcasters at a luncheon meeting in October 1943 that "the poor relation who gets the free time cannot hope to attract the attention that the time buyer builds up with his day-by-day bombardment." Moreover, Fly denounced the code for limiting radio to the sale of merchandise and services. To restrict broadcasting to this single function "is to betray the very foundations of a free radio." The opening up of microphones to labor was a key component to protecting freedom of speech on radio.[87]

Fly punctured the first hole in the NAB code. In 1943, NBC was in the process of selling one of its networks, but it needed FCC approval for the transfer of licenses. Fly used the proceedings to put pressure on the new network to abrogate the NAB policies. During the hearings, Fly quizzed the future chairman and president of the new network, Edward J. Noble and Mark

Woods, respectively, about their loyalty to the code. Woods explained that he would sell time to Ford Motor Company and any other business sponsor to sell goods or to maintain the public's "goodwill." What if, Fly asked, the AFL wanted time for a similar purpose? "'No, sir,' said Woods, 'We will not sell them time because they have a particular philosophy to preach.'" Do not expect approval of the transfer, warned Fly, unless you reconsider your broadcasting policies. Labor, he advised the witnesses, "doesn't want a handout"; it wanted the same rights as business to buy time on the air. The new owners did reconsider. Noble promised, in writing, to judge requests for time from "all classes and groups" with an open mind, strictly on their "individual merits" and "without arbitrary discrimination." Thus, the new network, which would be known as ABC, offered access to organized labor.[88]

With the code cracked, in the spring of 1944 the CIO intensified its efforts to open the airwaves to labor. Determined to use every medium of communication on behalf of the campaign to reelect Roosevelt and congressional liberals, the CIO-PAC emerged as the new leader of the drive. Technically, during political campaigns, labor had equal access to radio, since the one exception to the prohibition against selling time for controversial issues concerned political broadcasts. The code allowed stations to air paid broadcasts connected to political campaigns. The Communications Act of 1934 did not require stations to accept such programming. However, if a station aired advertising on behalf of one candidate, it was obligated to provide equal time to all rivals. Also, censorship of political broadcasts was forbidden.[89]

When drafting the code in 1939, the NAB recognized that it could not limit political broadcasting to sustaining time. In the 1930s, radio had developed as a powerful political tool, exploited by an array of national and local politicians. By the 1940 election, the two major parties were spending a third of their budgets on broadcasts, representing the single largest expense of the campaigns.[90]

Similarly, the CIO had shown an early interest in using radio to promote its political interests. Before the 1936 election, the newly formed CIO created Labor's Nonpartisan League as a union campaign organization. The Nonpartisan League devoted significant resources to radio in addition to the traditional techniques used by unions to encourage workers to vote for labor candidates. In Ohio, it sponsored daily broadcasts during the last thirty days of the campaign. In a speech that was part of a series of talks broadcast nationally over CBS, the vice president of the United Mine Workers, Philip

Murray, declared bluntly that the central issue in the campaign could be stated in nine words: "Economic and political tyranny versus economic and political liberty." He advised his listeners, "[I]f you value your political and economic freedom," you must reelect Franklin Roosevelt, thus safeguarding it from the "economic royalists."[91]

Despite initial success in 1936, labor's political media campaign appeared stillborn. Defeats in 1937 and internecine struggles between the AFL and CIO derailed the Nonpartisan League and diminished the force of labor's political voice. Republican victories in the 1942 congressional elections, growing antilabor sentiment, and the passage of anti-union legislation pushed the CIO in 1943 to form a new, more powerful national political arm, the CIO-PAC. Its primary goal was the reelection of Franklin Roosevelt. Citing low voter turnout as a contributing factor to the failures in 1942, the CIO-PAC focused on mobilizing the working class as well as progressive allies.[92] It bombarded workers with its message through millions of pieces of campaign literature and a constant stream of articles, pictures, and cartoons distributed to the nation's 1,200 union and 230 African-American newspapers. Efforts to place positive stories about the CIO-PAC in the commercial press, with its much broader audience, proved less successful. Much of the newspaper and editorial coverage of the CIO-PAC was hostile. It became clear to PAC leaders that the most effective means of winning the sympathy and support of the general public was through the use of "the most important medium of mass communication in America—radio."[93]

The CIO-PAC organized a radio division in April 1944 and launched what it characterized as the first "coordinated program for nation-wide labor participation in radio." Headed by Emil Corwin, the brother of the screenwriter Norman Corwin, and with legal guidance from Eugene Cotton, a former top attorney of the FCC, the radio division's first step was to publish and widely distribute a radio handbook that defined the people's rights to radio airtime. Observing that many unions had not yet realized the importance of radio as a communications medium, the handbook instructed locals on how to secure time and how to protest if stations treated them unfairly. It advised, "[W]hen you shout—make it loud." If a station manager turned a deaf ear to requests for free or paid time, CIO members were to get the refusal in writing and then send it with an explanation of why the refusal was unfair to James Lawrence Fly, chairman of the FCC. The radio handbook also provided technical suggestions for programming that would "capture audience interest" and "a sampling of scripts and spot announcements." One such spot advised listeners that by voting for PAC-endorsed candidates they could help determine "how secure our peace will be. And whether we shall have full employment and win our fight over Poverty, Illness, and Ignorance."[94]

The CIO-PAC handbook attracted nationwide interest, serving as the subject of numerous articles in the daily press and in radio trade publications. For *Variety*, it represented "the first move in labor's drive for airtime." The entertainment newspaper *Billboard* praised it and urged every station operator to obtain a copy. "Never in the past," *Billboard* observed, has labor had such "a logical and workable approach to radio." A *Daily Worker* columnist, Peter Ivy, characterized the pamphlet as "dynamite." To Ivy, it was evidence of the CIO's new awareness of radio's importance, the true beginning of labor's fight for freedom of the air. In a burst of hyperbole, Ivy asserted that "for the radio Bourbons, looking down from their high offices, it means defeat," but for "54 million American toilers, it means the right to be fully heard, the right to rebut slanders, the right to 'the air which belongs to the people.'"[95]

The trade magazine *Broadcasting*, reflecting the interests of the NAB, was appalled by the publication of the *Radio Handbook*, regarding it as part of a well-organized campaign to "obliterate" the NAB code. *Broadcasting* condemned the CIO-PAC publication as a "brazen impudent effort" to pressure broadcasters into yielding free time to CIO unions. It urged station owners to resist the CIO's "strongarm" tactics. According to the trade magazine, the CIO can "shout to the high heavens if it wishes" because the decision to grant airtime "still rests with station management."[96] Release of the *Radio Handbook* also brought an immediate reaction from NAB, which had ordered one hundred copies from the CIO. President J. Harold Ryan defended the code, contending that "in intent and in practical application" it assured labor a "fair allocation of radio time." The code reflected years of experience by broadcasters in meeting conflicting demands. "Without the guiding hand of the code," Ryan warned, "chaos would result," and he urged broadcasters to apply the code's guidelines "carefully and faithfully."[97]

Although the networks warned that the NAB code prohibited dramatizations of political issues, the CIO-PAC radio division produced a series of musical and dramatic programs to be sponsored by local unions that focused on the importance of registering and voting, the meaning and purpose of political action, jobs for the returning veteran, farm-labor unity, and the reasons for supporting progressive candidates. As the director of the radio division, Emil Corwin, saw it, "[I]f entertainment and showmanship can sell soap, coffee, and cigarettes, it can sell ideas." The CIO-PAC also developed a series of short spot announcements that were played six thousand times in fifteen critical states during the last week of the campaign. Moreover, it distributed recorded talks by well-known liberals such as the actor Orson Welles and the writer Edna Ferber, who explained why they were voting for Roosevelt. The Ohio CIO Council was especially pleased with the spots, reporting that they "had a terrific wallop to them."[98]

In the face of CIO-PAC pressure, some broadcasters began to interpret the NAB code more liberally. Local unions throughout the country convinced stations to air the PAC recordings. In Ohio, Republican Senator Robert A. Taft sent telegrams to radio stations urging them to refuse time to labor for the broadcast of CIO-PAC programs exposing his "obstructionist record." The Ohio CIO Council immediately sent a protest to the FCC, and the CIO-PAC succeeded in placing its anti-Taft recordings with many of the radio stations in the state. An angry Taft yelled "bloody murder, which was very effective," according to the assistant director of the CIO-PAC, Garland Ascraft of Cincinnati.[99] More unions, both AFL and CIO, also bought time for regular weekly programs, during which they presented the material developed by their national office as well as local programming aimed at their own community. The director of the northwest regional PAC, Jerry J. O'Connell, for instance, reported that unions in Aberdeen, Everett, Bellingham, Longview, and Vancouver, Washington; Wallace, Idaho; and Great Falls, Montana, sponsored weekly programs. In evaluating radio's effectiveness in the Northwest, O'Connell asserted that the use of radio in the political campaign had truly awakened members to its value. "They see in it a chance to counteract the vicious falsehoods of the controlled press against labor." The people too, he continued, "generally, have a better appreciation of the role of labor, and are enthusiastic for a greater utilization of the power of Radio by Labor." Utilization of radio, however, varied across the nation. The director of the West Virginia PAC, John B. Easton, admitted that "our boys were slow in realizing the importance of radio." In addition, some stations continued to resist selling or giving labor airtime.[100]

The CIO, the ILGWU, and the Teamsters also bought network time over NBC and CBS to boost Roosevelt's reelection. Recognizing Hollywood's ability to draw listeners, the ILGWU enlisted major show-business personalities, including James Cagney, Edward G. Robinson, and Paulette Goddard, who appeared with prominent political figures in broadcasts produced and coordinated by Morris Novik. Garment workers held radio parties, gathering in groups to listen to their union's program. On one October program, Frank Sinatra joined Ethel Merman, who sang "Don't Look Now, Mr. Dewey, but Your Record Is Showing." One listener, Ruth M. Eddy, "a Rooseveltian," wrote to the ILGWU that "Sinatra's speech was pretty good for a swoon crooner. But Ethel Merman certainly went to town with that song."[101]

In early September 1944, seeking to gain fairer treatment from network radio, CIO president Philip Murray met with members of the commentators' Association of Radio News Analysts. He explained CIO positions on a variety of public issues and answered "a flock of questions." According to *Billboard*, "everyone came away from this meeting with a feeling of mutual benefit and understanding." CIO-PAC staff members also began providing commentators with pro-labor spins on news stories. According to Paul Lazarsfeld, the radio division also hoped to interject social issues into network entertainment programs. Corwin and his staff began contacting writers and producers of network programs that regularly attracted audiences of millions, suggesting nonpolitical, nonpartisan themes of importance to labor that might be integrated into their scripts. For instance, the CIO-PAC suggested to writers of radio dramas that they tell about some interesting incidents relating to the history of the right to vote. This theme tied in with the CIO voter-registration campaign. By early August 1944, Corwin reported that the CIO-PAC had secured "important plugs" on the shows "The Great Gildersleeve" and his brother's program, "Columbia Presents Corwin."[102]

The CIO-PAC, however, was not content to rely solely on radio's obligation under the code to provide even-handed treatment to organized labor. In a move that *Billboard* charged thwarted the goodwill generated by Murray's lobbying, the radio division set up a monitoring system using the content-analysis technique developed by the political scientist Harold Laswell to keep track of what national commentators were saying about labor and the CIO-PAC. A staff of volunteer listeners, with two listeners assigned to each program, analyzed thirty-three of the most popular network news and comment shows.[103] The service revealed the extent to which prejudice dominated network news. The monitors' survey of network broadcasts from mid-September to mid-October 1944 found that for every favorable item broadcast on labor there were six unfavorable ones. Moreover, the survey revealed that network commentators repeatedly charged that the CIO-PAC used "coercive tactics," that it was "linked up with the Communists," that strikes were harming the war effort, and that increased wages were dangerous and inflationary.[104]

The CIO used its findings to put pressure on the networks to drop pundits such as Henry J. Taylor and Upton Close, who regularly attacked unions. Just before election day, Emil Corwin presented the radio division's analysis of Taylor's broadcasts to G. W. Johnstone, the head of the Blue Network's

(ABC) News and Special Events Division. The report showed that only 8 percent of Taylor's material was factual; the rest, stated Corwin, was "just his cockeyed opinions." According to the CIO-PAC study, Taylor's major themes were that PAC leaders were linked to the Communists, that the PAC controlled the Democratic party, that Sidney Hillman had ties to criminals, and that PAC leaders were all foreign-born. Corwin bluntly asked Johnstone, "What are you going to do about Taylor's deliberate misrepresentation, lies, and slander?"[105]

Monitors also listened to local newscasts and business broadcasts for antilabor bias or one-sided coverage of controversial issues to pressure stations into giving labor equal time. To make its case, the CIO-PAC pointed to the FCC's 1941 Mayflower Decision, which obligated stations to present "all sides of important public questions fairly and objectively, and without bias." Emil Corwin, who was helping out with the monitoring project, spotted the NAM's series "Businessmen Look to the Future" on the New York station WOR. Arguing that the program presented only the business side of postwar problems, the CIO-PAC asked for and received equal time to present labor's viewpoint on the issue. The CIO-PAC also received time on WWRL to clarify misstatements about the CIO made by one of its commentators during the Philadelphia transit strike. C. B. Baldwin, the assistant CIO-PAC chairman, urged all the regional directors of the PAC to be as aggressive as the New York and Philadelphia unionists in monitoring broadcasts and in requesting airtime to refute programs unfriendly to labor.[106]

The CIO-PAC was pleased with labor's growing access to local radio stations, but it also wanted a nationwide audience. In late summer of 1944, prodded by the radio division, Philip Murray went to the networks and began negotiating for regular weekly national radio programs that would counteract the antilabor bias being documented by the monitoring service.[107] Murray singled out the free time given to NAM for "Businessmen Look to the Future," pointing out that requests by labor for a similar program had often been denied. At the same time, AFL president William Green took similar demands to network officials. The AFL had begun to awaken to the importance of reaching the public with labor's message. By 1944, wartime business attacks against labor had sparked new interest within the AFL's ranks in creating a public relations program. The AFL now recognized that labor needed to win "the sympathy and support of public opinion," and it could not do this "through a prejudiced press." Radio was the most effective medium of reaching the public available to labor, the Executive Council decided. Its value in developing goodwill "cannot be overestimated." With a new interest in expanding its radio activities, Philip Pearl, who had previously praised network cooperation with labor, joined the CIO in criticizing the networks for their failure to provide regular time to labor after the cancellation of "Labor for Victory."[108]

In October 1944, in response to pressure from labor, the ACLU, and the FCC, the three largest networks agreed to allot the AFL and CIO free time for weekly programs beginning in January 1945. The AFL and CIO each sponsored thirteen weeks of an NBC Sunday-afternoon panel talk show, "America United." Business and farm organizations took over the program during the rest of the year. The AFL also had "American Federationist of the Air," a Saturday-evening weekly news magazine broadcast over ABC, and "Builders for Victory," broadcast over CBS for twenty-six weeks on Saturday afternoons, which focused on the exploits of Seabees, the majority of whom were members of the AFL's building and metal trades unions. CIO programs included "Labor USA" and "Jobs for Tomorrow," which focused on reconversion problems and plans, presenting dramatic scripts about the impact of the transition from a wartime to peacetime economy on individual workers. "Labor USA," which aired on ABC and shared its Saturday-evening time spot half the year with the AFL, used music, stories, and interviews as "a good antidote to the anti-strike poison you get from newspapers and from many radio commentators."[109]

An early review of labor's network programs reflected the CIO's more extensive experience with radio. *Variety* welcomed the new shows and patted the networks on the back for keeping pace with the "social and economic forces that have projected labor into a key position" in American society. The launching of the new labor programs, observed *Variety*, "represented a far cry from the days not so long ago when socially-minded guys who recognized the necessity of labor getting a hearing were obliged to knock at the doors of broadcasters and plead for a break." While the AFL's segment of "America United" was "too general, tried to include too many statistics and . . . failed to hold sustained listener interest," *Variety* praised the CIO shows "Jobs for Tomorrow" and "Labor USA" for making effective use of dramatic formats. The first "Jobs for Tomorrow," for instance, opened with a UAW ballad, accompanied by the strumming of a guitar. It then picked up a conversation between a union representative and a girl who knew nothing about organized labor. In a brief imaginary trip, the unionist made "real and understandable" the work of the UAW and its expectations for the future. He also emphasized the autoworkers' stand against racial discrimination and its support for equal rights for working women. According to *Variety*, the show effectively conveyed the idea that the UAW was proud of its past and looked forward to a future "it was determined to help mold."[110]

By early 1945, according to *Business Week,* the muzzle was "part-way" off. In addition to pressure from unions and other reformers, the need for wartime unity, which required enlisting the support of all elements of society on behalf of the war effort, also pushed broadcasters to open the airwaves to the voices of labor as well as minorities. The networks began giving unions a more significant voice through weekly sustaining or free programs, and more unions were able to buy time on local stations as well. As the "public interest" began to be defined more broadly, even some of the most controversial issues were no longer considered taboo in some localities. In January 1945, for instance, during a factional fight within the UAW over retention of the union's no-strike pledge, the bloc supporting the pledge succeeded in purchasing eleven hours of broadcasting, spread in quarter- and half-hour programs over twenty-one stations, in the auto and aircraft production centers. While some stations quietly ignored the code, New York City's most prominent independent station, WMCA, in open defiance of the NAB code publicly announced its willingness to sell time to unions for the discussion of controversial issues.[111]

At the same time, a few antilabor voices were brought down a notch. Shortly after the 1944 election, the Blue Network dropped Henry J. Taylor's commentary, and NBC dropped Upton Close, though both were ultimately picked up by the smaller Mutual Network. *Billboard* credited the CIO-PAC's monitoring system for contributing to the break between Taylor and the Blue Network.[112] In addition, the PAC's demand that stations adhere to their obligation to present all sides of public issues seemed to be having an impact on station programming. A NAM representative to the NAB's fall 1944 meeting found that as a result of labor pressure, stations were less willing to take NAM shows, like the "Businessmen Look to the Future" series, or wanted modifications in business programming. The station owners suggested that they "could uphold their position to labor critics a little better" if only one of the thirteen broadcasts in the series included a labor representative. Thus, the CIO-PAC drive succeeded in weakening the NAB code and in raising important questions about the equitable treatment of labor on the airwaves.[113]

❖ ❖ ❖

In the summer of 1945 the FCC dealt the final blow to the NAB code. Throughout the war, unions had been filing protests with the FCC over denial of airtime. The UAW was among the most vigorous unions to defend labor's rights to air, and it was a UAW complaint that led the FCC to officially rule on the legitimacy of the code. In June 1943, Columbus, Ohio, UAW Local 927, which represented fifteen thousand workers at the Curtiss-Wright aircraft plant, bought a weekly half-hour program on WHKC. At that time, the aircraft company had been sponsoring a commercial half-hour weekly program on WHKC for more than a year. Curtiss-Wright, which built dive bombers at the Columbus plant, used its program to plug its contribution to the war effort and occasionally to recruit workers. According to UAW president R. J. Thomas, the show also "subtly propagandized for the Curtiss-Wright point of view."[114]

While Local 927 was interested in touting labor's contribution to the war effort and winning public sympathy for the union cause, it was also seeking a vehicle for communicating with its membership. Like many CIO unions, Local 927 struggled to reach new members, who were at best apathetic and at worst had "negative views" of organized labor. The majority of the plant's workers came from rural areas and had little experience with factory labor or unions. With a shortage of housing near the plant, many of the employees lived as far away as fifty or sixty miles. The long commute and gasoline rationing made it difficult for even motivated workers to attend union meetings. Urged on by Richard Evans, the local's education director who during the 1930s had helped produce a labor show in Portsmouth, Ohio, the union leadership decided that radio was the "best instrument" for educating its members about the aims, principles, and achievements of organized labor.[115]

Local 927 approached WHKC about buying airtime. A Mutual Network affiliate and a member of the NAB, WHKC had never aired a regular labor program, although it had broadcast on sustaining time occasional speeches by union leaders. Before selling the airtime, the station's general manager, C. M. Everson, sought assurances that labor relations were amicable at the Curtiss-Wright plant and that the union had no intention of discussing race, religion, or politics on the air. He asked Evans, who was to produce the union program, "[Y]ou don't want to do anything in this program that is going to disrupt . . . friendly relations . . . with the management at Curtiss-Wright?" According to Everson, Evans promised that Local 927 would abide by the NAB code prohibiting the broadcast of controversial issues on paid time. Everson later testified to the FCC that he sold the union time on the condition that it would be used only to inform the public about labor's contribution to the war effort and that he gave Evans a copy of the code.[116]

Evans had much more ambitious goals for his local's new program. Despite his assurances to the station manager, Local 927's "Labor Leads the Way" used dramatizations performed by workers and talks by the rank and file and union officers to defend labor's war record, educate members about the workings and benefits of the union, and promote the CIO's political agenda. For instance, on June 13, 1943, an aircraft worker, Lucille Dodd, read a letter she had recently sent to her brother, Paul, who was in the armed forces. Her brother had written, asking, "What can those strikers back there be thinking of? Don't they realize that we want to get back home as soon as we can?" She replied that before working at Curtiss-Wright she used to hate unions, but after she started working at the airplane plant, she saw the department steward protect one of her fellow workers from an unfair discharge. Inspired by this event, Lucille joined Local 927 and learned that its members "aren't just a bunch of trouble-makers and agitators. They want to work; they want to help in the war effort." Her union, she declared over the air, "is the most democratic organization imaginable. . . . I love my union; I love the way these people stand by each other, the way they will stand by me, if I ever need them." Moreover, she assured her brother that her local was not going to strike. "We've given up our right to strike for the duration. We will work and sacrifice and buy bonds and give our blood right along with you boys until it is over, and we're all together again." A number of the programs followed the fictional exploits of Jack Elverson, a brand-new aircraft worker who, like the real-life Lucille Dodd, learns that workers gain strength through collective action. After joining the union, Elverson uncovers a company stooge, helps stop a wildcat strike, and helps track down saboteurs responsible for the crash of a new bomber. Instead of a conventional commercial, the typical union messages encouraged listeners to register and vote, spoke of labor's role in promoting racial harmony, or emphasized the importance of winning the peace through equitable postwar planning.[117]

Citing the NAB code, WHKC repeatedly censored Local 927's program. From the union's fictional serial about Jack Elverson, the station took out a scene in which the foreman tries to prevent workers from joining the union. The station's program director argued that accusing even a fictional company of using underhanded tactics might create friction between union members and Curtiss-Wright management. The station also cut a voter-registration appeal that charged that Congress, under the influence of "poll-taxers and reactionaries," was "deliberately and systematically taking away labor's rights" and "helping millionaires make more millions."[118] In August 1943, the UAW's vice president, Richard T. Frankensteen, attempted to deliver a

speech attacking business and reviewing the voting and political records of
the Ohio politicians Robert A. Taft and John M. Vorys. Asserting that the
talk was controversial and not in keeping with the purpose of the program,
the station management cut the speech to pieces, deleting all criticism of
Taft and Vorys. Among the statements cut was Frankensteen's assertion that
while America had suffered no major military defeats in 1943, "she has suffered a major defeat in Congress; she has suffered the perversion of her central democratic institution to selfish and sinister political purposes." He was
also not permitted to say that Senator Taft "can tell you why the cost of war
must be paid out of your slender wallet instead of out of the swelling bank
accounts, reserve funds, and 'reconversion' allotment of big business."[119]

While the local had acquiesced to the earlier censorship, Frankensteen
was furious. He fired off a complaint to the FCC, requesting time on WHKC
to deliver the uncensored speech. The FCC asked for an explanation from
the station but refused to intervene further. Encouraged by the CIO-PAC,
the UAW petitioned the FCC to cancel WHKC's license, which was up for
renewal, on the grounds of censorship and failure to operate in the public
interest. The commission denied the petition and in May 1944 renewed the
station's license for the normal three years. Three months later, after strong
protest from the CIO and its supporters in Congress, the FCC agreed to reconsider and hold a hearing.[120]

In preparing for the August hearing, the Ohio CIO Council sent the FCC
thousands of petitions signed by Ohio workers and sympathetic citizens. The
petitions, which were part of the council's Fair Play on the Air Campaign,
stated that the station had "deliberately and consistently followed a policy of
presenting the news and issues of the day in a biased, unfair, and distorted
manner" and urged the FCC to take "corrective action." The CIO-PAC encouraged unions throughout the nation to support the petition drive, observing that the results of the hearing "will have nation-wide implications . . . it
is a case testing the principle of FREEDOM OF THE AIR."[121] Also prior to
the start of the hearing, the UAW asked the FCC to subpoena the scripts of
the Mutual Network commentators heard over WHKC, including those of
Upton Close, Fulton Lewis Jr., and Robert McCormick. C. J. Durr, the commissioner who had earlier criticized the NAB code and was openly sympathetic to organized labor's case, issued the subpoenas for the commentators' scripts.[122]

The UAW also sought to demonstrate how the NAM used the economic
power of its membership to pressure radio stations into accepting its programming. The union asked the FCC to subpoena General Motors chairman

Alfred P. Sloan, Standard Brands president James S. Adams, and William S. Rainey, radio director of the NAM. Their names had appeared on a letter sent by the NAM to every radio station in the country requesting them to carry NAM's "Businessmen Look to the Future" series. The NAM letter advised station managers that employers in their communities would be notified of the local station's decision whether or not to cooperate. Besides this veiled threat, the UAW pointed out that the 3.5 million dollars spent by Sloan's and Adams's companies on network advertising as well as advertising dollars spent locally by these firms "might be expected to have at least a minor influence" on stations. FCC commissioner Ray C. Wakefield, however, denied the subpoena request.[123]

During the hearings, the UAW tried to prove that the station's programming failed to maintain a balanced treatment of controversial issues. It charged that while the station either refused airtime to unions or censored UAW speeches, it did not interfere with the "venomous talks of Fulton Lewis Jr., kingpin of the hate-labor chorus." The UAW entered parallel scripts into evidence to show that while Local 947's program was not allowed to attack speculative builders in its discussion of housing, Fulton Lewis Jr. was permitted to praise the real-estate interests and criticize the National Housing Agency. WHKC's station manager, Carl Everson, denied that his station had ever been antilabor and claimed that it offered a balanced program, giving all sides of the picture. As for the commentators, Everson explained that their programs came live from the Mutual Network, and it was impossible for the station to screen for objectionable material prior to broadcast. Moreover, he argued that there was no need to censor Lewis because he was "absolutely neutral" in his opinions. The UAW "punctured that illusion" by submitting the results of a content analysis expert whose study of 175 of Lewis's broadcasts demonstrated that 57 percent of the time he attacked labor, and he was favorable to labor only 5 percent of the time.[124]

Towards the end of the weeklong hearing, Everson announced that he had decided to scrap the NAB code, since it was impossible for the station to apply it equally to local and network programming. Subsequently, WHKC reached an agreement with the UAW, promising to eliminate the code restrictions and to adopt a nondiscriminatory policy in regard to labor broadcasts. It was a "clear-cut triumph for labor" and a "sharp repudiation" of the NAB code.[125] The union and the station then joined in asking the FCC to renew the station's license. The FCC acceded to their request and, in a decision issued on June 29, 1945, applauded the UAW-WHKC agreement and attacked the NAB code. It declared that radio was "to be an instrument of free speech"

and that the operation of any station "under the extreme principles that no
time shall be sold for the discussion of controversial issues" was "inconsistent with the concept of public interest established by the Communication
Act."[126] The FCC had all but destroyed the code.

In August 1945, with the handwriting on the wall, the NAB abolished the
code and substituted new standards that left decisions about broadcasting
controversial issues entirely up to the individual station managers.[127] Two
months later, the CIO took its case for a wage increase to the American public through a series of paid broadcasts over ABC. This was the first time that
organized labor had the opportunity to buy time over network airwaves.
Labor's struggle for access, however, was not entirely over. While the ABC
and Mutual networks began selling time to labor, it was not until 1950 that
NBC and CBS adopted a similar policy. Some local stations also continued to
censor or refused to sell or give time to unions, particularly during strikes or
electoral campaigns. As during the war, CIO unions aggressively challenged
stations' denial of airtime, frequently turning to the FCC and threatening to
intervene in license-renewal proceedings. After the WHKC decision, however, the FCC more actively interceded on labor's behalf. The CIO's victory
in its long battle to open the airwaves to organized labor showed the potential of reform groups to democratize radio. In fact, it served as the lightning
rod for a much broader campaign to reform broadcasting in the immediate
postwar era.

(( ))

5   Protecting Listeners' Rights:
     Radio Reform, 1945–48

ON MAY 8, 1947, an overflow audience of more than fifteen hundred crowded
into New York City's Town Hall to participate in a rally called by the Voice
of Freedom Committee (VOF). Hundreds of others were turned away from
the packed hall. Headed by the writer Dorothy Parker, the Voice of Freedom
Committee had formed two months earlier to protest the silencing of liberal
radio commentators. Since the end of the war, progressives had disappeared
from the airwaves while conservative voices remained strong. The most recent casualty was William Shirer, one of CBS's acclaimed wartime corre-
spondents. To dramatize the threat to democracy from the loss of diverse
political perspectives in broadcasting, actors on stage at the rally presented
an imaginary radio show that took the audience three years into the future
for a glimpse of life in the United States.

    The imaginary broadcast emanated from an "underground" radio sta-
tion on an island off the Atlantic coast, "behind the intellectual barbed wire"
of an America ruled by "Republocrats," who have banned dissent, outlawed
progressive organizations, and intimidated minorities. John E. Rankin, the
chair of the House Committee on Un-American Activities (HUAC) in 1947,
was now head of the U.S. thought police. The commentator William Gailmor
related how Americans had let "reactionaries drive freedom underground
by throwing liberal voices off the air." He reminded the audience that only
"a few years ago, when we warned that this might come, people didn't listen,
until they were no longer able to hear us. We now call on the people of the
United States to recapture their lost freedom." At the end of the imaginary
show, the commentator Frank Kingdom, borrowing a slogan from the CIO's

Radio Handbook, declared that the "air belongs to the people." Business's influence over broadcasting, he asserted, meant that radio was ruled by "greed and fear," the "seeds of fascism."[1]

To recapture this vital medium, the Voice of Freedom Committee circulated petitions urging the FCC to ensure that radio stations provide impartial comment on world and national affairs, give time to organized labor equal to that available to industry, and support high-quality dramatic and musical programming. These petitions represented the goals of a wide-ranging reform movement that raised fundamental questions about the American broadcasting system during the mid 1940s. By the end of World War II, many of the concerns that labor had voiced about business control over the mass media meshed with a swelling critique of radio. The CIO's victory against the NAB code served as a green light for attacking corporate control of the media.

In the immediate postwar years, a variety of individuals and groups spanning the political spectrum—from public intellectuals and members of the FCC to organized labor and the leftist cultural or popular front—demanded reform. The CIO was an important part of this loose coalition, which fought unchecked commercialism, promoted public service, and sought to make radio more representative and democratic and to increase community control. One of the key battles in the campaign for a more democratic media contested the distribution of FM licenses. This new broadcasting system could potentially break the monopoly control of advertisers and networks over radio and open station ownership to previously excluded groups. Thus in the immediate postwar years the CIO focused its attention on its continuing campaign to reform broadcasting and on developing a strong voice on radio through both local and network programming. This chapter examines the postwar radio reform movement; the following chapters explore how labor used its airtime at the height of union power in America.

❖ ❖ ❖

In the mid-1940s, a chorus of voices condemned almost every aspect of American broadcasting. Books and magazine articles charged that radio had become a handmaiden to advertisers. The public's desire for news about the war had helped increase the number of listeners, and advertisers flocked to the medium, making radio more profitable than ever. Radio's critics blamed weak-kneed broadcasters for acceding to advertisers' demands, for commercials of "dubious taste and in many cases dubious honesty." Moreover, most programming, which advertisers shaped to their own special interest—the selling of goods—was mediocre. According to the Scripps-Howard columnist

Robert Ruark, excessive commercialism made nearly everything in radio either "corny, strident, boresome, florid, inane, repetitive, irritating, offensive, moronic, adolescent, or nauseating."[2]

Morris Ernst, the ACLU counsel and a prominent defender of civil liberties, Senator Burton K. Wheeler, a leading congressional progressive, and the FCC commissioner Clifford Durr argued that networks had concentrated the control of radio and warned of the dangers of media monopoly. In 1944, two-thirds of the stations, including almost all of the most powerful stations, were affiliated with the networks, which themselves fell under the influence of a few big advertisers and advertising agencies.[3] Advertiser control not only resulted in mediocre programming but tended to reduce the diversity of voices on the air. Prior to the war, stations offered many of the best arts and public affairs programs on a sustaining (nonadvertising) basis. But the selling of virtually every moment of prime time during the war forced noncommercial programs off the air or relegated them to less desirable late-night or Sunday-morning time slots. These programs had been the primary vehicles for broadcasters to fulfill their service to the public interest. The decline in public service programming made it more difficult for minorities or groups such as organized labor to gain sufficient opportunity to be heard on controversial issues.[4]

Critics also worried that sponsors exercised too much ideological control over radio news. Most stations and networks allowed sponsors to choose their own news analyst or commentator. This gave big business tremendous influence over what Americans heard in the way of news and discussion of national and world issues. Not surprisingly, conservative sponsors such as Pure Oil or General Motors hired like-minded commentators. The liberal commentator Quincy Howe, for one, admitted that news analysts might be tempted to slant their interpretation "the way he thinks his sponsor might like to go." The radio editor of the *New York Times,* Jack Gould, fretted about the implications of commercial sponsorship of the news, noting that advertisers were being permitted to determine "what news is to be put on the air." This gave sponsors powers that were "antithetical to sound principles of journalism," according to Gould. In the spring of 1947, this concern over private interests' power to shape the news led the Commission on Freedom of the Press to recommend that the radio industry take control of its programs from advertisers.[5]

Organized labor ranked among radio's strongest critics. Even after the favorable 1945 WHKC decision, which gave labor greater access to radio, unions still had a litany of complaints about the broadcasting industry. Foremost was labor's continued difficulty in gaining airtime. In 1948, the CIO noted that there had been some gradual improvement in the radio industry's treatment of labor, but the "road to radio utopia" was "still long and hazardous."[6] Radio stations in some communities continued to censor or refused to sell time to unions. During the 1946 campaign, for instance, the Iowa station WMT refused to broadcast a series of political announcements by CIO groups, contending they were controversial. In Ohio, the Brush-Moore newspaper chain, which controlled stations in Portsmouth and Canton, declared that only parties certified on the state ballot could sponsor political broadcasts, effectively excluding the CIO-PAC's voice. In California, the Don Lee Network denied the PAC paid airtime for an address by CIO president Philip Murray.[7] Efforts to gain airtime during strikes or organizing campaigns also proved contentious. In February 1946, General Electric's Schenectady station, WGY, refused to sell time to the United Steelworkers but allowed the American Iron and Steel Institute to broadcast several programs. In the midst of the 1946 GM strike, stations in Anderson, Indiana, and Bay City, Michigan, refused the UAW time. Eight months later, six unions met with the FCC to discuss the refusal of Milwaukee stations to sell or give them time to discuss the Allis-Chalmers strike.[8]

Labor had a particularly difficult time in the South, especially when broadcasts dealt with issues such as race or organizing. In December 1947, WFOR of Hattiesburg, Mississippi, cut the CIO's civil rights forum on the "America United" broadcast off the air after nineteen minutes, charging that it was too controversial. Program participants had just begun to discuss revelations from a Senate investigating committee about Mississippi state officials preventing blacks from participating in the 1946 election. The station manager explained to the CIO national office, "We are in the Deep South, and you got off on the racial questions. We cut it off . . . telling the radio audience this is a controversial issue and that both sides were not represented." By both sides, the manager said that he meant "someone representing the South and someone representing the colored people." Of the program participants, two were southern whites and one was an African American, Leslie Perry of the NAACP. The CIO immediately fired off a sharp letter of protest to the FCC, asserting that WFOR's action was a serious violation of the principles of free speech and asked that the incident be considered when the station's license was up for renewal. The following spring, a Blackstone, Virginia, station kept the CIO's southern organizing committee off the air as it prepared for an NLRB election. The station cited the excuse that the material was too controversial, although the town's other station had been "most cooperative in selling time." Elsewhere in the South, stations refused access for fear of antagonizing local business.[9]

The CIO's critique of radio extended beyond the issue of union access. Like other critics, labor was concerned about the influence of business on program content. The CIO's assistant publicity director, Henry C. Fleisher, affirmed that audiences wanted something "more profound to chew upon than chewing-gum commercials, soap operas, or whodunits." Labor felt even more strongly about the anti-union propaganda that it believed business injected in radio programming. The antilabor diatribes from business-backed conservative commentators were mentioned specifically, but even fictional programs created unflattering images of unions. An October 1946 *Variety* story confirmed unionists' suspicions that some sponsors were using their shows to portray labor in a negative light. Sponsors pushed writers of major radio shows to promote the "ideals of private enterprise," *Variety*'s radio editor, Saul Carson, reported. In at least one instance, a sponsor requested that the scriptwriter of a mystery show make the murderer in the story a member of the Maritime union.[10]

Labor critics traced radio's problems to the patterns of ownership in the broadcasting industry. According to the CIO, a corporate monopoly controlled most of the radio stations and newspapers in the nation. A relatively small group of manufacturers, bankers, and the nation's six main newspaper chains owned or controlled 568 of the 912 radio stations operating in 1944, including the vast majority of the most powerful stations. The *CIO News* accused these "moneyed masters" of letting loose "their mechanized hounds of the press and radio . . . after the American working people and their unions." It was no coincidence that newspapers denounced labor during strikes and that unions struggled for access to the airwaves. In fact, unionists believed that newspaper-owned radio stations affiliated to chains such as Hearst and Gannett were among the most hostile to labor. They pointed to incidents like the denial of airtime in Milwaukee during the Allis-Chalmers strike by two Hearst-owned stations.[11]

❖ ❖ ❖

After World War II, the disappearance of commentators who had defended labor and the Left seemed to epitomize the power of networks, station owners, and sponsors to restrain free speech and limit radio's political diversity. During the war, the expansion of news commentary had enabled a host of liberal commentators to find homes on the airwaves. Commentary by Frank Kingdon, Robert St. John, William L. Shirer, Raymond Swing, and

Organized labor charged that business used its control over radio to attack unions.
Reprinted from *Reading Labor Advocate*, Feb. 4, 1947.

John Vandercook had helped offset the big-business, antilabor messages of conservative commentators. A *Variety* survey of thirty of the top analysts conducted in July 1945 found remarkable balance between conservative and liberal voices.[12]

Within two years of the end of the war, that balance had disappeared. In part due to the political chill from the emerging domestic cold war, networks and local independent radio stations pushed out liberal and leftist commentators or pressured them to "tone down" news sympathetic to progressive causes.[13] Even before the end of the war the vulnerability of liberal commentators was evident. In March 1945, KFI in Los Angeles, one of the nation's largest independent stations, announced that all commentators would be employees of the station and promptly replaced all six of its pundits, three of whom were decidedly liberal and pro-labor, with a conservative lineup. The station owner, Packard car distributor Earl C. Anthony, a conservative who considered the Democratic party, the New Deal, Roosevelt, and labor unions "communistic," declared that he was fed up with "personal opinions and interpretations" and wanted "direct economic control over persons broadcasting news and opinion forming programs."[14]

KFI proved to be the vanguard of what *Variety* characterized as a "quiet but effective campaign to drive from the airwaves every radio gabber ever-so-slightly left of center." On the West Coast, the number of progressive commentators dropped from fourteen to three, while the number of conservatives climbed to thirty-five. One Los Angeles station manager ordered his newscasters never to mention the names of Franklin Roosevelt or Henry Wallace on the air. Asked, "What if Wallace dies?" he replied, "Just say the 'secretary of commerce.'" On the East Coast, the House Committee on Un-American Activities, angry at being "slandered, maligned, and ridiculed by certain commentators," led the charge against the progressives.[15] In the fall of 1945, claiming that it had received letters from listeners complaining of "communistic" views, HUAC requested the scripts of seven mostly New York–based commentators with the intention of holding hearings on their political ideology. "The time has come to determine how far you can go with free speech," explained a committee spokesman. The hearings never occurred, but after analyzing the scripts, the committee accused the seven (who supported full employment, better health and medical protection, and higher wages, and who questioned the growing tension between the United States and the Soviet Union) of promoting pro-Russian and pro-Communist propaganda. HUAC chairman John S. Wood introduced a bill designed to impose controls on radio stations and their news commentators.[16]

Fallout from HUAC's attack came quickly. Shortly after being named by the committee, Hans Jacob lost his job. To Jacob, an antifascist refugee, the episode was eerily reminiscent of events in Germany during the 1930s. Johannes Steel, also one of the HUAC's targets, warned that "liberal commentators like myself are being subpoenaed in a pressure campaign which is designed to intimidate radio stations and get us off the air."[17] Within a year, broadcasters dropped Steel, a ten-year broadcast veteran, and Frank Kingdon, whom *Variety* characterized as the "fastest rising commentator on the national scene," and cut the airtimes of two others. Stations claimed no available sponsor or time spot as explanations. It was not surprising that stations shied away from Kingdon. He had acquired a reputation as a "fighting progressive" and had recently become chairman of the National Citizens Political Action Committee (NCPAC), the CIO's organization to mobilize liberals outside the ranks of labor.[18]

The networks also cleaned house. In 1946 NBC dismissed the liberals John Vandercook, Robert St. John, Don Hollenbeck, and Don Goddard. A conservative analyst took Vandercook's spot, and St. John was replaced by an audience-participation show. According to NBC, there was no conspiracy, but broadcast insiders asserted that the network was making a "concerted long-range effort to get liberals out."[19] Former New York City Mayor Fiorella La Guardia's popular ABC Sunday-evening commentary was also canceled in 1946. Morris Novik had convinced *Liberty Magazine* to sponsor the former mayor as a weekly commentator. La Guardia's liberal stances and his defense of strikers and criticism of railroad operators angered the business community, which pressured *Liberty* to drop the show. Justifying its decision, *Liberty* claimed that public interest in the show was waning, but the NAM later took credit for helping drive La Guardia off the air.[20]

In March 1947, the J. B. Williams Company, a soap manufacturer, canceled William Shirer's sponsorship contract. With an audience of about five million, Shirer had the highest Hooper rating of all daytime programs on CBS, but the network refused to continue broadcasting his program without a sponsor. Shirer believed that CBS gave into "Wall Street and allied pressure." George Herman, a CBS news writer, later recalled that everyone in the office was aware that "sponsors were beginning to be afraid" of Shirer's liberalism.[21] Less than a year later, ABC dropped the distinguished broadcaster Raymond Swing, another liberal broadcasting fixture named by HUAC in the fall of 1945. On the air since 1935, he had various commercial sponsors over the years. By late 1947 he was sponsorless, with the network carrying him on a sustaining basis. Known for his integrity, Swing had negotiated a contract from sponsors guaranteeing him absolute editorial control. During the war, public association of Swing with his 10 P.M. time slot was so powerful that characters in two detective novels used listening to his show as alibis. Swing was a staunch opponent of fascism, an advocate of women's and workers' rights, and a proponent for world control of nuclear power, all of which made him vulnerable to right-wing attacks. After he went off the air, Charles Siepman wrote that Swing disdained to curry favor and never hesitated to speak out. "His appeal was always to our conscience, and though we might wince, we could not protest, for we knew that he spoke from his own troubled concern about the world." By early 1948, with CBS analysts such as Edward R. Murrow and Eric Sevareid barred by their network from interpreting the news, the network airways had a decidedly conservative cast. Aside from the liberal Elmer Davis on ABC, the only commentators heard more than once a week on network prime time were the conservatives H. V. Kaltenborn, Earl Godwin, Fulton Lewis Jr., Henry J. Taylor, and Gabriel Heatter.[22]

The attack on liberals touched off a wave of protest that began on the floor of Congress and spread across the nation. In the House of Representatives a number of legislators immediately denounced HUAC's demand for scripts and its proposed legislation. Representative Hugh DeLacey, a Washington Democrat, characterized the committee as "congressional thought police" who threatened commentators with government surveillance and placed their thoughts "under House arrest." HUAC's investigation sent a message to radio stations that if they wanted to stay "out of the center of smear controversy, they had better get other commentators," according to the California Democrats Ellis Patterson and Helen Gahagan Douglas. The *New York Times* worried that HUAC might succeed in scaring the networks so that they would hesitate to permit free expression of opinion. This "indirect suppression would be as 'un-American' an activity as some others the committee is gunning for."[23]

Many Americans took their concerns about the disappearance of liberals directly to the FCC. In September 1946, M. J. Bablich of West Allis, Wisconsin, and R. D. Shields of Toledo, Ohio, were among the many who wrote concerning the dismissals of Vandercook and St. John. Both worried about the chilling influence of big business on the media. Bablich believed that the commentators were fired because of their "defense of the common citizens' interests and attacks on big business." Shields charged that the "pressure of the N.A.M. . . . . is far too serious for the public to ignore—it becomes sinister."[24] Mrs. Raymond P. Keesecker of Cleveland wanted NBC to understand the importance of St. John's commentary in her community. She described how at 8:45 each morning, radios throughout her entire Shaker Heights apartment building could be heard "one after another, tuning in to hear Robert St. John." She reported that "we, in Cleveland, have a sense of consternation that such a program, one of the few to which those with a degree of intelligence can listen in the morning, is to be discontinued." H. Ross of New York City was even more direct about the importance of balanced programming, declaring, "We refuse to have one single rotten point of view poisoning our people in these trying days—We vets fought and died to wipe out Fascism, not to flagrantly bring it to life."[25]

❖ ❖ ❖

To many critics, the commentator controversy was symptomatic of radio's deeper problems, which centered on the power business exercised over the medium. They believed, for instance, that it was business's influence that resulted in radio's overcommercialization and the loss of liberal voices. In the years immediately after the end of World War II, these critics were the nucleus of a renewed media-reform movement. This loose coalition of reformers sought to reduce corporate influence over broadcasting. Some simply wanted to hear fewer commercials and higher-quality programming. Others feared the monopolization of the media and sought changes in the broadcasting system to make radio more representative and democratic. Among these reformers were advocates of a "listeners' rights" approach to broadcasting that "put the listener's freedom to hear a diversity of voices on par with the broadcast speaker's right to speak." Advocates of listeners' rights believed that citizenship participation was critical to a democratic broadcasting system.[26]

Labor and the Left were key elements of this reform movement. The CIO was at the forefront, with its political organization, the CIO-PAC, leading the way. Its victory over the NAB code during World War II served as a shining example of reform in action. Of its affiliates, the UAW was most aggressive in promoting listeners' rights. Until late in 1946, when ideological divisions over Communism split their alliance, the CIO worked closely with the National Citizens Political Action Committee to advance radio reform. The CIO formed the NCPAC during the 1944 election campaign to mobilize liberals outside the ranks of labor. Other liberal groups interested in radio reform included the Independent Citizens Committee of the Arts, Sciences, and Professions (ICCASP) and the Progressive Citizens of America, which was formed in December 1946 through a merger of the NCPAC and the ICCASP. Active in these organizations were progressives, Socialists, and Communists,

many of whom backed labor, civil rights, and international causes associated with the Popular Front. The Communist party was another significant
element of the reform movement, committed to fighting the monopoly interests that it argued controlled American broadcasting.[27]

Most postwar reformers never questioned the existing commercial basis of
radio but looked to the FCC to ameliorate broadcasting abuses. While strong
conservative elements within the commission were responsive to industry
demands, the reform movement had friends on the FCC. Indeed, in the mid
1940s, some members of the FCC were in the forefront of the campaign to
reform radio. During World War II, chairman James L. Fly and commissioner
Clifford Durr had been strong advocates of the public interest in broadcasting
and critics of unregulated corporate powers. A vigorous proponent of intellectual and ideological diversity on the air, Fly was an early advocate of the
concept of the freedom to listen.[28] His successor as chairman was the New
Dealer Paul Porter. He and Clifford Durr, who upon Fly's retirement emerged
as the strongest voice for reform on the commission, believed strongly in public ownership of the airwaves and encouraged citizen participation. In the fall
of 1945, they urged radio listeners to help shape the content of programming
by writing to station operators, to the commission, and to Congress. Durr
called for a democratic radio system that would be regulated by the people
and "scrupulous in its regard for minority rights."[29]

The FCC actually took the lead in fighting excess commercialism. In the
spring of 1945, Porter made it clear to the radio industry that he intended to
"build upon the foundation of activism started by Fly." He warned broadcasters that the FCC planned to take a closer look at station performance.
When broadcasters applied for permits, they gave pledges that time would
be available for public service programs. Although stations often failed to
fulfill these promises, the commission traditionally renewed licenses automatically for a three-year period. In April, the FCC jolted the industry when
it began putting stations on probation.[30]

During the summer of 1945, the FCC conducted a wide-ranging survey
of radio programming, and in March 1946 it issued a report, *Public Service
Responsibility of Broadcast Licensees,* known popularly as the Blue Book because of its cover. The Blue Book was a groundbreaking document that represented the commission's first systematic effort to regulate program content.
As the legal scholar Amy Toro has observed, it was "a bold step in asserting
the FCC's regulatory authority." Arguing that too many broadcasters had
"abdicated to advertisers the control over their stations," the report documented the abuses that radio's critics had been discussing for years and laid

out new criteria to determine if stations were fulfilling their public service responsibility.[31]

The FCC proposed four key guidelines for stations to meet: 1) carrying noncommercial sustaining programs, 2) carrying local live programs, 3) airing discussions of public issues, and 4) avoiding advertising excesses. When renewing licenses, the commission planned to give "particular consideration" to these areas. These guidelines were meant to increase airtime given to nonprofit educational, civic, religious, agricultural, and labor organizations as well as guarantee the broadcasting of programs serving minority tastes and interests.[32] The insistence on live local programs was designed to reduce network control over broadcasting and to provide an opportunity for community participation in radio. Clifford Durr viewed such participation as critical to the operation of a democratic society, which he contended thrives "more on participation at its base than upon instruction from the top." Durr believed that radio could be more than a one-way pipeline of news, ideas, and entertainment. Enforcement of the Blue Book guidelines could ensure that radio would serve as an outlet for full information and free expression, "uncurbed by commercial [or] by political restraint."[33]

If the FCC was at the front of the campaign to improve programming quality, labor and the Left spearheaded the drive for diversity in the media. In late October 1945, delegates from twenty national and local educational, fraternal, civic, political, and union organizations interested in the preservation of civil liberties met in New York City to form a "Mobilization against Thought Police in the USA." Led by the acclaimed radio writer Norman Corwin, the group denounced HUAC's attack against freedom of speech in broadcasting and called upon network executives to join their fight. The following month, this group, which included representatives from the Southern Conference for Human Welfare, the National Negro Congress, the NAACP, the National Farmers' Union, the Brotherhood of Railway Trainmen, and the ICCASP, met to develop a campaign to defeat the Wood bill and to seek to abolish HUAC. The Wood bill never came to a vote, but HUAC continued to target commentators that it considered subversive.[34]

Labor also defended liberal commentators. The American Federation of Radio Artists telegraphed protests to HUAC after the committee's demand for liberal scripts. Philip Murray asserted that although the CIO had been the victim of biased radio commentary, it was "unalterably opposed to attempts to censor or gag radio broadcasts." When a New York station ended Frank Kingdon's daily commentary, the CIO-PAC, the NCPAC, and the ICCASP sent a joint protest to the FCC against this "crusade to keep liberal commentary from the people."[35] Shirer's removal from CBS in March 1947 touched off even more protests. CIO-PAC's director, Jack Kroll, demanded that the FCC investigate Shirer's dismissal. A month later, the newly formed Progressive Citizens of America held a "Crisis in Radio" conference in New York City, resolving that American radio failed to speak for all the people. Among those denied a voice were union members, racial and religious minorities, and liberals.[36]

In early February 1947, a group of writers, intellectuals, and artists met over dinner in New York City to discuss the state of broadcasting. Most were leftists involved in a variety of progressive causes, and all were incensed over the curtailment of free speech over the radio. The gathering formed the Voice of Freedom Committee, with the writer Dorothy Parker as chair. Other supporters of the committee included the actors Will Geer, Edward G. Robinson, Orson Welles, Jack Gilford, and Judy Holliday, the composer Harold Rome, the poet Langston Hughes, the commentators Algernon D. Black, Frank Kingdon, and William Shirer, and the sociologist Henry Pratt Fairchild.[37] The VOF envisioned itself as a watchdog on behalf of democracy in the media. It fought for balanced coverage of the news, higher-quality programming, and racial equality in broadcasting, urging the removal of racist stereotypes and the hiring of more African Americans. As the anti-Communist blacklist descended on radio, the VOF also mobilized in defense of its victims. The organization sponsored rallies and meetings, lobbied the networks and the FCC, and participated in hearings in Washington, D.C., related to broadcast legislation. Its representative testified against the White-Wolverton bill, which would end limits on the number of stations owned by corporations or individuals. By April 1948, VOF boasted that it had "become feared in the offices of Radio City." Dorothy Parker's involvement meant that the organization would not be easily ignored. It had enough clout that CBS chairman William Paley met with a VOF delegation to defend dropping Shirer's broadcast.[38]

Most broadcasters tended to dismiss the VOF's charges that liberals, labor, and the Left faced discrimination in the media. In April 1947, the Mutual Network's vice president, A. A. Schechter, explained to participants at a City College Radio and Business Conference that declining audiences rather than bias against liberals was the reason for the reduction in the number of radio commentators. Schechter argued that the demand for news during the war led to the hiring of some relatively ineffective commentators. With the war over and interest in the news dwindling, these commentators were expendable. Audiences wanted to be entertained, "to listen to a commentator with a pleasing voice, integrity, and opinion." No sponsor, declared Schechter, would ever fire a commentator, conservative or liberal, who could deliver a large audience. In any case, in the view of the industry trade journal, *Broadcasting,* networks or sponsors had the prerogative to make programming changes. Norbert Muhlen, *Broadcasting*'s radio editor, asserted that the fervor over the purging of liberals was being orchestrated by the Communists. In particular, he contended that the commentators Johannes Steel and Lisa Sergio were Communists and thus deserved to be fired.[39]

❖ ❖ ❖

While reformers hoped that the more vigorous FCC oversight outlined by the Blue Book might significantly improve the existing AM broadcasting system, many envisioned FM as a second chance to create a more democratic and diverse broadcasting medium. Invented by Edwin Armstrong and patented in 1933, FM radio is a radically different method of transmission that produces greater fidelity of sound than AM and is relatively immune to electrical interference and static. Resistance from AM broadcasters, who feared competition, and the wartime freeze on the civilian electronics industry slowed FM's development. In 1944 there were only forty-six commercial FM stations in operation. The FCC's decision in January 1945 to shift the FM band to a higher frequency, making the half-million existing FM sets obsolete, further slowed the system's momentum. Nevertheless, as the war drew to a close, expectations for FM's future were bright. In August 1945, during hearings before the FCC, the leading network broadcasters admitted that they anticipated that FM, if given a chance, would soon be the dominant broadcast service.[40]

FM's proponents expected that this new broadcasting system would make possible a large number of small independent stations, perhaps as many as three thousand, which could be developed at relatively low cost. A huge expansion of radio stations could break the monopoly control of networks and advertisers, opening station ownership to small businesses, veterans' groups, unions, churches, and colleges, groups that had all been largely excluded from AM. In May 1940, when the FCC authorized FM broadcasting, it asserted that "the opening of a new band for commercial broadcasts will help to correct numerous defects and inequalities now existing in the standard broadcast system."[41]

The possibilities of FM broadcasting caught the imagination of important elements of the labor movement and the Left. According to the CIO, FM was "a shining hope for the future" because it would enable labor to bypass the big commercial interests controlling radio, many of whom "took in the welcome mat when they saw labor coming up the steps." Union FM stations could provide to the public high-quality programming, rather than the "hokum of commercial copy-writers," while serving labor directly as an organizing medium and as a means of promoting labor's political and economic goals. In November 1944, the CIO convention urged labor to get in on the ground floor of FM broadcasting. Hoping to preclude FM from becoming monopolized by the same antilabor forces that controlled AM broadcasting, the CIO urged unions to apply for FM station licenses where financially possible or consider joining with other progressive community groups to establish public service stations.[42]

Labor dove into FM. In December 1944 the UAW applied for FM licenses in six major cities for noncommercial stations that would give all groups and classes such a "freedom of speech and opportunities for discussion as to be unparalleled in history." By the fall of 1945, the ILGWU and the ACWA had applied for licenses in multiple locations, promising that their stations would emphasize public service and that they would use the airwaves for the "primary purpose of bettering the lives of their listeners."[43] Stymied in their attempts to acquire an AM station during the war, New York City unionists eagerly embraced FM. The National Maritime Union, the United Electrical Workers, and the Fur Workers joined the ILGWU and the ACWA in exploring FM broadcasting in the city. The Chicago Federation of Labor, owner of the long-standing labor AM station WCFL, also filed for an FM station. Many other labor bodies, ranging from national unions to state and city central organizations to locals, also explored the possibility of operating FM stations. When building their new headquarters, the Detroit and Wayne County Federation of Labor even considered constructing an FM station on the top floors.[44]

Community groups, often with close ties to labor and the Left, also hoped to get in on the ground floor of FM. Among leftist organizations applying for licenses in New York City were the People's Radio Foundation (PRF) and the Debs Memorial Foundation; in Washington, D.C., the Potomac Cooperative Federation; in Los Angeles, the Hollywood Community Radio Group; and in Berkeley, California, the Pacifica Foundation.[45] The story of the PRF is particularly revealing of these efforts. In the early 1940s, a small group associated with the International Workers Order, a Communist party–backed fraternal-insurance organization, began to explore the ownership of FM stations by labor, fraternal, and community groups. Joseph R. Brodsky, an attorney who gained national recognition in the 1930s defending the Scottsboro Boys, and the artist and radical political activist Rockwell Kent were the moving forces behind this effort.[46] If FM was to represent a community of progressive interests, Brodsky and Kent believed that it must be closely linked to the labor movement. In October 1944 they called a meeting in New York City attended by fifty trade unionists, writers, artists, and activists. After viewing a promotional film on FM, participants formed the People's Radio Foundation and applied for an FM station in New York City. Promoters envisioned that "for the first time a radio station will be owned and operated in the interest of the community, free from business pressures." The PRF founders promised that their station would offer honest labor news, promote international friendship, fight race hatred, educate the community, and offer opportunity to developing artists.[47] The PRF planned to promote a network of community-operated radio stations, owned by progressive organizations, in which labor would play an integral role. The left wing of the labor movement was strongly represented at the initial meeting. Among the charter members of the new organization were Joseph Curran, president of the National Maritime Union, Ben Gold, president of the International Fur and Leather Workers, John T. McManus, president of the Newspaper Guild of New York, Arthur Osman, of Local 65 of the Wholesale and Warehouse Workers, and Joseph P. Selley, president of the American Communications Association. Ultimately, nine CIO unions, mostly New York City locals with ties to the Communist party, endorsed the foundation.[48]

Labor and the Left joined what was shaping up to be an increasingly chaotic race for FM. With the war drawing to a close in the summer of 1945, advertisers, networks, AM stations, newspapers, and small businesses scrambled for places in the spectrum, submitting hundreds of applications for stations to the FCC. In some places there were many more applications than available channels, while in others applications were sparse. FM allocation policy determined to what extent the new spectrum would fulfill the hopes of reformers. Under chairman James Fly, the FCC's initial rules governing FM encouraged diversity of ownership, setting aside every fifth channel for nonprofit educational broadcasting and capping the number of stations granted to any one interest at six. The FCC was aware that AM station owners might seek to acquire FM licenses as a defensive measure and simply duplicate their schedule. Thus, the FCC required that jointly owned FM-AM stations devote at least part of the day to programs not broadcast simultaneously over both stations. This requirement would encourage consumers to buy FM radios. Moreover, under Fly, the rules gave an advantage to applicants who proposed to provide a service distinct from any already available to the community.[49]

After Fly left the FCC in early 1945, Clifford Durr continued to push for ownership diversity. He felt that "too exclusive occupation of the air by one small group to the exclusion of other groups can be as effective censorship as government censorship." He urged that the FCC give preference to newcomers who demonstrated a sense of public responsibility and a commitment to "new concepts" in broadcasting. In May 1945, when the commission floated its new allocation plan for FM, Durr's influence was evident. Under this plan, the FCC proposed to hold back for later assignment 20 percent of the channels (beyond those already reserved for educators). Fearful that once FM licenses became available all the best transmitter sites and frequencies might be gobbled up by existing AM operators, this was designed to give newcomers a better chance at acquiring a station license. Justifying the plan, the FCC observed that it was "economically and socially unwise to concentrate the control of broadcasting facilities in the hands of a select few, and it is economically and socially essential to keep the door open to the fullest extent possible for newcomers."[50]

With expectations running high that FM would offer a fresh start for radio, reformers were disappointed when the FCC backed away from its commitment to protecting FM development and promoting diversity of ownership. Yielding to substantial industry pressure, in August 1945 the FCC dropped the requirement that FM stations owned by AM operators carry independent programming and reversed its plan to assist radio newcomers by reserving 20 percent of FM channels for future assignment. The commissioners justified these decisions as necessary for the rapid development of the new medium. To that end, it announced October 7, 1945, as the closing date for filing FM license applications.[51]

Reformers condemned these decisions. Within the commission, the reformer Clifford Durr offered a dissenting opinion, asserting that the use of two radio channels for the same service was not only a waste of frequencies but would "retard the development of FM broadcasting." With identical programs available on their old AM radios, listeners would have little reason to invest in an expensive new FM set. He was equally upset about establishing such an early application deadline. Applications for licenses involved complicated technical, legal, economic, and organization data that took time to complete and required substantial financial resources. Durr and other reformers feared that small businesses, labor unions, community groups, and veterans were unprepared to meet these requirements and would be frozen out of FM. The FCC's early deadline drew scores of complaints from these groups. Veterans' protests were so scorching that the secretary of war, Robert P. Patterson, sent a formal protest in their behalf to the FCC.[52]

The NCPAC, working with the CIO, immediately organized a campaign to "protect the people's right to the air." It circulated to "action groups" throughout the nation a hundred thousand copies of an eight-page analysis of the FCC plan. Of the hundreds of FM applications currently on file, the NCPAC noted, all but a few were from existing broadcasting stations or newspapers. It asked whether the American people would permit those who "have failed to fulfill their pledge of public service" to dominate FM radio. Worried about the "monopolizing of the information and opinion-molding media," the report included a petition urging the FCC to grant no more than one-quarter of available FM channels to existing standard broadcast stations and newspapers; the remainder should go to small businesses or farm, labor, cooperative, and citizens' groups, which had been previously excluded from radio.[53]

In October 1945, the FCC began consideration of nearly seven hundred applications for new FM stations, granting sixty-four conditional licenses. All but ten went to existing standard stations, some of which were owned by newspapers. C. B. Baldwin, the executive vice president of the NCPAC, wired the FCC chairman, Paul Porter, protesting the commission's allocation of these frequencies without public hearings. He argued that in many communities, dual newspaper–FM radio ownership would effectively create a media monopoly, posing a "grave threat to effective freedom of speech and press." Baldwin again urged that the FCC provide ample opportunity in FM broadcasting for newcomers.[54] Porter assured Baldwin that the commission had given careful consideration to each application before granting a license. Moreover, according to Porter, the commission "unreservedly" welcomed the submission of any facts related to a "particular applicant's qualifications to operate its proposed station in the public interest." Finally, he promised that in the future if there were any question about an applicant, the commission would schedule a hearing.[55]

Unconvinced by Porter's assurances, the NCPAC, working closely with the CIO-PAC, continued to push the FCC to reserve every fifth channel for later assignment. This liberal-labor coalition gained a powerful ally when the Senate Small Business Committee took up their cause. One committee member, Glen H. Taylor, a liberal Iowa Democrat and former radio cowboy singer who believed that "radio broadcasting need not be exclusively a big business game," spearheaded a congressional drive to defend newcomers' rights in radio. In late October 1945, the Small Business Committee launched an investigation of the FCC's FM-allocation policy. It reported six months later that the FCC had betrayed the public's high hopes for a democratically controlled FM system by allocating 70 percent of FM grants to AM broadcasters or newspapers. The Senate committee observed that nothing is "more important to the health and vitality of our democracy than the wide distribution of the control of the media" and urged the commission to relax regulations to permit those of limited means to enter the FM field.[56]

Throughout the spring and early summer of 1946, Taylor's committee, the CIO-PAC, and other labor, liberal, veteran's, and farm organizations pressured the FCC to hold some FM channels in abeyance. In July, despite fierce opposition from networks and the NAB, the commission again reversed course, announcing its intention to promote an equitable distribution of FM frequencies by reserving for a year every fifth FM channel for latecomers. Although a far cry from the NCPAC's original demand that three-quarters of all licenses be allocated to newcomers, the decision was a victory, albeit a small one, for radio reformers.[57]

❖ ❖ ❖

Winning a slightly improved FM allocation plan was only part of the battle for a democratic media; implementation of the plan was even more critical. FCC decisions regarding licensing and renewals in the FM and AM spectrums would determine who had access to the air. After the war ended, the FCC plunged into a licensing frenzy. It opened up FM while at the same time is-suing licenses for hundreds of new AM stations, made possible by a decision to reduce the required bandwidth distance between stations. Adding to this workload was the ongoing task of license renewal for established stations, which the Blue Book made more complex.[58] In the midst of this activity, several liberal reform groups, advocates of "listeners' rights," began urging citizens to become more involved in the regulatory process. Groups like the NCPAC called for hearings in local communities on all license applications, both new and renewals, so that members of the public might present their points of view. They also asked that all applications for license renewals be advertised in local newspapers well in advance of the hearing to ensure the widest possible citizenship participation. In cases where community mem-bers believed that stations had failed to uphold their duty to serve the public interest, the NCPAC encouraged citizens to vigorously challenge the station's license renewal. Essentially, the NCPAC was calling for greater community control over radio.[59]

Such activism divided the FCC. As the FM allocation decisions made evident, there were strong pro-industry elements within the commission. Still, the FCC's liberal supporters of radio reform—James Fly, Paul A. Porter,

Paul A. Walker, and Clifford Durr—exercised influence over FCC policy until the latter part of the 1940s.[60] The Blue Book, which in many ways was Clifford Durr's creation, encouraged listeners to exert their rights, advocating the formation of listener councils to "convey . . . the wishes of the vast but not generally articulate radio audience." Egged on by Durr and applauded by the NCPAC, the FCC encouraged public participation in the regulatory process by moving some licensing hearings out of Washington, D.C., and into local communities. This was a major shift in FCC policy, which previously had excluded listeners.[61]

The CIO's campaign to protect the "people's right to the air" put labor at the forefront of the movement for listeners' rights. The PAC's *Radio Handbook,* published during the 1944 campaign, began with the observation that if the U.S. Constitution were written today, the freedom to listen would appear before freedom of the press. Emphasizing the people's ownership of the airwaves, the *Handbook* asserted that the public has the right to hear labor's voice and balanced coverage of controversial issues. When stations abuse the airwaves by broadcasting statements unfair to labor or of a racist nature, or when stations refuse access to labor or other minority groups, the CIO-PAC urged unionists to assert their rights by complaining of unfair treatment to the stations, to the networks, and to the FCC.[62]

CIO unionists regularly took their complaints about censorship or lack of access to the commission, demanding enforcement of FCC rulings. They followed these complaints with interventions in the license renewal process, the next step in empowering listeners. In the spring of 1944, when the UAW made a concerted effort to overturn WHKC's license, it became one of the first citizen organizations to intercede in the licensing process. Previously, only third parties with technical or economic grievances like signal interference had been allowed to participate. Labor had an immediately significant impact. During the WHKC hearing, the UAW was involved in "cross-examining, calling witnesses, and presenting exhibits and expert testimony," and it provided the "settlement language that the Commission adopted almost verbatim."[63]

The FCC's ruling in the autoworkers' case firmly established that stations have a duty to cover controversial issues and to provide time for all points of view. This decision became one of the roots of the Fairness Doctrine, which governed American broadcasting until 1987. As the legal scholar Amy Toro notes, the Fairness Doctrine served as the most important tool for social-reform groups seeking to fight prejudice over the air. The WHKC case established another important precedent: the FCC began to review a station's overall programming when determining if a station operator was serving the public interest. The publication of the Blue Book in the spring of 1946 was a further affirmation of the commission's commitment to upholding public service standards. All this opened up the opportunity for citizenship involvement in the regulatory process, providing the incentive for reform groups to testify on behalf of or against station operators. This level of community involvement in licensing was unprecedented.[64]

In the first quarter of 1946, despite a backlog of more than a thousand pending applications, the FCC scheduled hearings for new stations in fifty-three cities throughout the nation. To the CIO-PAC and the NCPAC, the hearings were an "opportunity to educate the FCC Commissioners about the people's desires." The public could propose standards of broadcast operation for their own community and urge the FCC to refuse to grant any application that failed to meet these standards. Local groups could secure pledges from station operators to offer well-rounded discussion of local and national issues, free speech for local civic, farm, labor, and progressive groups, programs fostering racial and religious tolerance, fewer commercial interruptions, and better children's programming. With these promises on the public record, if a station failed to live up to its promises, citizens could seek redress from the FCC.[65]

The CIO-PAC and the NCPAC widely distributed the hearing schedule and an "action memorandum" that provided instructions on how to participate in the hearings, including how to obtain copies of license applications and other relevant public records. They advised citizens to closely scrutinize applications from local newspapers, suggesting that they should evaluate the paper's record of objectivity on political and social issues. Moreover, communities should consider if newspaper ownership of a local radio station would result in a "monopoly over the instruments of making public opinion." The CIO and the NCPAC also encouraged citizenship groups to pay close attention to applications from corporations operating stations in other cities. "If the stations they now operate are not of the type you want in your community," the memo urged, "oppose their invasion of your city."[66] The UAW's radio director, Allen Sayler, emphasized the importance of labor's participation, advising that labor's voice at these hearings might mean the "difference between reactionary and progressive radio service" in local communities.[67]

Unionists in many communities responded. In Pennsylvania, Berks County industrial unionists asked to testify at the hearing regarding the licensing of a new station in Reading, and the Meadville Textile Workers local opposed Dr. H. C. Winslow's application for a new radio station on the grounds that it was "derogatory to the best interests of the community." The Michigan CIO Council opposed the Fort Industry Company's application to purchase the Detroit station WJBK, asserting that the company already had three FM licenses, two television licenses, and at least seven AM stations. To August Scholle, president of the Michigan CIO Council, this was "a monopolistic development to which we object." Moreover, according to the CIO, the other stations operated by the company violated the FCC Blue Book prohibitions against excessive commercialism.[68]

In Ohio, CIO unionists opposed S. A. Horvitz's application for AM-FM permits in the towns of Lorain and Mansfield. The CIO argued that Horvitz already owned the only local newspapers in those towns and that he was antilabor. These stations would give him a monopoly on news coverage in the region. The unions in Lorain, as well as the CIO national office, successfully demanded that the hearing be shifted from Washington, D.C., to the local community, in the interest of citizen involvement. At the June 1946 hearing, four local CIO officials from Lorain testified, reiterating charges against Horvitz's newspaper, the *Lorain Journal*, asserting that it either ignored union activities or presented a distorted picture of organized labor. The Mansfield CIO Council supplied specific examples of the paper's biased treatment of unions.[69]

Elsewhere, unions began to more aggressively intervene in the renewal of station licenses. In Wilkes-Barre, Pennsylvania, Newspaper Guild and Textile Workers locals presented petitions in support of the station WBAX, which labor applauded for readily providing access to unions and other community groups. More routinely, unionists used the license renewal process as a weapon against stations that refused time to labor or censored scripts. West Coast industrial unionists, for instance, complained bitterly to the FCC after the San Francisco station KGO canceled a scheduled address dealing with issues related to an upcoming NLRB election covering seventy thousand workers in the canning industry. The FCC failed to intervene after the station asserted that the program was not of "sufficient interest to listeners." The Food, Tobacco, and Agricultural Workers' Union responded by asking to intercede in the KGO renewal hearing.[70]

Systematic censorship led textile workers in Griffin, Georgia, to oppose WKEU's application to renew its license and build a new station. Based on their complaints, the FCC conducted a hearing in Griffin in May 1946. Textile worker representatives recounted the history of the union's relationship with the station. A year earlier, the Textile Workers Union of America had sent Clara Kanun to organize workers in Griffin, a small mill town located about twenty miles south of Atlanta. Like most organizers operating in the South, she faced a hostile climate, including almost daily newspaper attacks against the union as an outside troublemaker. Nevertheless the union managed to gather enough signatures to schedule an August representation election at one local mill. Prior to the election, Kanum attempted to purchase radio time to reply to the newspaper and to gain community support. WKEU refused her request, but after the textile workers won the election, the station agreed to a ten-week contract for a fifteen-minute Saturday-morning show, "The Textile Workers Speak," beginning January 12, 1946.[71] During the first show, the local union leader Hozy Corley assured listeners that there "is nothing more native to . . . Georgia than the Textile Workers organization which is growing here" and compared the union to community organizations like the Red Cross and the American Legion. Subsequent programs explained the union's structure and operation, its educational work, its relationship with religion, and its benefits, including increased wages and purchasing power and protection from stretchouts and other forms of exploitation and discrimination.[72]

A battle over the scripts quickly ensued. According to Kenneth Douty, Georgia state director of the Textile Workers Union, the scripts were measured and educational, "controversial only in the sense that there are present in the Griffin community powerful representatives of management interests who are bitterly anti-labor." Nevertheless, the station began to censor the scripts, demanding that they be more generalized and avoid mention of local personages and organizations. Immediately, the organizer Clara Kanun complained to the FCC that the station sent the scripts for censoring to the attorney of the Thomaston Mill, where an NLRB election had been postponed due to union charges of unfair labor practices. At the end of the fifteen-week contract, WKEU refused the union's requests for renewal. The union submitted further evidence against the station, charging that it maliciously slandered Kanun by broadcasting a story alleging that she was an adulteress.[73]

In testimony to the FCC, the station manager, A. W. Marshall, admitted his reluctance to air the show because of concerns that it might be a program of agitation and propaganda. As his fears were realized, he claimed that censorship became necessary to remove libelous material. For instance, the station objected to the union's inference that the mills were a dictatorship. "The mills are no more dictatorships than any other large organizations or even the union itself," Marshall claimed. Even the theme song, "Solidarity," was offensive, since it tended to create "class versus class" feelings. Marshall confessed that he submitted the union scripts to the mill attorneys but claimed that there were no ties between the station and the mills. He refused to renew the textile workers' contract, he explained, because he had no opposing programs and he feared that the "public might feel that it was our viewpoint [and] we might be classed as a CIO station."[74] To Kenneth Douty, the director of the Textile Workers Union, the whole controversy revolved around listeners' rights. The right of free people in a democracy to listen to the widest possible discussion of all questions was at stake. As Douty saw it, what happened in Griffin amounted to a conspiracy between the radio station and mill managers to deny the union and the people of Griffin the rights guaranteed under the Bill of Rights.[75]

Unions were particularly committed to fighting for the public's right to hear about industrial conflict. In April 1946, the UAW asked the FCC to turn down the Cincinnati station WKRC's application for license renewal for a number of reasons covered by the Blue Book's admonition that radio serve the public interest. But the primary incident that sparked the UAW's intervention was the station's cancellation of a December 1945 broadcast entitled "The Rights of Labor," a program in which priests discussed the Catholic position on social issues, sponsored by the Archdiocese of Cincinnati. The station, owned by the son of the arch-conservative Republican Senator Robert A. Taft, canceled the show after discovering that the priests intended to discuss the ongoing General Motors strike.[76] Msgr. Clarence C. Issenmann of the Cincinnati Archdiocese learned that the station believed that "industrialists would object" to the program. Station executives were upset with paragraphs in the script comparing the automobile strikers to workers suffering from economic injustice during the French Revolution and praising the federal government for promoting the common good by supporting unions. Particularly objectionable was the concluding paragraph quoting Pope Pius XII: "Workers must come to each other's aid." Monseigneur Issenmann asked, "Does freedom of the radio mean that the station itself, or big business, or industrialists largely supporting it, shall determine what shall be permitted and what shall not be permitted on the air waves as a statement of Catholic position?" Widespread protest over the program's cancellation led *Billboard* to observe that the UAW's intervention was "an important milestone, indicating a new trend in the control of media of culture, information, and education dissemination."[77]

❖ ❖ ❖

In the latter part of the 1940s, groups such as the NAACP, the American Jewish Congress (AJC), and the Voice of Freedom joined the CIO in adopting a listeners' rights approach to broadcast reform. The NAACP urged its members to aggressively combat racism on the air with complaints to the FCC, and the AJC intervened in several high-profile cases against stations that had demonstrated a history of anti-Semitism. In New York City, for instance, there were nineteen applicants for five available FM channels. The AJC presented statistical evidence, modeled after the kind of evidence generated by the UAW in the WHKC case, against one of the applicants, the *Daily News,* contending that the newspaper had exhibited consistent bias and hostility against Jews and African Americans. In justifying its intervention, the AJC argued that the "freedom to listen is indeed the indispensable counterpart of the freedom to speak." After complex legal wrangling, the commission voted to officially ignore the AJC's evidence. Nevertheless, it refused to award a license to the *Daily News,* previously considered the front-runner.[78]

The Voice of Freedom's monitoring system was another tool used by citizens to promote fairness over the airwaves. In the spring of 1947, the VOF set up a network of "listening posts," monitors who listened to commentators' broadcasts for balanced coverage. By 1950, listening posts had grown from a few hundred in New York City to a web of three thousand monitors spread across the nation. When they heard what they believed to be misinformation or bias, monitors sent letters of protest or made calls to the commentator or the station. A New Jersey monitor, for instance, wrote to Fulton Lewis Jr., "[W]hy do you enjoy spreading fear in all your broadcasts?" Instead of balance, "[Y]ou almost always try to frighten your listeners with the 'red herring.'" On March 17, 1948, New York City monitors and their friends overwhelmed WOR's switchboards with complaints when the station refused to carry a debate on the Fair Employment Practices Commission (FEPC) between Congressmen Vito Marcantonio and John Rankin, being aired over the Mutual Network. Three months later, Chicago monitors joined other civic groups to protest WBBM's cancellation of the series "Report Uncensored," which was to include a story on racial restrictions in housing. Faced with a wave of protest, station executives backed down and aired the show the following week.[79]

At times the VOF took monitor complaints to the FCC. In June 1948, after monitors reported that NBC had failed to present both sides of the arguments on the Mundt-Nixon bill, Dorothy Parker and Stella Holt sent telegrams to the FCC requesting an explanation from the network. The VOF urged it members to "stand guard, and exercise your power as an alert listener." It assured its monitors that "those bullets of yours do hit their mark. Each one of them is carefully counted by the station, and the network nerves begin to rattle as the mailbags pile up."[80] The VOF also urged monitors to write in support of networks and stations that provided liberal commentary or sought to raise the educational and cultural content of radio. In June 1948, for example, the VOF urged its monitors to write CBS to praise Howard K. Smith, the network's European news chief, for his honest analysis of international news. Empowered listeners relished their sense of influence; a Minneapolis listener wrote: "[A]t last an organized effort to help the long-suffering public inundated by the radio flood of intellectual garbage and propaganda!"[81]

❖ ❖ ❖

In the years immediately after World War II, radio reformers felt optimistic about their progress. The FCC appeared ready to enforce Blue Book programming standards that promised to rein in the commercial excesses of radio. Only weeks after issuing the Blue Book, the commission rejected the long-pending transfer of WINS in New York from the Hearst Company to the Crosley Corporation. The FCC objected to the high sale price, arguing that it would be economically unprofitable for Crosley unless it flooded its programming schedule with commercials. It also condemned a condition of the transfer that required Crosley to reserve an hour every day for ten years for Hearst commercials. Through the balance of 1946, in an effort to avoid all-out war with a jittery broadcasting industry, the commission gave a clean bill of health to the vast majority of the stations that had been placed on probation, but it did schedule hearings for some that had failed to provide "a well-rounded program service."[82]

Industry observers believed initially that the Blue Book exerted considerable influence on station operations. Spurred by the FCC and by increasing indignation throughout the nation, elements of the radio industry seemed to be adhering to the Blue Book's plea for reduced commercialism. Anecdotal evidence suggested that stations paid more attention to public service programming and opened their microphones to civic groups. Moreover, when applying for new licenses, broadcasters began gearing their applications to meet the requirements of the new FCC program standards. By following the Blue Book's guidelines, these broadcasters were essentially acceding to the FCC's claim to the right to regulate programming through control of licenses.[83]

Reformers found evidence in FCC licensing decisions that their protests were having some influence. FM allocation decisions announced late in 1946 favored newcomers over established broadcasters and favored applicants most closely connected with the local community. Labor benefitted from the commission's receptivity to newcomers; the UAW, the ACWA, and the IL-GWU won licenses in twelve cities.[84] The commission also initially advanced the concept of listeners' rights by scheduling hearings in local communities. Its decision on the allocation of FM stations in Lorain and Mansfield, Ohio, demonstrated its commitment to listeners' rights. In a rare departure from its general practice, the commission denied the newspaper publisher S. A. Horvitz's licenses, citing the conduct of his newspapers as the sole basis for its decision. CIO representatives had charged that both newspapers were antilabor, while other witnesses charged the newspapers with trying to undermine local competitors. The commission concluded that these practices indicated a "lack of concern for the listening public."[85]

Unions enjoyed less success in using listeners' rights activism to open up broadcasting for organized labor. Most disappointing was the FCC's refusal to respond to many of labor's demands for hearings in the wake of censorship. Moreover, even when it held a hearing, the commission never denied a license renewal based on union complaints. For instance, the FCC renewed the Griffin, Georgia, station WKEU's license despite the compelling case built by the Textile Workers Union against its management.[86]

Still, the commission did not totally ignore labor's struggles for airtime. Secretary T. J. Slowie followed up on many union grievances, especially when station licenses were up for renewal. Slowie often asked for an explanation from the station and regularly cited the WHKC case, reminding stations that time must be made available to all parties to discuss controversial issues.[87] Often, the commission quietly settled differences between unions and broadcasters "out of court." WHBU in Anderson, Indiana, which had initially refused time to the UAW, acceded to the union's request after the FCC became involved. During the 1950 Chrysler strike, the FCC publicly rapped the knuckles of the Detroit station WWJ for refusing to sell or grant time to the UAW to present its side of the strike. It advised the station, which was owned by the anti-union *Detroit Evening News,* that its conduct was "not in accord" with FCC policy. Often the threat of FCC intervention was enough to open the airwaves. A CIO public relations official in the South reported that some labor-friendly station managers had asked him to threaten to report their stations to the FCC so that they would have an alibi to give to local businessmen after agreeing to sell time to labor. Review of FCC and labor records suggests that the commission's intervention made a difference. By the late 1940s, unions found that the airwaves especially outside the South were increasingly open.[88]

Listeners' councils, promoted by the Blue Book, were another segment of the radio reform movement. By late 1948 there were groups in California, Wisconsin, and Cleveland, with thousands of listeners monitoring broadcasts. Dorothy Parker's Voice of Freedom represented the left wing of the listeners' groups. The aims and methods of these groups were diverse. Some worked with the NAB, while others were independent and aggressive about goals ranging from restoring opera broadcasts to relegating network mystery shows to after 9:30 P.M., to getting William L. Shirer back on the air after he was bumped by CBS.[89]

To the broadcasters, however, all this was evidence that the reform movement posed a real threat to their control over the media. Although a few acknowledged that the radio reformers' criticisms had some validity, most viewed the Blue Book as a fundamental attack on radio's freedom. *Broadcasting* dismissed the "shrieks of over-commercialism" as emanating from those quarters occupied by the ACLU, various college forums, and "the anti-radio labor unions" who "would see radio Government-controlled for political or economic reasons." At minimum, the Blue Book seemed to portend stepped-up government involvement in programming decisions. The FCC's inclination to favor radio newcomers and to promote diversity of ownership also alarmed broadcasters.[90]

Broadcasters worried especially about the increased interest of labor and the Left in the media. Rumors swept the industry that labor and leftist organizations were plotting to capture American broadcasting, particularly FM. In April 1946, NBC's vice president, William C. Hedges, described this opposition as "Pinks and Commies" who sought "to gain control of broadcasting in order to implement their gaining control of the nation." *Broadcasting* characterized the NCPAC's campaign to limit existing stations and newspapers to one-quarter of available FM channels as an effort to throw existing broadcasters out of business. In October 1945, the magazine contended that unions wanted "everything in radio cleared with some CIO Sidney, so CIO can get all the free time it wants."[91]

❖ ❖ ❖

The broadcasting industry mobilized across a broad front against the reform movement, launching an assault that ultimately overwhelmed most of the reform agenda. The Blue Book, the CIO, and leftist groups such as the People's Radio Foundation and the Voice of Freedom were primary targets. Exploiting the emerging cold war, opponents attempted to delegitimize the broadcast-reform movement, tarring even the most politically moderate radio reformers as Communists out to destroy the American broadcasting system. The fact that some of the reformers were Communists made the entire group more vulnerable to attack. Conservative business and patriotic organizations such as the NAM and the American Legion were important allies in the broadcasters' campaign. In September 1947, the chairman of the NAM, Robert R. Watson, addressed the NAB, urging them to "clean out [the industry's] remaining Communists and fellow travelers." He promised that "both industry and commerce will join you to restore freedom to the radio industry." The American Legion worried that "subversive and left wing groups" had already made significant headway into FM broadcasting, which it anticipated becoming "a decidedly important propaganda and information medium on the American scene." Pinning the red-subversive label on a range of Socialists, liberals, and labor unions, including groups that were strongly anti-Communist, the legion pledged its resources in the battle to protect American broadcasting.[92]

The NAB led the attack against the Blue Book. Justin Miller, who in October 1945 had left the U.S. Court of Appeals to take over as president of the NAB, spearheaded a high-level offensive against the Blue Book, emphasizing legal and constitutional issues. In public meetings and in the press, he attacked the report as an invasion of "free radio." It amounted to censorship, violating the constitutional guarantees of the First Amendment and the statutory limitations on FCC power. Miller questioned the right of seven men in Washington to pass judgment on programming, branded the talk about "the people owning the air" as a "lot of hooey," and dismissed Blue Book advocates as "communist stooges."[93]

The NAB looked to its friends in Congress for support. Throughout the Roosevelt administration, there had been tremendous political pressure on the FCC. While liberals in Congress provided key support, conservative anti–New Deal legislators were ardent opponents of the regulatory agency. One of Congress's favorite pastimes was to haul FCC commissioners in for interrogation and debate the merits of legislation reducing the commission's power. The Blue Book was a touchstone. In May 1946, Representative B. Carroll Reece of Tennessee, chairman of the Republican National Committee, argued that the Blue Book was laying the groundwork for government regimentation of radio. "American Radio offers the finest quality and variety of programs in all the world," he boasted, pointing out that "American radio has been a private commercial operation where success depended entirely upon its ability to please the listener." Reece promised to introduce legislation stifling the FCC. In July 1946, Senator Charles W. Tobey, a New Hampshire Republican, called for a full-scale probe of the commission. The following year the NAB released its own draft of a new radio bill banning any future FCC interference in programming.[94]

Culminating the campaign to emasculate the Blue Book was a public relations drive on behalf of "free radio." As the historian Michael J. Socolow has observed, the Blue Book touched a nerve, acting as a "catalyst for the most widespread public discussion of advertising and broadcasting in American history."[95] Broadcasters felt threatened by this often extremely critical discussion of radio's performance. In May 1946, NAB president Justin Miller assured CBS president Frank Stanton that the NAB could successfully overcome the immediate regulatory threat posed by the Blue Book but that the "groundswell of opinion" against radio posed a far greater long-term danger. To offset the drive to "destroy freedom of speech over the radio," Miller proposed a campaign to build support for the private, advertiser-supported broadcasting system. The networks and the NAB began independent efforts to promote "free radio." CBS aired a number of programs defending the commercial basis of American radio, and in the spring of 1947 the NAB launched an elaborate grassroots public-relations drive highlighting the broadcasting industry's constructive contributions to American society. To further undercut radio's critics, the NAB also passed a new, voluntary code of ethics designed to address the worst of the abuses identified by the Blue Book.[96]

As the backlash against the FCC intensified, the commission's new chairman, Charles Denny, promised that the Blue Book would never be "bleached." However, in September 1947, *Variety* observed that the FCC was indeed giving the program report the "clorox treatment." A shift in the composition of the FCC was one factor in the weakening of the Blue Book. Charles Denny never had Fly's or Porter's commitment to reform. His sympathies lay with the broadcasters. In October 1947 he left the FCC to become vice president and general counsel of NBC. His quick exit left critics wondering exactly when he had been offered the network position, especially since his "muddled leadership" of the FCC, at least one historian contends, contributed to the Blue Book's demise.[97]

Declining political support for reform was another factor in the commission's weakening resolve. The immediate postwar period was an inauspicious time for the FCC to engage in broadcasting reform. In the fall of 1946, Americans elected a Republican majority to Congress, signaling rough sledding for the FCC at the hands of some of its sharpest critics. Led by a chairman with little stomach for reform and with its members under attack, including a HUAC investigation, the FCC backed away from the Blue Book. It renewed all of the stations previously cited in the Blue Book for excessive commercialism and, over Clifford Durr's strong dissent, awarded FM grants in Chicago to three AM stations that demonstrated virtually no commitment to public interest programming. As early as January 1947, a disappointed Saul Carson, the radio editor for the *New Republic,* caustically observed that the FCC might expound very revolutionary ideology, but the Republican party and big business had no reason to feel threatened. "If the commission ever mounts the barricades, it will be on the side of the guy with the frock coat."[98]

Broadcasters also attacked listeners' councils. Recognizing their growth and influence, the NAB hired a coordinator of listener activities and sought to bring the councils under its umbrella. According to the NAB, the first concern of radio councils should be to ensure that the FCC did not extend its powers beyond its charter. In August 1948, Leslie Spense of the Wisconsin Joint Committee for Better Radio Listening reported to Clifford Durr that the NAB had successfully infiltrated virtually all of the national women's organizations.[99] Red-baiting was another means to undercut groups—such as the Voice of Freedom—that were the most vocal advocates of listeners' rights. HUAC repeatedly labeled the VOF a Communist-front organization, and in 1949 the American Legion denounced the VOF after it defended the radio director William H. Sweets, a blacklist victim. American Business Consultants, an anti-Communist group, used membership in the VOF as a criterion for inclusion in their publication *Red Channels,* a compendium that listed 151 entertainers and their supposed Communist connections. In a three-day tirade in February 1950, the conservative commentator Fulton Lewis Jr. asserted that the VOF was "dangerous" and "diabolical" with many "Communist-front affiliations," charges circulated widely by the Hearst press. By the end of the 1940s, broadcasters had tamed the activities of organized listeners.[100]

Broadcasters also targeted the CIO-PAC. During the 1946 election, the CIO used radio as a political weapon, touting it as "the most effective means of reaching millions daily." In early September, the CIO-PAC launched its "air battle" for a large voter turnout by distributing nineteen records with short "register-vote" announcements, songs by Tom Glazer and Pete Seeger, and dramatic skits by Hollywood actors. The CIO-PAC considered these spots urging Americans to participate in the electoral system to be public service announcements that should be broadcast without charge.[101]

Broadcasting protested, charging that the CIO-PAC was trying to bulldoze broadcasters with veiled threats of potential investigations by the FCC. It urged radio operators to resist the efforts of any political organization to "wheedle free time" under the guise of public interest. Pointing out that the singers Glazer and Seeger had been cited by HUAC, the trade magazine advised the public and station owners that if they looked closely they would see that the CIO-PAC's radio announcements were tinged with red. NAB's supporters in Congress assisted. In late September 1946, the House Select Committee to Investigate Campaign Expenditures announced that it was scrutinizing the CIO-PAC's air campaign, looking for possible violations of the Communications Act. As a result, during the 1946 electoral campaign numerous stations refused labor's political broadcasts, either on paid or free time.[102]

❖ ❖ ❖

Hopes for FM as a vehicle for reforming radio also began to fade. Despite the heady predictions that it would quickly supplant AM, the new spectrum faced unexpected barriers. The biggest problem was the lack of audience. In 1949 the manager of an FM station in Cleveland remarked, "If I went on the air at high noon, and talked obscenity into my microphone, no one would be the wiser." Reformers charged that AM broadcasters, working hand in glove with set manufacturers, were retarding FM's development. Those AM broadcasters who also owned FM stations were purposely failing to promote their new outlets, they claimed, and investment capital was going into continued development of AM at the expense of FM. In June 1946, furious that manufacturers were devoting 90 percent of their production capacity to old-style AM sets, Senator Glen Taylor and the UAW asked the Justice Department to investigate the radio industry for possible antitrust violations. The future for FM seemed so bleak that in March 1947 one hundred applicants withdrew their bids for FM stations.[103]

Those on the left wing of the radio reform movement, who had anticipated that FM would open up the airwaves to the entire range of political thought, were especially disappointed. While organized labor's anti-Communist wing, which included the UAW, the ILGWU, and the ACWA, had enough political and economic clout that it could not be frozen out of FM, organizations with any links to the Communist party faced a much rockier road in their quest for a radio license. FCC policies and attacks from the anti-Communist forces, including elements of organized labor, presented significant barriers to the most radical voices trying to find a place on the FM dial. The chilling winds of the cold war doomed the efforts of much of the Left to gain a broader audience through operating FM stations.[104]

The contest in New York City for FM licenses provides a good example of the forces arrayed against the left wing of the reform movement. As noted earlier, New York City trade unionists and radio reformers were excited by FM's potential. By 1946, five groups committed to reform, including three unions (the ILGWU, the ACWA, and the Maritime Workers) and two groups with close ties to labor (the People's Radio Foundation and the Debs Memorial Radio Fund), had thrown their hats into the crowded FM New York City radio ring. While the ILGWU and the ACWA had strong anti-Communist credentials, the Maritime Workers and the PRF had close affiliations with the Communist party. Anti-Communists cheered when the ILGWU appeared on the scene as a competitor to the PRF. The Debs Memorial Fund, which operated WEVD, was no friend of the Communists, but its Socialist tradition certainly made it suspect. These reformers were part of a pool of eighteen competitors fighting for only five licenses when the FCC conducted hearings in New York City in July 1946.[105]

Each group endorsed the goals of the Blue Book and promised a high standard of public service with minimal commercialism. They pledged innovative programming that encouraged the development of local talent, reached out to minorities, and responded to the needs and interests of the local community. The ILGWU, for instance, proposed programs for the various nationality groups in the city as well as "Inquiring Reporter," a daily program interviewing the "man on the street" about the state of the city. It also promised to set up a dramatic workshop and production unit to showcase the talents of local artists. The PRF offered "The Minorities Are Major," alternating dramatic, musical, and documentary formats designed to help the community understand and overcome racism and anti-Semitism. The PRF also promised "Past, Present, and Future," to explore the role of women in shaping history, and experimental children's programs to replace the "present commercialized and distorted 'chamber of horror' programs."[106]

Not surprisingly, all of the reformers promised access to organized labor. But the ILGWU and the ACWA downplayed the labor connection, contending that they planned on operating as community rather than union stations. They were aware that the FCC generally shied away from granting licenses to "special interest" stations. Both unions promised to combine "hard commercial thinking" with a devotion to meeting the needs of the entire community. They pointed to their unions' elaborate adult-education and cultural programs that were designed not only to improve their members' lives but to "make them better citizens of their communities." The Debs Memorial Fund also emphasized the community orientation of WEVD and their proposed FM station.[107]

Behind the ILGWU's radio strategy was Morris Novik. Passionately pro-labor with a genuine commitment to public service, Novik prided himself on being a realistic, hard-nosed radio man. Aware of the rumors circulating about labor "taking over" FM, he understood the importance of reassuring the commission that an ILGWU station would avoid overtly promoting labor's cause. Testifying before the FCC examiner, the ILGWU's executive secretary, Frederick Umhey, who had been tutored by Novik, pledged that "there will be no concentration on programs that you might call labor activity programs." When asked if the station will be used to propagandize for unions, he responded, "Definitely not."[108]

In contrast, the People's Radio Foundation and the Maritime Workers based their claims to broadcast solely on labor's inability to receive equality on the air from existing stations. To counterbalance this discrimination, they intended to devote a significant amount of programming to working-class issues and unions. Most of the Maritime Workers' projected program schedule focused on the lives of sailors or programs for unions. The PRF had a richer and more diverse program lineup, with shows on topics ranging from health and fashion to current events and history, but it too was proud to label itself a "labor station." Both took a much more populist approach to broadcasting than most elements of the broadcast reform movement, which tended to promote elite-oriented, high-tone educational and cultural programs. The Maritime Union, for instance, expected its shows to reflect the interests of its members and intended to draw upon them for program material and talent. The PRF promised listener control of programming. Joseph Brodsky, head of the PRF, hoped to stimulate "creative expression on the part of the people in this area to produce music, people's music, people's drama, people's presentation."[109]

In openly promoting labor, the PRF and the Maritime Workers directly challenged FCC policies. However, their ties to the Left were perhaps the most critical barrier to winning a license. The Maritime Workers, whose application had been hastily assembled, appeared to have little chance, but the PRF had generated significant public interest and support. Its Advisory Council included such respected writers and artists as Rockwell Kent, Norman Corwin, Peter Lyon, Harold Rome, and Eugene O'Neill, and it had strong support from the left wing of the local labor movement. The PRF mobilized a parade of witnesses to speak on its behalf at the FCC hearings. Unionists such as Howard Edelson of the United Electrical Workers, representatives of civic, political, and fraternal organizations like the Hellenic American Fraternal and the League of Women Shoppers, among many others, testified on the PRF's behalf.[110] Almost a thousand organizations and individuals wrote letters of support. Some emphasized the importance of giving labor or liberals a radio voice in a city where such voices were "stifled to such a degree" that they were rarely heard. Others addressed the PRF's impressive commitment to exposing the "miserable injustices" to which minorities had been subjected.[111]

Recognizing that it faced an uphill battle for a license, the PRF took its project to the public. It rented New York City theaters and presented radio scripts that typified the sort of programs planned for the new FM station. On December 13, 1946, seventy-five actors and technicians simulated a regular broadcast with full radio equipment. They performed three shows termed too controversial by the networks. The scripts dealt with the lynchings that occurred the previous spring in Columbia, Tennessee, a musical tribute to a war hero, and a fantasy about the threat of atomic warfare. Building on these performances, the PRF established a mobile company of actors, writers, and engineers, which gave performances to organizations throughout the city. Presented over microphones like actual radio programs, the scripts satirized commercial radio and addressed political and social issues such as the postwar housing crisis. The PRF also formed a speakers' bureau of young people from colleges, unions, and veterans' groups, which appeared before numerous city organizations, recounting the foundation's story and appealing for assistance.[112]

An array of anti-Communist forces, fearful that well-meaning liberals on the FCC might consider granting a license to the PRF, worked to keep the organization off the air. A series of exposés accused the PRF of Communist ties. Just before the New York City hearing, the conservative *New York World Telegram* ran a story about the PRF with headlines that blared "Reds in Drive for Foothold in FM Radio." The foundation was also featured in a series on the Communist Fifth Column in the *Chicago Journal of Commerce,* which argued that the Communists wanted an FM channel to propagandize for their "masters in Moscow." The author of the series, Andrew Avery, warned that the group had attracted "deluded unionists and liberals" and was winning wide support. Similarly, *Broadcasting* repeatedly referred to the PRF's Communist connections, noting that Joseph Brodsky had been chief counsel to the Communist party for over twenty years.[113] Letters from legislators and individuals urged the FCC to deny the PRF's application. In one widely distributed newsletter, the American Legion identified the PRF as one of the organizations attempting to subvert radio. HUAC investigators also made an appearance at the July 1946 hearing in New York City, offering the FBI files on several of the foundation activists.[114]

Anti-Communists within the labor movement contributed to the red-baiting. Anxious to eliminate competition for a license, lawyers for the Debs Memorial Foundation and the ILGWU made frequent references to the PRF's ties to Communist groups and its supposed allegiance to foreign powers.[115] In the spring of 1947, just before the FCC issued its preliminary decision, So-cialist and labor newspapers joined in the attack, publishing detailed analyses of PRF associates. They asserted that most of the organizations backing the PRF were Communist front groups and that the eight unions involved with the PRF were led by party-liners. Moreover, they charged that the officers of the PRF were trying to hide their links to the Communist party. The Socialist paper *New Leader* concluded that there "was little doubt that the comrades want to go beyond their street corner days and shout their political wares into every radio set in the country, if they can."[116]

The FCC's decision, issued in the spring of 1947, was a partial victory for reformers. The commission decided to assign one of the five available chan-nels to organized labor. The Debs Memorial Fund, which had a history of feuding with the FCC, was rejected on the basis that its AM outlet WEVD was "overcommercialized." Given the strength of the anti-Communist cam-paign, it was little surprise to the leaders of the PRF and the National Mari-time Union that the FCC rejected their bids. The FCC praised the ILGWU's and ACWA's applications, noting that both "offered well-balanced program services" and neither would operate as a labor station. Impressed with the ILGWU's previous radio experience and with its plans to promote FM by arranging with a manufacturer for the production of a large number of FM sets for sale at low cost to its members, the FCC gave the nod to the ILGWU. New York City radicals never made it to the air, but in May 1949, liberals cheered the debut of the ILGWU's FM station, WFDR.[117]

By the end of 1948, reformers' expectations that the postwar era would see sweeping changes in American broadcasting had diminished, although labor's FM stations still offered a small ray of hope. Increasingly, there was little place on the FCC's agenda for regulatory activism. In the face of fierce broadcaster opposition, the Blue Book was fading into memory, and in June 1948, Clifford Durr, the strongest advocate of reform, left the com-mission. It would be twenty years before the FCC, under pressure from the civil rights movement, again allowed citizenship participation in licensing decisions. Pressure from the Left also receded as the People's Radio Founda-tion disbanded and the rest of the left wing of the reform movement began disappearing into the vortex of anti-Communism. Moreover, FM's future remained uncertain. Even labor's enthusiasm seemed to be flagging. The

ACWA, which had been authorized to operate a station in Rochester, New York, returned its permit to the FCC and withdrew its other applications. Similarly, the ILGWU and the UAW scaled back their ambitious FM plans, opening five rather than their planned twelve stations.[118]

Still, the garment workers and autoworkers remained committed to station ownership, seeking AM stations to bolster their FM operations. Moreover, in the postwar years, AFL and CIO unionists aggressively sought airtime on local stations and the networks and significantly strengthened organized labor's voice in the media. Liberals eagerly anticipated the debut of the union stations, and business kept a wary eye on labor's broadcasting efforts. The business community had been stunned by the results of the 1948 election, and it attributed at least part of Truman's victory to the strong support of the AFL and CIO. At the end of the 1940s, organized labor's influence seemed secure. Prior to the 1948 election, the Harvard economist Sumner Slichter asked, "Are we becoming a laboristic state?" In December 1948, *Fortune* noted that the five licensed labor FM stations were enough to form "the nucleus of a pro-labor network blanketing the major U.S. metropolitan areas."[119]

PART 3

Postwar Broadcasting

6 Competing Voices: Business and Labor in Local Postwar Broadcasting

WITH A BRONZE BUST of the late Franklin Delano Roosevelt spotlighted on the stage, the ILGWU's new FM station, WFDR, made its debut in a two-hour broadcast from Carnegie Hall in New York City. The June 19, 1949, program included musical performances by Broadway stars, speeches by dignitaries such as Eleanor Roosevelt and former treasury secretary Henry Morgenthau Jr., messages of welcome from the leaders of France, India, Italy, and Chile, and a star-filled tribute from Hollywood, featuring Ronald Reagan, Eddie Cantor, Gene Kelly, and Milton Berle. All of the speakers extolled the achievements of the former president, and Eleanor Roosevelt observed that the station exemplified organized labor's new political and economic status. She proclaimed that as a result of its many achievements and contributions to society, labor was fully entitled to "have its own voice." The president of the ILGWU, David Dubinsky, promised that WFDR would be a station that "will talk and sing" in the "spirit of the great re-builder of America," a leader who understood the masses longing for security.[1]

WFDR and the four other labor FM stations that went on the air in the late 1940s epitomized labor's commitment to media reform. They were dedicated to improving broadcasting by making radio more representative and culturally uplifting and less commercial. Just as unions had "forged industrial democracy in the plants," labor's FM stations would "create a kind of electronic democracy in radio." By focusing on economic, social, and political issues mostly ignored by mainstream radio, labor broadcasting would educate and mobilize listeners. In her remarks during the debut, FCC commissioner Frieda Hennock anticipated that the ILGWU would "always place public service above all else" in its operation of its FM stations.[2]

But labor also had much more pragmatic goals for FM broadcasting, viewing its radio stations and its other broadcasting initiatives as weapons in the continuing union struggle against business. The postwar era brought escalating labor-management conflict. Unlike Eleanor Roosevelt, important elements of the business community were alarmed at labor's new status. Postwar business attempted to rein in organized labor through tough collective bargaining and by intensifying its wartime public relations campaign. As a part of its strategy, business began pouring more resources into broadcasting. Recognizing the power of this ideological assault, key segments of organized labor sought to contest business efforts to shape worker consciousness. Business and union voices competed at the national level through network broadcasting. But they also struggled for the loyalty of workers and the support of local communities through programs originating at the local level. In most cities these shows were broadcast over commercial AM radio stations, but in five cities for a brief period labor also took its message to the public through its own nonprofit FM stations.[3] Local business and labor broadcasting, both AM and FM, is the focus of this chapter.

❖ ❖ ❖

Bitter labor struggles and high-stakes political campaigns marked the decade after World War II, as unions and business fought to shape the postwar American political landscape. Labor stood ready to exercise its economic power, and union activists like Walter Reuther of the UAW had ambitious plans to advance a wide-ranging social democratic agenda. Given the politicized relationship between unions, business, and the state, labor and employers understood the importance of maintaining a strong relationship with workers as well as winning broader public support. Business and labor conflict coalesced around a number of major issues that remained unresolved at the end of the war, including the relationship of government and the economy, the proper size and activities of the welfare state, and the scope of union power.[4]

On the heels of Japan's surrender, a cascading wave of strikes swept the nation. To employers, the strikes epitomized the union threat to their control over the workplace. Business leaders also feared the continued expansion of wartime government regulation and planning, or as they called it, "creeping socialism." Moreover, they worried about the public's apparent attraction to what they considered collectivist measures guaranteeing security for the working class, including unionization. In fact, while the public expressed frustration with the disruptive effects of postwar strikes, labor found significant support in some communities. Employers were disturbed by opinion polls that showed a widespread distrust of the business community and its individualist ethics. Polls in August 1945, for instance, found that Americans by a margin of two to one supported major political influence in the nation passing from big business to labor and that 76 percent of Americans favored the expansion of social security and government public works programs. As the staunchly conservative steelmaker Ernest Weir saw it, the New Deal had nicked away at individual freedom and individual incentive, the cornerstones of the American way. But in the postwar era, government was attempting to "take away all freedom and incentive, and concentrate complete control of the economy" in the hands of the state and labor.[5]

Threatened by New Deal liberalism and the increasing presence of unions, business launched a long-term campaign to discredit the ideological underpinnings of New Deal liberalism and to undermine the legitimacy and power of organized labor. While much of the postwar struggle between business and labor occurred in the realms of politics and collective bargaining, an important element was ideological. Corporate leaders sought to delegitimize the New Deal political ideology, which emphasized the public good, social and economic justice, and a more equal distribution of wealth, and replace it with an individualistic ideology that associated freedom with increased productivity, individualism, and unregulated business behavior. Large corporations as well as national umbrella organizations and industry trade groups such as the National Association of Manufacturers, the Chamber of Commerce, and the Iron and Steel Institute took their message to their workers and the public with expensive public relations campaigns that used newspapers, magazines, pamphlets, lectures, radio, and later, television. The corporate offensive directly targeted the workplace through sophisticated human relations, communications, and educational programs and reached into the community through schools, churches, and recreational activities. Through all these means corporate leaders attempted to shift the political climate in a more conservative direction. They sought to construct a vision of Americanism that emphasized social harmony, free enterprise, individual rights, and abundance. As part of their campaign to teach Americans about the benefits of capitalism and the dangers associated with government and unions, corporate leaders readily exploited anti-Communism, using it as a tool to "tar government intervention in the economy" and organized labor with the brush of Socialism.[6]

Use of the mass media, and especially radio, was a key element in the business community's effort to magnify its public voice. Corporations and industry trade organizations continued to use the networks to reach a national audience, a subject that will be addressed in the next chapter. But as companies expanded their community relations programs in the postwar era, local broadcasting was an essential component of their strategy.

The NAM stepped up its radio activities as part of the intensified postwar campaign to promote the free enterprise system. The manufacturers' association already had a significant presence in the media, but after the war the NAM sought to further strengthen its influence, especially in local communities. It began sending representatives to meet regularly with local station managers, commentators, and program directors of radio shows. Through increased personal contact, it hoped to boost the number of stations carrying NAM programming and to encourage the "incorporation of more of our thinking in program scripts." It also doubled its distribution of "Briefs for Broadcasters," a weekly service that provided commentators with pro-business news stories and editorials. To reach the audience more directly, the employers' organization furnished a recorded news commentary entitled "Your Business Reporter" to 250 local radio stations. The NAM continually emphasized the need to maintain "firm faith in the benefits and opportunities provided by the American free enterprise system in the face of constant attacks from the left."[7]

Individual companies followed the lead of the NAM by significantly expanding their public relations programs. They placed high priority on reaching local communities and forging ties with schools, churches, and community organizations. Business relied on all kinds of media to communicate its message, using newspaper advertising, films, mailings to community leaders, and even pamphlets strategically placed on racks in the factory or in local barbershops or waiting rooms. But radio remained an essential component of their media strategy. The postwar era saw an expansion in business's use of radio at the local level.[8]

Local business associations and even some small firms inaugurated weekly or daily radio programs aimed at teaching the public about the centrality of their industry to community well-being. In Wisconsin, the Racine Manufacturers' Association's program, "The Cavalcade of Racine Industry," dramatized the "history and romantic growth" of local industry, while the Oshkosh Associated Industries' "Wings of Industry" presented the perspective of "ordinary working people" on the role of industry in community life. Each program featured a member firm offering a description of the company, the investment required for each employee, details of plant growth and sales volume, and interviews with the firm's factory workers. According to one employer, the show demonstrated that "what is good for business is good for everybody."[9] The Bridgeport, Connecticut, Chamber of Commerce aimed at reaching women. Each week a local firm's officials took three wives or mothers of their employees on tours of their plant, pointing out the advantages of working there. During the tour, the women visited with their relatives and learned about their jobs and working conditions. Later that week, the women shared their experience during the chamber's "Round the Town" morning radio program, using a script based on discussion generated during the tour.[10]

Companies found radio an effective community relations tool, especially during times of conflict. In the 1930s, companies and unions had used radio to argue their case to the public during labor conflict. This practice continued in the following decades. During the postwar strike wave, for instance, General Motors made heavy use of radio in strike-affected communities. Its radio spots were single-idea, "punchy pieces" that implied that the UAW was striking against the country's reconversion efforts rather than against the company. One ad asserted, "What America needs right now is production, production, and more production. And what is America getting? Strikes, strikes, and more strikes."[11]

Radio could generate goodwill by associating the company with popular community activities. Armco Steel, Yale and Towne Manufacturing Company, Gardner Board and Carton Company, and the GE Electronics Department in Syracuse broadcast high school football and basketball games, using the commercials to explain the company's accomplishments and contributions to community welfare.[12] In 1950, as a service to local groups, Ansul Chemical Company began sponsoring a short daily program, "Your Social Reporter," which announced meetings, bazaars, school and sports events, and other community activities, identifying the company only at the opening and closing of the program.[13]

Other programs helped integrate the company into the community. In the fall of 1947, Armstrong Cork Company of Lancaster, Pennsylvania, hired a full-time radio program director to produce a program to air on Thursday evenings. It soon reached three-quarters of the listeners in the region, mixing company reports with musical entertainment, featuring company employees and members of the community. Alcoa had a series called "Let's Go Calling" in which the announcer interviewed plant workers in a series of imaginary visits to the company's plant in Lafayette, Indiana.[14] In 1949, to counter the high level of distrust of business among residents of its community, Gerity-Michigan Corporation began sponsoring a daily radio program in Adrian, Michigan. The weekday program, aimed at children, stressed safety, while

Radio programs enabled firms to build ties with local communities. This photo-
graph shows a machinist, Clyde King, being interviewed on the Keystone Steel
and Wire Company's program, "Sounds of Our Times." Reprinted from *American
Business,* June 1953.

the Sunday "hit parade" featured songs suggested by employees. In the mid
1950s, Keystone Steel and Wire Company's "Sounds of Our Times," Mooresville Mills' "Voice of Mooresville," and F. E. Myers and Brothers' "Ashland
Today" brought the plant directly into local homes. Taped in the shop, the
shows interspersed the sounds, voices, and news of the plant with music and
announcements of forthcoming community activities.[15]

The merits of the free enterprise system were a recurrent theme of many
of these programs. Some featured stories of "eminent Americans who took
advantage of the opportunities that exist only in this country." Others were
harder-hitting. Youngstown Sheet and Tube Company's daily program pointed out the importance of profits in the "American free enterprise system"
and warned of threats to our "American way of life" from those who would
undermine individual freedom with a "welfare state." Watch out for government handouts, the company advised, for they are the first step to social-

ism.[16] The Detroit Trust Company was worried that business had overlooked women. Beginning in 1949, it sponsored a series of radio forums aimed at the female audience, in an effort to convince them that "knowledge of economic realities" is the most important "safeguard against complete government control." Many of the hour-long programs, taped before an audience of 350 club women, addressed the profit motive, but others focused on contemporary political issues, attacking President Truman's proposed housing and health-care programs.[17]

Timken Roller Bearing Company of Canton, Ohio, had one of the most comprehensive local media programs. It was the centerpiece of an elaborate community relations effort that included institutional advertising in local papers, public meetings, weekly mailings to five thousand community leaders, and regular open houses. These activities were aimed at reducing organized labor's influence on Timken's workers. While its plants were organized, the company refused to accept the legitimacy of organized labor and had a sharply adversarial relationship with its unions.[18] The company believed that one reason for the continuing conflict was its failure to effectively communicate with its workers and the public. Timken's president, William E. Umstattd, believed that the more the employees and the public know about company, problems, policies, and goals, the less chance "for the growth of false and harmful misconceptions" that lead to conflict.[19] By 1948, Timken was paying for five radio programs, a daily half-hour of recorded popular music, a weekly hour of classical and semiclassical music, daily sports and news shows, and a news commentary program featuring Fulton Lewis Jr. Each carried commercial announcements from the company. Timken donated some of this time to local or national drives of charitable or patriotic organizations, while the rest went to a mixture of institutional and advocacy advertising. Each week during its classical music program, listeners heard about different aspects of the company's operations and learned how various products, like seamless tubes or rock bits, were made.[20]

The company used its programs to correct the "misconception" that Timken was "antilabor" and "anti-union." "We at Timken," Umstattd assured the radio audience, "believe in honest collective bargaining." He blamed the recurring labor conflict on the policies and practices of union leaders, who created friction by magnifying the complaints of a small "minority of malcontents." Timken's messages during Fulton Lewis Jr.'s program were often political, calling for such things as reductions in taxes and government spending. Timken urged listeners to write to their congressional representatives and "tell them you're fed up with this spending orgy perpetrated against, and not for, the taxpayer." All of the company's programs regularly promoted the fight against Communism and the necessity of preserving "our free enterprise system of business."[21]

Like Timken, the Employers Association of Detroit worried that "there are among us many people actively working to overthrow" the American way of life and to substitute "a socialistic or communistic form of government." In the fall of 1948, the association launched one of the most creative and ambitious of the local business programs, "The Mark Adams Show." Broadcast for four years, it reminded listeners of the benefits they enjoyed under capitalism and projected the association's view of life under a Socialist or Communist system. The program gave Detroit business the "opportunity to tell its side of the story—to prove that management is not a monster, but the hand that feeds our entire economy—the hand that has built our high standard of living—the hand that has protected individual freedom as set down in our Constitution."[22]

The show centered around Mark Adams, a fictional radio commentator and crusader for the free enterprise system. Each week Adams introduced a radio play that dramatized some aspect of the American economic or political system, contrasting it with conditions in Soviet-dominated Eastern Europe. The show often told the story of an immigrant who succeeded in America through hard work and determination and because of the opportunity for personal advancement provided by private enterprise. In episode after episode, characters discovered the "fruits of initiative and the joy of profits," or the consequences of business being crippled by taxes and government regulation. One 1949 broadcast dramatized the story of Will Scott, who operates a small canning company that has been the economic mainstay of the town of Pine Falls. A political reform movement results in the passage of a series of taxes and unnecessary regulations, and workers strike for "impossible demands." Harassed, Scott closes his plant and leaves the town to its own destitution. In his summary, Mark Adams observed, "Pine Falls learned that America is as rich as it is, as free as it is, only because business itself has grown freely." He warned, "There are no jobs where there is no private enterprise."[23]

One particularly revealing program exemplified the show's message. In an episode entitled "Security Island," a crafty corporate leader allows his workers to set up a socialistic welfare state that establishes a minimum wage, a profit-sharing plan, decent housing, and health, old age, and unemployment insurance. At first it seems like Utopia, but then the residents discover that they have lost many of their freedoms, including the freedom to choose among consumer items. Bathing suits, for instance, come only in black. Since security is assured, production lags and prices rise. Government-sponsored health care is also a disappointment, as the system is overtaxed and burdened with red tape. Ultimately, the experiment descends into an impoverished police state, essentially offering false security. Mark Adams concluded the episode with the observation that "there is nothing so impossible as 'perfect security' ... there is no possible substitute for the incentive, the individual profit or the reward, of private enterprise."[24]

Unions were deeply concerned about the impact of this business programming on audiences. Labor had long condemned business's efforts to use the media to sell its ideology. During the war, unions had worried about the impact of the business campaign to paint labor as an "uncooperative, greedy, or unpatriotic institution and to tar government as a bureaucracy that stomped on cherished individual freedoms." There was certainly evidence, as the historian Gerd Horten has contended, that as a result of its wartime propaganda campaign, the business vision of a "privatized, consumer-oriented" economy had begun to be "relegitimized and affirmed." Wartime public opinion polls, for instance, found frustration with the government's intrusive wartime economic regulations and revealed that while a majority of Americans still favored organized labor, support for unions fell.[25]

Neither business nor labor, however, felt comforted by the results of postwar surveys of public opinion. The polls revealed confused public attitudes towards unions, corporations, and the government. This confusion fed the anxiety of business and labor about the public's loyalty to their institutions. There was evidence that the Depression-spawned distrust of business and attraction to government-guaranteed economic security had not abated among workers. Yet these same postwar polls also reflected hostility towards unions and government: 74 percent of the public wanted the government to crack down on labor and get production moving, and 54 percent called for less government regulation. An August 1945 Minnesota poll found 50 percent saying that unions had too much power during the war, while 29 percent said their power was about right. In a Gallup poll conducted at the same time, 50 percent of respondents supported increasing legal restrictions on unions.[26]

The postwar strike wave certainly had some impact on opinions towards labor, but it was not difficult for unions to find other evidence in the immediate postwar period of resurgent corporate influence. The destruction of price controls, the election of a Republican majority in Congress in 1946, and the passage of the Taft-Hartley Act the following spring suggested that the business message captured a public impatient with labor strife and demobilization turmoil. Labor and liberals also read the silencing of liberal radio broadcasters as symptomatic of the business community's success in shaping a more conservative postwar political climate. In December 1947, the *New Republic* observed, "Liberal commentators have an unfortunate tendency to lose their sponsors, while commentators who belabor unions in every case of industrial strife somehow seem to hold their contracts without trouble." It was clear to the UAW that with "audiences running into millions of persons," network radio commentators were "playing an important role in the cultivation of a lynch psychology against organized labor."[27]

❖ ❖ ❖

Organized labor challenged the growing business domination of political discourse through several strategies. In addition to working with the radio reform movement to promote a more democratic media, union leaders tried to expose employer propaganda. They warned workers that business was funding a "vast outpouring of propaganda" designed to convince the American people that labor was a "monopoly" and that unions should be weakened to "give business an even break." Drawing on the critique developed by the media reform movement, unions charged that the class nature of the mass media hindered fair coverage. Since most newspapers and radio stations were linked to a vast interlocking web of corporations, the CIO pointed out, it was not surprising that the press damned labor "at every opportunity." *Pennsylvania Labor News* warned its readers against listening to newscasters like Fulton Lewis Jr., who did the bidding of the Republican party and the NAM. One UAW foundry worker, Leroy Krawford, cautioned workers against trusting the antilabor Detroit media: "Believe only our union press and radio hookup which is paid for by you and staged by you to tell you the score."[28]

As the antilabor assault escalated, unions aggressively contested the portrayal of labor in the mass media. The AFL and CIO continued to complain regularly to the FCC about the antilabor bias of news broadcasts in an effort to pressure stations to provide fairer coverage. The CIO urged its members to renew and expand the monitoring service initiated during the 1944 election and to demand time for rebuttal for attacks on labor. Monitoring paid off. In late 1946, when the commentator H. V. Kaltenborn "beat his gums too freely one night about the Allis Chalmers strikers," the UAW local, citing the Fairness Doctrine, received time from NBC on Kaltenborn's program to "speak the truth." About the same time, the Mutual Network opened its microphones to Walter Reuther to reply to Henry J. Taylor's attacks against the UAW.[29] In the summer of 1947, fed up with the anti-union propaganda "blasted over radio loudspeakers these days," a conference of AFL central labor unions in eastern Pennsylvania sent committees in each community to meet with the management of local radio stations and local merchants who sponsored antilabor commentators. The AFL unionists pressed stations to provide equal time to liberal commentators to offset the spokesmen for big business. Unionists in Geneva, New York, took stronger action: in 1948 they launched a consumer boycott against Geneva Federal Loan, the sponsor of Fulton Lewis Jr.'s commentary on their local radio station.[30]

Finally, important elements of the labor movement embarked on an ambitious plan to use the radio to directly compete with business for worker loyalty and public sympathy. Unions pursued two radio strategies, both of which originated during the war years: One focused on establishing nonprofit labor stations and promoting FM, which labor and other media reformers viewed as a second chance at ownership by groups excluded from AM. The second involved purchasing or obtaining free time on the networks and local commercial AM stations. The balance of this chapter examines labor's use of broadcasting at the community level through sponsoring shows on local AM stations and through its experiment with FM, while the final chapter focuses on network radio.

❖ ❖ ❖

Local labor programs sprang up across the nation in the late 1940s and early 1950s, partly as a result of the CIO's aggressive campaign for access to the air and for listeners' rights. While there were still instances of censorship or refusal of airtime, especially in the South, labor's right to broadcast was a firmly established principle. Another factor behind the growth of labor programs was the increased availability of airtime. After World War II, the FCC not only licensed hundreds of FM stations but also rapidly expanded the AM spectrum. These new stations were hungry for business. Moreover, increased competition from television caused network radio broadcasting to recede, leaving local stations with yet more open airtime to fill.[31]

Some of the early postwar programs were an outgrowth of labor's search for community support during the postwar strike wave. The programs sponsored by the Greater Flint Industrial Council and the Lansing CIO Council, for instance, began during the GM strike but continued as regular offerings into the 1950s. During the UE's 1946 nationwide strike against General Motors, General Electric, and Westinghouse, electrical workers in major industry centers from New York to Lima, Ohio, made effective use of radio to reach the public. Some UE locals continued to broadcast after the strike, including those in Schenectady, New York, Bridgeport, Connecticut, and Fort Wayne, Indiana, where programs were still on the air two years later.[32]

Other programs originated from labor's political activities. During the electoral campaign of 1946 and in the spring of 1947, as labor mobilized against Taft-Hartley, the CIO-PAC pushed local unions and councils to seek airtime for political broadcasts. In March 1947, CIO unionists in New Orleans launched a thirteen-week series to combat antilabor legislation. In Detroit, during the fall of 1946, UAW Plymouth Local 51 initiated a weekly roundtable discussion program that took potshots at the NAM's "vicious propaganda" campaign against unions and encouraged workers to vote Democratic. Disastrous results in the election did little to discourage Local 51's opinion that radio was a "very forceful instrument in molding public opinion and a very effective educational weapon." Through 1947, "The Voice of Local 51" defended striking miners, lampooned "hate labor" commentators for placing a "halo of pious patriotism upon the employers," and encouraged workers to listen critically to business propaganda. In a February 1947 show, one local officer observed that "corporate interests of our country are sharpening their knives and preparing to slit the throat of organized labor." He dismissed business charges that labor had become a monopoly and a threat to free enterprise as lies. To the local president, Frank Danowski, it was clear that the real threat of monopoly came from business, which dominated Congress and shelved the "people's legislation," including funding for veterans' housing. Four rank-and-file members, all veterans, echoed Danowski, sharing their struggles to find housing and concluding that the solution was political action.[33]

As the antilabor assault intensified, the CIO urged more locals to take to the air. Through programs such as "The Voice of Local 51," unions hoped to compete with business for worker loyalty and counteract "the daily dose of anti-union poison" spread by the commercial press and radio. Recognizing the importance of community goodwill, the CIO also hoped that local programs, combined with its other community activities, would help establish unions as useful, responsible, and civic-minded organizations. The president of the Michigan CIO, August Scholle, argued that the only way for labor to increase its political effectiveness was by enabling the public to "learn the truth about us." With no expectation of fairness from the commercial press, Scholle believed that labor could level the playing field with radio.[34]

At the city and state levels, CIO unions organized radio councils or departments to provide support for local labor broadcasting. The radio councils offered weekly scripts and news summaries as well as training programs. Weekend workshops and weeklong institutes taught interested union members how to write and produce for radio. They also raised workers' consciousness about the implications of corporate control of the media, teaching unionists how to identify propaganda and how to listen critically to radio news. Michigan CIO Radio Council classes, for instance, pointed out that most of the news printed in newspapers and broadcast over radio came from the "same reactionary news services." Newspapers presented "reaction for the eye," while radio presented "reaction for the ear."[35]

During a typical 1950 class in Bay City, Michigan, members of the Steelworkers, Autoworkers, and Utility Workers unions practiced newly learned radio techniques by staging mock broadcasts. Four months later, the "Bay County CIO News" was on the air each Sunday at 1:30 P.M. over the station WGRO. The program began by advancing labor's political agenda, focusing on housing and health care. Later, Bay City labor commentators defended the head of the Bay County Council of Churches against attacks from the business community, which opposed his citywide referendum to build public housing. When prominent employers threatened to cut financial support to the Council of Churches, Bay County CIO commentators exposed this attempt to use money to pressure ministers to back away from public housing and denounced the "moral turpitude" of the local manufacturers and businessmen. They urged the community to support the referendum and to increase their donations to the Council of Churches to fill the newly created hole in its coffers.[36]

At the national level, the CIO-PAC and its Publicity Department as well as key CIO unions—the UAW, the UE, the International Association of Machinists, and the Packinghouse Workers—provided similar kinds of support for local broadcasting. The UAW urged its local affiliates to "ride the air waves" with campaigns for fair prices, housing, and fair employment practices. In August 1946 it warned, "If your local is not talking over the radio it is still talking in a whisper." The UAW Education Department provided scripts and recording, conducted radio workshops, and taught locals how to obtain free time over community stations. Even the AFL joined in. Stunned by the success of business's postwar antilabor campaign and the passage of the 1947 Taft-Hartley Act, the federation created a counterpart to the CIO-PAC, Labor's League for Political Education (LLPE), to increase its political voice. In 1950, LLPE's radio department offered to local unionists a recorded program for broadcast over public service time. "What's the Answer," broadcast over eighty-five stations, focused on political issues such as rent control, public housing, the expansion of social security, health insurance, and federal aid for education.[37]

Local radio shows often drew upon prepared scripts or recordings, but the Michigan Radio Council, under the leadership of William Friedland, urged unionists to develop their own programs. Friedland was the son of immigrant Jews who left Russia after World War I. As a teenager in the late 1930s, he was involved with the vibrant New York City Left. During World War II, Friedland moved to Detroit and became active in the UAW. Attracted to the union's cultural activities, he took up the guitar and began entertaining fellow unionists and leftists with songs and skits. In the late 1940s, he joined the Michigan CIO staff to promote radio. Friedland envisioned the CIO as a democratic mass movement of working men and women with close ties to local communities. He believed that "an intensely democratic life" is integral to unionism and that unions need to inculcate members in this tradition. Thus Friedland urged rank-and-file involvement in every aspect of the union's activities as well as in their local communities. In terms of radio, this meant that programs should be developed, produced, and performed by local unionists. These ideas meshed with the concerns of postwar broadcast reformers, captured in the goals of the FCC's Blue Book. Friedland was aware that there were some drawbacks to putting on shows with amateurs who had just spent the day laboring on an assembly line. But he believed that with training, local unionists could create "listenable programs" with a local slant that would empower members and do a better job of attracting an audience than "a soap opera with Hollywood talent and the best writers and promotion agents that money can buy."[38]

"Flint Labor Talks" was among the shows that broadcast the creative work of local unionists. One script, written and performed by members of UAW Local 649, told the story of Joe Worker, who runs a press on the fender line in an auto plant. On the ship returning home from World War II, Joe befriends John Wallace, an African American who had worked, before the war, as a janitor in the same auto plant as Joe. Wallace hopes to move to the all-white production line, which pays more. When the train carrying the two soldiers pulls into their hometown station, Joe, who before his years in the service disliked blacks and resented working with them, surprises his wife by proudly introducing his new friend. Confused, his wife later hesitantly asks her husband if he had changed his racial attitudes, and Joe confides that combat taught him "no matter what color a man is, he's still an American, and he feels love, hate, and homesickness just like I do." All Americans, Joe has come to realize, are entitled to constitutional rights. Returning to the shop, Joe Worker finds continued prejudice, which has tragic results. When John Wallace realizes his hopes of moving into the production line, a racist foreman keeps riding the new hire, hoping to drive him off the line. Working at an unsafe pace, Wallace's arms are caught in the press and mangled. Joe is devastated when he learns that his friend has died from the accident, but the incident has a lasting impact on the shop floor. "Somehow," Joe recalls, John Wallace "left the feeling that he had belonged there and the men began to see why a colored man has to have a job too." Perhaps implausibly, the play implies that the tragedy changes ingrained racist patterns among white workers. When a petition endorsing the state Fair Employment Practice bill is circulated, everyone in the plant eagerly signs it. The program concludes with Joe speaking directly to the audience, urging them to join in the campaign for racial equality and to write to their state representative in behalf of FEPC legislation.[39] While the script was perhaps overly idealistic, considering the racial tension on the postwar shop floor, it captured the ideas circulating in the workshops and classes of the CIO's more racially progressive unions.

Labor's radio mobilization amplified the union voice in communities across the nation. By the early 1950s, Michigan alone had sixteen weekly local CIO radio programs, and fifteen unions across Ohio were using the Ohio CIO Council Radio Department's weekly news script as the basis for their shows. In New York and New Jersey, the AFL and CIO state central bodies set aside their differences to sponsor "Labor Speaks," which was broadcast over six stations. In Pennsylvania, the ILGWU was on the air on five stations, and the following year trade unionists in Pottsville and Delaware County joined eighty-three other AFL central labor bodies in sponsoring the LLPE program. The UAW local in Lockport, New York, broadcast its show from the radio station WUSJ, which was conveniently located in the union headquarters. AFL members in Boston and St. Joseph, Missouri, CIO textile workers in Maine, steelworkers in Birmingham, Alabama, electrical workers in Rock Island, Illinois, among many others sought to get their stories across to the public with broadcasts. Unionists also periodically purchased time for "special events" on local radio and TV stations. And, of course, WCFL in Chicago continued to bring an array of labor programming to the Midwest.[40]

❖ ❖ ❖

Most labor programs consisted of news commentary or panel discussions. Combating corporate domination of the media, UE Lancaster Local 124 introduced its 1954 program as "The Voice of Radio Free Lancaster," piercing "the iron curtain of the local press, radio, and tv monopoly," and Buffalo unionists promised that their show, "News on the Niagara Frontier," would provide the "news of labor as it really happened." WCFL's listeners in Chicago could also always count on hearing news from a labor perspective. In the late 1940s, the Indiana CIO Council had radio news shows in Elkhart, Indianapolis, and South Bend, while the neighboring Kentucky State Federation of Labor sponsored a news program in Frankfort. The Central Labor Council of Santa Clara in San Jose, California, began broadcasting on a regular basis in 1950 and by the late 1950s had three shows on the air, world news at 5 P.M. each day, labor news at 7:15 P.M., and a fifteen-minute "Labor Forum of the Air" on Sunday mornings.[41]

Sponsored by the San Francisco CIO Council for over five years beginning in 1946, Sidney Rogers broadcast a progressive news commentary from the powerful station KYA to audiences of more than three hundred thousand, five nights a week between 1946 and 1951. The *New Republic*'s radio columnist Saul Carson praised the professional quality of Rogers's newscast, produced by the CIO Council's Radio Department. Impressed with the hard-hitting nature of his commentary, Carson observed that Rogers "says what he pleases—and, what very few radiomen have ever said on commercial programs." The CIO credited Rogers with giving labor in Northern California a significant economic and political lift.[42]

Despite the best efforts of unions to develop local talent, some unionists recognized that much of labor's local programming was considered dull listening, lacking in showmanship and the personal touch. In 1947, Ben Segal, an Operation Dixie organizer who was producing a new labor program in Lynchburg, Virginia, wanted to avoid "straight talks," believing that they "aren't worth much." Segal proposed broadcasting some "soap opera stuff." Allan Swim, public relations director for the CIO, agreed that unions needed to enliven their shows, although he cautioned that "a 'professional' program with non-professional talent" usually falls "flat on its face." Instead, he recommended "folksy" programs that let "ordinary workers tell ordinary stories in their own language."[43]

Talk continued to dominate labor radio, but some union broadcasters tried to attract audiences by mixing it with entertainment. This typically involved music, though sometimes labor programs offered short dramatic skits and occasionally longer dramatizations with economic and political messages. Seeking to enliven his 1948 Rock Hill, South Carolina, show, David Burgess wrote a series of short plays about the daily lives of local textile workers, with scenes from home and on the job that demonstrated how unions improve lives. CIO staffers played the roles of an antagonistic foreman, mill workers, an anti-union minister, and a union organizer. WCFL sought to attract listeners with "Labor's Own Amateur Hour," a weekday-afternoon program featuring rank-and-file workers. Other programs across the nation blended entertainment with the voices of real workers. Akron rubber workers used vignettes, some serious, others humorous, to deal with workplace, community, and political issues ranging from safety and compensation to the Taft-Hartley Act and the public school crisis. Each program concluded with interviews with rank-and-file workers. *Billboard* applauded the Rubber Workers' show, observing that the program "utilized sound and musical effects with telling effect." The personal stories were convincing, "told tastefully and simply," and the reviewer concluded that this "well-produced" show made for "good listening."[44]

Sports provided labor programs with another vehicle for reaching members. The Minnesota Federation of Labor sponsored broadcasts of Minneapolis high school basketball games on Friday nights, while Packinghouse Workers Local 46 and UAW Local 838 sponsored the broadcasts of the University of Iowa's football games. In 1951 the Teamsters' Joint Councils in Chicago and Philadelphia snagged sponsorship of Notre Dame football broadcasts in their cities. Instead of commercials for razors or beer, audiences heard labor's take on such issues as the reasons for high prices and the need to repeal the antilabor laws and learned about unions' service to the community. The Iowa broadcasts began with the announcer declaring, "The men and women of the CIO like football because it's the game where you carry the ball. That's what the CIO is doing across the country—carrying the ball," and concluded with, "Football is a great American sport, and organized labor is a great American institution."[45]

Appealing labor programming was especially imperative in the postwar South, which remained a bastion of anti-unionism. Operation Dixie, launched by the CIO in 1946, sought to organize low-wage southern workers and to reshape the region's political landscape. While unions established some beachheads in communities such as Winston-Salem, North Carolina, and Rome, Georgia, many cities and mill towns remained inhospitable territory. Organizers often faced apathetic, indifferent, or fearful workers. Moreover, company intimidation and violence, unfriendly community leaders, ministers who preached against the CIO, calling it the "mark of the beast," and a hostile media made forming unions in the South a difficult task.[46]

Like their predecessors during the great organizing drives of the 1930s,

Operation Dixie organizers turned to radio, which offered an "alternative public space" where unions could speak directly to workers and the broader community. Many organizers had a great deal of faith in radio's power and made it an integral part of their organizing strategy, either broadcasting weekly programs as they planted the seeds of unionization or broadcasting intensively with multiple short announcements in the days just before an election. Reliance on radio began early in Operation Dixie. During its 1946 organizing drive against the Cannon Mills in North Carolina, the state director, William Smith, reported that house-to-house contacts with textile workers found that "these people listen to the radio very carefully." The local CIO staff decided that radio was the answer to streamlining their publicity campaign, a decision endorsed by many organizers across the South.[47]

Radio was a central part of the 1948 campaign to organize textile workers in and around Rock Hill, South Carolina. Six months before the NLRB election at Aragon Mill, David Burgess began a one-hour Sunday afternoon program to "lift the pall of company-induced fear." The Textile Workers lost the election but kept broadcasting, broadening the union's message to include workers at the neighboring Republic and J. P. Stevens Mills. By 1950, Franz Daniel reported that the show had built up a good following and was of "great value." One indication of its impact was the company's launch of a competing show on another station during the same time slot. The Textile Workers also had a long-standing program broadcasting out of Rockingham, North Carolina, which in June 1949 paid unexpected dividends. After listening to the weekly broadcasts, a group of low-paid clothing workers at a small plant in nearby Pembroke asked the Textile Workers for assistance in organizing. The Textile Workers put them in touch with the ACWA, and they quickly won a certification election.[48]

In early 1950, at a point when Operation Dixie was staggering, the national director, George Baldanzi, turned to radio to "penetrate the iron curtain of reaction" that existed in the South. According to Baldanzi, southerners completely misunderstood the CIO because of a long-standing campaign of "vicious and distorted propaganda." His solution was a radio campaign aired on seventy-five southern stations that presented the program, policies, and purposes of the CIO. Blending the CIO's message with cultural symbols that appealed to local workers, the show featured Texas Bill Strength, a young, popular country singer. Each program consisted of country music and a few minutes of dialogue, with Texas Bill asking George Baldanzi questions about the CIO in a light, folksy manner. Their conversations covered such issues as the CIO's history, its role in the community, its relationship with religion, its struggle against Communism, and its commitment to obtaining a greater share of the nation's wealth for the people. While CIO unionists often spoke strongly in support of civil rights on programs aimed at northern workers, Baldanzi referred only vaguely to the organization's commitment to social justice and greater racial understanding. Fearful of alienating white southern workers, Baldanzi and other CIO organizers avoided explicitly attacking segregation. Ironically, the first show began with Texas Bill singing the song that would become the anthem of the civil rights movement of the 1960s, "We Shall Overcome." Although the show lasted only one year, Strength stayed on the CIO's payroll, appearing on CIO radio shows throughout the South and singing at organizing rallies.[49]

Despite Baldanzi's enthusiasm, radio was no panacea. Indeed, reliance on radio underlined one of the weaknesses of Operation Dixie, its inability to form cadre groups within the mills. Moreover, censorship and denial of airtime remained a problem in the South, since in some communities local employers controlled the radio stations. In 1946, for instance, the organizer Ruth Gettinger found the manager of a Gastonia, North Carolina, station anti-union, uninformed, fearful of antagonizing the church, and determined to prevent the broadcast of anything controversial about the local company. David Burgess secured airtime in Rock Hill but struggled endlessly with station management over the content of the program. Forced at times to "practically castrate the radio script by taking out all references to the boss," Burgess was convinced that the station was trying to push the organizers off the air. In Kannapolis, the Textile Workers joked that the radio station's motto was "Hear no unionism, speak no unionism, see no unions." Ultimately, Cannon Mills prodded the radio station WGTL to abrogate its contract with the Textile Workers.[50]

Anderson, South Carolina, exemplified the difficulties organizers faced in gaining access to broadcasting in some communities. Organizers began seeking airtime in Anderson in late 1949. The local radio station sold time to the Citizens Committee, which filled the airways "with the most vicious anti-union propaganda imaginable," but rebuffed the CIO, fearing a business boycott. Finally, in the spring of 1951, after vigorous protest to the FCC, the station agreed to sign a broadcasting contract with the CIO Organizing Committee. Texas Bill Strength was a regular on the program with the organizer Dick Conn, who refuted the accusations of Communism that were leveled against the CIO in the local newspaper and on the Citizens' Committee show. The union program spoke directly to listeners, emphasizing the role of unions in bringing democracy to the workplace, improving wages and conditions, and boosting the community's buying power. Like many other southern programs, the union emphasized a strong attachment to religion, recognizing its central role in southern mill towns. Nevertheless, the program experienced increasing censorship, with the station management insisting on documentary proof of all points included in the script. Complaints to the FCC had initially helped get labor airtime in Anderson, but by the early 1950s the commission showed little concern with protecting labor from censorship, especially in the South. In 1952, one of the attorneys representing the CIO noted that "these days" the FCC was a "pretty milk-toast affair." Some of the commissioners were openly antagonistic to organized labor, a tendency exacerbated by the ascendancy of Republicans to the White House in 1953. In the spring of 1953, with no way of compelling stations to live up to their contracts, the CIO Organizing Committee began to reconsider how much of its resources it should allocate to radio in the South. By no means, however, did southern organizers totally abandon radio. When the Textile Workers Union began to organize the carpet industry in northwest Georgia in the 1960s, it sponsored a daily broadcast that included music and union announcements on two radio stations in the town of Dalton.[51]

For a short while, in a small number of communities, labor was able to reach the public through its own stations. By the summer of 1949, the ILGWU and the UAW had five FM stations on the air. They joined WCFL, the Chicago Federation of Labor's AM station, and WCFM, a Washington, D.C., cooperative FM station, in an informal liberal-labor network that shared some programming. The ILGWU stations were located in Chattanooga, Los Angeles, and New York City, and the UAW stations were in Detroit and Cleveland. While the ILGWU built a station in Chattanooga in the hopes of strengthening labor's presence in the South, the other cities reflected high concentrations of garment workers or autoworkers. Almost three-fourths of the UAW's membership was in the reception area of the union's Cleveland (WCUO) and Detroit (WDET) stations. Operating at fifty-two thousand watts, WDET was one of the most powerful FM stations in the country, reaching towns within a sixty-mile radius of Detroit.[52]

A strong commitment to education and political action drew the ILGWU and the UAW to FM radio. Both organizations viewed broadcasting not only as a way to defend labor against business attacks but as a means of promoting a progressive political agenda that would improve the lives of all Americans. Historically, the garment workers had pursued ambitious and innovative agendas in education and politics. The ILGWU offered an array of educational, recreational, social, and cultural activities designed to make unionism a way of life. In the 1930s, when thousands of new members flocked to the union, ILGWU locals turned to radio to communicate with workers, and the national union staged radio shows supporting the Democratic party starting in 1940. Operating FM stations was thus a natural extension of the ILGWU's ongoing educational and political activity.[53]

The UAW was also no stranger to education, politics, or radio. Its constitution required that two cents of every dues dollar be devoted to educational activity, and from its inception the union had used radio in its organizing and political campaigns. The UAW had been a leader in the broadcast reform movement, constantly fighting the entrenched interests in radio. During the war it led the charge against the NAB code, and after the war it continued to battle for labor's access to the air, while also fighting for the establishment of a democratic FM system.[54]

Walter Reuther's election as UAW president in the spring of 1946 ensured that broadcasting would remain a top priority for the union in the postwar years. The son of a German-American socialist, Reuther had risen quickly through the ranks of the UAW. He had an expansive view of the role of unions in American society. During World War II, he gained national attention when he proposed a bold plan to build "500 Planes a Day" by using idle automobile plants and included provisions for involving workers in production decisions. In the immediate aftermath of the war, he shocked the auto industry with the demand that GM grant a major wage increase without boosting car prices. Reuther's concern about inflation reflected his belief that the union's and the community's interests were intertwined. Thus, under his leadership the UAW fought not only for better contracts to benefit members but also for social and political reforms designed to improve the lives of all Americans. When he ascended to the presidency, he already had a reputation in the broadcasting industry of being "hep to radio," which he believed could be a powerful instrument for social change. The establishment of a national network of labor and cooperative-owned stations had for years been a Reuther dream.[55]

It was clear to Reuther that if labor was to counteract the powerful forces mobilized against it, unions needed to reach the public with labor's message while recasting the consciousness of industrial workers, "making them disciplined trade unionists, militant social democrats, and racial egalitarians." Making the union an integral part of workers' lives was the key to building the ranks of dedicated unionists. During the 1930s, the UAW had engaged in a variety of social and cultural activities, hoping to unite a diverse work-force. But the war and internal union factionalism had disrupted the UAW's effort to create a "culture of unity." Reuther believed that revitalizing and expanding nonworkplace activities would help the union reclaim worker loyalty. Under his leadership, the UAW developed a wide range of programs for members in education, sports, retirement, health, and community ser-vice and even created union-sponsored bookstores and consumer co-ops. Radio offered another important means of reaching the rank and file as well as extending the institutions of the union into the community. Reuther be-lieved that FM radio provided a unique opportunity for unions to serve the community while advancing labor's political and economic goals. He regu-larly argued that what is good "for the community as a whole is good for the union and its members."[56]

The UAW and ILGWU had ambitious goals for their new stations. They intended to create a "new kind of democracy on the air" by cutting through the "iron curtains" that hid the "inequalities and injustices" of the American economic and political system. Reuther anticipated that labor stations would be powerful instruments for "propaganda-free news." He argued that the importance of impartial coverage could not be overestimated, especially "in a city like Detroit where the daily newspapers consistently distort the news." Labor's FM stations, which would operate on a nonprofit basis without ex-cessive commercialization, planned to open the air to all groups, races, and religions. The ILGWU intended to make WFDR "the most articulate town meeting hall, the outstanding music hall, the most attractive cultural center in the community."[57] Similarly, WDET wanted to be the "people's station, where all the problems, social, political, economic—which affect labor and the community generally can be talked about openly and honestly." To en-sure that its stations avoided "raw commercial exploitation" and responded to the needs of the community, the UAW established advisory boards made up of community, religious, and minority leaders to help shape broadcast-ing policies.[58]

❖ ❖ ❖

Programming for labor's FM stations reflected the influence of Morris No-vik, who served as radio consultant to the ILGWU and the UAW. Many of Novik's ideas came from his experience as program director of the New York station WEVD during the 1930s. In radio circles, he was considered the moving spirit behind the ILGWU's broadcasting operations, as it was No-vik who interested ILGWU president David Dubinsky in FM broadcasting

during World War II. Dubinsky then hired Novik to write the FCC applications for station licenses and to begin developing programming schedules.
A friend of Walter Reuther, Novik also served as his informal radio advisor
until January 1948, when the UAW hired him as a consultant to assist in establishing the Detroit and Cleveland stations. Novik worked closely with all
the labor FM stations, providing advice on programming, technical issues,
hiring personnel, and marketing. Like most radio reformers, he was disgusted
with the excessive commercialism of American broadcasting and the failure
of radio to provide public service. Novik believed that FM gave labor the
opportunity to show how a local station could effectively serve the public
interest; labor's stations would thus provide a yardstick by which listeners
could measure other stations. He advocated that labor-owned stations avoid
acting as "special peddlers" for organized labor, urging unions instead to
operate community stations that promoted local talent, emphasized serious
music and unbiased news, and most importantly, developed a wide range of
public service programming.[59]

Under Novik's guidance, labor's FM stations provided a significant
amount of cultural and educational programming. The stations avoided
the types of programs that reformers considered the worst examples of advertising excess and bad taste, in particular soap operas, mystery shows,
and children's adventure stories. Instead, the stations carried music, news,
"quality" children's programs, and "intelligent discussion" of community
and national problems. The music varied, but most stations broadcast more
classical and semiclassical than popular music. Although the emphasis was on
highbrow culture, labor's FM stations also sought to represent the authentic expressions of the people. The ILGWU's stations in New York and Los
Angeles, for example, mixed in jazz and folk music with programs featuring
the symphony, ballet, and opera. The ILGWU's Chattanooga station carried
classical music produced by local artists but also reflected its southern roots
with gospel shows and country music from Texas Slim.[60]

The program schedules for labor-owned FM stations made clear that they
took "public interest, convenience, and necessity" seriously. As one reviewer
noted, the audience of "KFMV, WDET, and WCUO must take Gilbert and
Sullivan, Beethoven, and an occasional play with generous sprinklings of the
American Cancer Society, health programs, [and] the U.N. Story." Much of
this public interest programming was broadcast in prime evening hours,
rather than buried late at night, as was the common treatment of noncommercial programs at most radio stations. WFDR's public service programs
included "Civil Defense Reporter," a weekly roundup of civil defense news,

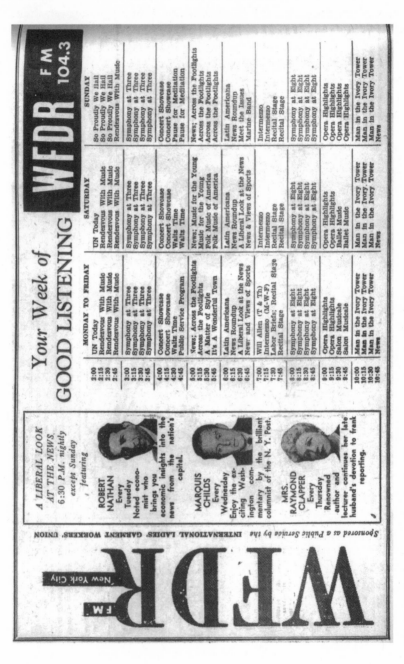

Weekly WFDR program list. *Justice*, Sept. 15, 1949; courtesy of UNITE HERE.

"The Power in Your Purse," a consumer co-op program, and "Skidmore Scans the Books," a Sunday-afternoon book discussion program featuring professors at Skidmore College. A *Variety* reviewer found the Skidmore program, which was also broadcast by the labor stations in Chattanooga and Cleveland, "listenable and literate," and not "too highbrow." Intent on addressing civic issues affecting the lives of listeners, in December 1949 WFDR responded to a municipal water crisis with a special Wednesday-night program with city officials and on-the-scenes reports explaining why water was scarce. The ILGWU's Chattanooga outlet was the first radio station in the city to take its microphones into City Hall and broadcast public hearings on community problems.[61]

WDET's public service offerings included "WDET Roundtable," a panel discussion of local legislative, social, and economic issues, "You and Your Health," a show produced in cooperation with the city's health department, and "Great Books on the Air," with "ordinary" people tackling everything from the Declaration of Independence to Plato, Aristotle, and Sophocles. Through "WDET Roundtable," the station hoped to bring the city of Detroit directly into the homes of radio listeners, with city officials and community representatives discussing housing problems, schools, tax levels, and recreation. Pledged to improving children's radio, the station's lineup included the teen forums "Young Americans Town Hall" and "Young Americans Look at Books" and "Storytime," with the Marygrove College professor May Jane Mossett reading children's stories to groups of boys and girls in the WDET studio. Mossett tried to "take the blood and thunder out of the typical children's story and yet make the tales interesting." Unafraid of controversy, the UAW's Detroit station broadcast a forum on "What Should Michigan Do about the Sex Deviate?" It also provided coverage of an ACLU conference considering whether Communists' civil rights were being violated, while WCUO in Cleveland aired a dramatic show entitled "Daddy, Am I White?" the "true experience of a Negro in war and peace."[62]

Union stations reflected much better than commercial radio the diverse makeup of American society. The war years had seen a precipitous decline in foreign-language broadcasting. In February 1948, despite its large immigrant population, the last ethnic shows went off the air in Detroit. The stations justified these cancellations by claiming that the foreign-language programs carried "a tinge of red." Disappointed immigrant organizations organized protests, asserting that foreign-language speakers had lost "their medium of expression." WDET helped address this loss with its cosmopolitan programs, tailored to the cultural interests of Italian, Yiddish, Polish,

Greek, and Ukranian speakers. With a blend of music, news, and cultural programming, the ethnic shows found an appreciative audience and were among the station's most commercially viable programs. (Like labor's other FM stations, WDET was nonprofit but sold advertising to support the cost of operations.) After starting out in less prominent time slots, by early 1952, foreign-language music programs anchored the late afternoon and early evening broadcast schedule.[63]

African Americans were also largely "rendered invisible" by mainstream radio, an injustice that labor's FM stations sought to redress. Committed to combating racial discrimination, WDET was the first Detroit station to appoint African Americans to its professional staff, placing Jerry Hemphill, a composer and music instructor, in charge of musical programming and making Bob Gill staff director. WDET also featured a black disc jockey, Ernie Durham, who spun jazz and popular music weekdays in the early afternoon. Other union-owned stations also promoted black on-air talent. Recognizing that the Los Angeles African American community had "no radio voice," the ILGWU station broadcast "The Joe Adams Show," featuring a black disc jockey. A show on the Chattanooga ILGWU station spotlighting African American teens earned immediate attention from an appreciative black community. The station manager, Joe Siegel, reported, "Negroes stop me on the street and thank me because the station carried the program."[64]

Union stations addressed racial issues that local broadcasters ignored or deemed too controversial. Fighting racism was a top priority for the UAW's Detroit station. Located in a city where racial tensions were constant and formidable, WDET sought to promote interracial understanding and to advance the cause of civil rights. Such programs as "Community Clinic," a roundtable discussion moderated by members of the Detroit Mayor's Interracial Committee, and "Let Freedom Ring" were designed to combat discrimination and bigotry. Each Monday evening on "Community Clinic," members of the Mayor's Committee and special guests from the community wrestled with contentious civil rights issues such as employment discrimination, segregation in housing, and the relationship between the police and minorities.[65]

Housing was a particularly hot-button racial issue to which WDET paid special attention. In March 1950, for instance, WDET was the only Detroit station to broadcast a two-hour Detroit Common Council hearing on rezoning a neighborhood to prevent the construction of a union-backed cooperative housing project that was committed to racial integration. Packed galleries at the hearing reflected the intense community interest in the issue. WDET's broadcast enabled listeners to hear civic, labor, and religious leaders defend "interracial living" as well as neighborhood property owners deny that their objections to the development were based on racial prejudice.[66]

In December 1949 the station launched a campaign aimed at exposing the discriminatory practices of a prominent civic group, the Detroit Tuberculosis Association. The Detroit school board had approved the sale in the public schools of the association's Christmas seals, despite opposition from groups, including the Michigan CIO, charging that proceeds of the sale were used to support a tuberculosis camp that admitted only white children. WDET sought to broadcast a roundtable discussion on the topic, but the association refused to participate, essentially quashing the broadcast. Following the Tuberculosis Association's rejection, WDET recorded one-minute personal statements by labor, religious, and civic leaders denouncing discriminatory practices, which it broadcast at frequent intervals during the ten days before Christmas. The station manager, Ben Hoberman, explained that "while it is uncommon for a radio station to take an active hand in such matters, we consider the present situation too clear-cut a violation of democratic American practice to go unchallenged."[67]

Civil rights were only part of the union stations' promotion of a progressive agenda. As promised, the union FM stations provided a forum for liberal and labor voices that had been largely silenced by the commercial media. The liberal commentator Helen Gahagan Douglas, for instance, provided reports on the Washington political scene for the ILGWU's Los Angeles station. WFDR and the two UAW stations broadcast "A Liberal Look at the News," a daily evening program developed by Morris Novik. It featured commentary on national and international events by prominent liberals, including Robert Nathan, a progressive economist who helped shape the CIO's postwar economic policy, John Carmody, a former New Dealer, and John Herling, Washington correspondent for the International Labor News Service. Beginning in January 1950, all the labor stations broadcast "Washington Report," which featured the journalists Joseph C. Harsh and Marquis Childs, both of whom had impeccable liberal credentials. About the same time, labor's FM stations began airing nightly news commentary by Frank Edwards, sponsored by the AFL. Edwards's link to the CIO's rival AFL did not prevent the UAW from praising the "witty, pleasant-listening" newscaster for his independent thinking and his "crusading spirit" on behalf of progressive objectives.[68]

Local labor commentators also brought a liberal perspective to their news analysis, presenting labor's position on local and national questions and drawing attention to issues ignored by the mainstream press. The UAW Cleveland station broadcast "Labor News and Views," a Sunday-evening program featuring the labor editor of the *Cleveland Citizen,* A. I. Davey. In Detroit, WDET carried "The Voice of the CIO," a Sunday-afternoon program with the *Michigan CIO News* editor Ted Olgar. During early 1950, Olgar advocated closing corporate tax loopholes, took Michigan Republicans to task for undermining efforts to improve the state's unemployment compensations law, and admonished Congress for passing a "toothless, spineless" Fair Employment Practices bill that had no provision for enforcement. Olgar regularly defended the welfare state, noting that business leaders' attacks on

Flyer promoting Guy Nunn's daily news commentary program, which was initially broadcast on WDET and then over the more powerful Canadian station CKLW. Courtesy of the Archives of Labor and Urban Affairs, Wayne State University, Detroit.

social security as evidence of the drift towards Communism ignored government largess for corporations in the form of subsidies and tax breaks.[69]

Guy Nunn's daily news and commentary program over WDET was the most popular of the FM labor news shows. In April 1950, he gained additional exposure when the UAW, frustrated with the press's failure to provide balanced coverage of its strike against Chrysler, began broadcasting Nunn's program in the early evening over the station CKLW, a powerful fifty-thousand-watt AM station in Canada that could be heard in most of Michigan, Indiana, and Ohio, and in parts of New York, Pennsylvania, and Illinois.[70] On the air back-to-back with Fulton Lewis Jr. over CKLW, Nunn quickly surpassed the conservative commentator in popularity. Guy Nunn had a colorful and dramatic career before joining the UAW's staff as WDET's news editor. Although a graduate of Occidental College and a Rhodes scholar, he inherited his railroading father's strong union convictions. An economist by training, before the war he worked as a labor analyst for the Federal Reserve, an investigator of unfair labor practices for the NLRB, and as FEPC regional director in California, where he helped thousands of African Americans and Mexicans gain jobs in the aircraft industry. That experience strengthened Nunn's lifelong commitment to civil rights. During the war, he served a stint with the Office of Strategic Services behind enemy lines and was captured and imprisoned by the Germans. Upon his return, he became a newscaster for a Detroit radio station but was kicked off the air for providing even-handed coverage of the 1946 GM strike. Nunn's run-in with the conservative owner of the station brought him to Walter Reuther's attention. Once hired by the union, Nunn quickly became known as the "Voice of the UAW." During the 1950s and early 1960s, Nunn was the most listened-to radio personality in Detroit. At one point, he was on the air three times a day for the UAW, on the radio at 6:15 A.M. and 2:30 P.M. and on television at 11:15 at night.[71]

Nunn's commentary took conservatives and business to task in a hard-hitting, caustic style. His open advocacy of liberal causes, particularly civil rights, and his promotion of the UAW's legislative and political objectives gave his opponents fits. In the spring of 1949, in a typical swipe at the Detroit media, which the UAW viewed as mouthpieces for the auto industry, Nunn noted that a *Free Press* editorial "was as twisted as a pretzel and as benevolently neutral as a clip-joint slot machine." According to Nunn, *Free Press* editorials were so poisonous against labor that their sale "should be made illegal unless accompanied by a stomach pump." Frustrated with moderate congressional Democrats who failed to support civil rights legislation, he observed that unlike Dixiecrats, these politicians did not "scream their heads off against civil rights" but did little to advance the cause. As Nunn saw it, on issues as important as fair employment and lynching, "a sin of omission is a great as any other." He warned that labor considered it "high time that some of Mr. Truman's old but not so reliable wheel-horses were put out to pasture."[72]

❖ ❖ ❖

The UAW's FM stations also had more specific union functions. WDET's weekly program, "Brother Chairman," visited a different union each week, introducing the listeners to officers who discussed the local's history and activities. The UAW's magazine, *Ammunition,* claimed that when "some of the people start to talk on this program, you can almost hear the fore-man coming up behind you in the shop, it brings your shop experiences so close to you." Programs like "Inside the UAW Political Action Committee" helped keep members abreast of union activities and developments. Larger locals, such as Ford Local 600 and Dodge Main Local 212, spoke directly to members through their own programs. These shows, produced, written, and

UAW Local Seven's show on WDET. *United Automobile Worker,* Apr. 1950; courtesy of the Archives of Labor and Urban Affairs, Wayne State University, Detroit.

performed by rank-and-file members, served as an outlet for workers' self-expression. As Jerry Sherman of Local 3 saw it, part of WDET's mission was to serve as an "extension of the actual voices of honest-to-God, rank-and-file trade union people!"[73]

WDET provided critical support during the 1949 Ford strike and the 1950 Chrysler strike. With Detroit's three daily papers siding with management, Ford workers grew to depend on WDET for coverage of their side of the dispute. WDET was on the picket lines from the start, taking spontaneous comments from the marchers. It went into union halls and interviewed local officers, committeemen, and soup-kitchen operators. A sound truck fitted with an FM tuner broadcast Guy Nunn's evening news commentary, which included progress reports on the strike, to the men and women on the picket lines. Emil Mazey recalled that "these broadcasts were terrific morale builders," for "every picket knew that his story was being beamed to thousands of listeners in southeastern Michigan." During the Chrysler strike, Guy Nunn added a special series of weekday-afternoon programs to his regular evening broadcast. Hundreds of Chrysler workers gathered in their local union halls to hear Nunn's latest strike news as well as interviews with striking union members. Special bulletins provided information about union meetings and how to obtain strike assistance from local community-service committees. To help boost morale, every Saturday night, WDET broadcast amateur-night programs, featuring songs, music, and comedy performed by Chrysler strikers and their families.[74]

The UAW and ILGWU actively promoted their stations. Like many FM outlets in the early 1950s, labor's stations struggled to find an audience. One problem was the high cost of FM receivers, which the unions tried to address by offering inexpensive FM converters to their members and making arrangements with dealers for discounts on new sets. To increase the audience, they ran listener contests, attached cards with the station's schedules to new FM receivers in local stores, placed banners on city buses, and plastered posters in union halls. Mildred Jeffrey, head of the UAW Radio Department, recalled lugging heavy FM equipment to countless union meetings, dances, and hot, dusty picnics in an effort to gain the members' attention. She urged local officers to encourage members to buy receivers, pointing out that the success of the UAW's program was "in direct proportion to the number of conscientious loyal members."[75]

The desire to boost audience size and attract union listeners created some conflict over the stations' programming philosophies. Novik urged labor's FM stations to keep a distance from their union sponsors and emphasize

In an effort to build its audience, the UAW's FM station, WDET, ran listener contests, placed banners on city buses, and plastered posters in union halls. Courtesy of the Archives of Labor and Urban Affairs, Wayne State University, Detroit.

high-quality programming. Ultimately, Novik left a stronger imprint on the ILGWU stations, especially in New York and Los Angeles, than on the UAW stations, although classical music and public service programming certainly remained key elements of the schedules of all the labor stations. But UAW president Walter Reuther, who took an active interest in the operation of WDET and WCUO, urged that they project a stronger public identification with the autoworkers. He also wanted additional distinctly labor programs that promoted the economic and political goals of the UAW as well as popular programming attractive to working-class listeners. Mildred Jeffrey agreed that while "we want to make both stations community-minded in their general orientation . . . in the final analysis we are not going to make WDET a success unless we build up first of all a loyal and devoted group of listeners among UAW and organized labor."[76]

As a result, WDET and WCUO began regularly broadcasting announcements like, "This is station WDET-FM, owned and operated by a million members of the UAW-CIO," and expanded their union-oriented programming. They also began offering more popular music, ranging from Dixieland to light-classical, and more sports. The Cleveland station scheduled high

The UAW's FM station, WDET, tried to attract young listeners with programs like Teen Tempo. Bob Hope appeared on the inaugural broadcast in September 1949. Courtesy of the Archives of Labor and Urban Affairs, Wayne State University, Detroit.

school football games, and Detroit began airing live broadcasts of the "Fight of the Week." Seeking to attract autoworkers' children with lighter programming, WDET created "Teen Tempo." The Saturday-morning show was produced by a group of teenagers with aid from the station staff. The program included music, a Teen Book-of-the-Week, high school notes, and appearances by visiting show-business celebrities. Early guests included Bob Hope, the musician Spike Jones, the singer Lena Horne, and President Truman's daughter, Margaret. Seeking to broaden its audience, the ILGWU's Chattanooga stations broadcast a revival meeting by a nine-year-old preacher.[77]

Still, many of those who wrote to WDET cherished the broadcasts of classical music and welcomed the educational programming. C. J. Major of Wyandotte, Michigan, wrote that he enjoyed the radio concerts, observing that it was "gratifying . . . that at least one station in this area tries to satisfy the tastes of true music lovers." For Charles Adrian, WDET was a "breath of *fresh air.*" Another listener found the station to be a "bright spot in the generally dismal and depressing condition" of Detroit radio. Others reported that they regularly listened to Guy Nunn for the "true slant of the news." One Detroit couple tuned into WDET religiously. For them, the evening symphony hour was "very precious and a wonderful antidote after a dull day at work." Moreover, the "speeches and treatment of economic problems" were "gems." Marion H. Bemis, assistant director of the Citizens' Housing and Planning Council of Detroit, particularly enjoyed the symphony hour and the "Great Books" roundtable discussion. She urged the station manager, Ben Hoberman, to stand firm against any pressure to popularize the station's programming. The station did more than preach to the choir. Bemis reported that one of her workers who was "exceedingly anti-union" regularly listened to WDET. "Perhaps," she hoped, "you are making some converts whether you know it or not."[78]

❖ ❖ ❖

Labor's FM stations won numerous accolades. In December 1949, Maxwell Fox of the Advertising Council praised a WFDR special-events program promoting blood donations. He characterized the broadcast as one of "the most intelligent examples of radio public service I have ever heard." The ILGWU won compliments from a Southern California listeners group, and in March 1951 the Los Angeles City Council passed a resolution praising the union for operating KFMV in the public interest. In 1950, KFMV and WFDR earned awards in *Billboard*'s annual radio promotion competition, with WFDR being recognized for innovations in FM programming. That year, KFMV garnered a Peabody Radio Award, and WDET won a *Variety* Show Management award, one of radio's top industry honors. *Variety* was particularly impressed with the station's forthright stand on behalf of civil rights. Finally, during 1951, WFDR won one of the media's most coveted citations, the Page One Award of the Newspaper Guild of New York, as well as a *Variety* award. The Newspaper Guild award cited the station for consistently championing "liberalism and labor's rights" and "for its responsibility to the public." *Variety* applauded WFDR for recognizing that a substantial portion of the New York audience was weary of soap operas and whodunits and demanded programs "produced with intelligence and imagination for adult minds." In November 1950, after reviewing the operation of the Los Angeles, Cleveland, and Detroit stations, the radio analyst Pat Peterman concluded that labor's FM stations were fast becoming "an instrument of force in the hands of labor."[79]

WDET won *Variety's* show management award in 1950. *Pictured left to right:* Ben Hoberman, station manager; George Rosen, *Variety* radio manager; Walter Reuther; Morris Novik. *United Automobile Worker,* July 1950; courtesy of the Archives of Labor and Urban Affairs, Wayne State University, Detroit.

Despite these high hopes and the many awards won by union stations, labor's experiment with FM was short-lived. The expected large audience for FM would not materialize for many years. As a result of financial losses, by the spring of 1952, all of the stations had folded, leaving a void unfilled by mainstream radio. *Justice,* the ILGWU's newspaper, observed that in a medium "swamped with commercialism," WFDR had provided an "auditory oasis for the intelligent listener." Daniel Strassberg of New York City mourned the closing of the station, observing that the city had lost "its only progressive radio voice." Similarly, the discontinuation of WDET brought sadness to a Detroit machinist, who wrote that "it is one of the best stations in the area and we need more like it." For the Chattanooga station manager, Joe Seigel, the closing of his station struck a critical blow at efforts to promote liberalism and labor in the South. He observed that "this city desperately needs a liberal outlet" and predicted that the station's demise "will be bad for the union and unionism."[80]

Labor's FM experiment was the victim of the manufacturers' refusal to develop low-cost AM-FM receivers, the radio industry's failure to promote FM, and increasing competition from the fledgling television industry. In March 1952, for instance, the UAW reported that despite an aggressive campaign to encourage workers and others to purchase FM sets, FM ownership among its members was still "woefully small." Mildred Jeffrey recalled that getting autoworkers to buy the expensive FM sets proved an "insurmountable problem." Instead, the UAW members were choosing to buy televisions. FM's format, with its emphasis on classical music and public interest programming, may have also hindered the development of a substantial audience. Surveys indicated that most listeners were professionals, intellectuals, and other members of the middle class. Jeffrey later concluded that "maybe our thinking [about programming] was a little highbrow." It was difficult for the ILGWU and the UAW to justify continued investment in a medium that was missing an important part of their target audience.[81]

Finally, hostility and suspicion towards labor hurt the stations in some cities. Newspapers often refused to publish program listings. In Detroit the school board turned down WDET's request to broadcast high school football games, which the station hoped would boost audiences. Guy Nunn concluded that there was "little question that CIO prejudice went into the decision." Although the stations were nonprofit, the unions hoped to secure enough advertising revenue to help cover operating expenses. Station staff pounded the pavement seeking advertisers. Trading on workers' consumer power, they targeted local merchants who wanted labor's goodwill as well as labor's business. WDET also sought sponsorship from larger firms with which the UAW had union contracts. In an ironic twist, given labor's bitter memories of "The Ford Sunday Evening Hour," the station even asked the Ford Motor Company to sponsor its evening symphony program. It proved exceedingly difficult, however, for union stations to find sponsors, mostly because of the small FM audience. But there was also a reluctance among many advertisers to be associated with union-owned stations, especially in times of labor conflict. After almost a year on the air, it had become clear to Mildred Jeffrey that advertisers "both large and small" were suspicious that WDET would be a "CIO propaganda outlet" and thus withheld their business.[82]

By the spring of 1952, labor's venture into FM broadcasting was over. The only union station left on the air was Chicago's WCFL, which operated like a conventional commercial station and was in the process of deemphasizing its labor connection. The UAW and ILGWU had established lofty goals for their radio stations. By seeking to privilege the public interest, they attempted to challenge America's commercial broadcasting system, which emphasized profits over public service. This commitment to innovation and public service broadcasting placed these unions at the forefront of the media reform movement. Enthusiastic unionists, however, had perhaps too lofty expectations about their ability to reshape the American broadcasting system and perhaps not enough appreciation of the many difficulties that they would face. Optimistic UAW radio enthusiasts believed that an expanding chain of community service stations modeled on labor's FM stations would break the domination of radio by the "commercial Goliath" before the end of the 1950s. They were, of course, wrong.[83]

In the wake of the closing of the last union FM station, however, the employers' magazine *Factory* warned that labor's voice was still "on the air waves, plenty," reminding readers that unions continued to bring their message to their members and the public via local and network AM radio programs and even television.[84] Labor's venture into media reform may have failed, but unionists' interest in using the mass media remained strong.

(( ))

7   Union Voices in a "Wilderness
      of Conservatism"

AFTER WORLD WAR II, the American labor movement was at the peak of
its economic power, and the union voice in broadcasting was stronger than
ever before or since. Despite the failure of FM, ongoing efforts to open the
airwaves enabled organized labor to use the AM spectrum—through local
and network programming—to speak directly to the public with ever greater
volume. Unlike today, in the postwar era the nation's union leadership was a
familiar presence on network radio and television. Postwar listeners became
accustomed to hearing labor leaders regularly spar with their business coun-
terparts on the network's sustaining public affairs and news shows. Moreover,
unions took advantage of the newly won ability to buy network airtime, experimenting first with national campaigns to promote their collective bargaining and political goals and then settling on daily news commentary as a
means of gaining a powerful national voice. By 1956, labor's national radio
news commentators provided some of the few liberal voices in a media that
was described by the pollsters Pulse, Inc., as a "wilderness of conservatism."[1]
Through all these broadcasting initiatives, unions contested the business
community's aggressive postwar anti-union campaign, strengthened a union
identity among workers, provided support for labor's collective bargaining
goals, and promoted a liberal democratic political agenda.

❖ ❖ ❖

In the postwar era, business continued to attack labor and liberalism and to
promote free enterprise ideology via network broadcasting. At the end of
the war, while many liberals were driven off the air, Fulton Lewis Jr., Henry

J. Taylor, Sam Pettingill, and a host of other business-sponsored conservative commentators regularly spiked their observations of the news with attacks on organized labor and liberalism. Lewis continued to be one of the public's favorite radio commentators. At the height of his popularity, his nightly audience on the Mutual Network approached ten million. Nicknamed "radio's silken voice of reaction" by labor, he regularly defended the freedom of individual enterprise as the most "important, the most vital freedom of all." A June 1945 commentary flatly stated, "If something is done by a Government, it's most likely to be bad." An ardent defender of Joseph McCarthy in the 1950s, he was known for his venomous attacks on labor and the Left, declaring, "I love this God-damned country of ours. It's a religion with me, and I'm not going to stand by idly while a bunch of CIO-backed Communist left-wing cracks try to wreck it."[2]

After the 1944 election, the CIO had successfully pressured NBC to drop Henry J. Taylor's program, but in late 1945 General Motors hired Taylor, shifting his commentary to the Mutual Network. For more than ten years on Monday and Friday nights, Taylor railed against the expansion of the welfare state, which he equated with socialism, increased taxes (especially on corporate profits), and the growing power of unions. He acknowledged the American desire for security but urged resisting the temptation to turn to the government. "Radicals all over the world," Taylor advised audiences, "seek to place us in the hands of a state government," but government is the "greatest thief of individual freedom and personal security." In 1947, he urged passage of the Taft-Hartley Act, warning that "as citizens we face monopolistic labor combines. We've all seen the paralyzing results. The public must be protected and quickly." During 1949 and 1950, when unions were striking to gain pensions, Taylor argued that this benefit would "destroy the individual incentive and freedom on which the prosperity of the whole country depends."[3]

The National Association of Manufacturers and the Chamber of Commerce also had a network presence. Representatives of both organizations regularly appeared on the popular debate and forum-style programs like "Town Hall of the Air." However, business groups worried that busy and ill-equipped employers were ineffective against opponents "trained in public brawling, armed to the hilt with facts and figures, and bug-eyed with zeal for the Leftist side of the debate," so in 1946 the NAM began providing special training to its debaters. The business organizations also had their own programs provided free of charge by the networks, except for production costs. In early 1945, as a result of the CIO's campaign for access, the FCC forced networks to begin offering labor time on the air. To balance the union perspective, the networks also gave the NAM and the Chamber of Commerce airtime. ABC split a time slot between the two business organizations, allowing them to create and produce their own programs. The business programs often aired back-to-back with the labor shows.[4]

The NAM went on the air with "It's Your Business," which became the granddaddy of all business public-service programs. Before settling into a formula of panel interviews with business leaders, the NAM experimented with a variety of formats in an effort to compete with the CIO's program. Reviewers often compared the labor and business shows, mostly to the detriment of the NAM. In early 1947, the *Variety* reviewer praised "It's Your Business" for using music and a dramatic skit to illustrate the plight of underpaid school teachers, which proved that "manufacturers are just as friendly to little people as any unionist could be." However, if the CIO show was "surefire," the business program "didn't quite come off." Subsequent reviews were significantly harsher. In January 1948, *Billboard* critiqued a program on price controls, dismissing the business leaders' opposition to the Office of Price Administration as "word weaseling" and "specious drivel." Later in the year, *Variety* carried lukewarm reviews of the show's experiment with a quiz format, which was dull and "about as subtle in plumping for the virtues of business (big and little) as a bass drum." Undeterred by the poor reviews, the NAM remained pleased with its opportunity to give the public the "facts" about industry and labor.[5]

In 1950 the NAM turned to television, launching a weekly program, "Industry on Parade." A sustaining program broadcast as a public service by more than 241 stations, it showcased firms, explaining how products are made and demonstrating what industry gives to the nation and its communities. Though production of new segments stopped in the 1960s, the program continued to air into the 1970s. Adopting a more subtle approach than its radio programming, the goal was to show that business is "the symbol of progress and hope for the majority of the people." The program had an immediate impact. In early 1952, Oklahoma City reported that the series ranked among the first five programs in popularity, and Milwaukee gave "Industry on Parade" a higher audience rating than "Meet the Press," broadcast at the same time. The broadcasting industry was so pleased with the response to "Industry on Parade" that the Dumont Television Network asked the NAM to develop a spinoff entitled "Meet the Boss." Designed to humanize industry and its executives, the show featured interviews with top executives from the firms spotlighted in "Industry on Parade."[6]

Immediately after World War II, business used institutional programming as part of its effort to "reconstruct a cultural climate conducive to the autonomous expansion of enterprise." Du Pont's "Cavalcade of America" selectively interpreted the past to sell free enterprise. One executive, William H. Hamilton, characterized the show's editorial goal as "positive Americanism." According to Hamilton, Du Pont "endeavored to acquaint our listening audience with a keener, broader understanding and appreciation of the freedoms that have secured for America the highest standard of living of any country in the world—the belief in the individual which strengthens our democracy politically and affords us tremendous economic strength." U.S. Steel's "Theatre Guild on the Air," a highly regarded dramatic anthology series, enabled the company to describe its contributions to the American economy and explain its policies to the American public. Like Du Pont, U.S. Steel emphasized the significance of the individual to the American way of life. Intermission talks by the announcer, George Hicks, a former ABC radio newsman, proclaimed the firm as the "Industrial Family That Serves the Nation." Hicks's institutional messages emphasized U.S. Steel's commitment to improving consumer products through research, to plant safety, to rehiring and training veterans, and to providing opportunity for each individual to rise up through the company's ranks. In U.S. Steel's world, only "the capabilities of the individual" stand in the way of success. While expensive, the company considered the program a worthwhile investment. It publicized responses from listeners who praised U.S. Steel for informing the public of what the company means to "this wonderland of ours." Another thanked the steel firm for the "lift" it "gives us in these times of confusion. Your radio plays are escape pleasure; your commercial messages are spiritual nourishment."[7]

In the early 1950s, business began to shift its network institutional programming out of radio and into television. In 1952, U.S. Steel transferred its "Theatre Guild on the Air" to television, and the following year Du Pont's "Cavalcade of America" made the jump. They joined other corporate giants—Alcoa, Ford, Firestone, Reynolds Metals, and General Electric—who had already taken their institutional messages to television. According to Gallup polls, General Electric's program, hosted by Ronald Reagan, was "the leading institutional campaign on television for selling ideas to the public." Du Pont's "Cavalcade" continued to teach Americans that "progress in this country has come about through our free enterprise system—not through a government controlled social state." Bohm Aluminum and Brass Corporation sponsored a program with commercial messages warning the public about the dangers of "Socialistic schemes" that look safe but are actually a "deadly poison" to freedom. Even local firms moved into television. Caterpillar, for one, sponsored a weekly half-hour news, weather, and sports program in Peoria, Illinois, that carried messages about the company.[8]

Business institutional programs, especially those based on a theater format, usually posted decent audience ratings. If reviewers were often impatient with the NAM's strident advocacy of the free enterprise system, they were more respectful of corporate institutional shows such as "Ford Theater" or U.S. Steel's "Theatre Guild on the Air." Media reviews praised the heavily financed programs for the quality of production and for institutional ads that were typically brief, effective, and in good taste. U.S. Steel understood that the way to attract audiences was to "put on an all-star dramatic hour like *The Theatre Guild on the Air* and millions of folks will gladly (and of their own accord) glue their ears to their radios. Week after week too!" In September 1947, however, *Variety* did poke fun at "Cavalcade" for its glorification of American industrial leaders of the past and its insistent emphasis on the superiority of the American economic system. "If you listened carefully," according to the reviewer, "at the sign-off, you might have heard Capitalism's sigh of satisfaction."[9]

"Cavalcade" fan mail and surveys indicated that many listeners and viewers were taking the company's message to heart. Postwar surveys found that audience members easily remembered Du Pont's slogan, "Better Things for Better Living through Chemistry," and that listeners characterized the firm as "a very good company" that "did a lot for humanity" and "for the betterment of society." It was "always looking in the future for your benefit and mine." One viewer described the ads as concerning mankind and confided, "I sort of like that. Makes me feel good." Writing in the mid-1950s, Harold Koster of Kansas thanked Du Pont "for putting on such a wonderful program to help Americanism," and Joan Christiansen of Massapequa Park, New York, reported that "our whole family always enjoys your program dedicated to building *up* America instead of tearing down." Likewise, Alvin Wingfield, of Charlotte, North Carolina, responded positively to the show's emphasis on the importance of individual freedom in the American economic system. He observed that "in a day when many great corporations are striving to find security and prosperity for themselves in a friendly alliance with omnipotent government, it is gratifying to see one not be afraid to support the idea that liberty and honor are more important than security, prosperity, or even peace."[10]

❖ ❖ ❖

The business voice on network radio was not uncontested. Through the first half of the 1950s, all the major networks provided the AFL and CIO with free time for weekly public service programs featuring the labor perspective. NBC had "America United—Labor-Management Talks" and then "Viewpoint, USA." On CBS, unions participated in "Cross-Section," a Saturday-afternoon interview show. ABC provided time on Saturday evenings for back-to-back labor and business shows and allowed each group to develop its own programming. The AFL and CIO each received twenty-six weeks a year divided into two thirteen-week segments. Over the years, the CIO sponsored "Labor USA," a variety show ("It's in the Family"), a labor-quiz show, and news commentary by the liberal economist Robert Nathan. The AFL public service program, "As We See It," consisted of interviews with union officials and government and political leaders.[11]

Most of these public service programs consisted of panel discussions, commentaries, or interviews. Sparks could fly, particularly on the forum programs, which featured debates on current labor and economic issues between representatives from unions and management. In early 1952, the Chamber of Commerce and the NAM refused to participate any further in the highly popular "America United," asserting that the show had degenerated into a "hog-calling contest" in which union officials overmatched employers. As a result, NBC changed the format to a more staid interview program with only one point of view represented, leading to a sharp drop in the number of listeners. The AFL and CIO denounced the employers' refusal to engage in a debate "in which some of their hypocritical pronouncements might be exploded in their faces."[12]

NBC and CBS controlled the formats of their public service labor programs, but ABC gave labor complete freedom. While the AFL program, produced by its publicity director, Philip Pearl, kept to an interview format, the CIO's Len De Caux began with a more imaginative approach. De Caux explained that "Labor USA" emphasized "simple popular presentation," using the "most modern and professional techniques of dramatization, music, and entertainment to attract and hold listeners of all kinds." To achieve this goal, DeCaux hired Peter Lyon, a top-notch radio writer who had worked on "The March of Time" and "Cavalcade of America." Flexible in format, shows in late 1946 presented a Christmas parable about Tiny Tim and a "flint-hearted" department store owner named Mr. Gotrocks, satirized the NAM's promises for a better tomorrow, interviewed CIO families in their homes, and presented brief talks by CIO leaders. The show also featured a twelve-man band and the twangy folk songs of Tom Glazer, who sang of "broken purse strings and anti-labor laws." In one typical tune Glazer linked the CIO drive for higher wages to Americanism:

> I am an American working man and I'll tell you what I want,
> I ain't got no fancy words so I really must be blunt.
> I want to make a living wage with prices that I can pay,
> 'Cause I'm an American working man and that's the American way.[13]

In July 1947, De Caux left the CIO, the victim of anti-Communist house-cleaning. But his influence on programming continued. In January 1948, the CIO began a new radio show in its ABC time slot that emulated popular quiz shows. "It's in the Family" featured rank-and-file CIO families competing for a savings bond by answering questions about labor and current issues, such as civil rights, wages, food prices, and foreign affairs. Occasionally, the quiz master, Joe O'Brien, also directed a few questions at CIO officials about collective bargaining or other labor issues.[14]

Reviewers preferred the livelier CIO shows over the straight-talk NAM program that immediately followed. *Variety* described "Labor USA" as "credible" and "warm, ingratiating, human ... down-to-earth ... close to the people for whom it speaks," while the "exact antonyms" characterized the business pitch, which had a stuffy quality. Moreover, "[Y]ou can't balance the voice of ex-NAM prexy Ira Mosher against Tom Glazer accompanying himself on the guitar ... and expect anyone to cheer for the NAM." The CIO's quiz show did equally well. *Billboard* described "It's in the Family" as a "frank pitch" by the CIO for "better understanding of labor and its problems." The format was "pleasantly unencumbered" and made for "easy listening." *Variety* praised the quiz show for its showmanship, observing that it made good use of the "intimacy of radio to sell its ideas." Moreover, "sandwiched in with the entertainment," labor's ideas "unquestionably" got across in an "unobtrusive, inoffensive, and therefore effective manner." The quiz show matched up well against NAM's weekly "look-what-a-good-boy-I-am spiel" that relied on old-fashioned platform oratory. In early February 1949, even H. V. Kaltenborn, certainly no fan of organized labor, admitted that the CIO had bested business, at least on the radio. Kaltenborn found "It's in the Family" to be an "amusing fast-moving show with lots of human interest" that subtly but effectively promoted CIO ideas. The NAM show, which sought to define the meaning of the word "capital," was "so dull and stodgy" that Kaltenborn's wife made him turn it off.[15]

Despite such positive reviews, by the end of 1949, the CIO abandoned its efforts to entertain and teach on its ABC sustaining show, turning instead to a more traditional format with commentary by the economist Robert Nathan. The reasons for the shift are not clear; perhaps it was an effort to reduce production costs, or perhaps it reflected the change in leadership or program goals in the CIO's publicity department. Instead of aiming at the rank and file, Nathan's commentary targeted a higher-tone intellectual and liberal radio audience.[16]

The union voice on the network was not limited to public service programming. Through the 1950s, the radio networks continued to provide time for speeches by the leaders of the AFL and CIO, including Philip Murray, Walter Reuther, George Meany, and James Carey. On Labor Day, network television news anchors routinely interviewed the heads of both federations. Unionists also regularly participated in public affairs shows on radio and television, such as "American Forum of the Air," "Town Hall," "Meet the Press," and "Capitol Cloakroom," as well as commercial news and variety shows such as "Today" and "The Kate Smith Show." In 1953, CIO head Walter Reuther had a standing invitation to participate in the ABC show "Crossfire" and Mutual's "Reporters Roundup."[17]

Such exposure meant that labor often had the opportunity to explain its position or quickly respond to attacks through the national media. For instance, in November 1959 in the midst of the steel strike, Walter Reuther, George Meany, and Emil Mazey, the UAW's secretary-treasurer, lit into President Eisenhower for issuing an injunction to restart the mills. Mazey charged that the injunction was a political payoff, and Reuther compared Eisenhower's behavior to the authoritarian behavior of the Soviet leader Nikita Khrushchev, suggesting that there is little democracy when cronies shape policy and compel employees to work against their will. In turn, commentators and editorialists rushed to Eisenhower's defense, attacking the union leaders as intemperate, illogical, and full of nonsense. Fulton Lewis Jr. charged that "in their fanaticism," Reuther and his "strong-arm chieftain" Mazey "had completely lost their heads" and were running "verbally amok." Within thirty-six hours of Lewis's attack, Reuther appeared on the "Today" morning show on NBC television, where he argued that the propaganda issued by the steel industry made it impossible for the public to learn the economic truth and called for the appointment of a nonpartisan fact-finding board.[18]

❖ ❖ ❖

In sharp contrast to the NAB-code era, the networks, particularly Mutual and ABC, also sold time to unions, greatly amplifying labor's ability to reach the public with its message. In October 1945, shortly after the FCC decision that overturned the broadcasters' code, the CIO spent a hundred thousand dollars to buy time on ABC for a series of four broadcasts entitled "CIO for America." This was the first time that a network sold time to labor for the discussion of controversial issues, and the programs were heavily advertised in newspapers and through radio spot announcements. During the broadcasts, CIO president Philip Murray took labor's case for a wage hike directly to the American people, arguing that mass purchasing power was critical to continuing economic growth. The programs also featured dramatic skits and conversations with rank-and-file CIO families, who explained what declining wages meant in their lives. Jean Marrone of Belleville, New Jersey, a member of Westinghouse's UE Local 426, for instance, saw her wages drop over 50 percent at the end of the war as a result of downgrades and reduced hours. This disabled veteran's wife had spent most of her bonds and cut back on gas, electricity, and food. She shared with the audience her fears and frustrations for her family, asking, "If we could have security during the war, why can't we have it now?"[19]

Labor waged its 1947 campaign against the Taft-Hartley Act on network radio. To arouse public opinion against legislation being touted by business and much of the mass media as "labor reform," the AFL bought network airtime for the first time in its history. To defeat Taft-Hartley, the AFL and CIO had relied on intensively lobbying Capitol Hill, rallies in scores of cities, letter-writing campaigns, and airtime on local stations around the nation.[20] The ILGWU radio consultant Morris Novik, however, believed that labor faced a crisis; more needed to be done "to stop some of the wild charges against labor" and to mobilize public opinion against the antilabor act. In April, with the support of ILGWU president David Dubinsky, Novik convinced the AFL to authorize four hundred thousand dollars to conduct a radio campaign and encouraged representatives of show-business unions—actors, singers, musicians, writers, directors, and press agents—to form the AFL Entertainment Unions Committee to produce the programs. While Novik negotiated for network airtime, some of the best writers and directors in New York and Hollywood began applying their talent towards creating the shows, the first of which aired within one week of the committee's formation.[21]

For six weeks beginning on May 5, as Congress debated the Taft-Hartley legislation and President Truman considered whether to veto the act, the AFL sponsored three series over ABC and Mutual designed to awaken the nation to the threats Taft-Hartley posed to their economic security. Almost six hundred entertainment union members participated in the campaign. One of the series, "Labor Must Be Free," aired on Tuesday evenings and featured a variety of civic, religious, and industrial leaders, who explained why they opposed the bills. The other two series built on the idea that if entertainment-oriented programming could sell "cheese and soap," it could also sell labor. Recognizing the bifurcated radio audience, the AFL took a two-pronged approach, directing some of its entertainment programs toward the entire family through star-studded evening shows and others at women through daytime soap operas. Like the worker films of the 1920s and 1930s, this was "entertainment in the pursuit of activism," mobilizing Americans to help defeat the antilabor legislation by writing to their congressional representatives and to the president.[22]

The variety show "Story from the Stars" featured top talent from Hollywood, Broadway, and radio, ranging from Gregory Peck and Milton Berle to Dinah Shore and Benny Goodman, all working at the industry's minimum scale. Broadcast on Thursday nights and rebroadcast Sunday afternoons, the show used music, comedy, and dramatic skits to attack the Taft-Hartley Act. The first program closed with a satirical skit by Arthur Miller depicting the sufferings of a lowly factory worker, Alfred Higgins, who is driven to exhaustion by the speedup system. Enter the unions, which save Higgins, until Taft-Hartley. A nasty-sounding boss boasts to Higgins, "Soon as they pass them bills, you boys're gonna be running around these machines like jack rabbits. You're gonna sweat again." Superman comes to the workers' rescue, advising listeners, "Your voice, the voice of the American people, is the only thing that can kill these slave-labor bills."

In the last program of this series, in a skit that challenged the contention that Congress had a public mandate for antilabor legislation, Melvyn Douglas played a pollster, asking members of the public their opinion about Taft-Hartley. Probably the funniest response came from the comedian Jimmy Durante. "Dey did'n ast me," Jimmy declared. "Maybe dey ast Umbriago!" his mythical sidekick. The most moving response, however, came from the retired steel worker Tom De Lacey, a veteran of the 1892 Battle of the Barges labor war in Homestead, Pennsylvania. He told the story of the battle on the Monongahela River between workers and scabs aided by Pinkerton detectives and recalled the twelve-hour days and oppressive working conditions of the non-union era. Labor, he predicted, would not take Taft-Hartley lying down. "We don't want to go back to 1892 again," he declared.[23]

The daytime serial *The Best Things in Life* focused on the lives and problems of ordinary working people. Like the variety show, it featured some of the best writers and actors in the business. The first series starred Frederic March and Florence Eldridge, and the second starred Arlene Francis and Sam Wanamaker. During the fifth week, Ed Begley and Arthur Kennedy, who were then playing the leads in Arthur Miller's hit Broadway play *All My Sons*, took a break each day from the theater to participate in the union production. Each series started on Friday in the hope that this cliffhanger technique would hold listeners' interest over the weekend. Hard-hitting commercials aimed at derailing Taft-Hartley tried to grab the attention of the mostly female audience. Recognizing women's role as consumers, the ads emphasized that unions were fighting for higher wages and lower prices and that organized labor, not business, gave American families security. "Lady," one warned, "down in Washington they're trying to push through a slave-labor bill that will slice your husband's envelope right down the middle." For six weeks, the afternoon airwaves rang with the cry, "Kill the Taft bill . . . Kill the Hartley bill!"[24]

The union message came through the stories as well as the commercials. Like the worker-made films of the 1920s and 1930s, the afternoon serials used melodrama to promote a political message and give "voice to workers' desires, dreams, and discontents," as the film scholar Steven Ross puts it. Scripted by experienced soap opera writers, *The Best Things in Life* drew from the conventions of daytime serials with narratives that focused on marital discord, illness, and crime—although the AFL soaper also took on issues rarely treated by daytime radio, such as racial prejudice. The stories also reflected the anxieties of the postwar period, particularly the concern over the emotional condition of veterans and the fear that they might inflict violence at home. Finally, they gave voice to the expectation that strong, loving women in traditional female roles could help their husbands restore order to their families and to the nation.[25]

But while conventional soap operas of the era tended to blame society's problems on dysfunctional relationships, the AFL's serial focused on the psychological impact of economic insecurity. In the second series of *The Best Things in Life*, entitled "Nothing to Fear," an ex-Marine named Jim Richards chafes bitterly at his inability to meet the household bills because of rising prices. He worries constantly about supporting his family and the uncertainty of the future. He is angry at business "for squeezing profits right and left" and for attempting to "smash organized labor" and thus "force down wages to make still more profits!" The depressed veteran laments that "after losing four years of my life in the war . . . to come back to this! It takes the heart clean out of you." A sense of isolation intensifies Jim's despair as he remembers with nostalgia that in the Marine Corps he had the feeling of belonging—of fighting an enemy together. Now, for Jim, "It's like fighting in the dark. You can't get your hands on him. And besides, you're fighting alone." Overwhelmed by his worries, Jim is tired and has little energy for his bright, sweet, seven-year-old son, Petey. He quarrels with his wife Sally over grocery bills, and she is shocked and frightened when she realizes that her husband seems overwhelmed by the social forces threatening to destroy him and his family. Finding that Petey has overheard their quarreling, Sally is deeply concerned about their son's sense of well-being and security as well.

The drama reaches a climax when the worried but stalwart seven-year-old decides to resolve the family's financial woes by going on his own to the bank for money, but he becomes lost and wanders in the streets in the midst of a thunderstorm. After a frantic search, Charlie Case, one of Jim's co-workers, discovers Petey, now sick from exposure. Charlie, a union activist, and Petey's doctor urge Jim to fight his sense of helplessness and isolation and to enlist in the collective struggle being waged by organized labor to restore every American family's sense of security. "Don't try to conceal that there are things wrong in the world," advises the doctor. "But let Petey know that you are fighting to put them right." Charlie urges Jim to start attending local meetings: "We're out to beat those anti-labor bills up before Congress. That means work . . . resolutions, petitions." The episode ends with a more optimistic Jim vowing to take an interest in the union struggle against Taft-Hartley. In the last scene, Jim tucks Petey into bed with the story of a Marine who was lost in a very dark tunnel. He "couldn't find his way out anywhere, till he finally saw a little ray of light," which he followed and found a procession "made up of almost all the people in this whole country." The scene ends at that point, but the announcer urges the audience to join in the procession: "You and your neighbors and friends—all of us must join together in one great swelling chorus which will be heard!"[26]

In the series "A Woman's Place," financial troubles create an even more desperate situation. Joe and Ellen Kierney had been a happy, loving couple with a young son and infant daughter, but Joe is changing, and the life that Ellen had built is crumbling around her. Like Jim Richards, Joe is a veteran with a good union job, but he is increasingly on edge, fighting with his wife over bills and alternately ignoring or hitting his eight-year-old son. Joe's problems stem less from maladjustment to civilian life than from economic stress due to the increased cost of living. Once price controls were lifted, the money they had set aside for Johnny's education went into household expenses, and their standard of living had declined. A sick baby who requires expensive medical attention puts further strain on the family's resources. Though he is working steadily, Joe's hopes of participating in the new consumerist ethos promoted by business evaporate. High prices keep him from buying his wife a washing machine or even considering replacing his old jalopy with one of the new cars that he helps build. Moreover, there is little hope of controlling prices or raising wages because an indifferent public believes the corporate propaganda that blames organized labor for inflation.

The crisis in the family arrives when Joe Kierney returns home from the plant one day to learn that Ellen, without his knowledge, has taken their sickly baby daughter to a free clinic for treatment. Enraged and accusing Ellen of advertising to their friends that he can not support his family, Joe shouts that they ought to put the baby up for adoption, slaps his wife, and storms out of the house. Ellen's mother, who is visiting, urges her to leave her husband, declaring, "When a man starts beating his wife it's time to forget him." Convinced that Joe was overwrought and did not mean to hit her, but aware that Johnny is now afraid of his father, Ellen is torn between helping her husband and protecting her children. Trying to reassure her son, she insists that Joe is "not mean or cruel . . . just terribly, terribly unhappy" because he has been robbed of his self-respect.

Ellen finally decides to send her children off with her mother, while she waits at home to face Joe. Her concern for his well-being is intensified when Joe's shop steward, Bill Lipson, stops by and reveals that the company doctor has found that Joe, who had internalized his anxiety about his family's financial situation, has developed ulcers. After six hours of walking the streets, Joe returns home to ask his wife's forgiveness for his violent outburst. While sympathetic about his sense of inadequacy, she observes that he is not "the only man in this kind of jam . . . but maybe other guys don't sit around and stew about it." She chastises him for keeping his health problems secret, observing that their keeping secrets was symptomatic of the problems in their marriage. Finally, Ellen screws up her courage and announces that she is leaving Joe because she has grown afraid of him and because the "family hasn't been making you happy." An angry Joe demands, "Haven't I been a good husband? Do I kick you around—do I go and spend half my pay on dames or drinks? What've you got be afraid of?" At the climax of the episode, Joe admits that he has been afraid and connects the family's problems to the nation's indifference to the attack on labor.

> I've been working for 20 years—I remember what things were like before labor got a decent Bill so we could organize and bargain for wages so a man could give his family a few of the good things of life. Now take a look at what's happening in Washington. Men like Hartley and Taft want to throw working-men back 50 years. Those great big ads big business puts in the papers—all the power and money of those big boys is undermining the faith of the public in collective bargaining. Sure I'm scared silly—why wouldn't I be?

The series ends with the conflict between Ellen and Joe resolved as they promise to give each other another chance and to address their personal fears by becoming engaged in the political struggle against Taft-Hartley. At the very end, symbolically linking labor's struggle to the New Deal, Ellen declares, "I guess there are no truer words—'the only thing we need to fear, is fear itself.'"[27]

One element of the AFL's productions that stood in stark contrast to the conventions of variety shows and soap operas was the actors' open and proud identification with organized labor. To kick off the first of the Thursday-evening variety shows, the DeMarco Sisters paged "Mister Public," playing upon their opening of the popular Fred Allen program, and a voice responded, "It isn't the NAM, kiddies." Emcee Bert Parks introduced himself and added, "I hold union card 16780 in the American Federation of Radio Artists." Similarly, each episode of the soap opera began with the stars identifying themselves as union members and giving their card numbers. In one variety show, Edward G. Robinson stepped out of character and spoke directly to the audience. "As a union member and citizen," he asserted, "this bill can be stopped if President Truman vetoes it. And the president will veto it if we the people—all of us—make him know we want him to." Morris Novik hoped that defining all union members as workers with common interests would help overcome the anti-union sentiment that coursed through much of American society. Identifying the stars with unions would encourage the "ordinary listener who is at times even ashamed that his father or her husband is a member of the union" to be proud of their union connection.[28]

The AFL's campaign against Taft-Hartley received many rave reviews. Not surprisingly, John McManus, the radio columnist for the liberal/leftist newspaper *PM*, praised the AFL's programs, declaring its soap opera the "most urgent serial" on the air. Less partisan *Billboard* and *Variety* reviewers were impressed with the quality and effectiveness of the labor shows. The first variety-show segment "delivered a potent message on trade unionism," said the *Billboard* reviewer, and the open and hidden commercials against Taft-Hartley "were done in a humorous ingratiating manner." The *Variety* reviewer wrote that the Milton Berle–Henry Morgan comedy skit, along with the singing of the DeMarco Sisters and the Arthur Miller sketch, "had all the elements that make for a prize entertainment package." *Billboard* applauded *The Best Things in Life*, noting that it achieved "far more interest and impact than average soapers." Furthermore, the commercials were powerful, full of "forthright talk" about the "group cleavages within the country." *Variety* praised the labor serial's realism in comparison to the "routinized pap" of normal afternoon fare, judging it "more probing to the nerve tissue of human personality, more complex in its definition of the common man's problem, and less afraid to educate by shock rather than by saccharine."[29]

Others, however, condemned the AFL shows, charging that they were heavy-handed and inappropriate. The *New York Times* radio columnist Jack Gould criticized the shows for jamming propaganda "down the listener's throat" in the "guise of sugar-coated entertainment." The AFL, he concluded, had ill served labor's cause by "cheapening its position through recourse to the worst features of hucksterism." Similarly, the *New Republic* reported that even some liberals believed that labor had acted with "juvenile thoughtlessness" by using soap operas and variety shows to promote a serious political issue. They worried that unions were now guilty of breaking the "bars of radio's 'impartiality.'" The AFL responded that it was only matching the expensive entertainment programs that business had used to promote its philosophy.[30]

Surviving letters and postcards from listeners reflect the divided reception that the campaign received from professional critics. Charles and Shirley Vinning of Newark, Ohio, were among those praising the variety show. "God bless you for not being afraid to speak out for labor. We're not a communist, not a religious fanatic, but just working folks and proud of it." Mrs. Vitsilakes of Brooklyn wrote, "Bravo, Bravo! Bravo! The program was wonderful!" She thanked the actors and artists who were helping to awaken Americans to the "monstrous dangers which threaten working people and our unions." Other listeners were pleased that labor finally had a chance to speak and reported that they had sent letters to their congressional representatives and the president. The soap operas evoked a strong response among some women for whom they were a relief from the "inane and insipid day time serials." Arline J. Baum of Hartford, Connecticut, sent her congratulations to the cast and crew of the *The Best Things in Life* for "giving us women an intelligent afternoon radio program." For Lorena Keefe of Trenton, New Jersey, Joe and Ellen Kierney's story struck close to home. She wrote that the "entire story was identically the outline of my twenty-three years of trying in vain to keep my home together. Unfortunately today I am one of those parents, particularly mothers, who has been all through each and every step in the story. Today I am certain the exact incidents have been the cause for our home having been broken." Lorena continued that she, too, had "lived in fear because my husband lived a life of fright."[31]

Other listeners, many of whom were already angry at labor for the strikes in the immediate aftermath of the war, were not touched, enlightened, or entertained by the AFL's programs. According to D. A. Lindsay of New Jersey, the variety show was "unadulterated bunk" that should have been preceded by the announcement, "Written by imbeciles for the entertainment of morons." Edith Lockard of Mushofee, Oklahoma, complained to the AFL that its "vicious propaganda program" cluttered the air just as "unions have cluttered our lives and safety" through their strikes. Hostile listeners described the soap operas as "full of half-truths and deliberate falsehood." One episode from the first installment was enough to turn Norman Nash's stomach. He complained that of "all the unadulterated pap that has poured out of the country's radio, your story ranks as the worst." Similarly, an angry Mrs. E. Dasch of Colfax, Washington, scolded the AFL for attempting to "twist the straight thinking of the people with your not-so-subtle propaganda." She declared that unions, which denied citizens the right to work, corrupted elections, were contemptuous of law and authority, and sought to destroy the free enterprise system, had become a greater menace to the nation than any business monopoly. For some of these listeners, the programs had an unintended impact, inspiring them to write to their political leaders in support of Taft-Hartley. Morris Novik's effort to identify actors with workers also backfired with listeners like Donald Shoemaker of Detroit, who wrote, "These high pay brackets radio stars presenting themselves as 'working people' was particularly nauseating."[32]

Despite top stars and heavy production budgets, the AFL-sponsored shows failed to draw large audiences. The national Hooper ratings were low, with the soap opera pulling a 1.5 and the Thursday-evening variety show a 2.9. In comparison, Proctor and Gamble's serial, "Guiding Light," averaged 5.7, and Philco Radio's Bing Crosby show averaged 16.8. But *Variety* reported that AFL leaders were satisfied with the campaign's results, believing that the programming had helped generate a powerful public response. During the ten days in June when Truman considered vetoing the Taft-Hartley bill, over 845,000 telegrams, postcards, and letters poured into the White House. An informal survey showed that the bulk of communications appeared in response to the radio shows. Truman vetoed the bill, but within days Congress voted to override the veto.[33] Labor's first big venture in network commercial radio failed to halt the Taft-Hartley Act.

❖ ❖ ❖

Unionists who believed in the power of the mass media to shape ideology, however, kept at it. The United Electrical Workers Union had been appalled at the firing of liberal commentators after the end of World War II and became convinced that labor needed to directly answer conservative commentators who had helped create the sentiment that led to Taft-Hartley. From mid-1947 to early 1950, the UE sponsored a series of weekly news commentaries over the Mutual Network at the cost of $250,000 per year. Leland Stowe and then Arthur Gaeth interpreted the news with a progressive left-wing slant. Gaeth, for instance, supported the 1948 presidential campaign of Henry Wallace and deplored the growing cold war at home and abroad. He appealed for more conciliatory attitudes towards the Soviet Union and warned that the fear and hysteria associated with anti-Communism had led Americans to "accept an invasion of civil liberty," which, if continued, could only "produce a police state." Gaeth dramatized the housing woes of workers and sympathetically covered strikes. During the 1948 packinghouse workers strike, he provided a vivid description of Kansas City police stoning workers and breaking into and smashing their union headquarters. He routinely focused on African Americans' struggle against discrimination and racial violence. In February 1949 the UE commentator related the story of Isaiah Nixon's murder when attempting to vote in Georgia, and he exposed discriminatory hiring in the Detroit automobile industry. But the financial burden caused by the UE's own participation in the labor movement's internal war against Communism forced it to abandon its program in January 1950. The *New Republic* lamented that the "CIO's Right-Left split has knocked Gaeth off his Monday-night perch on the ABC network."[34]

In the summer of 1947, encouraged by Morris Novik, the AFL built on the Taft-Hartley campaign and vowed to make more extensive use of the mass media. After several false starts, the federation moved away from the idea of mixing entertainment with pro-union messages and settled on sponsoring a news show. Its goal was "to provide intelligent interpretation of the news from a liberal point of view." The AFL's "Frank Edwards Show" began in

January 1950 and aired five nights a week over 176 stations at ten P.M. at the cost of $750,000 per year. It originated in the same month that the UE pulled the plug on Arthur Gaeth.[35]

By early 1953 the CIO had joined the AFL in committing significant financial resources to a network radio program. After the radio enthusiast Walter Reuther assumed the presidency of the CIO in late 1952, he urged the adoption of an ambitious public relations program that centered on broadcasting. The Republican 1952 election victory and the CIO's continuing difficulties in organizing in the South convinced Reuther that the CIO needed to step up efforts to change the climate of opinion in the nation and improve the public image of labor. While he believed that labor needed to use both "highways of the air" to reach people in their homes, available airtime on the new medium of television was limited and costly. Moreover, although television had captured the imagination of many Americans and was potentially a tremendous educational force, radio was still "alive and kicking." It remained the primary form of mass media and the major source of news for much of the public. Not only were television sets expensive, but by 1953 there were only 108 stations broadcasting, leaving many Americans without access. In 1953, forty-six million homes had radios, while eighteen million had televisions. Given these factors, the CIO decided to pin its broadcasting hopes on radio. Impressed that the AFL's show gave it a "terrific shot in the arm," the CIO appropriated one million dollars for a public relations program, featuring a fifteen-minute daily news commentary by the progressive journalist John W. Vandercook. This was a major investment for the CIO, representing 20 percent of the organization's annual receipts. But Reuther believed that the venture paid immediate dividends. Within six months, the CIO boasted that Vandercook attracted equal or larger audiences than the conservative Fulton Lewis Jr. in thirteen of thirty-six surveyed cities.[36]

Broadcast over 150 ABC stations at seven in the evening, the CIO show sought to offset the antilabor propaganda that inundated the media and to spread the messages of the labor movement and democratic liberalism. The CIO hoped to convince Americans that labor was not another selfish interest group but instead that it sought "solutions to the problems of all the people." Although the CIO hoped eventually to reach large numbers of people outside the labor movement, cost considerations meant that it tended to place the show in areas where its membership was strongest or in regions targeted for organizing. For example, nine stations in Alabama and ten stations in Georgia carried Vandercook. Perhaps naively, Reuther believed that if southerners heard "straight" instead of biased news, the CIO could overcome anti-union sentiment. Seeking to strengthen its political influence and enlist the support of farmers, the CIO also selected stations such as KXEL in Waterloo, Iowa, that reached rural audiences. After the merger of the AFL and CIO in 1955, the new organization maintained both radio shows but cut Vandercook's broadcast to five minutes, a demonstration of the AFL's superior strength.[37]

The Edwards show (and that of his successor, Edward P. Morgan) opened with the statement that it was sponsored by eight million members of the AFL. Commercials on the AFL and CIO shows aimed to demonstrate that "unions don't have horns" and to identify organized labor with Americanism. While the business version of Americanism emphasized individualism, the union version stressed the "common good," with a focus on social justice and economic security for all. Thus labor's commercials ranged from public service announcements for the Red Cross or local community chests to statements about labor's ideology, emphasizing, for instance, the CIO's commitment to racial equality and democracy. The AFL and CIO commercials emphasized labor's long history of support for free public schools and economic justice, especially its fight for the abolition of child labor, the shorter work week, better wages and working conditions, and health insurance and pensions. Other commercials emphasized unions as citizens and neighbors. Stories of labor's public service recounted how sixty members of the painters union from a variety of faiths volunteered on weekends to redecorate a Chicago synagogue and how members of the building trades unions battled a flood that threatened Tulsa, Oklahoma.[38]

As charges of union corruption intensified in the mid- to late-1950s, the commercials stressed labor's legitimate role in American society. Big business, the AFL contended in 1955, exerted powerful pressure for its own interests, and organized labor provided a critical counterbalance. "Day in and day out," the AFL assured its listeners, "the man on the street has no better friend in America than the trade union movement." Unlike business, organized labor is dedicated to serving the "interests of all the American people" and to combating the forces that seek to "undermine the democratic institutions of our nation and to enslave the human soul."[39]

The programs' commercials also allowed labor to address current economic and political issues. In 1958, they discussed right-to-work laws, contested the charge that inflation is caused by wage increases, and urged support for bills increasing Social Security payments, expanding the coverage of the minimum wage, and establishing a health care program for the elderly. Ads often encouraged listeners to lobby for these measures by writing to their legislators. In early January the AFL-CIO sought to enlist the audience's support for retail workers fighting for democracy on the job. The commercial pointed out that most retail workers labored long hours at low wages, without insurance or pensions, in contrast to the benefits and protections won by industrial workers through collective bargaining. "We in the AFL-CIO," the announcer declared, "think they have a right to decent wages, sensible hours, and other benefits. Most of all, we think they must have a voice in determining their own economic future."[40]

As for the program content, the labor shows featured a mixture of commentary and straight news reporting. Certainly the commentary of Edwards, his successor Edward Morgan, and Vandercook was more politically moderate than the UE's Gaeth, particularly on foreign policy issues. Nevertheless, throughout the 1950s, they all provided sharp critiques of the Republican administration and the business community. Labor's news commentators exposed violations of civil liberties and brought to public attention union struggles ignored or distorted by the mass media. In 1953, for instance, Vandercook criticized the Eisenhower administration's support of a national sales tax and argued that its policies towards organized labor proved that government was now being "run by big business." He charged that the federal firings of security risks without explanation constituted "one of the worst blackouts of legitimate news in recent history." Typical Morgan broadcasts in 1959 publicized the plight of agricultural labor and migrant workers.[41]

Labor's national commentators strongly supported the emerging civil rights movement. Edward P. Morgan had a close relationship with the Southern Regional Council, a civil rights advocacy group. In his commentary, he condemned the White Citizens' Councils, and after the Brown decision he urged Eisenhower to push for rapid desegregation of public schools. Morgan was one of the first network journalists to support the Montgomery bus boycott, observing that the protest sprang "from the innards of some of the gentlest souls God ever fashioned, to choose their own seat on a municipal bus, to travel afoot or on horseback, in a Cadillac convertible or to stay at home."[42] Morgan also regularly scolded organized labor for its racism. For instance, in October 1955, he admonished a group of rubber workers in Waco, Texas, who did the cause of labor "no credit" in calling a wildcat strike to protest the assigning of a black worker to a previously all-white department. The following year Morgan took to task southern trade unionists who had joined the White Citizens' Councils, pointing out that the councils included business leaders whose desire to suppress black rights was "matched by their strenuous efforts to suppress labor's right to organize and bargain."[43]

Morgan's staunch support of civil rights evoked strong responses from some listeners. In February 1956, Cleveland Jones of the Mount Zion Baptist church in Anniston, Alabama, thanked Morgan for his excellent coverage of the Montgomery bus boycott. "You appear," Jones observed, "to have a complete appreciation for our struggle here in Alabama, and in the 'Deep South.'" Other listeners were less grateful for Morgan's advocacy of civil rights. V. R. Bowman of Berkeley, California, tired of hearing Morgan's "sob-sister stuff about school integration." He stated that labor should stay away from civil rights: "[W]e have got enough problems of our own without getting mixed up with integration of the races." A Texas listener was even more blunt in his criticism, asserting that Morgan was "desirous of destroying the white race by mixing it with the black race so that this country will eventually become a land of a mongrel race and mulatto, neither white nor black."[44]

❖ ❖ ❖

While all three commentators strongly supported labor and liberalism, there were some significant differences in their approaches to broadcasting. Frank Edwards, the AFL's first commentator, adopted a colorful radio style and a crusading spirit for progressive objectives. He was also the most controversial of the labor commentators. Hailing from Indianapolis, where his local labor commentary had aired immediately after Fulton Lewis Jr.'s, his consistent espousal of liberal causes stood in sharp contrast with Lewis's conservatism and won him large audiences among unionists, who appreciated his aggressive campaign against Taft-Hartley. Indiana labor leaders lobbied hard for Edwards's appointment as the AFL's commentator. Edwards sought to speak to "common, everyday Americans" and took pride in digging for the "story behind the story." As the AFL commentator, he never feared swinging the axe at employers or at the Eisenhower administration, which he breezily tagged the "happiness boys" or the "grabbag boys." He was so tough on Republicans that some labor leaders wondered how the AFL could expect any cooperation from Republican congressional leaders in advancing labor's legislative agenda "if we are fighting them on the radio every night." Edwards won praise from some media critics, who found his hard-hitting commentary "forthright" and "intelligent, liberal, and informed," but others condemned his aggressiveness. *Time* noted that he "usually sounds willing to punch anyone who disagrees with him."[45]

Edwards had an immediate impact. Six months after he was hired by the AFL, an independent survey conducted by Mutual Research found that, with thirteen million listeners, Edwards was pulling a significantly larger

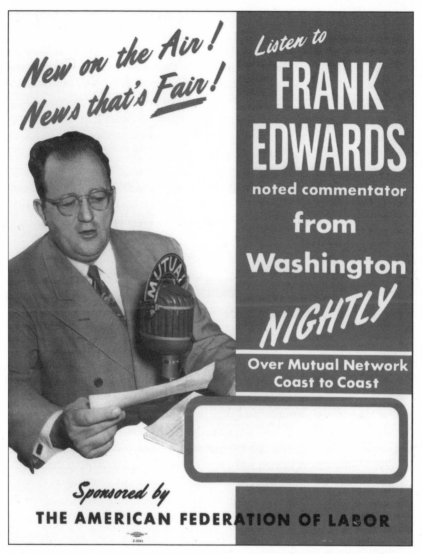

New on the Air!
News that's Fair!

Listen to
FRANK EDWARDS
noted commentator

from

Washington

NIGHTLY

**Over Mutual Network
Coast to Coast**

Sponsored by
THE AMERICAN FEDERATION OF LABOR

From 1950 to 1954, Frank Edwards served as the AFL's popular yet controversial national commentator. ILGWU Papers, Kheel Labor Management Documentation Center, Cornell University; courtesy of UNITE HERE.

share of the audience than Fulton Lewis Jr. Only Edward R. Murrow and Lowell Thomas topped his popularity, according to *Motion Picture Daily.* Up to a thousand listeners wrote to him each week, and his special offers, such as pamphlets listing the voting records of legislators, generated up to fifty thousand requests. When Edwards asked listeners to send postcards to a nine-year-old Kentucky boy dying of a rare blood disease, three hundred thousand responded.[46] In early 1950, he helped pry loose U.S. surplus food for distribution to distressed areas, and he mobilized public opinion against the Kerr bill, which would have removed federal control from the natural gas industry. Leaders in troubled communities were so impressed with Edwards's influence that they begged him to come visit with the hope of gaining the nation's attention to their needs. Kansas City, Kansas, for instance, asked Edwards to make an inspection tour and report on damage from a recent flood. Afterwards, the Chamber of Commerce thanked the AFL for its support and praised Edwards's "eloquence in describing our problems." Wilkes-Barre, Pennsylvania, was struggling with a different kind of disaster: widespread unemployment. In April 1951 the Central Labor Union pleaded with AFL president William Green to send Edwards to their community, hoping that the resulting publicity might bring new industries and jobs. According to the local union leader Leon Decker, Edwards's "help was the spark that was needed to set our course toward the solving of our community problems."[47]

Many listeners, including members of the middle and professional classes, shared Decker's enthusiasm for Edwards's commentary. According to Monroe Sweetland, a Democratic National Committeeman in Oregon, Edwards's broadcasts countered reactionary commentators and had become the "principal radio source of factual information and liberal interpretation." The Rural Electrification Administrator Claude R. Wickard applauded Edwards for exposing the South Carolina Electric and Gas Company's campaign of "untruths and misrepresentation" and observed that he brought facts to the public that "often do not reach them in the press." An attorney, Lester Collins, wrote that he and his wife never missed an Edwards broadcast. "He is the only commentator on the air who now represents labor and the liberal elements left in the U.S. His fight on the off-shore oil lands alone has been and will be worth millions of dollars to the American people; just to think that there is still someone on the air who speaks for the people and not the corporations is a great service."[48]

But Edwards's strongest support came from unionized workers. Desiring to share the benefits of his broadcast, numerous central labor bodies asked that their local stations be added to the list of those carrying the show. The UAW's FM stations proudly broadcast the AFL commentator, and Edwards's success inspired the UAW and CIO to sponsor their own commentators, Guy Nunn and John W. Vandercook. In 1952 California machinists reported that Edwards's "fearless" exposés were "tremendously popular with working people" throughout the state. Carpenters in Anchorage, Alaska, characterized Edwards as "truly a great voice for labor," and the AFL unionist Fred Bugby of Los Angeles urged that his broadcasts be increased to twice a day to further fight the "mercenary, unscrupulous Jackals" in Washington, D.C., who were "looting and pillaging without hardly a voice raised against them." According to a Pennsylvania unionist, "[M]embers have become more union-minded and more impressed with the solidarity of labor, through listening to the Frank Edwards program," and in Minnesota one railway officer observed that Edwards reached beyond union activists and liberals to help legitimize unions for farmers and workers who some assumed were Republicans.[49]

Frank Edwards had many admirers, but he also annoyed quite a few listeners, including some in the labor movement. Don Connery of *Time* magazine believed that Edwards badly needed some "good-sense and good-taste," and James R. Jones of Glenside, Pennsylvania, found that Edwards's constant knocking of big business and soft pedaling of strikes gave him a *"pain."* Dr. S. H. Wetzler of Milwaukee denounced Edwards for disseminating and fomenting "hate, dissension, and dissatisfaction," and the former FCC general counsel Walter B. Stiles asked the FCC chairman why the commission did not halt Edwards's "crucifixions of public servants."[50]

More troubling to the AFL, however, were his journalistic flights into the realm of fantasy, including reports on flying saucers and cancer cures. AFL officers also objected to his positions on foreign affairs and even his tough stance on industry. In September 1950, for instance, the Amalgamated Meat Cutters and Butcher Workmen took exception to an Edwards broadcast blaming the A&P Company for high grocery prices. According to the union president, Earl W. Jimerson, A&P was a unionized firm that paid high wages and provided good benefits; Edwards should be urging workers to vote in the upcoming election "instead of attacking decent employers."[51]

Edwards never had uniform support from the AFL's Executive Council. Morris Novik, the federation's radio consultant, was no fan of the commentator, whom he viewed as a sensationalist. To gain greater control over the show, the AFL assigned an editor to work with Edwards and considered canceling his contract, but a wave of protest kept him on the air. Finally, in August 1954, the federation fired him, replacing him briefly with the AFL publicist Harry Flannery and then with Edward P. Morgan. Publicly, AFL president George Meany asserted that the AFL dropped Edwards because he failed to draw a line between news and opinion and because his obsession with flying saucers was embarrassing to the labor movement. Union members protested the firing, but to no avail.[52]

Neither Morgan nor the CIO's Vandercook were as flamboyant or as controversial as Edwards. Vandercook was a veteran newspaper journalist who joined the NBC news staff in 1939 and broadcast from European battlefields during the war. Although he was one of the network's most popular commentators, Vandercook was among the liberals knocked off the air after World War II. Listeners of his CIO show praised the "sparkle and punch" of his delivery and welcomed his liberal perspective. Helen Fahey of Van Nuys, California, felt that "messages of intolerance" and "seemingly deliberate distortion of the news" from commentators like Fulton Lewis Jr., George Solkosky, and Henry J. Taylor made it "imperative that men of Mr. Vandercook's integrity and knowledge" be heard. John O'Donnell thanked Vandercook for being "one of the few commentators with the courage to face the wrath of McCarthy . . . and his pathetic and, worse, fanatic mob of followers." Don Kehoe, who was a young college student when Vandercook took to the air in 1953, was a devoted listener. He recalled that he was impressed with how courageously Vandercook took on McCarthy, "without any compromise."[53]

Like Vandercook, Edward P. Morgan was a respected veteran network reporter. Morgan, who came to the AFL from CBS, emerged as one of the most prominent voices of liberalism in his twelve years as the voice of the AFL. In his first broadcast, he advised listeners that he was particularly pleased about having a sponsor who was "not allergic to the word 'liberal'" or thought the label "an obscenity." Morgan won praise for presenting news "cooly and articulately" and for commentaries that were "liberal and literate" as well as "incisive, sane, courageous, and—when they can be—humorous."[54] Listeners were also impressed with Morgan's freedom to criticize organized labor. Aware of the AFL's conflict with Frank Edwards, Morgan insisted that he be employed by ABC, the network broadcasting the AFL show, and that the federation abide by a policy of noninterference. Morgan took pride in his independence and ability to criticize his sponsor and was unafraid of sharing with listeners his "frustration and dismay at the sometimes narrow, self-seeking tendencies of the labor movement." At least publicly, the AFL asserted that it was proud of Morgan's freedom of expression and that it never attempted to influence the content of his broadcasts. According to Al Zack, head of the Public Relations Department, when Morgan scolded labor, "all

CIO ON RADIO

John W. Vandercook

and the News

EVERY MONDAY
THRU FRIDAY
on
ABC Network

Station: _ _ _ _

_ _ _ On your dial

Time: _ _ _ _ _

Impressed with Frank Edwards's success, in 1953 the CIO began sponsoring the veteran liberal news commentator John W. Vandercook. Southern Labor Archives, Georgia State University; courtesy of the AFL-CIO.

we can do is gulp." But at least one high-level union official complained, "I don't mind his being critical. But does he have to hate us?"[55]

Morgan, with his calm, dispassionate style, stood in sharp contrast to Edwards. There was no sensationalism in his show, no scoops, exclusives, or appeals to the audience. He carefully separated his news report from his commentary. Morgan was described by one listener as "well trained in the art of shooting down the precise middle." Reviewers characterized the program, which over a decade won numerous broadcasting awards, as less partisan and "less of a propaganda piece" than its predecessor. While some unionists acknowledged that Morgan was fair to unions, others missed Edwards's "fire" and wanted a program that was more openly "pro-labor." Some middle-class listeners argued that Morgan's show was more effective because it was not "offensively pro-labor." They contended that he was winning new friends for the AFL-CIO. One listener argued that Morgan was "breaking down prejudice." She noted that "people who would tune out" strident commentators

In 1954, Edward P. Morgan replaced Frank Edwards as the AFL's news commentator. A respected veteran network reporter, he served as the voice of the AFL-CIO until 1966. Courtesy of the George Meany Memorial Archives, Silver Spring, Md.

"listen to Morgan with respect, and I can witness to their changing attitude toward Labor." Another audience member wrote that Morgan counteracted many citizens' fears about "dictatorship in Labor." A California listener reported that since becoming a regular listener, "I have become almost tolerant, certainly more open-minded about unions in general."[56]

❖ ❖ ❖

Of course, labor programs rankled the business community and conservatives. *Business Week,* for instance, charged Edwards with "merchandising verbal poison," and the National Association of Manufacturers and the Chamber of Commerce called the AFL commentator a "hate monger." To refute Edwards, employers in Utah hired the former CBS newscaster Paul Sullivan to give industry's side of the news immediately after labor's broadcast. Similarly, General Motors sought radio time in Detroit right after Guy Nunn's UAW morning program to broadcast "Truth in News," which the autoworkers sarcastically tagged "the gospel according to Du Pont." Vandercook also worried business. Employers in Tennessee objected when CIO unionists posted flyers in the plants publicizing his show.[57] In the fall of 1953, shortly after Vandercook began broadcasting, the Iron and Steel Institute hired Hill and Knowlton, the nation's foremost public relations firm, to provide a weekly digest of his daily newscasts. Two years later, a gleeful Walter Reuther reported to the CIO Executive Boards that corporations had made at least twenty surveys of the program to judge its effectiveness. Similarly, the NAM kept close watch on union broadcasts.[58]

Labor programs so irritated business and conservatives that in some communities they pressured stations to remove the shows. Meanwhile, stations owned by conservatives sometimes refused to accept the broadcasts. In 1947, Pacific Gas and Electric, a major power company in California, campaigned to drive Sidney Rogers, the CIO's commentator in San Francisco, off the air, and in 1950 Chrysler tried to pressure CKLW to cancel Guy Nunn's evening commentary. Industrialists in Pottstown, Pennsylvania, did everything in their power to persuade the owner of WPAZ to cancel the UAW's morning show, "Eye Opener." When the UAW decided to end the program, the local conservative newspaper crowed that it was because of business pressure that the show was taken off the air. In Birmingham, Alabama, the mayor was so angry at an Edward P. Morgan broadcast condemning segregated facilities at the local airport that he demanded that WBRC cancel the show, silencing the "one voice of dissent" in the media available to Birmingham citizens.[59]

The strongest effort to silence the labor movement's media voice occurred in Michigan, where the UAW had a powerful presence on radio and television in the 1950s. Walter Reuther considered communicating with members to be one of the union's most serious problems and believed that radio and television were the most effective means of reaching the membership.[60] Under his leadership, the autoworkers developed an innovative, ambitious, and wide-ranging media program, much of it directed by Guy Nunn. At first, the UAW's broadcasting efforts focused primarily on promoting local union shows and its short-lived FM stations. Then, in the midst of the 1950 Chrysler strike, Nunn went on the air in Detroit with a nightly program of news, analysis, and interviews over WDET and the powerful AM station CKLW. By 1954, listener surveys indicated that "Labor Views the News" had an audience of close to half a million, which included significant numbers of middle-class listeners. Eighteen months after launching its evening radio commentary, the union began a weekly half-hour television program hosted by Nunn on WWJ-TV in Detroit. Oriented to broad community appeal, "Meet the UAW-CIO" presented a wide variety of political and economic subjects, ranging from the need for increased taxes for public schools to workman's compensation and bargaining and strike updates. Films depicting the union's recreational activities, its children's summer camp, its adult summer schools, and its retiree program brought to members and the general public a broader picture of the UAW's services and activities. Under various titles and shifting formats, the show was on the air for twelve years, mostly on Sunday afternoon. The union also sponsored special television programs. For a month before the 1954 election, for instance, the UAW broadcast a daily half-hour television program at noon to stimulate the interest of members and their families, retirees, and the unemployed in the political campaign. It featured appearances by Michigan Governor G. Memmen Williams, Patrick V. McNamara, who was in a tight congressional race against Republican Homer Ferguson, and almost all the other PAC-endorsed candidates for Congress. Williams was reelected by a large majority, and McNamara's win helped restore Democratic control of Congress.[61]

In April 1954, "Eye Opener," an innovative early-morning show, hit the airwaves in Detroit. Recognizing the emergence of new listening patterns as more automobiles were equipped with radio, "Eye Opener" targeted male commuters but also sought to attract wives who arose early to help husbands get off to work. Hosted by Guy Nunn and his partner, Joe Walsh, "Eye Opener" greeted bleary-eyed autoworkers driving to the plant at 6:15 in the morning with a cheery, "Hi there, Early Birds!" More informal than the UAW's other broadcasts, a typical show kept listeners up to date on the

Guy Nunn interviewing UAW president Walter Reuther on the UAW's popular drive-time morning radio show, "Eye Opener." *Sponsor,* Apr. 2, 1956.

news and union affairs and on key political developments on the community, state, and national levels. Time checks, music, sports updates, consumer tips, comedy skits, and jokes and banter between the hosts helped maintain a light atmosphere. At the same time, the union regularly inserted political, economic, and social messages, raising issues such as equal pay for women and corporate control over the media. Civil rights was another important theme emphasized by "Eye Opener." The program closely followed the Emmet Till case in the fall of 1955, with the UAW's education director, Brendan Sexton, a frequent guest on the show, observing that "justice has been mocked in Mississippi under the guise of law enforcement."[62]

Many autoworkers were devoted listeners of "Eye Opener." In 1955, General Motors checked six thousand cars in one of its plant's parking lots and found that half were tuned to the program. Listeners praised the show for "giving us the kind of news none of the other stations ever touched." The former UAW president Douglas Fraser recalled that Guy Nunn, with his "sharp tongue" and sarcastic, abrasive tone, was "our advocate" and was very popular among the membership. According to Fraser, "managers hated him," but "activists loved him." Impressed with the show's effectiveness and popularity, the UAW expanded the program's geographic coverage to reach all the major concentrations of autoworkers. By 1957, it was carried on forty stations, with cutout time provided for local union participation. That year the UAW eliminated Nunn's evening commentary show but substituted "Shift Break," a version designed to reach workers on the afternoon shift.[63]

A focus on politics coursed through all the UAW broadcasts. They featured appearances by politicians endorsed by the autoworkers. Although Nunn invited Republicans to participate in the panel programs, few accepted the offer. According to Nunn, "[T]hey seem to think we might ask a few loaded questions." The UAW programs openly advocated for the Democratic party and liberal causes, and Guy Nunn's sharp and stinging news commentaries "drove almost every Republican politician in Michigan to despair." During a typical "Labor Views the News" commentary in 1956, Nunn accused the Eisenhower administration of favoritism to business and cronyism. In a tone dripping with sarcasm, Nunn observed that if there was "one major figure in the Eisenhower administration who does not come from a specially favored class, business and big business at that, it has been a vastly kept secret." Democratic political candidates routinely credited their appearances on the UAW broadcasts and telecasts as decisive factors in their winning elections.[64]

Angry Republicans were determined to quash the UAW's media politics. They complained to the FCC and had Reuther, Nunn, and UAW secretary-treasurer Emil Mazey hauled before congressional committees to justify the UAW's political uses of radio. Senator Barry Goldwater charged that Nunn's evening commentary show was "vindictive and dangerous." After the 1954 congressional elections, when PAC candidates swept into office in Michigan, the frustrated state Republican leaders John Feikens and Arthur Summerfield demanded that the Justice Department investigate the UAW's use of dues for political activity. They pointed specifically to the union's partisan television and radio programs, which they argued violated Taft-Hartley Act provisions against union contributions to political parties. Guy Nunn replied that the "GOP, you see, isn't satisfied with having every daily paper (but one) in the entire state on its side—or owning the majority of commentators on the radio. They believe in the two party system so strongly that they want to close down virtually the only programs in the state that aren't full of Republican propaganda."[65]

In July 1955, a federal grand jury indicted the UAW on charges of violating the Federal Corrupt Practices provision of Taft-Hartley by using television and radio to support Democratic candidates in the 1954 primary and general elections. The UAW declared that it welcomed the GOP-inspired probe of its political activities and viewed the attack as an indication that its use of media had effectively reached workers and the public. To Reuther, the indictment was part of a campaign on the part of "reactionary and conservative political forces generally, to disfranchise the American labor movement and to disfranchise the people whom the American labor movement speaks for."[66] After a series of legal maneuvers and court decisions, in October 1957, the UAW went on trial in federal court in Detroit. The trial focused on nine telecasts from "Meet the UAW," paid for out of union dues, which the government argued were aimed at promoting the election of Democratic candidates. Reuther and Mazey testified that they were part of a year-round educational program that dealt with a variety of subjects, political and nonpolitical, and were voluntarily supported by members of the union. The UAW's chief counsel, Joseph Rauh, contended that if the UAW was in violation of the law, then so too were the sponsors of "Fulton Lewis's programs and those of a host of well known commentators who comment on candidates at election time." On November 6, 1957, after less then two hours of deliberation, the jury found the UAW not guilty of the charges. A jubilant Mazey hailed the decision as a definitive endorsement of labor's political voice in the media. Lawrence Lindemer, the Michigan Republican chairman, warned ominously that the verdict made the auto union "the political colossus of Michigan."[67]

Lindemer's comments said more about the Republican party's anxiety and frustration than the power of labor's media presence to fundamentally reshape attitudes and political beliefs. Yet, as Nelson Lichtenstein has observed, despite the image of the 1950s as a "'conservative' decade in which an affluent working class turned its back on the radical values" of the 1930s, autoworkers remained class-conscious, if often disengaged. Among autoworkers, union broadcasting certainly helped reinforce and legitimize a working-class political, cultural, and economic perspective that was suspicious of business power. The UAW's aggressive media program got the union message out to members and the public, helping the autoworkers in Michigan exercise considerable political power and strengthening working-class support for the Democrats. But there were real limits to labor's ability to reshape social and cultural attitudes through the media. All of the autoworkers' programming, for instance, steadily fought racism and promoted civil rights, but to little avail. As Thomas Sugrue has shown, despite the efforts of the UAW leadership and broadcasters, racial conflict and tension continued to plague the factories and neighborhoods of postwar Detroit.[68]

In mid-1949, the *New York Times* columnist Arthur Krock charged that

a newly articulate labor movement working closely with liberals was taking "full advantage of government-licensed radio" to promote its cause on
the air. The conservative *Saturday Evening Post* chimed in with dire warn-
ings about labor's exploitation of broadcasting. In a March 1950 editorial, it
charged that labor's new FM network and Frank Edwards's five-times-a-week
radio commentary were part of a nefarious campaign to "push the country
faster and faster toward the handout state." Obviously, the United States did
not move faster and faster toward the feared welfare state in the 1950s. But
in the increasingly conservative political atmosphere of that decade, labor
used radio to provide an important alternative political perspective, one that
helped nurture unionism "as a culture of beliefs and behaviors" that helped
sustain liberalism into the 1960s.[69]

Epilogue

IN EARLY 1954, *Variety* surveyed labor's involvement in broadcasting. It was enthusiastic about labor's progress, but its understanding of the movement's history was a bit truncated. *Variety* marked early 1946 and the ILGWU's and UAW's decision to file for FM applications as the beginning of labor's venture into radio, thus overlooking the founding of WCFL, labor's use of radio in the 1930s, the wartime struggles for access, and union involvement in the movement for media reform. According to *Variety*, in their quest to promote FM radio, unions, like many others, had been misled by the "Nostradamuses" who had predicted that the FM spectrum was going to rapidly supplant AM. The broadcasting magazine concluded that although labor's "Noble Experiment" in FM had failed, unions had preformed "valuable services" to their listeners by offering a superior lineup of programs that emphasized public service and by effectively publicizing the role of labor in society.[1]

Variety was also impressed with other elements of labor broadcasting. It pointed to a Morris Novik–inspired concentrated radio and TV campaign to win longshoremen's support for an AFL drive to supplant the corrupt International Longshoremen's Association in New York City. That campaign failed, but Novik sprang into action again the following year when media charges of sabotage, shootings, and rioting as well as reports of back-to-work movements began undermining public and worker support for a strike against the Louisville and Nashville Railroad. The first railroad strike in twenty-five years, it affected communities in sixteen southeastern states. After a month of railroad ads and broadcasts stirring up hostility against the strikers, the railroad unions appealed to the AFL for help, and Novik, dropping everything, quickly organized a hookup of eighty-nine stations, which enabled the unions to speak directly to members and the public through twice-daily strike reports. The railroad unions won a decisive victory, and a jubilant Railroad Telegraphers president G. E. Leighty thanked AFL president George Meany for Novik's assistance. "Radio," he proclaimed, was "our most valuable link with the rank and file strikers" and "proved to be of tremendous importance in the great victory that we have achieved."[2]

Variety also praised labor's less dramatic and more measured use of radio, noting the public relations boost from the Teamsters' sponsorship of Notre Dame football and from labor's effective use of its free time on the networks, especially the AFL's public service program on ABC, "Both Sides." Similarly, the Taft-Hartley campaign and the inauguration of the Frank Edwards news show were noted as important milestones. *Variety* reported that Edwards's show was one of the top-rated news programs on the air, soundly beating out his ideological rival, Fulton Lewis Jr., for listeners in a recently conducted audience survey. *Variety* marveled at Edwards's ability to mobilize the public, observing that his campaign on behalf of a little girl suffering from polio led to the installation of dozens of iron lungs in community hospitals. His campaign against ceding oil-rich coastal lands to states for private development resulted in a deluge of thousands of letters and telegrams to Congress. Edwards's program was so successful that it inspired the UAW and CIO to sponsor their own nightly newscasts, all of which had large audiences and a wide following among non-union and union members of the listening public. Summing up, the show-business trade journal concluded that labor's record of accomplishments in radio in a few short years had been "quite outstanding."[3]

When *Variety* published this survey, the union voice in broadcasting was still expanding. Five years later, however, labor's presence in the media and labor as an economic and political force in American society had begun to slowly but steadily contract. In terms of broadcasting, there had always been doubting Thomases within the labor movement for whom education, communication, and public relations were of secondary importance. Others questioned the effectiveness of labor's programming. In 1954, Robert Oliver, Walter Reuther's assistant, urged reconsidering the CIO's sponsorship of John W. Vandercook. He advised Reuther, "[C]onfidentially, I have not found anyone, and I have asked many people, who thinks the program is worth a damn; that is, no one outside the Publicity Department." I. W. Abel of the Steelworkers agreed with Oliver. In 1957, to counter rank-and-file indifference and a grassroots insurgency movement, the Steelworkers began sponsoring the program "TV Meeting of the Month." In early 1959, while preparing for nationwide contract negotiations, the program featured the singer Phil Regan. Abel could see "no gain" from this activity. In his opinion, radio, newspaper ads, and television were all "lousy." Moreover, as labor—even the UAW—became increasingly oriented to a service model of unionism that emphasized the delivery of wages and benefits, there was less interest in communicating with and mobilizing the membership.[4]

Over the course of six years, the UAW virtually abandoned its ambitious and innovative broadcasting program. The first cuts came in 1958, when union membership plummeted in the midst of a major economic recession, and the UAW adopted an austerity program. Hard-pressed for funds, the union chopped its broadcasting schedule to pieces, dropping twenty-three of the forty stations carrying "Eye Opener" and reducing the program's operating budget. Next it cut the Detroit afternoon drive-time show, "Shift Break," and then in August 1963 the union canceled its twelve-year-old television program, asserting that it was not reaching enough of an audience to justify the expense. At the same time, the union continued to drop the number of stations contracted to broadcast "Eye Opener." Finally, in late 1964, the autoworkers canceled the morning show, the most popular part of its broadcasting program, despite Reuther's praise for the show's sustained support of the civil rights movement, its attention to the persistence of poverty in the United States, and its encouragement to listeners to actively support the legislative and political programs of the UAW and the AFL-CIO. The UAW told disappointed listeners that it intended to continue using media. It produced a few documentaries for airing on television, but by 1968 the Radio and TV Department had been disbanded, and Nunn had left the union.[5]

While auto executives heaved a sigh of relief at Guy Nunn's silencing, listeners—union and non-union—pleaded with the UAW to restore him to the air. A tool and die maker from Marion, Ohio, who listened to Nunn on his way to work every morning asked, "Why did you have to take Guy Nunn and his great program off the air?" He asserted that "we got more real truth from his program than from all the country's newspapers combined." In Southern California, where the "suburban warriors" described by Lisa Mc-Girr were helping to shift the political climate to the right by championing individual economic freedom, Nunn's show had served as a flashpoint of liberal sentiment. For the autoworker V. V. Roe of LaPuente, California, the abandonment of "Eye Opener" came as a "great shock and disappointment." He reported that "for all of us here" it was "the only island in the local sea of vicious employer-inspired propaganda and poisonous diversionary korny

During the 1950s and 1960s, the UAW's Guy Nunn was the most listened-to radio personality in Detroit. At one point, he was on the air three times a day for the union. Courtesy of the Archives of Labor and Urban Affairs, Wayne State University, Detroit.

krap." Michael Berg of Glendale, California, agreed, contending that "to us in the land of reaction and looming fascism, it came a great relief from the retarded monotony many regard as freedom." From the Midwest, A. Hewitt of Chicago implored Reuther to reinstate the show, declaring, "Eye Opener must come back—it's the best thing the union . . . does. . . . There is just nothing to take its place—it oriented us daily to our work lives, as citizens, as human beings."[6]

"Eye Opener" was equally important to middle-class listeners. For years, Ruth Miller, a New York City writer who worked into the early morning hours, made a special effort to wake up for the 6:00 A.M. broadcast. She praised the UAW's use of culture, comparing the comedy skits on Nunn's show to the tradition of the ILGWU's "Pins and Needles," and lamented that "there's darn little of that tradition left." Miller confided to Reuther that while she had always favored unions, her enthusiasm for labor had diminished steadily in recent years. Only "Eye Opener" had helped revive her flagging enthusiasm and understanding of organized labor. According to Miller, except for Edward P. Morgan's show, "Eye Opener" was the only source of information about labor easily available to New York City listeners. While one listener, Lewis Waldrup, did not always agree with the show's conclusions, he felt that it said "lots of things that needed very much to be said." Who else, he asked, "will say them, if not some progressive backed by labor?"[7]

In the years after the UAW halted them, its broadcasting activities became even more apparently important to some unionists. Responding to an audience survey conducted after all the shows were off the air, one local officer observed, "Guy Nunn's television and radio programs were truly the only 'spokesman' for union members." He further contended that "labor's views were completely shut off when Nunn's programs were taken off the air" and that "Republicans, Big Business, Birchists, and other antilabor organizations rejoiced" when he was silenced. To another respondent, the ending of the UAW broadcasts had important political implications. He argued that "it was a grave mistake to take off both the Radio and Television shows in the Midwest. We in the labor movement lost many candidates running for state and federal offices because of this." Thirty-five years later, Oscar Paskal, chief steward at DeSoto in the 1950s, recalled that the Nunn's shows elevated the consciousness of many workers, and John D'Agostino, a retiree, mused, "[W]e didn't realize what we had till we lost it."[8]

The phasing out of the UAW Radio Department and its broadcasts reflected the union's "increasingly narrow political orthodoxy," according to Nelson Lichtenstein. While many listeners appreciated Nunn's militancy, his programs often embarrassed some UAW officers and over the years created opposition to the Radio Department among the UAW Executive Board. Some Executive Board members felt that the tone of Nunn's broadcasts was too belligerent and that his views were not "sufficiently representative of the union." Indeed, Nunn overshadowed much of the UAW high command. To many listeners and much of the rank and file, "Guy Nunn *was* the UAW." Jealous regional directors felt that the commentator was not only explaining but attempting to make union policy. Moreover, his aggressive support of civil rights, a contentious issue within the UAW, made him particularly vulnerable to attack. Nunn was far ahead of many of the members as well as much of the leadership on the issue. Oscar Paskal remembers that local officers and regional directors heard complaints from irritated members of the rank and file, who asked, "[W]ho the hell was Guy Nunn to make great statements about civil rights—why is he always harping on that?"[9]

The AFL-CIO's broadcasting program took somewhat longer to disappear. After the merger in 1956, the AFL-CIO cut Vandercook's time back to five minutes, and in 1957 the Executive Council gave serious consideration to canceling both programs. In the late 1950s, however, the intensification of an ongoing corporate antilabor campaign brought a renewed commitment on the part of the AFL-CIO to reaching the public through the mass media. The McClellan Committee union corruption hearings of 1957 and 1958 raised the specter of irresponsible union power and dealt a blow to the legitimacy of organized labor. Exploiting the committee's revelations, employer organizations stepped up state-level right-to-work campaigns, and the NAM intensified its legislative drive for a national labor reform act. To counteract the antilabor drive, the AFL-CIO responded with a "crash" public relations program to bring the truth about the labor movement to the public. The federation increased its public relations budget by 58 percent to $1.2 million a year. Broadcasting was at the center of the program. The AFL-CIO expanded the number of stations carrying the Vandercook and Morgan programs, began issuing television news releases, and developed a public service television program, "America at Work," which portrayed workers' contributions to "America's industrial might." It also developed several new weekly public affairs radio programs that were broadcast over free time.[10]

Once the crisis passed, in the 1960s, the AFL-CIO increasingly settled into a somnolent complacency. While membership figures grew, the proportion of workers in unions declined. For those who were organized, wages were high and benefits were good. AFL-CIO president George Meany, however, had little interest in expanding the core of the unionized sector through mass-organizing campaigns, mobilizing the membership, or promoting social reform. Furious at the AFL-CIO's lack of social vision and crusading spirit, a disgusted Walter Reuther complained, "We don't have a labor movement. We have a club. It's a very exclusive club; stays in the best hotels, in the finest resorts in the Western hemisphere. But it isn't doing a job." In 1966, the labor writer John Herling observed that while corporations were vigorously trying to organize public opinion in their plants, unions were losing touch with their rank and file.[11]

With little interest in serving as a vital force for social change or mobilizing its membership, the AFL-CIO in the 1960s scaled back its public relations program and discontinued most of its broadcasting activities. Its public relations budget dropped from 14 percent of total expenses in 1960 to 2 percent in 1968, and the ensuing years saw the initiation of few new projects to reach members or the public. When Vandercook's health failed in mid-1960, the AFL-CIO made no effort to replace him on the air. In 1967, the federation ended "As We See It," a weekly public service radio program featuring interviews with union leaders that had been broadcast for more than seventeen years, and withdrew from circulation the "Americans at Work" films. This left only one weekly union network public affairs program on the air. That same year, Edward P. Morgan left his program for a position with educational television. Months before his resignation, the Public Relations Department had called for the continuation of the program, asserting that Morgan had developed "so much favorable AFL-CIO identification that abandonment would be a disaster."[12]

Nevertheless, the Executive Council voted to drop the program after sixteen years of sponsorship. Meany had regularly questioned the effectiveness of the news programs in improving labor's image, and union leaders were often irritated with Morgan's criticism of organized labor. In 1959, for instance, while the textile workers appreciated Morgan's coverage of its yearlong strike against the Henderson Cotton Mills in North Carolina, president William Pollok was appalled that the commentator characterized aspects of the union's conduct of the strike as "overly class-conscious, an anachronistic attitude in itself." Similarly, the UAW secretary-treasurer Emil Mazey lit into Morgan for characterizing the Democratic party in Michigan as "labor-dominated."[13]

Listeners lamented the loss of the program and the decline of labor broadcasting. Alan G. Clive of Detroit, who had listened to the program for eight years, regretted the loss of the "last voice of sanity left on the networks." Sidney Seifer of New York City was stunned when he learned that Morgan was leaving the air, confiding to Morgan that "whenever I felt bewildered by the day's news I would turn to you, to your program and as if by some magical process my bewilderment would turn to enlightenment." For Lawrence C. Sullivan, the executive secretary-treasurer of the Greater Boston Labor Council, the ending of the Morgan show "dealt a damaging blow" to organized labor's effort to speak to the public.[14]

Throughout the nation, labor's voice receded while public support for unions declined. In Chicago, for instance, WCFL, whose coverage of labor had been declining since the 1950s, became primarily a cash cow for the Chicago Federation of Labor. In 1978, when the CFL sold the station to Amway, it was so devoid of any union or public service programming that few listeners realized that WCFL had a connection to organized labor. Attempts to reverse the trend away from broadcasting were unsuccessful. The International Association of Machinists inaugurated twice-weekly five-minute news spots in 1964 entitled "The World of Labor," which eventually reached seventy-two cities. The Machinists hoped in part to offset the AFL-CIO's withdrawal from radio. Five years later, however, the program was discontinued because of lack of funds. It is impossible to show any direct connection between the decline of labor broadcasting and falling public approval for labor, but there is a circumstantial link. Public support for unions declined sharply—from 76 to 63 percent—in the midst of the corruption charges during the late 1950s, rallied briefly in the early 1960s, and then continued to drop, down to 55 percent in 1979, the lowest in 43 years. To this day it remains at that level.[15]

Labor never totally abandoned broadcasting. In the mid-1970s, the ILGWU ran its celebrated "Look for the Union Label" advertising campaign on network television. In the early 1980s, as the auto industry faced plant closings and massive unemployment, the UAW sponsored extensive, but short-term, advertising campaigns, calling for strengthening the industrial base of the economy. Facing similar challenges, the National Education Association and the American Federation of State, County, and Municipal Employees also conducted national media advertising campaigns to build support for public education and to improve the image of public employees. Through the 1980s, the UAW and occasionally other unions also utilized the Fairness Doctrine, which required broadcasters to provide fair and accurate coverage of controversial issues, to gain airtime to counter blatant attacks against labor. But for much of the latter part of the twentieth century, unions had little sustained presence in broadcasting.[16]

In sharp contrast, business never stepped back from the media. By the early 1960s, in over five hundred communities, conservative corporate activists with links to the John Birch Society, the Manion Forum, and the National Economic Council were sponsoring a wide range of radio programs attacking organized labor and the state, essentially laying the seeds for a rightward shift in American politics. By the mid-1970s, much of the rest of the business community felt the need to help. Facing shrinking profits and increased regulation and worried about the loss of public confidence, business organizations launched a massive assault on the labor movement and fought to undermine regulation and the remaining structures of the New Deal welfare state. Equally important was the ideological contest. Business-backed economic-education programs selling free enterprise proliferated, and institutional and advocacy advertising also shifted into high gear. The Chamber of Commerce sponsored major campaigns, as did individual firms like the W. R. Grace Company, whose television ads emphasized the principles of freedom and small government. By the end of the 1970s, total estimated corporate spending on this kind of advertising amounted to a billion dollars a year.[17]

This wholesale business assault on labor and the social-justice political agenda worked. Union membership declined dramatically, falling from 29 percent of the workforce in 1973 to about 16 percent in 1991. Real wages stagnated, and income inequality increased. In the context of stagflation, rising unemployment, rising welfare costs, busing, affirmative action, and court rulings on abortion and school prayer, the anti-tax, antigovernment, and antilabor campaigns helped push the ideological center of gravity to the right, creating a more conservative, pro-business political culture.[18] With no sustained voice in the media, organized labor was unable to publicly defend itself against the massive corporate assault against the labor movement in the 1970s.

Today, workers face a media that is even more completely dominated by corporate capitalism than the media of the post–World War II era. The fears of postwar reformers, including the declining diversity of ownership and the marginalization of local broadcasting, have become today's frightening reality. Media concentration has increased dramatically since the mid-1990s, and localism, especially in radio, has virtually disappeared. Deregulation and the overturning of the Fairness Doctrine in 1987 by a Reagan-appointed FCC has made it even easier for business to use broadcasting to promote its conservative message.[19]

In contrast, organized labor, weakened by a thirty-year economic, political, and ideological assault, has dissipated as a social force in American society and virtually disappeared from the mass media except for negative coverage during strikes. Recently, however, American labor has shown new signs of life, with a renewed commitment to organizing and defending the interests of the working class. At least some within the union movement have begun to understand that to rebuild organized labor, unions need to "engineer a political and cultural breakthrough that sways the hearts and minds of millions and millions of people who today see the unions as irrelevant, or even hostile, to their interests." This breakthrough will require labor to challenge the individualistic ethos of free market ideology and to articulate a vision based on solidarity, equality, community, and democracy. But to have an impact, American labor needs to effectively communicate its values and ideals to workers and the broader public.[20]

Labor's experience during the CIO era suggests that it is possible to challenge the capitalist broadcasting system and to use the media to help achieve organized labor's goals. There have been encouraging signs that some unionists are again ready to "take back the airwaves." There are over sixty locally produced labor radio and television programs on the air, and in 2001, labor educators in Madison, Wisconsin, created the Workers Independent News Service (WINS), which produces two- and three-minute daily news broadcasts and several weekly feature stories. Listeners in over a hundred communities can hear WINS broadcasts, which focus on lives and concerns of working people. Yet, as the communications scholar Robert W. McChesney suggests, in addition to creating their own programs, unions again need to join with other progressive democratic forces in opposing corporate control of the media.[21] If we are ever to recapture the true promise of American democracy, the voice of workers must again be heard in the mainstream media.

NOTES

List of Abbreviations

ACLU	American Civil Liberties Union Papers, Seeley G. Mudd Library, Princeton University, Princeton, N.J.
ACWA	Amalgamated Clothing Workers of America Papers, Kheel Center for Labor-Management Documentation and Archives, M. P. Catherwood Library, Cornell University, Ithaca, N.Y.
ALUA	Archives of Labor and Urban Affairs, Walter P. Reuther Library, Wayne State University, Detroit
ALUCP	American Labor Unions' Constitutions and Proceedings, Microfilm edition (Glen Rock, N.J.: Microfilming Corporation of America, 1975).
CUA	Department of Archives and Manuscripts, The Catholic University of America, Washington, D.C.
FCC	Federal Communications Commission Records, RG 173, National Archives and Records Center, College Park, Md.
FP	Federated Press Papers, Rare Book and Manuscript Library, Butler Library, Columbia University, New York
GMMA	George Meany Memorial Archives, Silver Spring, Md.
HCLA	Historical Collections and Labor Archives, Patee Library, Pennsylvania State University, University Park
HML	Hagley Museum and Library, Wilmington, Del.
ILGWU	International Ladies Garment Workers Union Records, Kheel Center for Labor-Management Documentation and Archives, Martin P. Catherwood Library, Cornell University, Ithaca, N.Y.
KLMDC	Kheel Center for Labor-Management Documentation and Archives, Martin P. Catherwood Library, Cornell University, Ithaca, N.Y.
LC	Library of Congress, Washington, D.C.
NAB	National Association of Broadcasters Papers, SHSW, Madison, Wis.
NARA	National Archives and Records Center, College Park, Md.

NAM   National Association of Manufacturers Records, Hagley Museum and Library, Wilmington, Del.
NBC   National Broadcasting Company Records, State Historical Society of Wisconsin, Madison.
NBC-LC   National Broadcasting Company Records, Library of Congress, Washington, D.C.
SHSW   State Historical Society of Wisconsin, Madison
UE   United Electrical Workers Archives, University of Pittsburgh
WVRHC   West Virginia and Regional History Collections, West Virginia University Libraries, Morgantown

Introduction

1. Richard Klimmer, interview with the author, Jan. 28, 2001.

2. Elizabeth A. Fones-Wolf, *Selling Free Enterprise: The Business Assault on Labor and Liberalism, 1945–60* (Urbana: University of Illinois Press, 1994). See also Alex Carey, *Taking the Risk out of Democracy: Corporate Propaganda versus Freedom and Liberty* (Urbana: University of Illinois Press, 1995); and Howell John Harris, *The Right to Manage: Industrial Relations Policies of American Business in the 1940s* (Madison: University of Wisconsin Press, 1982).

3. Susan J. Douglas, *Listening In: Radio and the American Imagination, from Amos 'n' Andy and Edward R. Murrow to Wolfman Jack and Howard Stern* (New York: Times Books, 1999), 9; Warren Susman, *Culture as History: The Transformation of American Society in the Twentieth Century* (New York: Pantheon, 1984), 228; Michele Hilmes, *Radio Voices: American Broadcasting, 1922–1952* (Minneapolis: University of Minnesota Press, 1997), 6; Douglas B. Craig, *Fireside Politics: Radio and Political Culture in the United States, 1920–1940* (Baltimore: Johns Hopkins University Press, 2000), 218.

4. Barbara Dianne Savage, *Broadcasting Freedom: Radio, War, and the Politics of Race, 1938–1948* (Chapel Hill: University of North Carolina Press, 1999), 11; Michael Denning, *The Cultural Front: The Laboring of American Culture in the Twentieth Century* (London: Verso, 1996).

5. Douglas, *Listening In*, 6; Hilmes, *Radio Voices*, 46; S. H. Walker and Paul Sklar, "Business Finds Its Voice," *Harper's*, Jan. 1938, 122.

6. Savage, *Broadcasting Freedom*, 2. Historians are beginning to explore the role of radio and television in the civil rights movement. In addition to Barbara Savage's work, see Kay Mills, *Changing Channels: The Civil Rights Case that Transformed Television* (Jackson: University Press of Mississippi, 2004); and Brian Ward, *Radio and the Struggle for Civil Rights in the South* (Gainesville: University Press of Florida, 2004).

7. Elliott Shore, *Talkin' Socialism: J. A. Wayland and the Role of the Press in American Radicalism, 1890–1912* (Lawrence: University of Kansas Press, 1988); Steven J. Ross, *Working Class-Hollywood: Silent Film and the Shaping of Class in America* (Princeton, N.J.: Princeton University Press, 1998); John Bodnar, *Blue-Collar Hollywood: Liberalism, Democracy, and Working People in American Film* (Baltimore: Johns Hopkins University Press, 2003); Lary May, *The Big Tomorrow: Hollywood and the Politics of the American Way* (Chicago: University of Chicago Press, 2000).

8. Nathan Godfried, *WCFL: Chicago's Voice of Labor, 1926–1978* (Urbana: University of Illinois Press, 1997); Robert W. McChesney, *Telecommunications, Mass Media, and Democracy: The Battle for Control of U.S. Broadcasting, 1928–1935* (New York: Oxford University Press, 1993).

9. William J. Puette, *Through Jaundiced Eyes: How the Media View Organized Labor* (Ithaca, N.Y.: ILR Press, 1992); Jo-Ann Mort, "How the Media 'Cover' Labor," *Dissent* 39 (Winter 1992): 81–85; Ross, *Working-Class Hollywood*, 243; Christopher R. Martin, *Framed: Labor and the Corporate Media* (Ithaca, N.Y.: ILR Press, 2004).

10. Roland Marchand, *Creating the Corporate Soul: The Rise of Public Relations and Corporate Imagery in American Big Business* (Berkeley: University of California Press, 1998); William L. Bird, *"Better Living": Advertising, Media, and the New Vocabulary of Business Leadership, 1935–1955* (Evanston, Ill.: Northwestern University Press, 1999); Ross, *Working-Class Hollywood*; Godfried, *WCFL*; McChesney, *Telecommunciations, Mass Media, and Democracy*. See also Kathy M. Newman, *Radio Active: Advertising and Consumer Activism, 1935–1947* (Berkeley: University of California Press, 2004). Newman's innovative study explores labor boycotts of business broadcasting in the 1930s. See also Vincent J. Roscigno and William F. Danaher, *The Voice of Southern Labor: Radio, Music, and Textile Strikes, 1929–1934* (Minneapolis: University of Minnesota Press, 2004), for a suggestive sociological study of the role of radio and music in creating an oppositional culture.

11. Amy Toro, "Standing Up for Listeners' Rights: A History of Public Participation at the Federal Communications Commission" (Ph.D. diss., University of California at Berkeley, 2000), 11; Robert W. McChesney, *Rich Media, Poor Democracy: Communication Politics in Dubious Times* (Urbana: University of Illinois Press, 1999).

12. On the concept of listeners' rights, see Toro, "Standing Up for Listeners' Rights," 14.

13. The end of the Fairness Doctrine and deregulation during the 1980s again put a tight lid on citizenship involvement in the regulatory process. Mills, *Changing Channels*, 244–64; Ward, *Radio and the Struggle for Civil Rights*, 275–77.

Chapter 1: Putting Class on the Air

1. Barry D. Karl, *The Uneasy State: The United States from 1915–1945* (Chicago: University of Chicago Press, 1983), 12; Lizabeth Cohen, *Making a New Deal: Industrial Workers in Chicago, 1919–1939* (Cambridge: Cambridge University Press, 1990).

2. Douglas B. Craig, *Fireside Politics: Radio and Political Culture in the United States, 1920–1940* (Baltimore: Johns Hopkins University Press, 2000), 9; Cohen, *Making a New Deal*, 133–34.

3. Susan J. Douglas, *Listening In: Radio and the American Imagination, from Amos 'n' Andy and Edward R. Morrow to Wolfman Jack and Howard Stern* (New York: Times Books, 1999), 75; Cohen, *Making a New Deal*, 133–38; Jacquelyn Dowd Hall et al., *Like a Family: The Making of a Southern Cotton Mill World* (Chapel Hill: University of North Carolina Press, 1987), 259–61.

4. Craig, *Fireside Politics*, 18–71; Robert W. McChesney, *Telecommunications, Mass Media, and Democracy: The Battle for the Control of U.S. Broadcasting, 1928–1935* (New York: Oxford University Press, 1993), 115–16.

5. Michele Hilmes, *Radio Voices: American Broadcasting, 1922–1952* (Minneapolis: University of Minnesota Press, 1997), chaps. 3–7; Douglas, *Listening In,* 161–86.

6. Craig, *Fireside Politics,* 12–13; Harvey Green, *The Uncertainty of Everyday Life, 1915–1945* (New York: Harper Collins, 1993), 188; Richard Butsch, *The Making of American Audiences: From Stage to Television, 1750–1990* (Cambridge: Cambridge University Press, 2000), 196.

7. Craig, *Fireside Politics,* 13; Cohen, *Making a New Deal,* 327; Bruce Lenthall, "Radio Waves: Tuning in to a Changing American Culture in the Great Depression" (Ph. D. diss., University of Pennsylvania, 1999), 31–38; Hall et al., *Like a Family,* 258–59; Butsch, *Making of American Audiences,* 198.

8. AFL, *Proceedings* (1925), 316, reel 9, ALUCP; Steven Ross, *Working-Class Hollywood: Silent Film and the Shaping of Class in America* (Princeton, N.J.: Princeton University Press, 1998), 63–69, 73–76.

9. AFL, *Proceedings* (1930), 130, reel 10, ALUCP.

10. Ross, *Working-Class Hollywood,* 156.

11. AFL, *Proceedings* (1921), 345; AFL, *Proceedings* (1925), 316, reel 8, ALUCP; AFL, *Proceedings* (1937), 378, reel 12, ALUCP; McChesney, *Telecommunications, Mass Media, and Democracy,* 69–70; Ross, *Working-Class Hollywood,* 230–34.

12. Ross, *Working-Class Hollywood,* 230–33; AFL, *Proceedings* (1925), 316; "Radio Broadcasting," AFL Records microfilm, reel 33, GMMA; AFL, *Proceedings* (1929), 103–4, reel 10, ALUCP; *Labor's News,* Dec. 21, 1929; *Federated Press Labor Letter,* Feb. 9, 1928.

13. Craig Phelan, "William Green and the Ideal of Christian Cooperation," in *Labor Leaders in America,* ed. Melvyn Dubofsky and Warren Van Tine (Urbana: University of Illinois Press, 1987), 138–48.

14. Emanie N. Arling, "Report on NAB Code," Feb. 1, 1940, vol. 2212, ACLU.

15. Nathan Godfried, *WCFL: Chicago's Voice of Labor, 1926–78* (Urbana: University of Illinois Press, 1997), 197–98; AFL, *Proceedings* (1929), 103, reel 10, ALUCP; Michael Kazin and Steven J. Ross, "America's Labor Day: The Dilemma of a Workers' Celebration," *Journal of American History* 78 (Mar. 1992): 1312–13.

16. AFL, *Proceedings* (1932), 99, 185, 271, reel 10, ALUCP; AFL, *Proceedings* (1934), 149, reel 11, ALUCP; AFL, *Proceedings* (1935), 314, reel 11, ALUCP; AFL, *Proceedings* (1938), 188, reel 12, ALUCP; AFL, *Proceedings* (1939), 273, reel 12, ALUCP; *Federation News,* Sept. 10, 1932; "Report of the Executive Committee, Workers Education Bureau of America to the Twenty-Fifth Anniversary Convention," Apr. 5–6, 1945, box 11, file A, series 8, Files of the Director of Research, AFL Papers, SHSW.

17. This discussion of the history of WCFL and of WEVD draws primarily from Godfried, *WCFL.*

18. Ibid., 118, 46–124.

19. Ibid.

20. G. August Gerber to Friend, Apr. 17, 1929, Vertical File (Radio Station: New York, N.Y.), Tamiment Library and Robert F. Wagner Labor Archives, New York University; Nathan Godfried, "Legitimizing the Mass Media Structure: The Socialists and American Broadcasting, 1926–1932," in *Culture, Gender, Race, and U.S. Labor History,* ed. Ronald C. Kent, Sara Markham, David R. Roediger, and Herbert Shapiro (Westport, Conn.: Greenwood Press, 1993), 123–49.

21. Godfried, "Legitimizing the Mass Media Structure," 132.

22. Lawrence W. Levine, "The Folklore of Industrial Society: Popular Culture and Its Audiences," *American Historical Review* 97 (Dec. 1992): 1393; Craig, *Fireside Politics*, 154–57, 159–61; Alan Brinkley, *Voices of Protest: Huey Long, Father Coughlin, and the Great Depression* (New York: Vintage Books, 1983), 82–101, 169, 193.

23. Alan R. Raucher, *Public Relations and Business, 1900–1929* (Baltimore: Johns Hopkins University Press, 1968); Roland Marchand, *Creating the Corporate Soul: The Rise of Public Relations and Corporate Imagery in American Big Business* (Berkeley: University of California Press, 1998); Roland Marchand, "Where Lie the Boundaries of the Corporation? Explorations in 'Corporate Responsibility' in the 1930s," *Business and Economic History* 26 (Fall 1997): 85.

24. Eric Foner, *The Story of American Freedom* (New York: W. W. Norton and Co., 1998), 196; Cohen, *Making a New Deal*.

25. Michael Denning, *The Cultural Front: The Laboring of American Culture in the Twentieth Century* (London: Verso, 1996); Lary May, *The Big Tomorrow: Hollywood and the Politics of the American Way* (Chicago: University of Chicago Press, 2000), 75; John Bodnar, *Blue-Collar Hollywood: Liberalism, Democracy, and Working People in American Film* (Baltimore: Johns Hopkins University Press, 2003).

26. Richard S. Tedlow, *Keeping the Corporate Image: Public Relations and Business, 1900–1950* (Greenwich, Conn.: JAI Press, 1979), 59; Barton quoted in Denning, *Cultural Front,* 43; Marchand, *Creating the Corporate Soul,* chaps. 6–7; Marchand, "Where Lie the Boundaries of the Corporation?" 85.

27. Quoted in S. H. Walker and Paul Sklar, "Business Finds Its Voice," *Harper's,* Jan. 1938, 122.

28. Lazarfeld's study quoted in William Stott, *Documentary Expression and Thirties America* (New York: Oxford University Press, 1973), 80–82.

29. Walker and Sklar, "Business Finds Its Voice," 122; Marchand, *Creating the Corporate Soul,* 192–93; "Wheeling Steel's Show," *Printers' Ink,* Dec. 27, 1940, 16.

30. S. Prakash Sethi, *Advocacy Advertising and Large Corporations: Social Conflict, Big Business Image, the News Media, and Public Policy* (Lexington, Mass.: Lexington Books, 1977), 7–10; Harvey Pinney, "The Radio Pastor of Dearborn," *The Nation,* Oct. 9, 1937, 374; "Wheeling's Musical Steelmakers' Help Make Industrial Harmony," *Sales Management,* July 15, 1939, 22–24; "Wheeling Steel's Show," *Printers' Ink,* Dec. 27, 1940, 16.

31. Du Pont Press Release, Sept. 27, 1935, box 36, Acc. 1410, Du Pont Public Affairs Department Papers, HML; *Original Radio Script of Abraham Lincoln from the Cavalcade of America,* Feb. 13, 1940 (New York: Harcourt Brace Publishers, 1940), back cover; Marchand, *Creating the Corporate Soul,* 218–23; William L. Bird Jr., *"Better Living": Advertising, Media, and the New Vocabulary of Business Leadership, 1935–1955* (Evanston, Ill.: Northwestern University Press, 1999), 66–82.

32. Bird, *"Better Living,"* 98–119; Talbot Johns to James R. Angell, Dec. 4, 1939, Keith Kiggins to Station Managers, Nov. 30, 1939, W. G. Preston to John F. Royal, Dec. 1, 1939, folder 81, box 67, NBC; James Angell to Lammont Du Pont, Jan. 17, 1940; W. G. Preston to James R. Angell, Aug. 28, 1940, folder 67, box 76, NBC.

33. David L. Lewis, *The Public Image of Henry Ford: An American Folk Hero and His Company* (Detroit: Wayne State University Press, 1976), 241–65; Allan Nevins and

Frank Ernest Hill, *Ford: Decline and Rebirth, 1933–1962* (New York: Scribner, 1963), 55–54.

34. Lewis, *Public Image of Henry Ford,* 315–17, 326–29; "Farewell Ford," *Time,* Feb. 2, 1942, 53–54; Nora Huey to W. J. Cameron, Dec. 11, 1939, box 17, Acc. 23, Henry Ford Office Papers, Ford Motor Company Archives, Dearborn, Mich.

35. Marchand, *Creating the Corporate Soul,* 210–11; Lewis, *Public Image of Henry Ford,* 326; Paul Hutchinson, "Heretics of the Air III—Mr. Ford's Mr. Cameron," *Christian Century,* Apr. 17, 1935, 508; William J. Cameron, *The Ford Sunday Evening Hour Talks, 1934, 1935, 1936* (Dearborn, Mich.: Ford Motor Co., 1936), 18–19, 38–40, 112–14; William J. Cameron, *The Ford Sunday Evening Hour Talks, 1936, 1937, 1938* (Dearborn, Mich.: Ford Motor Co., 1938), 43–48, 82–86, 160–70; William J. Cameron, *The Ford Sunday Evening Hour Talks, 1940, 1941* (Dearborn, Mich.: Ford Motor Co., 1941), 63–65.

36. Cameron, *Ford Sunday Evening Hour Talks, 1934, 1935, 1936,* 53, 105–6, 175, 189–92; "The Ford Sunday Evening Hour," *Propaganda Analysis* 1 (July 1938): 57–60; Thomas S. Green, "Mr. Cameron and the Ford Hour," *Public Opinion Quarterly* 3 (Oct. 1939): 669–75; Cameron, *Ford Sunday Evening Hour Talks, 1936, 1937, 1938,* 30, 130–32, 258–60; Cameron, *Ford Sunday Evening Hour Talks, 1940, 1941,* 22–25.

37. Cameron, *Ford Sunday Evening Hour Talks, 1934, 1935, 1936,* 53; Pinney, "Radio Pastor of Dearborn," 376; Cameron, *Ford Sunday Evening Hour Talks, 1936, 1937, 1938,* 258–60.

38. Erik Barnouw, *The Golden Web: A History of Broadcasting in the United States, Volume 2: 1933–1953* (New York: Oxford University Press, 1968), 14–15, 34; Robert F. Burk, *The Corporate State and Broker State: The Du Ponts and American National Politics, 1925–1940* (Cambridge, Mass.: Harvard University Press, 1990), 124–36, 153, 176, 202–3.

39. *Variety,* June 1, 1936; *Chicago Industrial Worker,* July 18, 1936.

40. "'American Family Robinson' Program Now in Third Successful Year," *World News,* June 1937; Mrs. Geo. W. Ebert to Radio Station WWNC, June 17, 1935, box 156, series I, Acc. 1411, NAM (hereafter Acc. 1411, NAM I/156); *NAM Newsletter,* Nov. 3, 1939, 8; Bird, *"Better Living,"* 54–58.

41. Stuart Ewen, *PR: A Social History of Spin* (New York: Basic Books, 1996), 317–18; "National Industrial Information Committee 1939 Campaign—Goal $1,000,000," n.d., Acc. 1411, NAM III/843; James P. Selvage to Noel Sargent, July 2, 1935, Acc. 1411, NAM I/156. For NAM's 1930s public relations campaign, see Richard S. Tedlow, *Keeping the Corporate Image: Public Relations and Business, 1900–1950* (Greenwich, Conn.: JAI Press, 1979), 60–73.

42. "The American Family Robinson," scripts for programs 1–11, Synopsis of Succeeding Broadcasts of "The American Family Robinson," Nov. 1, 1934, Acc. 1411, NAM I/156.

43. Norbert Muhlen, "The Canned Opinion Industry," *Common Sense,* Oct. 1945, 9–11; Norbert Muhlen, "Radio: Political Threat or Promise? The Networks' Influence on the Public Mind," *Commentary* 3 (Mar. 1947): 203; Irving Fang, *Those Radio Commentators!* (Ames: University of Iowa Press, 1977), 3–14; David Holbrook Culbert, *News for Everyman: Radio and Foreign Affairs in Thirties America* (Westport, Conn.: Greenwood Press, 1976), 14–28.

44. Kathy M. Newman, *Radio Active: Advertising and Consumer Activism, 1935–1947* (Berkeley: University of California Press, 2004), 88; Culbert, *News for Everyman,* 34–59; Fang, *Those Radio Commentators!* 107–18; *Evening Public Ledger* (Philadelphia), June 24, July 14, Nov. 24, 1937.

45. "Self-Evident Subtlety," *Time,* Aug 1, 1938, 22; "L'Affaire Sokolsky," *New Republic,* Aug. 3, 1938, 360; *New York Times,* Mar. 17, 1937; *New York Herald Tribune,* June 8, 1936; Karen S. Miller, *The Voice of Business: Hill and Knowlton and Postwar Public Relations* (Chapel Hill: University of North Carolina Press, 1999), 12–18.

46. Fang, *Those Radio Commentators!* 35–38, 202–10; Culbert, *News for Everyman,* 153–72; Muhlen, "Canned Opinion Industry," 14; H. N. Oliphant, "Fulton Lewis, Jr.: Man of Distinction," *Harper's,* Mar. 1949, 77; Dixon Wecter, "Hearing Is Believing: Fulton Lewis, Jr.—Upton Close," *Atlantic Monthly,* August 1945, 54–55.

47. Harrison B. Summers, ed., *A Thirty-Year History of Programs Carried on National Radio Networks in the United States, 1926–1956* (New York: Arno Press, 1971), 67, 62; "100% Yardstick New York Radio Audience," Dec. 7, 1942, folder 6, box 1, Dec, 13, 1941, folder 1, box 1, Dec. 7, 1942, Monday to Friday, Apr. 1943, folder 1, box 2, Pulse Inc. Reports Papers, SHSW.

48. "Information on 'Cavalcade of America' Prepared for Educational Directors of the National Broadcasting Company," ca. Dec. 1939, folder 41, box 75, NBC; "Evidence of the Impact of 'Cavalcade,'" ca. 1956, box 8, Acc. 1803, Du Pont Advertising Department Papers, HML; Paul W. Sampson to W. S. Carpenter Jr., June 11, 1942, box 832, series II, pt. 2, Walter S. Carpenter Jr. files, Du Pont Company Records, HML.

49. A. R. Barbier to E. J. Condon, Mar. 21, 1940, box 20, Acc. 149, Advertising-General, Ford Motor Company Archives.

50. Walter S. Carpenter to Arthur C. Dorrance, Nov. 8, 1944, box 842, Carpenter files; Bruce Barton to Paul Markman, Mar. 12, 1956, box 76, Bruce Barton Papers, SHSW.

51. *Variety,* Oct. 16, 1935, Sept. 23, 1936, Oct. 6, 1937, Sept. 10, 1939, Sept. 11, 1946, Aug. 20, 1947, June 15, 1949, Sept. 7, 1949, Sept. 13, 1950, June 13, 1951, Sept. 3, 1952.

52. *Variety,* July 22, 1936, Feb. 2, 1938, Aug. 4, 1948, Feb. 27, 1946, Oct. 8, 1947.

53. Robert H. Zieger, *The CIO, 1935–1955* (Chapel Hill: University of North Carolina Press, 1995), chaps. 1–4.

54. *Wisconsin CIO News,* July 30, Nov. 14, Dec. 5, 1938, Feb. 20, 1939; *CIO News,* Dec. 15, 1937, Aug. 7, 1939; *United Automobile Worker,* Apr. 15, 1939.

55. Albert R. Priebe to FCC, Apr. 7, 1938, W. M. Hayman to Anning S. Prall, Feb. 4, 1936, box 190, General Corr., 1927–46, RG 173, FCC.

56. *West Side Conveyor,* Nov. 23, 1937.

57. *United Automobile Worker,* Oct. 18, 1937, Apr. 2, 1938, June 4, 1938, Feb. 28, 1940, Mar. 13, 1940.

58. *United Automobile Worker,* May 13, 1939.

59. See Newman, *Radio Active,* for a groundbreaking study of consumer activism and broadcasting; Ross, *Working-Class Hollywood,* 90–91.

60. Culbert, *News for Everyman,* 47–48; James B. Carey to Boake Carter, Nov. 2, 1936, Eleanor Fowler to James Carey, Oct. 31, 1936, box 41, Yellow Acc., UE Archives.

61. Newman, *Radio Active,* 81–108; Anita A. Brophy to Philco Radio Co., June 27, 1928, box A5-4, John Brophy Papers, Department of Archives and Manuscripts,

CUA; *Union Labor Record,* Aug. 6, 1937; James B. Carey to James Skinner, July 29, 1937, United Electrical Workers Local 101 to Leon Levy, July 29, 1937, box 41, Yellow Acc., UE Archives; "Resolutions" passed by Philadelphia Committee for Industrial Organization Council, Jan. 13, 1938, file 15, District 1 Records, Local Series, UE Archives.

62. *Variety,* June 30, Aug. 11, Nov. 11, Dec. 1, 1937, Jan. 5, 19, 26, Feb. 2, Mar. 16, Oct. 12, 1938; *Union Labor Record,* Jan. 21, 1938.

Chapter 2: Labor Radio

1. CIO Executive Board Minutes, July 2, 1936, box 14, Katherine P. Ellickson Papers, ALUA; UAW, *Proceedings* (1939 Special Convention), 106, 108, reel 22, ALUCP; Victor Reuther, *The Brothers Reuther* (Boston: Houghton Mifflin, 1976), 206.

2. Quoted in Melvyn Dubofsky and Warren Van Tine, *John L. Lewis* (New York: Quandrangle, 1977), 234, 250, 253.

3. *Variety,* Apr. 17, May 1, 15, 1935, Jan. 29, 1936; *Labor Herald and Citizen,* Sept. 21, 1935; CIO Executive Board Minutes, Nov. 7–8, 1936, reel 1, pt. 1, *CIO Files of John L. Lewis* (Frederick, Md.: University Publications of America, 1988); AFL, *Proceedings* (1935), 587; *ACLU Bulletin,* Oct. 25, 1935, Report on Los Angeles radio station by J. W. Buzzell, Oct. 7, 1935, vol. 770, ACLU.

4. Ronald L. Filippelli and Mark McColloch, *Cold War in the Working Class: The Rise and Decline of the United Electrical Workers* (Albany: State University of New York Press, 1995), 30; James B. Carey to John Edelman, Oct. 17, 1936, Carey to Joseph Nassau, Nov. 18, 1936, Carey to Edward N. Nockels, Dec. 18, 1936, box 41, Yellow Acc., UE Archives; CIO Executive Board Minutes, Nov. 7–8, 1936, reel 1, pt. 1, *CIO Files of John L. Lewis;* UE Executive Board Minutes, Dec. 3, 1936, UE Archives; *Radio Daily,* July 2, 15, Oct. 20, 29, 1937.

5. CIO Executive Board Minutes, Nov. 7–8, 1936, reel 1, pt. 1, *CIO Files of John L. Lewis;* James B. Carey to Joseph Nassau, Nov. 18, 1936, Report of Director John Brophy to the Meeting of the CIO in Atlantic City, Oct. 11, 1937, box 89, CIO Office of the Secretary-Treasurer Papers, ALUA; *ACLU Bulletin,* Oct. 25, 1935, Report on L.A. radio station by J. W. Buzzell, Oct. 7, 1935, vol. 770, ACLU; *Variety,* Oct. 20, 1937.

6. James Carey to M. S. Novik, Nov. 18, 1936, box 41, Yellow Acc., UE Archives; United Electrical Workers Executive Board Minutes, Dec. 3, 1936, UE Archives; *Labor Herald,* June 30, 1938.

7. Mark Starr, "Workers Education—CIO Model," reel 5, pt. 1, *CIO Files of John L. Lewis;* "CIO Placing Spots to Promote Cause," *Broadcasting,* Aug. 1, 1937, 23; *Variety,* May 19, 26, July 21, Sept. 1, 1937.

8. "CIO Placing Spots to Promote Cause," 23; *Variety,* July 21, 1937; Frank Fernbach Oral History Interview IV, July 25, 1975, HCLA; Transcripts, SWOC Sparrows Point Radio Program, box 5, Meyer Bernstein Papers, HCLA; James Carey to M. S. Novik, Nov. 18, 1936, box 41, Yellow Acc., UE Archives; *Variety,* July 21 and Sept. 1, 1937.

9. *Variety,* July 21 and Sept. 1, 1937; "CIO Placing Spots to Promote Cause," 23; Frank Fernbach Oral History Interview IV, July 25, 1975, HCLA; Gus Tyler, interview with the author, Nov. 12, 1998; Nathan Godfried, "Struggling over Politics and Cul-

ture: Organized Labor and Radio Station WEVD during the 1930s," *Labor History* 42 (2001): 351–52; *Daily Worker,* Dec. 28, 1938.

10. UAW Newsletter, June 19, July 23, 1936, box 6, Henry Kraus Papers, ALUA; Homer Martin Broadcasts, WCFL, Chicago, June 22, July 6, July 20, 1936, WJIM, Lansing, Mich., July 18, 1936, box 1, Richard Frankensteen broadcast, WMBC, Detroit, July 3, 1936, Delmond Garst Broadcasts, WTMV, St. Louis, Nov. 23, Nov. 25, Nov. 30, 1936, box 1, Norman Smith Papers, ALUA; *United Automobile Worker,* Sept. 1936, Feb. 23, 1937; Stanley Novak, Report at Organizers Meeting, Nov. 1936, box 7, Henry Kraus Papers, ALUA; Margaret Collingwood Nowak, *Two Who Were There: A Biography of Stanley Nowak* (Detroit: Wayne State University Press, 1989), 19–20, 77–78; "Motor Strike-National Job," *Business Week,* Jan. 23, 1937, 15.

11. Report of International Secretary Geo. F. Addes to General Executive Board, UAW, Sept. 13, 1937, box A-6, John Brophy Papers, CUA; *President's Report to Second Annual Convention of International Union, United Automobile Workers of America,* Aug. 1937, 42, 55, ALUA; *United Automobile Worker,* July 10, Aug. 21, Sept. 18, 1937, Mar. 12, 19, Apr. 30, 1938; *Detroit News,* June 5, 1937; *CIO News,* May 14, 1938; *Billboard,* Jan 1, 1938.

12. UAW Executive Board Minutes, May 9–25, 1938, box 2, ALUA; *Variety,* Mar. 30, 1938. Scripts of both factions' radio addresses are in box 4, Richard Frankensteen Papers, and box 4, Homer Martin Papers, ALUA.

13. *United Automobile Worker,* Sept. 13, 20, Oct. 4, Nov. 15, 29, Dec. 6, 1939; *CIO News,* Oct. 2, 1939; Steve Jefferys, *Management and Managed: Fifty Years of Crisis at Chrysler* (New York: Cambridge University Press, 1986), 81–87.

14. Scripts from the Ford drive can be found in box 30, UAW Public Relations Department Papers, and box 2, Maurice Sugar Papers, ALUA; *CIO News,* Oct. 7, 1940; *Variety,* May 14 and 21, 1941; *Ford Facts,* May 20, 1941.

15. Godfried, "Struggling over Politics and Culture," 357.

16. Morris S. Novik to Charles Zimmerman, Mar. 17, 1934, box 37, Charles S. Zimmerman Papers, ILGWU.

17. Godfried, "Struggling over Politics and Culture," 358–59; Publicity flyer for "The International Hour," box 7, Charles S. Zimmerman Papers, ILGWU.

18. Morris Novik interview by Nathan Godfried, Dec. 7, 1991 (transcript in author's possession); *Justice,* Jan. 15, Feb. 1, June 1, Sept. 15, 1935, Jan. 1, 1937; ILGWU, *Proceedings* (1953), 101, reel 48, ALUCP; *Justice,* Sept. 1, 1935, Jan. 15, 1936, Mar. 15, 1937; Publicity flyer for Local 22 Dressmakers Radio Hour, box 7, Charles S. Zimmerman Papers, ILGWU.

19. George Field to Charles Zimmerman, Jan. 9, 1935, "Facts in Brief about the Labor Hour," n.d., George Field to Zimmerman, June 11, Sept. 14, Oct. 11, 1938, Charles S. Zimmerman Papers, ILGWU; *Variety,* Feb. 24, 1937.

20. William Leader to John L. Lewis, July 31, 1936, reel 6, pt. 1, *CIO Files of John L. Lewis; Union Labor Record,* Aug. 6, 1936; William Dowell to Homer Martin, Apr. 23, 1935, Homer Martin to F. J. Dillon, Apr. 5, 1935, L. H. Turner to Radio Station WLBF, May 21, 1935, box 1, Homer Martin Papers, ALUA.

21. *Labor Review,* Jan. 4, 25, 1936.

22. *Shop Bulletin,* UE Local 1002, Jan. 30, 1939, box 70, Yellow Acc., UE Archives;

CIO News (Wisc. ed.), Aug. 20, 1938; *Variety,* Nov. 22, 1939; Lizabeth Cohen, *Making a New Deal: Industrial Workers in Chicago, 1919–1939* (Cambridge: Cambridge University Press, 1990), 343; *CIO News,* July 2, 1938; *Labor Herald,* Jan. 26, 1939; *CIO News,* Oct. 21, 1940.

23. Nathan Godfried, *WCFL: Chicago's Voice of Labor, 1926–78* (Urbana: University of Illinois Press, 1997), chaps. 6–8.

24. On the important role of radio in forging a collective oppositional consciousness, see Vincent J. Roscigno and William F. Danaher, *The Voice of Southern Labor: Radio, Music, and Textile Strikes, 1929–34* (Minneapolis: University of Minnesota Press, 2004).

25. Robert Zieger, *The CIO: 1935–1955* (Chapel Hill: University of North Carolina Press, 1995), 43–45; Philip Murray, "Report to the Steel Workers Organizing Committee," Sept. 29, 1936, reel 12, pt. 1, *CIO Files of John L. Lewis;* William L. Munger to John Brophy, Oct. 20, 1936, box 7–20, CIO National and International Union Files, 1935–56, CUA.

26. Reuther, *Brothers Reuther,* 172–78, 197–98; Clayton W. Fountain, *Union Guy* (New York: Viking Press, 1949), 48; Robert R. R. Brooks, *As Steel Goes . . . : Unionism in a Basic Industry* (New Haven, Conn.: Yale University Press, 1940), 112–13, 118; *Civil Liberties News,* Sept. 6, 1938, vol. 2021, ACLU; *CIO News,* Jan. 14, 1938; *United Automobile Worker,* July 31, 1937.

27. William Z. Foster, *Organizing Methods in the Steel Industry* (New York: Workers Library Publishers, 1936), 11–12; *Variety,* Dec. 8, 1937; Ford Organizing Program, WJBK, scripts, Nov. 7, 25, Dec. 13, 14, 1940, box 30, UAW Public Relations Department Papers, ALUA.

28. *United Automobile Worker,* Jan. 15, Mar. 12, 1938; August Meier and Elliott Rudwick, *Black Detroit and the Rise of the UAW* (Oxford: Oxford University Press, 1979), 96–97; Veal Clough Radio Address, Detroit, Jan. 24, 1941, Leonard Newman Radio Address, Detroit, Jan. 17, 1941, Luke Fennell Radio Address, Detroit, Dec. 13, 1940, box 30, UAW Public Relations Department Papers, ALUA.

29. *CIO News,* Dec. 8, 1941.

30. *Labor Review,* Oct. 27, Nov. 28, Dec. 19, 12, 1936; *The Advance,* Jan. 1937; *Steel Labor,* Jan. 9, 1937; Mary Heaton Vorse, *Labor's New Millions* (New York: Modern Age Books, 1938), 227.

31. *PM,* Feb. 13, 1941; *Justice,* Feb. 1, 15, Mar. 1, 1941.

32. *Justice,* Sept. 1, Oct. 1, 15, Nov. 1, 15, 1935.

33. Roscigno and Danaher, *Voice of Southern Labor,* esp. 104.

34. "Strike Sponsors," *Broadcasting,* Oct. 15, 1938, 44; *United Rubber Worker,* Apr. 1936; Daniel Nelson, *American Rubber Workers and Organized Labor, 1900–1941* (Princeton, N.J.: Princeton University Press, 1988), 193–97; P. W. Litchfield broadcast, Mar. 9, 1936, reel 26, Adolph Germer Papers, SHSW; Congress of Industrial Organizations, *How the Rubber Workers Won* (Washington, D.C.: CIO, 1936), in box 5, Meyer Bernstein Papers, HCLA.

35. Ruth McKinney, *Industrial Valley* (New York: Harcourt Brace, 1939), 307; Richard Frankensteen Radio Broadcast, July 10, 1936, box 6, Henry Kraus Papers, ALUA; *Labor Review,* June 20 and July 11, 1936.

36. *Socialist Call*, June 12, 1937; Henry Kraus, *Heroes of Unwritten Story: The UAW, 1934–39* (Urbana: University of Illinois Press, 1993), 306–7.

37. Frank Fernbach Oral History Interview, pt. IV, July 25, 1975, HCLA.

38. It was common for strikers to add new lyrics specific to their particular struggle to old melodies. Roscigno and Danaher, *Voice of Southern Labor*, 110; *New York Post*, Mar. 21, 1936; *Akron Times-Press*, Mar. 16, 1936; *The Advance*, Apr. 1936; Rose Pesotta, *Bread upon the Waters* (New York: Dodd, Mead, and Co., 1944), 221–22; John Brophy, *A Miner's Life* (Madison: University of Wisconsin Press, 1964), 264; Ruth McKinney, *Industrial Valley*, 359–65.

39. On industrial union culture in the 1930s, see Elizabeth Fones-Wolf, "Industrial Unionism and Labor Movement Culture in Depression-Era Philadelphia," *Pennsylvania Magazine of History* 109 (Jan. 1985): 3–26; Cohen, *Making a New Deal*, 333–49; Michael Denning, *The Cultural Front: The Laboring of American Culture in the Twentieth Century* (London: Verso, 1996), 67–77; *United Automobile Worker*, Nov. 1, 1941.

40. Bruce Lenthall, "Tuning in to a Changing American Culture in the Great Depression" (Ph.D. diss., University of Pennsylvania, 1999), 18; Susan J. Douglas, *Listening In: Radio and the American Imagination, from Amos 'n' Andy and Edward R. Murrow to Wolfman Jack and Howard Stern* (New York: Times Books, 1999), 23–24; *Justice*, Nov. 1934, Feb. 1, June 1, July 1, Oct. 1, 1935, Jan. 1, 1937.

41. *Variety*, Mar. 9, 1938; *CIO News*, May 14, 1938; *Billboard*, Jan. 1, 1938; *United Automobile Worker*, June 26, 1937, Jan. 8, Feb. 5, Mar. 12, 19, 26, Apr. 30, 1938.

42. Cohen, *Making a New Deal*, 346–49; *United Automobile Worker*, Dec. 11, 1937; UAW WJBK broadcasts, scripts, Nov. 12, 1940, May 8, 1941, box 30, UAW Public Relations Department Papers, ALUA; Norman Smith broadcast, Nov. 30, 1936, John Kociscak broadcast, Jan. 28, 1937, box 1, Norman Smith Papers, ALUA; *United Automobile Worker*, Nov. 29, 1939; *Labor Review*, Apr. 25, 1936.

43. *United Automobile Worker*, Mar. 14, June 26, July 10, Aug. 14, 1937.

44. *United Automobile Worker*, Nov. 15, 1939.

45. B. J. Damich Radio Address, script, Cleveland, July 12, 1937, reel 14, pt. 1, *CIO Files of John L. Lewis*.

46. John L. Lewis, *The Future of Organized Labor* (Washington, D.C.: Committee for Industrial Organization, 1935), in reel 1, pt. 1, *CIO Files of John L. Lewis;* Norman Smith Radio Address, Memphis, Oct. 6, 1937, box 1, Norman Smith Papers, ALUA; *Steel Labor*, July 28, 1939.

47. Address by Thomas Kennedy, Harrisburg, Pa., Aug. 3, 1937, box 5, Meyer Bernstein Papers, HCLA; John Brophy Labor Day Address, script, Sept. 6, 1937, box A5–5, John Brophy Papers, CUA; *Labor Review*, Jan. 18, 1936; A. J. Pickett Radio Address, East St. Louis, Ill., Dec. 2, 1936, box 1, Norman Smith Papers, ALUA.

48. John Brophy, New Haven radio talk, Oct. 3, 1937, box A5–5, John Brophy Papers, CUA; Delmond Garst, St. Louis, Nov. 25, 1936, Jan. 12, 1937, Norman Smith broadcast, Memphis, Oct. 5, 1937, box 1, Norman Smith Papers, ALUA; *United Automobile Worker*, Nov. 15, 1939.

49. John Brophy Labor Day Address, script, Sept. 6, 1937, box A5–5, John Brophy Papers, CUA. On unions and Americanism, see Gary Gerstle, *Working-Class Ameri-*

canism: The Politics of Labor in a Textile City, 1914–1960 (Cambridge: Cambridge University Press, 1989).

50. *Socialist Call,* Feb. 6, 20, 1937; Address by Norman Thomas, "President Roosevelt and the Share Croppers," NBC, Mar. 26, 1936, Address by Norman Thomas, "The Forgotten Men," CBS, Feb. 21, 1935, Address by Norman Thomas, "The Sharecropper and the AAA," NBC Network, Apr. 3, 1935, reel 1, *Southern Tenant Farmers' Union Papers, 1934–1970,* microfilm (Glenlock, N.J.: Microfilming Corporation of America, 1971).

51. *Journal of Commerce,* Jan. 28, 1937; Meyer Bernstein to Jacob Bernstein, Feb. 3, 1938, box 1, Meyer Bernstein Papers, HCLA.

52. *United Automobile Worker,* Oct. 9, 18, 1937; George Lambert, "Memphis Is Safe for Ford," *The Nation,* Jan. 22, 1938, 93; Perry C. Cotham, *Toil, Turmoil, and Triumph: A Portrait of the Tennessee Labor Movement* (Franklin, Tenn.: Hillsboro Press, 1995), 167–68.

53. Michael K. Honey, *Southern Labor and Black Civil Rights: Organizing Memphis Workers* (Urbana: University of Illinois Press, 1993), 177–213.

54. Pesotta, *Bread upon the Waters,* 191–92; *Justice,* Jan. 1, 1936.

55. Quoted in Roscigno and Danaher, *Voice of Southern Labor,* 107.

56. Nowak, *Two Who Were There,* 28–41.

57. CIO, *Proceedings* (1941), 69, reel 18, ALUCP.

Chapter 3: Codes of Silence

1. Elmer E. Smead, *Freedom of Speech by Radio and Television* (Washington, D.C.: Public Affairs Press, 1959), 48–49.

2. William S. Paley, *The American System of Broadcasting* (Chicago: N.p., 1937); John F. Royal to Niles Trammel, Dec. 12, 1939, folder 40, box 108, NBC.

3. Elizabeth Fones-Wolf, "Creating a Favorable Business Climate: Corporations and Radio Broadcasting, 1934–1954," *Business History Review* 73 (Summer 1999): 233–43; William L. Bird Jr., *"Better Living": Advertising, Media, and the New Vocabulary of Business Leadership, 1935–1955* (Evanston, Ill.: Northwestern University Press, 1999), chaps. 3–4; U.S. Congress, Senate Committee on Interstate Commerce, *Hearing on S. 814 to Amend the Communications Act of 1934,* 78th Cong., 1st Sess., 586.

4. Steven J. Ross, *Working-Class Hollywood: Silent Film and the Shaping of Class in America* (Princeton, N.J.: Princeton University Press, 1998), 108–10, 170–72, 196–96, 245–47; Gregory D. Black, *Hollywood Censored: Morality Codes, Catholics, and the Movies* (Cambridge: Cambridge University Press, 1994).

5. Daniel Czitrom, *Media and the American Mind: From Morse to McLuhan* (Chapel Hill: University of North Carolina Press, 1982), 81; Robert W. McChesney, "Public Broadcasting in the Age of Communications Revolution," *Monthly Review* 47 (Dec. 1995): 4; Robert W. McChesney, *Telecommunications, Mass Media, and Democracy: The Battle for Control of U.S. Broadcasting, 1928–1935* (New York: Oxford University Press, 1993), 94; Bruce Lenthall, "Critical Reception: Public Intellectuals Decry Depression-Era Radio, Mass Culture, and Modern America," in *The Radio Reader: Essays in the Cultural History of Radio,* ed. Michele Holmes and Jason Loviglio (New York: Routledge, 2002), 51–54.

6. McChesney, *Telecommunications, Mass Media, and Democracy;* Susan Smulyan, *Selling Radio: The Commercialization of American Broadcasting, 1920–1934* (Washington, D.C.: Smithsonian Institution Press, 1994).

7. Richard W. Steele, *Propaganda in an Open Society: The Roosevelt Administration and the Media, 1933–1941* (Westport, Conn.: Greenwood Press, 1985), 18.

8. Stuart Ewen, *PR: A Social History of Spin* (New York: Basic Books, 1996), 251; Steele, *Propaganda in an Open Society*, 17–25, 127–36; Erik Barnouw, *The Golden Web: A History of Broadcasting in the United States, 1933–1953*, vol. 2 (New York: Oxford University Press, 1968), 62–63, 115–16; *Variety*, Jan. 4, 1939.

9. NBC quoted in Douglas B. Craig, *Fireside Politics: Radio and Political Culture in the United States, 1920–1940* (Baltimore: Johns Hopkins University Press, 2000), 124; Report of the President of the National Broadcasting Company to the National Advisory Council, May 1935, David Rosenblum to R. C. Patterson Jr., Apr. 16, 1935, "Policy on Public Service Programs," and enclosed in R. C. Patterson Jr. to David Sarnoff, Apr. 30, 1935, box 359, Policy-Program Policies, 1934–37 folder, NBC-LC.

10. Barnouw, *Golden Web*, 70; Bird, *"Better Living,"* 17; Robert W. Snyder, "Big Time, Small Time, All around the Town: New York Vaudeville in the Early Twentieth Century," in *For Fun and Profit: The Transformation of Leisure into Consumption*, ed. Richard Butsch (Philadelphia: Temple University Press, 1990), 118–31; Burke Boyce to John F. Royal, May 20, 1935, box 359, Policy-Program Policy, 1934–37 folder, John F. Royal to Niles Trammell, Mar. 2, 1933, box 361, Policy-Program Policies, 1926–34 folder, NBC-LC.

11. Quoted in Nathan Godfried, *WCFL: Chicago's Voice of Labor, 1926–78* (Urbana: University of Illinois Press, 1997), 20.

12. Barnouw, *Golden Web*, 119; ACLU Press Release, Aug. 27 and 28, 1935, Norman Corwin to Clifton Read, Aug. 27, 1935, telegram, John L. Clark to Roger Baldwin, Aug. 27, 1935, ACLU; Clifton Reed, "Radio Censors Labor," *The Nation*, Sept. 25, 1935, 357.

13. American Civil Liberties Union, *Radio Is Censored!* (New York: ACLU, 1936), 20–21.

14. Mina F. Kassner to American Civil Liberties Union, Oct. 26, 1937, Memorandum Indicating the Necessity for the Radio Bills to Be Introduced in the Coming Session of Congress by the American Civil Liberties Union, enclosed with Mina F. Kassner to Hazel Rice, Dec. 1, 1937, vol. 1011, ACLU. In 1940, R. J. Thomas reported to the UAW convention that the union had met "with difficulty in purchasing an adequate amount of time from the large stations." *Report of R. J. Thomas, President, UAWA, July 29, 1940*, 50, ALUA.

15. American Civil Liberties Union, *Radio Is Censored!* 22; *Daily Worker*, Dec. 13, 1935; Ernest Besis to Roger Baldwin, June 28, 1935, ACLU Press Release, July 9, 1935, vol. 770, ACLU; *Variety*, June 12, 1935.

16. *Socialist Call*, Jan. 23, 1937; Mary Heaton Vorse, *Labor's New Millions* (New York: Modern Age Books, 1938), 138. The Canadian station CKLW, located just across the river from Detroit, however, refused to broadcast the second of a series of six UAW talks because the station manager believed the address to be too controversial. An angered UAW canceled the remainder of the series. *United Automobile Worker*, Jan. 22, 1937; *Variety*, Jan. 27, 1937.

17. Ruth Brindze, *Not To Be Broadcast: The Truth about the Radio* (New York: Vanguard Press, 1937), 181–82.

18. Ernest De Maio to Jerome M. Britchey, May 8, 1939, vol. 2104, ACLU.

19. Samuel S. White to Roger Baldwin, Jan. 28, 1937, Scripts from Dallas Dressmakers Union, n.d., *Dallas Ladies' Garment Worker,* Jan. 18, 1937, vol. 1060, ACLU.

20. *Federation News,* Mar. 6, 1937.

21. Alden Whitman to Roger Baldwin, May 20, 1937, Charles E. Clift to John Shepard, May 27, 1937, John Shepard to Charles E. Clift, May 31, 1937, vol. 1010, ACLU; *Variety,* May 26, 1937; Elizabeth McLeod, "Local Voices: The Don Lee and Yankee Networks," Broadcasting History Links, Jan. 24, 2006, http:www.midcoast.com/lizmcl/regional.html.

22. Memorandum Indicating the Necessity for the Radio Bills to Be Introduced in the Coming Session of Congress by the American Civil Liberties Union, enclosed with Mina F. Kassner to Hazel Rice, Dec. 1, 1937, vol. 1011, ACLU; *Report of R. J. Thomas, President, UAWA, July 29, 1940,* 50, ALUA; *Federated Press Labor Letters,* Mar. 8, 1928.

23. Louis F. Spisak speech, WHK, Jan. 25, 1937, Steve Jenso to Roger Baldwin, Jan. 26, 1937, vol. 1010, ACLU; *New York Times,* Feb. 2, 1937; *Variety,* Feb. 3, 1937; Steve Jenso to Federal Radio Commission, Jan. 14, 1937, Paul Miley Speech, ca. Jan. 1937, WHK, reel 1, pt. 1, *CIO Files of John L. Lewis* (Frederick, Md.: University Publications of America, 1988).

24. "CIO Cancels Program on Colonial, Objecting to Explanatory Remarks," *Broadcasting,* July 1, 1937, 70; *New York Times,* May 22 and 24, 1937; *Variety,* May 26, 1937.

25. *Variety,* May 26, 1937.

26. To Mr. Royal, June 2, 1938, box 357, Policy-Program Policies, 1938 folder, NBC-LC; Paley, *American System of Broadcasting.*

27. *Variety,* Feb. 9, 1937; Michael Denning, *The Cultural Front: The Laboring of American Culture in the Twentieth Century* (London: Verso, 1996), 302–3.

28. Memorandum for Labor Unions Indicating the Necessity for Supporting Bills S. 2755, S. 2756, S. 2757, and HR 3038, HR 3039, Introduced into 75th Congress, 1st. Sess., ca. Dec. 1937, vol. 1011, ACLU; Godfried, *WCFL,* 145; Harry Boyer to John L. Lewis, reel 6, pt. 1, Kathryn Lewis to Philip Murray, Dec. 24, 1936, reel 12, pt. 1, *CIO Files of John L. Lewis.*

29. Brindze, *Not to Be Broadcast,* 174–75; Thomas quoted in Godfried, *WCFL,* 150.

30. Alexander Ware, "U.S. Constitution: 'I Am the Law,'" *Christian Science Monitor,* July 1, 1939; John F. Royal to Janet MacRorie, Aug. 21, 1939, folder 70, box 77, NBC; John F. Royal to Niles Trammell, Dec. 14, 1939, folder 40, box 108, NBC.

31. Hazel L. Rice to John W. Love, Dec. 28, 1937, vol 1011, ACLU; Hannah Haskell to I. Lutsky, Apr. 18, 1938, Montreal Dressmakers Union Local 262 to Hannah Haskell, Apr. 14, 1938, William Ross to David Dubinsky, Apr. 15, 1938, box 80, David Dubinsky Papers, ILGWU; Kathryn Lewis to David Dubinsky, Aug. 17, 1937, Kathryn Lewis to Paul Fuller, Aug. 18, 1937, reel 12, pt. 1, *CIO Files of John L. Lewis.*

32. Barnouw, *Golden Web,* 29–36; Smead, *Freedom of Speech,* 45–57; Frank M. Russell to R. C. Patterson, Oct. 26, 1934, John F. Royal to Frank Mason, June 7, 1934, folder 29, box 25, NBC.

33. John F. Royal to William Hedges, Nov. 11, 1934, John F. Royal to Richard C. Patterson, Feb. 20, 1935, folder 40, box 39, NBC; Bird, *"Better Living,"* 28–29.

34. Barnouw, *Golden Web,* 14–15; Lenox R. Lohr to Jouett Shouse, June 18, 1936, folder 34, box 43, NBC.

35. Memorandum of Minutes of the Eleventh Meeting of the Advisory Council of NBC, Apr. 12, 1938, reel 21, NBC; L. H. Titterton to William Burke Miller, Jan. 11, 1937, Policy-Program Policies, 1929–50 folder, box 358, NBC-LC; John F. Royal to David Sarnoff, Jan. 25, 1937, folder 45, box 53, NBC.

36. Report of the President of the National Broadcasting Company to the Advisory Council of the National Broadcasting Company, Ninth Annual Meeting, May 27, 1935, vol. 769, ACLU.

37. NAM Public Information Program, June 20, 1940, box 114, series I, Acc. 1411, NAM (hereafter Acc. 1411, NAM I/114); *Variety,* Dec. 18, 1940; S. H. Walker and Paul Sklar, "Business Finds Its Voice," *Harper's,* Jan. 1938, 123.

38. Brindze, *Not to Be Broadcast,* 197–98; John F. Royal to M. H. Aylesworth, Oct. 29, 1934, folder 29, box 25, NBC.

39. Bird, *"Better Living,"* 51–52; William Millikan, *A Union against Unions: The Minneapolis Citizens Alliance and Its Fight against Organized Labor, 1903–1947* (St. Paul: Minnesota Historical Society, 2001), 284, 328.

40. *Report of R. J. Thomas, President, UAWA, July 29, 1940,* 50, ALUA; Samuel S. White to Roger Baldwin, Jan. 28, 1937, vol. 1060, ACLU; Nick Hughes to FCC, Nov. 13, 1937, vol. 1010, ACLU.

41. Hazel Rice to Henry J. Eckstein, Dec. 7, 1937, vol. 1011, ACLU; Brindze, *Not to Be Broadcast,* 116, 180–89, 196–214; Kathy M. Newman, "Poisons, Potions, and Profits: Radio Rebels and the Origins of the Consumer Movement," in *Radio Reader: Essays in the Cultural History of Radio,* ed. Michele Hilmes and Jason Loviglio (New York: Routledge, 2002), 167–69.

42. On KGCC, see T. J. Slowie to James D. O'Neill, Apr. 21, 1938, and letters from the Portland Industrial Union Council, the Ship Scalers and Painters, the Alameda County Industrial Union Council, and the Steel Workers Organizing Committee, among others, all in box 349, General Corr., 1927–46, FCC; T. J. Slowie to Frank Berson, May 13, 1938, box 184, FCC. For other protests to the FCC, see Nick Hughes to FCC, Nov. 13, 1937, and Resolution adopted by Seattle Labor Unity Council, Sept. 7, 1939, vol. 1010, ACLU, among many others.

43. T. J. Slowie to E. Anthony and Sons, Apr. 16, 1938, box 349, T. J. Slowie to S. H. Dalrymple, Nov. 7, 1939, Frank R. McNinch to Robert Wagner, Feb. 9, 1939, box 184, FCC.

44. Alden Whitman to Roger Baldwin, May 20, 1937, Charles E. Clift to Alden Whitman, May 27, 1937, vol. 1010, ACLU.

45. *Variety,* Oct. 20, Dec. 16, 1937; "Oct. 17 Tentative Date for Net Study," *Broadcasting,* Sept. 15, 1938, 3; "Chain-Monopoly Hearing Moved to Nov. 14," *Broadcasting,* Oct. 15, 1938, 17–18; Lee Pressman to T. J. Slowie, Sept. 23, 1938, box 349, FCC.

46. Steele, *Propaganda in an Open Society,* 130–31; Craig, *Fireside Politics,* 100–104; Harrison B. Summers, ed., *Radio Censorship* (New York: H. W. Wilson Co., 1939), 27–36; Philip Foster Napoli, "Empire of the Middle: Radio and the Emergence of an Electronic Society" (Ph.D. diss., Columbia University, 1998), 148–54.

47. Black, *Hollywood Censored.*

48. James D. Secrest, "Causes of the Friction in the Communication Commission," *Congressional Digest* 17 (Dec. 1938): 297; *New York Times,* Nov. 15, 1938; "Self Regulation Move Comes from Inquiry," *Broadcasting,* Dec. 1, 1938, 14; Neville Miller to Lenox Lohr, Dec. 8, 1938, folder 66, box 62, William S. Hedges to Lohr et al., June 12, 1939, Frank Russell to Niles Trammell, June 9, 1939, folder 78, box 70, NBC; "Debate Ends FCC Inquiry," *Broadcasting,* June 1, 1939, 56; Craig, *Fireside Politics,* 261.

49. *The Code of the National Association of Broadcasters, Adopted by the 17th Annual Convention of the NAB,* July 11, 1939, 3–4, folder 78, box 70, NBC; "Stringent Code Is Submitted to Industry," *Broadcasting,* June 15, 1939, 9, 66–67; "Code: Self Sacrifice," *Broadcasting,* June 15, 1939, 44; Craig, *Fireside Politics,* 264.

50. Ed Kirby to Neville Miller, Nov. 25, 1938, folder 66, box 62, NBC; NAB, *Code Manual* (1939), 15–17, box 355, NBC-LC; Report of Joseph N. Miller on Labor Programs, attached to Janet MacRorie to Niles Trammell, Apr. 6, 1939, folder 78, box 70, NBC; Elmer E. Snead, *Freedom of Speech by Radio and Television* (Washington, D.C.: Public Affairs Press, 1959), 48–49.

51. "Adopt Radio Code," *Business Week,* July 22, 1939, 33; "Radio Writes a Code for Itself," *Christian Century,* July 26, 1939, 917; T. R. Carskadon, "Radio Cleans House," *New Republic,* July 12, 1939, 274–75.

52. David Lawrence, "Radio's New Code," *U.S. News,* July 17, 1939, 14; "Elliott Roosevelt in Tiff with Coughlin Who Declines MBS Time Offer for Reply," *Broadcasting,* Aug. 1, 1939, 28; *Washington Post,* Dec. 17, 1939; "The Broadcasters' Code," *Publishers Weekly,* Dec. 9, 1939, 2141; *Variety,* Oct. 11, 1939.

53. Neville Miller, "The Code Preserves Free Speech," address over CBS, Oct. 22, 1939, folder 79, box 70, NBC; Neville Miller to Roger Baldwin, Dec. 23, 1939, vol. 2212, ACLU; Neville Miller, "Radio's Code of Self Regulation, *Public Opinion Quarterly* 3 (October 1939): 683–86.

54. Frank M. Russell to Niles Trammel, Oct. 10, 1939, folder 77, box 70, Nov. 30, 1939, folder 79, box 70, NBC; Sol Taishoff, "Fly's Approval Brings New Code Support," *Broadcasting,* Nov. 1, 1939, 13, 72; *Statement of Distinguished Groups Praising the New NAB Code,* pamphlet, ca. Oct. 1939, vol. 2107, ACLU; *Radio Daily,* Oct. 10, 1939.

55. Minutes of the Meeting of the Radio Committee of the National Council on Freedom from Censorship, May 25, 1939, Report of the Committee on Radio to the Board of Directors of the American Civil Liberties Union, July 24, 1939, vol. 2108, ACLU statement on NAB Code, ca. Nov. 1939, vol. 2212, ACLU.

56. McChesney, *Telecommunications, Mass Media, and Democracy,* 8, 80–85, 236–39.

57. ACLU statement on NAB Code, ca. Nov. 1939, vol. 2212, Minutes of the Meeting of the Radio Committee of the National Council on Freedom from Censorship, July 24, 1939, vol. 2063, ACLU; NAB Press Release, Oct. 7, 1939, folder 77, box 70, Frank Russell to Niles Trammell, Oct. 13, 1939, folder 79, box 70, NBC; *New York Post,* Oct. 9, 1939.

58. M. H. Aylesworth to William Green, Jan. 3, 1936, folder 47, box 46, NBC; Report of Joseph N. Miller on Labor Programs, enclosed in Janet MacRorie to Niles Trammell, Apr. 6, 1939, folder 78, box 70, NBC; Emanie N. Arling, Report on NAB Code, Feb. 1, 1940, vol. 2212, ACLU.

59. "First Code Act Brings NAB Discord," *Broadcasting,* Oct. 15, 1939, 72.

60. Henry Eckstein to Neville Miller, Oct. 23, 1939, folder 79, box 70, NBC; Eckstein to Hazel Rice, Oct. 23, 1939, vol. 2110, ACLU.

61. John A. Garraty and Mark C. Carnes, eds., *American National Biography,* vol. 7 (New York: Oxford University Press, 1999), 564–65; Morris L. Ernst, *The First Freedom* (New York: MacMillan Co., 1946), 125; Hazel Rice to RNB, Nov. 24, 1939, vol. 2061, *Traveler* (clipping), Oct. 14, 1939, vol. 2107, ACLU; "Broadcasters' Code," 2141.

62. Report of Joseph N. Miller on Labor Programs, enclosed in Janet MacRorie to Niles Trammell, Apr. 6, 1939, folder 78, box. 70, NBC; UAW Press Release, Oct. 12, 1944, vol. 2602, ACLU.

63. Henry Eckstein to Sidney M. Kaye, Nov. 2, 1939, Henry Eckstein to Quincy Howe, Nov. 2, 1939, vol. 2110, ACLU; *Union Labor Record,* Nov. 10, 1939.

64. James H. Wishart to Hazel L. Rice, Nov. 3, 1939, vol. 2104, ACLU; *United Automobile Worker,* Nov. 8, 1939; *Variety,* Nov. 8, 22, 1939.

65. T. J. Slowie to S. H. Dalrymple, Nov. 7, 1939, box 310, FCC; *Variety,* Nov. 15, 1939.

66. James Wishart to Hazel L. Rice, Nov. 3, 1939, Hazel Rice to Elizabeth Magee, Nov. 1, 1939, vol. 2104, ACLU; *Variety,* Nov. 15, 1939.

67. *United Automobile Worker,* Nov. 8, 15, 1939.

68. *CIO News,* Nov. 13, 1939; *United Automobile Worker,* Nov. 15, 1939; *Variety,* Nov. 8, 1939.

69. *Variety,* Nov. 22, Dec. 20, 1939; *CIO News,* Dec. 11, 1939.

70. *CIO News,* Oct. 21, Nov. 4, 1940; *New York Times,* Oct. 31, 1940. See box 349, FCC, for sixty-nine letters sent between Oct. 23, 1940, and Mar. 27, 1941, from West Coast unions protesting the cancellation of "Labor on the Air." Also see James L. Fly to Philip Murray, Dec. 4, 1940, and James L. Fly to John L. Lewis, Nov. 8, 1940, box 349, FCC.

71. Craig, *Fireside Politics,* 96–96; "FCC Starts Newspaper Ownership Drive," *Broadcasting,* Mar. 24, 1941, 7–9; "Running Account of Press-Radio Hearings before FCC," *Broadcasting,* Sept. 22, 1941, 24–26.

72. E. M. Stoer to John S. Brookes Jr., Aug. 30, Sept. 1, 1939, John S. Brookes Jr. to E. M. Stoer, Aug. 31, 1939, box 1938, docket 6051, FCC.

73. Clarence Lindner to John S. Brookes Jr., Jan. 11 and Feb. 17, 1940, box 1938, docket 6051, FCC.

74. E. M. Stoer to John S. Brookes, Jan. 18, 1940, E. M. Stoer to Reiland Quinn, Mar. 5, 1940, Grove J. Fink to R. L. Quinn, Apr. 19, 1940, box 1938, docket 6051, FCC.

75. Reiland Quinn to E. M. Stoer, May 21, June 4, 26, 1940, Stoer to C. B. McCabe, May 29, 1940, McCabe to Stoer, June 6, 1940, box 1938, docket 6051, FCC; Stoer testimony, Sept. 18, Hearings on Press Control of Radio Stations, box 1933, docket 6051, FCC.

76. Clarence Lindner to R. E. Berlin, Aug. 15, 1940, Harold Meyer to E. M. Stoer, undated telegram, ca. Sept. 1940, Stoer to Meyer, undated telegram, ca. Sept. 1940, C. B. McCabe to Stoer, Sept. 27, 1940, Stoer to Meyer, Oct. 2, 1940, Meyer to Stoer, Oct. 10, 1940, Stoer to James Lawrence Fly, Nov. 19, 1940, Charles Linder to Walter A. Haas, Oct. 14, 1940, Meyer to Stoer, Oct. 23, 1940 (Exhibit 157), Meyer to Stoer, Oct. 23, 1940 (Exhibit 158), box 1938, docket 6051, FCC.

77. CIO, *Proceedings* (1939), 24–25, 35, reel 17, ALUCP; CIO, *Proceedings* (1940), 52, 85, 309–10, reel 17, ALUCP; CIO, *Proceedings* (1941), 69–70, 291, reel 18, ALUCP.

Chapter 4: "The Air Belongs to the People"

1. Office of War Information, Bureau of Intelligence, Media Division, Weekly Media Report no. 30, Aug. 29, 1942, box 1720, Records of the Office of Government Reports, Bureau of Special Services, Office of War Information, RG 44, NARA.

2. AFL, *Proceedings* (1942), 138, reel 13, ALUCP; CIO, *Proceedings* (1943), 57, reel 18, ALUCP.

3. Robert H. Zieger, *American Workers, American Unions* (Baltimore: Johns Hopkins University Press, 1994), 62–99; Howell John Harris, *The Right to Manage: Industrial Relations Policies of American Business in the 1940s* (Madison: University of Wisconsin Press, 1982), 23–74.

4. Roland Marchand, *Creating the Corporate Soul: The Rise of Public Relations and Corporate Imagery in American Big Business* (Berkeley: University of California Press, 1998), 312–40; Robert Griffith, "The Selling of America: The Advertising Council and American Politics, 1942–1960," *Business History Review* 57 (Autumn 1983): 388–412; Frank W. Fox, *Madison Avenue Goes to War: The Strange Military Career of American Advertising, 1941–1945* (Provo, Utah: Brigham Young University Press, 1975).

5. "CIO's Heat Wave," *Broadcasting*, Aug. 28, 1944, 104.

6. Joel Seidman, *American Labor from Defense to Reconversion* (Chicago: University of Chicago Press, 1953), 67–73.

7. Donaldson Brown to W. P. Withrow, July 31, 1942, box 112, series I, Acc. 1411, NAM (hereafter Acc. 1411, NAM I/112); *NAM News: War Congress of American Industry,* Dec. 12, 1942, p. 13, Acc. 1411, NAM III/845.

8. Donaldson Brown to W. P. Withrow, July 31, 1942, Acc. 1411, NAM I/112.

9. *NAM News: War Congress of American Industry,* Dec. 12, 1942, p. 32, Acc. 1411, NAM III/845; C. E. Harrison to Mr. Weisenburger, Dec. 18, 1944, C. E. Harrison to NIIC Staff Executives, n.d., Acc. 1411 NAM III/845; National Industrial Information Committee, *Annual Report* (1943), Acc. 1411, NAM III/842.

10. Marchand, *Creating the Corporate Soul,* 312–15; Gerd Horten, *Radio Goes to War: The Cultural Politics of Propaganda during World War II* (Berkeley: University of California Press, 2002), 93–101; "Advertising in Wartime," *New Republic,* Feb. 21, 1944, 233–36.

11. Victor H. Bernstein, "The Anti-Labor Front," *Antioch Review* 3 (Sept. 1943): 330; "Advertising in Wartime," 235; Marchand, *Creating the Corporate Soul,* 321–24.

12. Erik Barnouw, *The Golden Web: A History of Broadcasting in the United States, 1933–1953,* vol. 2 (New York: Oxford University Press, 1968), 166; Horten, *Radio Goes to War,* 101.

13. Marchand, *Creating the Corporate Soul,* 332–33; Barnouw, *Golden Web,* 166.

14. Horten, *Radio Goes to War,* 105; Policyholders Service Bureau, Metropolitan Life Insurance Company, *Community Relations: Telling the Company's Story* (New York: Metropolitan Life Insurance Co., 1949), 18; "U.S. Rubber Co. Adopts Policy for Symphony Series," *Broadcasting,* May 24, 1943, 18; Marchand, *Creating the Corporate Soul,* 338.

15. Douglas B. Craig, *Fireside Politics: Radio and Political Culture in the United States, 1920–1940* (Baltimore: Johns Hopkins University Press, 2000), 217–21; Horten, *Radio Goes to War,* 25–33; "Interest in Newscasts Soared in 1943," *Broadcasting,* Jan. 24, 1944, 13; Susan J. Douglas, *Listening In: Radio and the American Imagination, from Amos 'n' Andy and Edward R. Murrow to Wolfman Jack and Howard Stern* (New York: Times Books, 1999), 189, 196.

16. Douglas, *Listening In,* 189, 196.

17. Irving E. Fang, *Those Radio Commentators!* (Ames: Iowa Sate University Press, 1977), 205; David Holbrook Culbert, *News for Everyman: Radio and Foreign Affairs in Thirties America* (Westport, Conn.: Greenwood Press, 1976), 169; H. N. Oliphant, "Fulton Lewis Jr., Man of Distinction," *Harper's,* Mar. 1949, 77–83; Dixton Wecter, "Hearing Is Believing: Fulton Lewis Jr.—Upton Close," *Atlantic Monthly,* Aug. 1945, 54–55.

18. Norbert Muhlen, "Radio: Political Threat or Promise? The Networks' Influence on the Public Mind," *Commentary* 3 (Mar. 1947): 204; Wecter, "Hearing Is Believing," 55–61; Fang, *Those Radio Commentators!* 121–29.

19. Culbert, *News for Everyman,* 67–90; Fang, *Those Radio Commentators!* 17–35; David G. Clark, "H. V. Kaltenborn and His Sponsors: Controversial Broadcasting and the Sponsor's Role," *Journal of Broadcasting* 7 (Fall 1968): 309–10.

20. Clark, "H. V. Kaltenborn and his Sponsors," 311.

21. David G. Clark, "The Dean of Commentators: A Biography of H. V. Kaltenborn" (Ph.D. diss., University of Wisconsin, 1965), 502.

22. Ibid., 499–502; Chester Giraud, "The Radio Commentaries of H. V. Kaltenborn: A Case Study in Persuasion" (Ph.D. diss., University of Wisconsin, 1947), 389–427, esp. 404 and 423; Address of H. V. Kaltenborn, Sept. 3, 1942, box 164, H. V. Kaltenborn Papers, SHSW; A. A. Schechter to C. L. Menser, Mar. 23, 1942, folder 3, box 88, NBC.

23. "Henry J. Taylor: Soft-Spoken Pegler," *New Republic,* Oct. 16, 1944, 490–91; David W. Shepard, "An Experiment in Content Analysis: The Radio Addresses of Henry J. Taylor, 1945–1950" (Ph.D. diss., University of Minnesota, 1953), 220–48.

24. Minutes, Sub-Committee on Radio, Mar. 31, 1941, Minutes, NAM Public Relations Committee Meeting, Apr. 11, 1941, Acc. 1411, NAM I/113; Minutes, Red Network Planning and Advisory Committee, NBC, Oct. 30, 1941, box 3, William Hedges Papers, SHSW.

25. *Variety,* Feb. 26, Mar. 26, 1941; "Highlights of the 1943 Public Information Activities," n.d., Acc. 1411, NAM 3/842; "Defense for America," script, June 21, 1941, box 418, Feb. 22, 1941, box 419, NBC; William L. Lawson to NBC, Oct. 20, 1941, "Plan of Operation—'Defense for America' Staff," Mar. 19, 1941, folder 66, box 82, NBC; *Variety,* Feb. 26, Mar. 26, and Apr. 23, 1941; Jess Swicegood to Niles Trammell, Feb. 27, 1941, folder 66, box 86, NBC.

26. National Industrial Information Committee, *Annual Report* (New York: NAM, 1943), 17, 24–25, Acc. 1411, NAM 3/842; National Industrial Information Committee of the NAM, *Interpreting Free Enterprise to Grassroots America* (New York: NAM, 1944), 12, Acc. 1411, NAM 3/845.

27. Scripts, *Businessmen Look to the Future,* Apr. 24, Aug. 24, 31, and Sept. 21, 1945, Nov. 9, 1944, Acc. 1411, NAM I/157.

28. AFL, *Proceedings* (1942), 138, reel 13, ALUCP; CIO, *Proceedings* (1943), 57, reel 18, ALUCP; Transcript, Testimony of Len De Caux before the FCC, n.d., ca. Sept. 1943, box 2, Len De Caux Papers, ALUA; *Variety,* June 30, 1943.

29. "Commentators' Week," *Time,* Apr. 6, 1942, 78; Charles Morrison and Anne Gerlovich to NBC, Mar. 31, 1942. Among many others, see also Glenn Chinander to NBC, Mar. 17, 1942, and Leonard Lageman to NBC, Mar. 16, 1942, folder 3, box 88, NBC.

30. William Cahn to FCC, Apr. 28, 1942, box 349, General Corr., 1927–46, FCC.

31. Philip Pearl to Kenneth H. Berkeley, Mar. 25, 1942, box 429, NBC-LC; *Radio Daily,* Oct. 21, 1943; *Labor Review,* Oct. 8, 1943.

32. *Variety,* June 30, 1943; Clark, "H. V. Kaltenborn and His Sponsors," 316–19; G. F. Kielhack to F. H. Marling, Apr. 28, 1942, J. E. Jones to F. H. Marling, Mar. 26, 1943. Among many complaints, see Hugo S. Peterson to Pure Oil Company, Mar. 3, 1942, Dan M. Gephart to Pure Oil Company, Apr. 8, 1942, and P. F. DeMore to Henry M. Dawes, Apr. 20, 1942, F. H. Marling to H. V. Kaltenborn, Apr. 29, box 150, H. V. Kaltenborn Papers, SHSW.

33. "Pure Oil Expands Kaltenborn's Time," *Broadcasting,* May 18, 1942, 34; Henry M. Dawes to F. H. Marling, Mar. 24, Apr. 3, 1942, H. V. Kaltenborn to Frank Ferrin, Mar. 22, 1943, H. V. Kaltenborn to F. H. Marling, Apr. 9, 1943, box 150, H. V. Kaltenborn Papers, SHSW; *Labor Review,* Dec. 3, 1941; Chester, "Radio Commentaries of H. V. Kaltenborn," 410–27.

34. A. L. Ashby to William Burke Miller, Apr. 6, 1942, folder 3, box 88, NBC; A. A. Schechter to Niles Trammell, June 3, 1940, folder 8, box 78, NBC; Clark, "H. V. Kaltenborn and His Sponsors," 319.

35. Fang, *Those Radio Commentators!* 9–10; Memorandum on Possible Revision of NAB code on Commentators, Sept. 18, 1941, vol. 2302, ACLU.

36. Steele, *Propaganda in an Open Society,* 128–31; C. L. Menser to Niles Trammell, Sept. 11, 1942, Frank M. Russell to Niles Trammell, Aug. 7, 1942, James F. Royal to Frank E. Mullen, July 18, 1944, C. L. Menser to Jules Herbuveaux, Sept. 11, 1942, folder 6, box 114, NBC; Wecter, "Hearing Is Believing," 59. For letters and petitions to the FCC, see Edith D. Moses to Paul Porter, Nov. 10, 1944, H. K. Taylor to Paul Porter, Dec. 11, 1944, Mabel Brothers to Niles Trammel et al., Mar. 22, 1945, box 196, FCC; *Billboard,* Nov. 18, 1944.

37. James Fly to Charles Webber, May 8, 1943, box 310, FCC.

38. *Variety,* June 9, 1943; Testimony of Len De Caux, in U.S. Congress, Senate Committee on Interstate Commerce, *Hearings on S. 814, a Bill to Amend the Communications Act of 1934,* 78th Cong., 1st Sess., 1943, 577.

39. *Radio Daily,* July 26, 1943; *Variety,* July 28, 1943; Joseph Miller to Edward Levinson, Aug. 3, 1943, Harry Camp to Bass Luckoff, July 9, 1943, Merle S. Jones to M. Pearl, July 9, 1943, box 4, Edward Levinson Papers, ALUA; Testimony of Len De Caux before the FCC, Sept. 20, 1943, box 2, Len De Caux Papers, ALUA; *United Automobile Worker,* Sept. 15, 1943.

40. Testimony of Len De Caux before the FCC, Sept. 20, 1943, box 2, Len De Caux Papers, ALUA; Clifford Judkins Durr, "Freedom of Speech for Whom?" *Public Opinion Quarterly* 8 (Fall 1944): 401–2; Emil Corwin and Alan Reitman, "Is Radio Going Liberal?" *New Republic,* Feb. 12, 1945, 218.

41. Testimony of Len De Caux before the FCC, Sept. 20, 1943, box 2, Len De Caux Papers, ALUA; *CIO News,* May 17, 1943; *Variety,* May 5, 1943.

42. *CIO News,* May 25, 1942; *Variety,* Sept. 23, 1942; "Labor Broadcast: Six-Station Hookup Plugs Utah AFL Employers," *Broadcasting,* Nov. 15, 1943, 56.

43. "Unions on the Air," *Business Week,* Sept. 12, 1942, 112; "L.A.'s Own War," *Business Week,* Mar. 14, 1942, 87; "Labor Radio Program Exposes Press Lies, Tells Unions' Story," Dec. 22, 1943, reel 9112, FP; Workers Service Program, scripts, Jan. 10, 1942, Dec. 27, 1941, Dane County Labor Defense Council Papers, SHSW.

44. *CIO News,* Mar. 16, 1942; Sterling Fisher to James Carey, July 1, 1943, box 25, CIO Office of the Secretary-Treasurer Papers, ALUA.

45. CIO Executive Board Minutes, Mar. 24, 1942, reel 1, ALUA; "Labor Goes on the Air," *Time,* Apr. 20, 1942, 69; Erik Barnouw, *Radio Drama in Action* (New York: Farrar and Rinehart, Inc., 1945), 80; Transcript, Interview with Peter Lyon, Nov. 27, 1944, file B0232, Bureau of Applied Research Papers, Electronic Data Service Offices, Lehman Library, Columbia University.

46. A. L. Ashby to William Burke Miller, Apr. 6, 1942, William Burke Miller to Al Kiefner, Apr. 8, 1942, William Burke Miller to Frank A. Bolka, Apr. 8, 1942, box 88, folder 2, NBC; Nathan Godfried, *WCFL: Chicago's Voice of Labor, 1926–78* (Urbana: University of Illinois Press, 1997), 209.

47. *Billboard,* Apr. 11, 1941; Len De Caux to All National and International Unions et al., Apr. 1, 1942, reel 7, pt. 2, *CIO Files of John L. Lewis* (Frederick, Md.: University Publications of America, 1988); *Pennsylvania Labor Record,* May 22, 1942; Barnouw, *Golden Web,* 230; Testimony of Len De Caux before the FCC, Sept. 20, 1943, box 2, Len De Caux Papers, ALUA.

48. Report for the Board of Directors' Meeting, Apr. 10, 1943, box 943, NBC-LC; William Burke Miller to Al Kiefner, Apr. 8, 1942.

49. Transcript, Interview with Peter Lyon, Nov. 27, 1944, file B0232, Bureau of Applied Research Papers, Electronic Data Service Offices, Lehman Library, Columbia University; Barnouw, *Radio Drama in Action,* 80–81; *Variety,* May 24, 1944; *Federation News,* Nov. 21, 1942; "Labor for Victory," script, July 4, 1943, box 443, NBC.

50. *CIO News,* June 29, Dec. 12, 1942, Jan. 10, 1944; Barnouw, *Radio Drama in Action,* 80–81; CIO Executive Board Minutes, Feb. 5–7, 1943, reel 2, ALUA.

51. "Labor for Victory," scripts, Nov. 21, 1943, June 27, 1943, box 443, NBC.

52. *CIO News,* Dec. 28, 1942; CIO Executive Board Minutes, Feb. 5–7, 1943, reel 2, ALUA.

53. *Variety,* May 24, June 4, 1944; Philip Murray to Niles Trammell, n.d., box 2, Len De Caux Papers, ALUA; *Daily Worker,* June 1, 1944.

54. U.S. Congress, Senate Committee on Interstate Commerce, *Hearings on S. 814,* 532; *Radio Daily,* Dec. 2, 1943; *CIO News,* Aug. 21, 1944.

55. *CIO News,* Sept. 29, 1941.

56. "Summary of Radio Procedures for Union Educational Committees," n.d., Testimony of Allan S. Haywood before the FCC, Sept. 25, 1941, box 2, Len De Caux Papers, ALUA; Alan Lomax, "A Right to the Airwaves," *Ammunition,* May 1944, 21; *CIO News,* June 19, 1944.

57. *CIO News,* Sept. 29, 1941; Testimony of Len De Caux before the FCC, Sept. 20, 1943, box 2, Len De Caux Papers, ALUA.

58. CIO, *Proceedings* (1941), 69, reel 18, ALUCP.

59. CIO, *Proceedings* (1940), 52, reel 17, ALUCP; CIO, *Proceedings* (1941), 291, reel 18, ALUCP; U.S. Congress, Senate Committee on Interstate Commerce, *Hearings on S. 814*, 582; Len De Caux to Quincy Howe, Apr. 8, 1941, vol. 2302, ACLU.

60. "St. Louis Blues," *Broadcasting*, May 19, 1941, 66; "Official Digest of NAB Code Interpretations," *Broadcasting*, 1941 Year Book Number, 314; Len De Caux to Quincy Howe, Apr. 8, 1941, vol. 2302, ACLU.

61. *Variety*, Jan. 21, 1942; NAB, *Annual Report*, May 15, 1942; *NAB Reports*, Sept. 3, 1943, 369.

62. Joseph L. Miller to the NAB Code Committee, Apr. 28, 1942, folder 52, box 85, NBC; *Billboard*, Jan. 22, 1944; Godfried, *WCFL*, 213; Report by Emanie N. Arling, Feb. 1, 1940, vol. 2212, ACLU; Memorandum on Code Committee Meeting, June 16–17, 1943, box 10, NAB.

63. Memorandum on Code Committee Meeting, June 16–17, 1943, box 10, NAB; Report by Emanie N. Arling, Feb. 1, 1940, vol. 2212, ACLU.

64. Roger Baldwin to William L. Cherney, May 23, 1940, vol. 2212, Quincy Howe to Len De Caux, Mar. 20, 1941, vol. 2302, ACLU.

65. Quincy Howe and Roger Baldwin to National Association of Broadcasters, July 28, 1940, vol. 2212, ACLU; Hazel L. Rice, "Report on the Panel on Censorship," Feb. 12, 1941, folder 56, box 81, NBC.

66. Roger Baldwin to H. Thomas Austern, Nov. 23, 1940, Roger Baldwin to Josephine H. Klein, Nov. 18, 1940, vol. 2212, ACLU.

67. Robert W. McChesney, *Telecommunications, Mass Media, and Democracy: The Battle for the Control of U.S. Broadcasting, 1928–1935* (New York: Oxford University Press, 1993), 81–84; Harriet F. Pilpel to Morris Novik, May 1, 1941, vol. 2302, ACLU; Report on the Panel on Censorship, Feb. 12, 1941, folder 56, box 81, NBC; Report by Morris Novik to Hazel L. Rice, May 5, 1941, vol. 2302, ACLU; Report by Emanie N. Arling, Feb. 1, 1940, vol. 2212, ACLU.

68. Hazel L. Rice to Roger N. Baldwin and Quincy Howe, Jan. 9, 1941, vol. 2351, ACLU; Minutes of ACLU Committee on Radio, Oct. 28, 1943, Paul F. Lazarsfeld to Roger N. Baldwin, Mar. 5, 1943, box 141, Paul F. Lazarsfeld Papers, Rare Book and Manuscript Library, Columbia University.

69. Roger Baldwin to William L. Chenery, May 23, 1940, vol. 2212, Thomas R. Carskadon to Neville Miller, June 24, 1943, Carskadon to Harold Fair, June 24, 1943, vol. 2494, ACLU.

70. Robert J. Landy to Roger Baldwin, Feb. 9, 1943, vol. 2494, Roger N. Baldwin to Norman Thomas, June 17, 1942, vol. 2352, ACLU; Norman Thomas to Burton K. Wheeler, Nov. 11, 1943, box 24, James Lawrence Fly Papers, Rare Book and Manuscript Library, Columbia University.

71. *Variety*, Feb. 19, 1941; Quincy Howe to Len DeCaux, Mar. 20, 1941, Minutes of ACLU Radio Committee, Apr. 24, 1941, vol. 2302, ACLU; William Burke Miller to Sidney Strotz, May 9, 1941, folder 56, box 81, NBC; *Radio Daily*, June 17, 1943; American Civil Liberties Union Bulletin 1109, Jan. 3, 1944, vol. 2493; Minutes of a Special Meeting with the Program Managers Committee of the NAB, Jan. 12, 1944, vol. 2602, ACLU; *Variety*, Jan. 12, 1944.

72. Memorandum on Code Committee Meeting, June 16–17, 1943, box 10, NAB.

73. American Civil Liberties Union Bulletin no. 1080, June 14, 1943, vol. 2494, Memorandum on Chairman Fly's Recommendations, Oct. 21, 1943, vol. 2680, ACLU.

74. Roger Baldwin to Norman Thomas, June 17, 1942, vol. 2352, Minutes of Meeting of ACLU Radio Committee, Dec. 17, 1942, vol. 2352, Memorandum on Chairman's Fly's Recommendations, Oct. 21, 1943, vol. 2680, Robert Landry to Roger N. Baldwin, Feb. 9, 1943, vol. 2494, ACLU.

75. Morris Novik to Hazel L. Rice, May 5, 1941, vol. 2302, Quincy Howe to Edgar Bill, May 9, 1943, vol. 2302, Thomas R. Carskadon to Joseph L. Miller, Apr. 20, 1943, vol. 2494, Memorandum to Radio Industry, Dec. 10, 1943, vol. 2680, ACLU.

76. *Variety,* June 23, 1943; Memorandum on Code Committee Meeting, June 16–17, 1943, box 10, NAB.

77. Larry Vail to Federal Communications Assoc., Nov. 26, 1941, T. J. Slowie to Retail Department Store Employees' Union Local 1100, box 264, T. J. Slowie to Joseph Ullman, Sept. 13, 1943, box 264, T. J. Slowie to George De Nucci, Nov. 4, 1944, box 349, FCC.

78. Testimony of Allan S. Haywood before the FCC, Sept. 25, 1941, box 2, Len De Caux Papers, ALUA.

79. Gary M. Fink, ed., *Biographical Dictionary of American Labor* (Westport., Conn.: Greenwood Press, 1984), 179; U.S. Congress, Senate Committee on Interstate Commerce, *Hearings on S. 814,* 582–86.

80. *CIO News,* July 16, Oct. 1, 1938; Michigan CIO Council, *Proceedings* (1939), 83–85, ALUA; U.S. Congress, Senate Committee on Interstate Commerce, *Hearings on S. 814,* 274, 265–66.

81. Barnouw, *Golden Web,* 168–72; Alan Brinkley, *The End of Reform: New Deal Liberalism in Recession and War* (New York: Alfred A. Knopf, 1995), 153.

82. "People in the Limelight: III," *New Republic,* Dec. 25, 1944, 856; Cifford Judkins Durr, "Freedom of Speech for Whom?" *Public Opinion Quarterly* 8 (Fall 1944): 398–400.

83. John A. Garraty, *American National Biography,* vol. 7 (New York: Oxford University Press, 1999), 152–53.

84. James Lawrence Fly, "Control of Broadcasting in War and in Peace," speech at the National Association of Broadcasters Convention, May 13, 1941, box 33, James Fly Papers, Rare Books and Manuscript Library, Columbia University; Barnouw, *Golden Web,* 169–70; *New York Times,* Sept. 29, 1943.

85. James Lawrence Fly, "Broadcasting as an Instrument of Democracy," address before the American Civil Liberties Union, Feb. 12, 1941, box 33, James Lawrence Fly, "Free Speech—An Exploration of the Broadcaster's Duty," speech at the Radio Executives Club, New York, Oct. 7, 1943, box 37, James Fly Papers, Rare Books and Manuscript Library, Columbia University.

86. *New York Times,* Sept. 14, 1943; "Notes on Informal News Conference," Sept. 13, 1943, box 37, James Fly Papers, Rare Books and Manuscript Library, Columbia University.

87. James Lawrence Fly to Karl E. Mundt, Oct. 26, 1943, box 311, FCC; James Lawrence Fly, "Free Speech—An Exploration of the Broadcaster's Duty," speech at the Radio Executives Club, New York, Oct. 7, 1943, box 37, James Fly papers, Rare Books and Manuscript Library, Columbia University.

88. Interview with Harry Plotkin, James Lawrence Fly Project, Oral History Research Office, Butler Library, Columbia University; Barnouw, *Golden Web,* 189–90; "Unions Must Get Time on Air, Fly Tells Radio Executives," Oct. 8, 1943, reel 9111, FP.

89. "The NAB Code," pamphlet, n.d. (ca. 1939), vol. 2212, ACLU; Craig, *Fireside Politics,* 115–16.

90. Craig, *Fireside Politics,* 164.

91. Philip Taft, "Labor's Changing Political Line," *Journal of Political Economy* 15 (Oct. 1937): 641–42; Melvyn Dubofsky and Warren Van Tine, *John L. Lewis: A Biography* (New York: Quadrangle, 1977), 252. See transcripts of radio speeches, box 218, XIV, Misc. Corr., ACWA; Transcript CBS broadcast of speeches by Charles P. Howard, William Green, Robert J. Wat, Frank X. Martel, D. B. Robertson, and Philip Murray, Oct. 28, 1936, box 15, pt. 1, series 1, Wayne County AFL-CIO Papers, ALUA; Radio Address of Philip Murray, CBS, Oct. 14, 1936, box 218, XIV, Misc. Corr., ACWA.

92. James Caldwell Foster, *The Union Politic: The CIO Political Action Committee* (Columbia: University of Missouri Press, 1975), 3–26.

93. CIO Executive Board Minutes, Nov. 16, 17, 19, 25, 1944, 189, reel 7, ALUA; Philip Schuyler, "PAC's Propaganda Drive Swings into High Gear," *Editor and Publisher,* July 19, 1944, 8; Foster, *Union Politic,* 27; Emil Corwin, "The Role of Radio in the CIO-PAC Election Campaign," Dec. 11, 1944, box 2, Len De Caux Papers, ALUA.

94. In the 1960s, civil rights organizations undertook a similar campaign to counter biased news coverage and to gain access to the southern media. Brian Ward, *Radio and the Struggle for Civil Rights in the South* (Gainesville: University of Press Florida, 2004), 156–57. "CIO Set to Invade Radio on all Sides," *Broadcasting,* Aug. 7, 1944, 12; Emil Corwin to Sidney Hillman and C. B. Baldwin, Nov. 13, 1944, box 17, C. B. Baldwin Papers, Special Collections Department, University of Iowa Libraries; *United Automobile Worker,* Feb. 1, 1945; CIO Political Action Committee, *Radio Handbook,* box 17, C. B. Baldwin Papers, Special Collections Department, University of Iowa Libraries.

95. C. B. Baldwin to Regional Directors, Sept. 11, 1944, box 17, C. B. Baldwin Papers, Special Collections Department, University of Iowa Libraries; *Variety,* July 12, 1944; Emil Corwin, "The Role of Radio in the CIO-PAC Election Campaign," Dec. 11, 1944, box 2, Len De Caux Papers, ALUA; *Billboard,* July 15, 1944; *Daily Worker,* Aug. 21, 1944; *New York Times,* Sept. 13, 1944.

96. "CIO's Heat Wave," *Broadcasting,* Aug. 28, 1944, 104; "CIO Radio Action," *Broadcasting,* Aug. 14, 1944, 38; "CIO Set to Invade Radio on All Sides," 12–13.

97. Interview with Emil Corwin, Nov. 25, 1944, file BO232, Bureau of Applied Research Papers, Electronic Data Service Offices, Lehman Library, Columbia University; "CIO Set to Invade Radio on All Sides," 12; *Billboard,* Aug. 12, 1944.

98. Emil Corwin to Philip Murray, Oct. 30, 1944, and attached list of stations, box A4–9, Philip Murray Papers, Department of Archives and Manuscripts, Catholic University of America; Radio Division, CIO–Political Action Committee, "Transcriptions Available without Charge for Radio Programs, Rallies, Sound Trucks," n.d., reel 41, *Operation Dixie: The CIO Organizing Committee Papers, 1946–1953* (Sanford, N.C.: Microfilm Corporation of America, 1980); Tom Downs to Emil Corwin, Sept. 28, 1944, box 17, C. B. Baldwin Papers, Special Collections Department, University

of Iowa Libraries; Emil Corwin, "The Role of Radio in the CIO-PAC Election Campaign," Dec. 11, 1944, box 2, Len De Caux Papers, ALUA.

99. "Taft Tries to Keep CIO off the Air," clipping, Oct. 26, 1944, reel 9112, FP; George DeNucci to All Radio Stations in Ohio, Oct. 19, 1944, George DeNucci to FCC, Oct. 19, 1944, box 17, C. B. Baldwin Papers, Special Collections Department, University of Iowa Libraries; Garland Ascraft to Emil Corwin, Nov. 13, 1944, box 2, Len De Caux Papers, ALUA.

100. *CIO News,* July 4, 1944; Jerry J. O'Connell to Roy W. Atkinson, n.d., box 2, Len De Caux Papers, ALUA; John B. Easton to Jack Kroll, Dec. 4, 1944, box 17, C. B. Baldwin Papers, Special Collections Department, University of Iowa Libraries.

101. *Variety,* Oct. 11, 1944; David Dubinsky, to All ILGWU Local Unions and Joint Boards Campaign Committees, Oct. 7, 1944, Telegrams from David Dubinsky, Oct. 11, 13, 14, 20, 23, 1944, J. S. Martin to David Dubinsky, Oct. 16, 1944, Ruth M. Eddy to ILGWU Campaign Committee, Oct. 26, 1944, box 139, David Dubinsky Papers, ILGWU.

102. *Billboard,* Sept. 16, 1944; Interview with Emil Corwin, Nov. 25, 1944, file B0232, Bureau of Applied Research Papers, Electronic Data Service Offices, Lehman Library, Columbia University; Functions of the Radio Division, memo attached to Emil Corwin to Ping Ferry, Aug. 4, 1944, box 17, C. B. Baldwin Papers, Special Collections Department, University of Iowa Libraries.

103. *Billboard,* Sept. 16, 1944; Leila A. Sussman, "How Radio Treated Labor in the Elections," *Common Sense,* Feb. 1945, 34.

104. *CIO News,* Feb. 26, 1945; "An Open Letter," *Ammunition,* Feb. 1945, 8; Leila A. Sussmann, "Labor in the Radio News: An Analysis of Content," *Journalism Quarterly* 22 (Sept. 1945): 207–14.

105. Emil Corwin to Sidney Hillman and C. B. Baldwin, Nov. 2, 1944, Leila Sussmann to C. B. Baldwin, n.d., box 17, C. B. Baldwin Papers, Special Collections Department, University of Iowa Libraries; Second Interview with Emil Corwin, Nov. 28, 1944, file B0232, Bureau of Applied Research Papers, Electronic Data Service Offices, Lehman Library, Columbia University.

106. C. B. Baldwin to Regional Directors, Aug. 8, 1944, box 17, C. B. Baldwin Papers, Special Collections Department, University of Iowa Libraries; Interview with Emil Corwin, Nov. 25, 1944, Bureau of Applied Research Papers, Electronic Data Service Offices, Lehman Library, Columbia University; Emil Corwin to Sidney Hillman and C. B. Baldwin, Nov. 13, 1944, box 17, C. B. Baldwin Papers, Special Collections Department, University of Iowa Libraries.

107. "Unions Seek Air," *Business Week,* Aug. 26, 1944, 88; *CIO News,* Oct. 30, 1944.

108. AFL, *Proceedings* (1944), 215, reel 14, ALUCP; Emil Corwin, "An Open Letter," *American Federation of Labor Weekly News Service,* Oct. 24, 1944; AFL Executive Council Minutes, Jan. 21–31, 1946, GMMA; *Radio Daily,* Nov. 10, 1944.

109. *CIO News,* Oct. 30, 1944, Jan. 28, 1946; *Variety,* Nov. 1, 1944; AFL, *Proceedings* (1946), 100–101, reel 14, ALUCP; AFL Executive Council Minutes, Jan. 21–31, 1946; CIO, *Proceedings* (1946), 65–66, reel 18, ALUCP; "Labor's Network Programs," *Business Week,* July 7, 1945, 96.

110. *Variety,* Jan. 10, 1945.

111. Barbara Dianne Savage, *Broadcasting Freedom: Radio, War, and the Politics of Race, 1938–1948* (Chapel Hill: University of North Carolina Press, 1999); "Labor's Case Goes on the Air," *Business Week,* July 7, 1945, 94; "WMCA to Take Programs Prohibited by the N.A.B. Code as Controversial," *Business Week,* Mar. 4, 1944, 98–99; "WMCA Policy on Controversial Issues Promotes Discussions, Straus Asserts," *Broadcasting,* Mar. 20, 1944, 66.

112. Emil Corwin to Sidney Hillman and C. B. Baldwin, Nov. 2, 1944, box 17, C. B. Baldwin Papers, Special Collections Department, University of Iowa Libraries; Second Interview with Emil Corwin, Nov. 28, 1944, Bureau of Applied Research Papers, Electronic Data Service Offices, Lehman Library, Columbia University; *Billboard,* Nov. 18, 1944.

113. "Labor's Case Goes on the Air," 95; C. E. Harrison to Mr. Weisenburger, Sept. 6, 1944, Acc. 1411, NAM 843/3.

114. R. J. Thomas testimony, U.S. Congress, Senate Committee on Interstate Commerce, *Hearings on S. 814,* p. 264; Report of Proceedings before FCC, United Broadcasting Co., Aug. 16, 1944, box 2238, docket 6631, FCC.

115. Zieger, *The CIO,* 149; Report of Proceedings before FCC, United Broadcasting Co., Aug. 17, 1944, box 2238, docket 6631, FCC.

116. Report of Proceedings before FCC, United Broadcasting Co., Aug. 16, 1944, box 2238, docket 6631, FCC.

117. Scripts, June 13, July 11, Aug. 30, Sept. 6, and 12, 1943, box 2235, docket 6631, FCC.

118. Report of Proceedings before FCC, United Broadcasting Co., Aug. 17, 1944, box 2238, docket 6631, FCC.

119. Report of Proceedings before FCC, United Broadcasting Co., Aug. 16, 1944, box 2238, docket 6631, FCC; "Station Censors Frankensteen Speech—Taft Taboo," Reel 9111, FP.

120. Richard T. Frankensteen to James Lawrence Fly, Aug. 19, 1943, C. M. Everson to T. J. Slowie, Sept. 1, 1943, box 2239, docket 6631, FCC; "Petition to Reconsider the Commission's Action Renewing the License of Station WHKC, Columbus, Ohio, Taken May 16, 1944, and to Designate for Hearing the Renewal Application of Station WHKC," to FCC, June 1, 1944, box 24, James Fly Papers, Rare Books and Manuscript Library, Columbia University; "Unions Seek Air," 88.

121. *CIO News,* July 31, 1944, Aug. 7, 1944; Jack Kroll to Assistant PAC Directors, West Virginia, Kentucky, box 27, West Virginia Industrial Union Council Records, Acc. 1449, WVRHC; *The Hell Diver,* July 27, 1944, box 36, UAW Region 2A Collection, ALUA.

122. "UAW Seeks Scripts of Fulton Lewis, Upton Close to Show Radio Bias," Aug. 10, 1944, reel 9112, FP; *New York Times,* Aug. 13, 1944.

123. *CIO News,* July 10, 1944, Sept. 15, 1944, "Petition for Issuance of a Subpoena," in re application of United Broadcasting Company (WHKC), Columbus, Ohio, for Renewal of License, docket 6631, box 17, C. B. Baldwin Papers, Special Collections Department, University of Iowa Libraries; Official Report of Proceeding before FCC, United Broadcasting Company, WHKC, Columbus, Ohio, box 2238, docket 6631, FCC; "Unions Seek Air," 88.

124. "Is Radio Going Liberal?" 219; Emil Corwin, "An Open Letter," *American*

Federation of Labor Weekly News Service, Oct. 24, 1944, 8; Report of Proceedings, United Broadcasting Co., Aug. 16, 1944, box 2238, docket 6631, FCC; *Variety,* Aug. 23, 30, 1944; *CIO News,* Aug. 28, 1944.

125. *Variety,* Aug. 23, 1944; "Is Radio Going Liberal?" 219.

126. *United Automobile Worker,* Nov. 15, 1944; "In re United Broadcasting Company (WHKC), Columbus, Ohio," June 27, 1945, box 2241, docket 6631, FCC.

127. "NAB Revises Code, Expands Labor Relations," *Broadcasting,* Aug. 13, 1945, 20.

Chapter 5: Protecting Listeners' Rights

1. *Variety,* May 14, 1947; *Daily Worker,* May 14, 1947.

2. By the 1930s, a group of public intellectuals had already developed a wide-ranging critique of radio. See Bruce Lenthall, "Critical Reception Public Intellectuals Decry Depression-Era Radio, Mass Culture, and Modern America," in *Radio Reader: Essays in the Cultural History of Radio,* ed. Michele Hilmes and Jason Loviglio (New York: Routledge, 2002), 41–62; Kathy M. Newman, *Radio Active: Advertising and Consumer Activism, 1935–1947* (Berkeley: University of California Press, 2004); Jennifer Hyland Wang, "'The Case of the Radio-Active Housewife': Relocating Radio in the Age of Television," in *Radio Reader,* ed. Hilmes and Loviglio, 346; Llewellyn White, "The Shortcomings of Radio," *Atlantic Monthly,* Apr. 1947, 66; "Radio Revisited," *New Republic,* Feb. 26, 1945, 297; and "The Revolt against Radio," *Fortune,* Mar. 1947, 101.

3. Morris L. Ernst, "Freedom to Read, See, and Hear," *Harper's,* July 1945, 52–53; *Broadcasting,* Aug. 2, 1943, 58; Burton K. Wheeler, "The Shocking Truth about Radio," *The Progressive: LaFollette's Magazine,* Nov. 6, 1944, 1, 10.

4. Bernard B. Smith, "The People's Stake in Radio," *New Republic,* July 3, 1944, 11–13.

5. Dixon Wecter, "Hearing Is Believing," *Atlantic Monthly,* July 1945, 55–57; Quincy Howe, "Policing the Commentator: A News Analysis," *Atlantic Monthly,* Nov. 1943, 47–49; *New York Times,* Jan. 5, 12, 26, Mar. 27, 1947.

6. Testimony of CIO before the FCC on the Mayflower Decision, presented by Henry C. Fleisher, ca. Mar. 1948, box 76, CIO Office of the Secretary-Treasurer Papers, ALUA.

7. CIO, *Proceedings* (1946), 303–4, reel 18, ALUCP.

8. *Variety,* Mar. 6, Nov. 20, 1946.

9. *Variety,* Dec. 17, 1947, Apr. 28, 1947; "FCC Gets CIO Protest in Program Censorship by Local Radio Station," Dec. 15, 1947, reel 9112, FP.

10. I. Keith Tyler and Nancy Dasher, eds., *Education on the Air* (Columbus: Ohio State University, 1947), 129–30; Testimony of CIO before the FCC on the Mayflower Decision, presented by Henry C. Fleisher, ca. Mar. 1948, box 76, CIO Office of the Secretary-Treasurer papers, ALUA; *Variety,* Oct. 2, 1946; *CIO News,* Dec. 9, 1946; Jack Lawrenson to Charles Denny, Nov. 22, 1946, box 349, General Corr., 1927–46, FCC (all citations to 1927–46, unless otherwise noted).

11. *CIO News,* Feb. 17, 24, 1947; *Ford Facts,* Feb. 8, 1947; *Variety,* Nov. 20, 1947.

12. *Variety,* July 25, 1945.

13. Bryce Oliver, "Thought Control—American Style," *New Republic,* Jan. 13, 1947, 35.

14. "Demand Probe of Station's Ban on Outside Commentators," Mar. 26, 1945, reel 9112, FP; *In Fact,* Mar. 19, 1945, 2; Wecter, "Hearing Is Believing," 57; Nathan Godfried, "'Fellow Traveler of the Air': Rod Holmgren and the Leftist Radio Commentary in the Cold War," paper presented at the Radio Conference: A Transnational Forum, Madison, Wis., July 28, 2003.

15. *Variety,* Dec. 25, 1946, Jan. 8, 1947; *CIO News,* Jan. 6, 1947.

16. U.S. House of Representatives, *Investigation of Un-American Activities and Propaganda,* House Report 2233, 79th Cong., 2d Sess., June 7, 1946, 9–13; *New York Times,* Nov. 7, 1945; *CIO News,* Jan. 6, 1947; "Free Speech Fight in Congress Seen," *Broadcasting,* Nov. 19, 1945, 100.

17. *American Thought Police: A Record of the Un-American Activities Committee* (New York: Civil Rights Committee, 1947), 8.

18. *Variety,* Dec. 18, 25, 1946, *CIO News,* Jan. 6, 1947; *PM,* Oct. 16, 1945.

19. *New York Times,* Dec. 23, 1946; Godfried, "'Fellow Traveler of the Air.'"

20. Morris Novik to D. Montgomery, June 1, 1946, box 25, Donald Montgomery Papers, UAW Washington Office Collection, ALUA; G. W. Johnstone to Stephen F. Dunn, June 28, 1957, box 156, series 1, Acc. 1411, NAM.

21. "The Shape of Things," *The Nation,* Mar. 29, 1947, 380–81; "Second Warning," *Saturday Review of Literature,* Sept. 27, 1947, 9; Stanley Cloud and Lynne Olson, *The Murrow Boys: Pioneers on the Front Lines of Broadcast Journalism* (Boston: Houghton Mifflin Co., 1996), 280.

22. Irving Fang, *Those Radio Commentators!* (Ames: Iowa State University Press, 1977), 160–69; *Variety,* Jan. 28, 1948; Charles Siepman, "The Passing of a Voice," mss., Reel 16, Edward R. Murrow Papers, LC.

23. *American Thought Police,* 8; "Rep. Patterson's Ire Aroused by Script Inquiry," *Broadcasting,* Oct. 22, 1945, 18; "House 'Liberals' Lead Fight against 'Un-American' Group," *Broadcasting,* Oct. 29, 1945, 93; *Billboard,* Nov. 3, 1945; *New York Times,* Nov. 8, 1945.

24. M. J. Bablich to FCC, Sept. 24, 1946, R. D. Shields to FCC, Sept. 17, 1946, box 219, FCC.

25. Mrs. Raymond P. Keesecker to NBC, Sept. 6, 1946, William T. Hade to FCC, Aug. 30, 1946, box 219, H. Ross to FCC, Dec. 27, 1946, box 188, FCC.

26. Amy Toro, "Standing Up for Listeners' Rights: A History of Public Participation at the Federal Communications Commission" (Ph.D. diss., University of California at Berkeley, 2000), 14.

27. "'Crusade' against Liberals Seen by 3 Left-Wing Groups," *Broadcasting,* Dec. 30, 1946, 22; *Daily Worker,* July 2, 1946, Apr. 19, 1947.

28. Toro, "Standing Up for Listeners' Rights," 22; "Freedom to Listen Basic Counterpart to Freedom of Speech, Fly Tells Club," *Broadcasting,* Oct. 4, 1943, 30; *New York Times,* Sept. 29, 1943; *Billboard,* Dec. 3, 1944; Lou Frankel, "In One Ear," *The Nation,* Jan. 25, 1947, 102.

29. "Dissent by Durr," *Tide,* Nov. 1, 1945, 114; FCC, *Public Service Responsibility of Broadcast Licensees* (Washington, D.C.: Government Printing Office, 1947), 55; Toro,

"Standing Up for Listeners' Rights," 22; I. Keith Tyler and Nancy Dasher, eds., *Education on the Air* (Columbus: Ohio State University, 1946), 77.

30. Michael J. Socolow, "To Network a Nation: NBC, CBS, and the Development of National Network Radio in the United States, 1925–1950" (Ph.D. diss., Georgetown University, 2001), 269; John A. Salmond, *The Conscience of a Lawyer: Clifford J. Durr and American Civil Liberties, 1899–1975* (Tuscaloosa: University of Alabama Press, 1990), 72–81; Richard J. Meyer, "The Blue Book," *Journal of Broadcasting* 6 (Summer 1962): 197–98.

31. Michael J. Socolow, "Questioning Advertising's Influence over American Radio: The Blue Book Controversy of 1945–1947," *Journal of Radio Studies* 9 (Dec. 2002): 287–88; Toro, "Standing Up for Listeners' Rights," 90; FCC, *Public Service Responsibility*, 18.

32. Jerry Spingarn, "The FCC Listens In," *The Nation*, Mar. 30, 1946, 368–69; FCC, *Public Service Responsibility*, 55.

33. FCC, *Public Service Responsibility*, 37; Clifford Judkins Durr, "Freedom of Speech for Whom?" *Public Opinion Quarterly* 8 (Fall 1944): 406.

34. *Variety*, Oct. 24, 1945; "House 'Liberals' Lead Fight against 'Un-American Group,'" 93; "Campaign Is On to Defeat Wood Bill," *Broadcasting*, Dec. 3, 1945, 18, 71.

35. "Campaign Is On to Defeat Wood Bill," 18, 71; "'Crusade' against Liberals Seen by 3 Left-Wing Groups," 22.

36. Jack Kroll to Charles R. Denny, Mar. 27, 1947, box 53, General Corr., 1947–56, FCC; *Billboard*, Apr. 26, 1947; *Variety*, Apr. 23, 1947.

37. *Voice of Freedom*, Apr. 1948, 2; Hearings before the Subcommittee of the Committee on Interstate and Foreign Commerce, U.S. Senate, 80th Cong., 1st Sess., S. 1333, US GPO, 1947, 509; *New York Times*, Aug. 29, 1947.

38. *Variety*, Feb. 8, 1950, June 4, Oct. 11, 1947; *Daily Worker*, June 19, 1947, Aug. 11, Oct. 11, 1949; *Voice of Freedom*, Apr. 1948, 2; William Paley to Jo Davidson, Apr. 7, 1947, Jo Davidson Papers, box 6, LC.

39. *New York Times*, Apr. 23, 1947, "Boys in the Bleachers," *Broadcasting*, Apr. 7, 1947, 48; Norbert Muhlen, "The State of American Radio Today," *New Leader*, Feb. 15, 1947, 5, 19.

40. Alan Barth and Eugene Katz, "FM and Freedom of the Air," *American Mercury*, July 1945, 36–37; "Broadcast Leaders See FM Replacing AM," *Broadcasting*, Aug. 6, 1945, 16.

41. Helen Fuller, "Radio's New Chance," *The Nation*, June 26, 1944, 841–42; "Radio's Second Chance," *The Nation*, Dec. 8, 1945, 613; National Citizens Political Action Committee, "Immediate Action: A Report to America on Radio Broadcasting," Oct. 1945, box 19, C. B. Baldwin Papers, Special Collections Department, University of Iowa Libraries (hereafter NCPAC, "Immediate Action").

42. *CIO News*, July 31, Aug. 14, 1944; CIO, *Proceedings* (1944), 238, reel 18, ALUCP.

43. The UAW applied for licenses in Detroit and Flint, Michigan; Cleveland; Los Angeles; Chicago; and Newark, New Jersey. The ILGWU applied for licenses in New York City, Philadelphia, Boston, and Chattanooga. The ACWA applied in Rochester, New York, New York City, Philadelphia, and Chicago. *CIO News*, Dec. 4, 1944;

"ILGWU Applies for Four FM Stations," *Broadcasting,* Oct. 15, 1945, 20; "Labor Unions Get Conditional Grants for Three FM Stations," *Broadcasting,* Feb. 18, 1946, 101.

44. *Billboard,* Feb. 19, 1944; "Labor Unions Request 16 FM Stations," *Broadcasting,* Nov. 26, 1946, 20; "Labor Unions Get Conditional Grants for Three FM Stations," 101; *Variety,* Feb. 13, 1946, Sept. 17, 1947; "Ford Local Prepares to Bid for Radio Station," Oct. 4, 1946, reel 9112, FP; *Billboard,* Feb. 19, 1944; Leonard C. Lewin to FCC, Apr. 15, 1946, box 349, FCC; P. V. McNamara to Paul Porter, Sept. 12, 1945, box 15, series 1, Wayne County AFL-CIO Papers, ALUA.

45. "Radio's Second Chance," *The Nation,* Dec. 8, 1945, 613.

46. Eugene Konecky, *The American Communications Conspiracy* (New York: People's Radio Foundation, 1948), 102; "Draft of Letter to Proposed F.M. Sponsors," n.d., box 19, International Workers Order Records, KLMDC.

47. Interview with Eugene Konecky, Nov. 28, 1944, file BO232, Bureau of Applied Research Papers, Lehman Library, Columbia University; "New Group Formed to Tap FM Radio Opportunities for Labor," Nov. 22, 1944, "Radio Station WPRF—The People's Choice," Feb. 6, 1947, reel 9112, FP; Konecky, *American Communications Conspiracy,* 102.

48. "New Group Formed to Tap FM Radio Opportunities for Labor," Nov. 22, 1944, reel 9112, FP.

49. *Daily Worker,* June 3, 1946; NCPAC, "Immediate Action"; Charles A. Siepmann, *Radio's Second Chance* (Boston: Little Brown and Co., 1946), 243–49.

50. "ACLU Backs World Freedom of Air," *Broadcasting,* Dec. 3, 1945, 70; *Daily Worker,* June 3, 1946; "FCC Visions FM as Major Radio Service," *Broadcasting,* May 28, 1945, 17; Siepmann, *Radio's Second Chance,* 243–49; NCPAC, "Immediate Action."

51. "FM Fog Cleared by FCC," *Business Week,* Sept. 1, 1945, 84; *Daily Worker,* June 4, 1946; NCPAC, "Immediate Action."

52. Konecky, *American Communications Conspiracy,* 73–74, 104; *Ammunition,* Oct. 1945, 9; Jesse Walker, *Rebels on the Air: An Alternative History of Radio in America* (New York: New York University Press, 2001), 47.

53. Minutes of Meeting of Steering Committee of NCPAC, Sept. 19, 1945, box 6, C. B. Baldwin Papers, Special Collections Department, University of Iowa Libraries; *Variety,* Oct. 3, 1945; NCPAC, "Immediate Action."

54. "FCC Approves 65 More FM Stations," *Broadcasting,* Nov. 5, 1945, 16, 84; "Ignoring Demands, Baldwin Declares," *Broadcasting,* Oct. 29, 1945, 95; *CIO News,* Oct. 29, 1945.

55. "CIO Protest Answered," *NAB Reports,* Nov. 9, 1945, 521–22.

56. R. J. Thomas to Glen Taylor, Dec. 14, 1945, box 18, R. J. Thomas Papers, ALUA; "What Future for FM?" *New Republic,* Apr. 22, 1946, 566; "One to Customer New FCC Policy," *Broadcasting,* Apr. 15, 1946, 17, 101.

57. "FM Set-Aside," *Business Week,* July 27, 1946, 33; *Ammunition,* Nov. 1945, 21; *Daily Worker,* June 4, 1946; *Variety,* June 12, July 24, 1946.

58. Susan J. Douglas, *Listening In: Radio and the American Imagination, from Amos 'n' Andy and Edward R. Murrow to Wolfman Jack and Howard Stern* (New York: Times Books, 1999), 224.

59. Toro, "Standing Up for Listeners' Rights," 14; NCPAC, "Immediate Action."

60. Toro, "Standing Up for Listeners' Rights," 22; *New York Times,* Sept. 29, 1943; *Billboard,* Dec. 3, 1944; Lou Frankel, "In One Ear," *The Nation,* Jan. 25, 1947, 102.

61. "Dissent by Durr," *Tide,* Nov. 1, 1945, 114; FCC, *Public Service Responsibility,* 55; Address by FCC commissioner Clifford J. Durr, Conference of the Independent Citizens' Committee of the Arts, Sciences, and Professions, New York City, June 23, 1943, box 30, Clifford J. Durr Papers, Alabama Department of Archives and History, Montgomery; Toro, "Standing Up for Listeners' Rights," 22; *Education on the Air* (Columbus: Ohio State University, 1946), 77.

62. CIO Political Action Committee, *Radio Handbook,* box 17, C. B. Baldwin Papers, Special Collections Department, University of Iowa Libraries.

63. Toro, "Standing Up for Listeners' Rights," 102, 113–15.

64. Ibid., 100–101; Steven J. Simmons, *The Fairness Doctrine and the Media* (Berkeley: University of California Press, 1978), 36–39.

65. T. J. Slowie to Alexander Nagy, Apr. 11, 1946, box 349, FCC; NCPAC, Action Memo, Jan. 15, 1946, box 18, C. B. Baldwin Papers, Special Collections Department, University of Iowa Libraries.

66. NCPAC, Action Memo, Jan. 15, 1946, and enclosed list of hearings, box 8, CIO-PAC Papers, ALUA.

67. Summary of the Proceedings of Editors Conference Sponsored by National CIO and CIO-PAC, Jan. 7, 1946, New York City, box 2, Len De Caux Papers, ALUA.

68. P. Speicher to T. J. Slowie, Jan. 22, 1946, T. J. Slowie to Robert Triolo, Mar. 11, 1946, box 2315, docket 6785, FCC; T. J. Slowie to Edward Pearson, Oct. 2, 1946, box 349, FCC; Michigan CIO Council News Release, May 23, 1947, box 13, Michigan AFL-CIO Council Papers, ALUA.

69. Harry Boyer to T. J. Slowie, Nov. 27, 1945, Thomas Pycraft to T. J. Slowie, Mar. 8, 1946, box 2736, Julius Uehlein to FCC, May 22, 1946, box 2735, Decision in re Applications of Laurence W. Harry, Mansfield Journal Company, Lorain Journal Company, Jan. 14, 1948, box 2736, Testimony, June 21, 1946, box 2735, docket 7356, FCC.

70. James B. Carey to T. J. Slowie, Apr. 10, 1946, box 38, CIO Office of the Secretary-Treasurer Papers, ALUA; *Billboard,* Sept. 7, 28, 1946; Paul A. Walker to Donald Henderson, Oct. 24, 1946, box 349, FCC.

71. Official Report of Proceedings of FCC at Griffin, Ga., May 27–28, box 2626, docket 7211, FCC.

72. Script, "The Textile Workers Speak," Jan. 12, 1946, box 2617, Official Report of Proceedings of FCC at Griffin, Ga., May 27–28, box 2626, docket 7211, FCC.

73. Official Report of Proceedings of FCC at Griffin, Ga., May 27–28, box 2626, T. J. Slowie to Radio Station WKEU, Feb. 15, 1946, WKEU to Kenneth Douty, Jan. 21, 1946, Memo for FCC from Textile Workers Union of America, CIO, Oct. 8, 1946, box 2617, docket 7211, FCC.

74. Official Report of Proceedings of FCC at Griffin, Ga., May 27–28, box 2626, A. W. Marshall to T. J. Slowie, Mar. 7, 1946, box 2617, docket 7211, FCC.

75. News Release, Statement by Kenneth Douty, Georgia State Director, Textile Workers Union of America, Griffin, Ga., May 28, 1946, box 2617, docket 7211, FCC.

76. *Variety,* May 1, 1946; *Billboard,* Jan. 19, 1946.

77. *Cincinnati Times-Star,* Dec. 6, 1946; NCWC News Service news release, Dec. 4,

1945, box 25, CIO Office of the Secretary-Treasurer Papers, ALUA. See also letters in reference to the case in boxes 264 and 349, FCC; *Billboard,* Jan. 19, 1946.

78. Toro, "Standing Up for Listeners' Rights," 51–54, 118–32, 134–51; Milton R. Konvitz, ed., *Law and Social Action: Selected Essays of Alexander H. Pekelis* (Ithaca, N.Y.: Cornell University Press, 1950), 143.

79. *Daily Worker,* June 24, 1947; *Voice of Freedom,* Feb. 1948, 3, Apr. 1948, 3, June 1948, 4.

80. Dorothy Parker and Stella Holt to FCC, May 19, 1948, T. J. Slowie to Dorothy Parker, May 24, 1948, Ken R. Dyke to T. J. Slowie, June 8, 1948, box 60, Gen. Corr., 1947–56, FCC; *Voice of Freedom,* Mar. 1948, 2.

81. *Voice of Freedom,* June 1948, 4, Apr. 1948, 2.

82. *Variety,* Sept. 25, Nov. 14, 1946; *Billboard,* Apr. 13, 1946.

83. Arthur Stringer to Judge Miller, Mar. 13, 1947, box 103, NAB; *Variety,* Mar. 12, Apr. 16, 1947; "Radio Listeners Be Damned," *Kiplinger Magazine,* Feb. 1947, 8; Elmer L. Smead, *Freedom of Speech by Radio and Television* (Washington, D.C.: Public Affairs Press, 1959), 95.

84. *Billboard,* Aug. 10, 1946; Proposed Decision, in re Applications of Laurence W. Harry et al., Jan. 10, 1948, box 2736, docket 7356, FCC.

85. Proposed Decision, in re Applications of Laurence W. Harry et al., Jan. 10, 1948, box 2736, docket 7356, FCC; *Variety,* Jan. 21, 1948; *CIO News,* Jan. 30, 1950.

86. Order in re Applications of Radio Station WKEU, June 17, 1947, box 2617, docket 7211, FCC.

87. See, for example, T. J. Slowie to McClatchy Broadcasting Company, Aug. 14, 1946, box 349, Slowie to Radio Station WISN, New York, Nov. 15, 1946, Slowie to WGAL, Lancaster, June 10, 1946, box 264, FCC.

88. *Variety,* Mar. 6, 1946; T. J. Slowie to R. J. Thomas, Mar. 13, 1946, box 349, FCC; Llewellyn White, *The American Radio: A Report on the Broadcasting Industry in the United States from the Commission on Freedom of the Press* (Chicago: University of Chicago Press, 1947), 175; *Variety,* Apr. 26, 1950.

89. Listeners' councils, mostly comprised of representatives of women's groups concerned about children's programming, had emerged in the earliest days of broadcasting, but their numbers increased in the 1940s. White, *American Radio,* 114–15; Saul Carson, "Radio: The Embattled Listener," *New Republic,* Jan. 17, 1949, 27–28.

90. Erik Barnouw, *The Golden Web: A History of Broadcasting in the United States,* vol. 2 (New York Oxford University Press, 1968), 231–32; "Program Report: VIII," *Broadcasting,* Apr. 29, 1946, 48; "P.R. Job Ahead," *Broadcasting,* Jan. 6, 1947, 46; "FCC at War—with FCC," *Broadcasting,* July 1, 1946, 48; *Billboard,* Oct. 2, 1946.

91. William S. Hedges to Frank E. Mullen, Apr. 16, 1946, folder 8, box 115, NBC; *Variety,* Oct. 2, 1946; "'Is This U.S.A. or . . . ,'" *Broadcasting,* Oct. 15, 1945, 54.

92. *PM,* Sept. 17, 1947; "NAM Chief Urges Anti-Truman Stand," *Broadcasting,* Sept. 22, 1947, 38; *In Fact,* Dec. 30, 1946.

93. Socolow, "Questioning Advertising's Influence over American Radio," 288–90; Barnouw, *Golden Web,* 231–32; "Miller Calls for United Radio Front," *Broadcasting,* Apr. 15, 1946, 18.

94. *New York Times,* May 19, 1946; "Tobey Promised Support for FCC Probe," *Broadcasting,* July 29, 1946, 15, 94; *Variety,* Sept. 10, 1947.

95. Socolow, "Questioning Advertising's Influence over American Radio," 287–88.

96. There was sharp disagreement between the Miller and the networks over how to respond to the Blue Book. While Miller was unwilling to admit that radio had any deficiencies, the networks acknowledged that radio was guilty of advertising excesses and should respond in a constructive manner to the commission's criticism. Justin Miller to Frank Stanton, May 27, 1946, box 103, NAB; *Billboard,* Oct. 19, 1946; Socolow, "Questioning Advertising's Influence over American Radio," 294–97; *New York Times,* Oct. 23, 1946, Sept. 21, 1947.

97. *Variety,* Sept. 24, 1947, Oct. 23, 1946; Hugh Richard Slotten, "'Rainbow in the Sky': FM Radio, Technical Superiority, and Regulatory Decision-Making," *Technology and Culture* 37 (Oct. 1996): 706; Barnouw, *Golden Web,* 243; Socolow, "Questioning Advertising's Influence over American Radio," 286.

98. *Variety,* Jan. 8, Feb. 3, Apr. 23, 1947; Barnouw, *Golden Web,* 233–34.

99. From the Report of Dorothy Lewis, Coordinator of Listener Activities, NAB, n.d. (ca. 1944), box 17, C. B. Baldwin Papers, Special Collections Department, University of Iowa Libraries; Leslie Spense to Clifford J. Durr, Aug. 23, 1948, box 1, Clifford J. Durr Papers, Alabama Department of Archives and History, Montgomery.

100. American Business Consultants, *Red Channels: The Report of Communist Influence in Radio and Television* (New York: American Business Consultants, Inc., 1950); *Variety,* Feb. 8, 1950; *Daily Worker,* Aug. 17, Oct. 11, 1949; American Legion National Americanism Committee, *Summary of Trends and Developments Exposing the Communist Conspiracy,* August and October 1949, box 50, American Legion Papers, Department of Wisconsin, SHSW; "On the Air," *New Republic,* Feb. 27, 1950, 23.

101. "PAC Urges Councils to Seek Free Time," *Broadcasting,* Sept. 9, 1946; "PAC Book Charts Plan for Air Time," *Broadcasting,* Sept. 30, 1946, 69; *Variety,* July 3, 24, Sept. 11, 1946.

102. "Raid-io, CIO Version," *Broadcasting,* Sept. 9, 1946, 46; "Observed by House Committee," *Broadcasting,* Sept. 23, 1946. For labor's difficulty gaining airtime during the 1946 election, see box 349, FCC.

103. "On the Air: WFDR," *New Republic,* July 4, 1949, 20–21; *PM,* July 20, 1946, Feb. 23, 1947; *Variety,* July 17, 1946, Mar. 5, 1947; *Billboard,* July 20, 1946.

104. Pacifica Radio is important exception.

105. "Radio of ILGWU to Oppose Reds," undated clipping, ca. Oct. 1945, *New York Journal American,* box 1, Morris S. Novik Papers, KLMDC; *Variety,* July 24, 1946.

106. Unity Broadcasting Corporation of New York Proposed Program Schedule, box 1, Morris S. Novik Papers, KLMDC; People's Radio Foundation, Inc., Proposed Program Services, box 1889, Official Report of Proceedings before FCC, July 16, 1946, box 1183, docket 6013, FCC.

107. McChesney, *Telecommunications, Mass Media, and Democracy,* 27, 75; *Variety,* July 3, 1946; Official Report of Proceedings before FCC, June 27, 1947, box 1881, docket 6013, Preliminary Decision, In re Applications WBNX Broadcasting Company, Inc., et al., Apr. 9, 1947, box 2628, docket 7225, FCC; *New York Times,* Apr. 13, 1947.

108. *New York Times,* Apr. 13, 1947; *Variety,* Apr. 3, 1946; WFDR Operating Policy, Digest from FCC Hearing Transcripts, July 25–27, 1946, box 44, Frederick F. Umhey Papers, ILGWU.

109. People's Radio Foundation, Inc., Proposed Program Services; Official Report of Proceedings before the FCC, July 16, 1946, boxes 1183 and 1184, July 23, 1946, box 1185, docket 6013, Preliminary Decision, In re Applications WBNX Broadcasting Company, Inc., et al., Apr. 9, 1947, box 2628, docket 7225, FCC.

110. Konecky, *American Communications Conspiracy,* 106–7; Official Report of Proceedings before the FCC, July 16, 1946, boxes 1183 and 1184, July 23, 1946, box 1185, docket 6013, FCC.

111. Edward Lindemann to FCC, June 30, 1946, Jack Anderson Spanagel to FCC, July 10, 1946, David Pressman to FCC, n.d., box 2625, Jonah E. Caplan to PRF, Nov. 27, 1945, box 2626, docket 7221, FCC.

112. Minutes of Stockholders Meeting, People's Radio Foundation, Inc., Sept. 23, 1946, box 36, IWO Papers, KLMDC; "Radio Artists Break Taboos, Show Radio As It Should Be," Dec. 16, 1946, "Radio Station WPRF—The People's Choice," Feb. 6, 1947, reel 9112, FP; *Daily Worker,* Jan. 26, 1947; Konecky, *American Communications Conspiracy,* 108–9.

113. *Daily Worker,* July 2, 1946; *New Leader,* Mar. 8, 1947, 5; *Chicago Journal of Commerce,* July 1, 1946; "Daily News Challenged in FM Hearing," *Broadcasting,* July 15, 1946, 90; "Six New York FM Applicants Must Still Present Evidence," *Broadcasting,* July 22, 1946, 84.

114. Alfred Kohlbert to FCC, July 2, 1946, Charles O. Andrews to Charles R. Denney, Charles Hubert to Vernon L. Wilkinson, Sept. 9, 1946, box 2626, docket 7221, FCC; *In Fact,* Dec. 30, 1946.

115. Official Report of Proceedings before the FCC, July 12 and 16, 1946, boxes 1183 and 1184, July 23, 1946, box 1185, docket 6013, FCC.

116. Charles O. Andrews to Charles R. Denny, Aug. 23, 1946, W. Lee Daniel to Denny, Oct. 17, 1947, box 2626, docket 7221, FCC; *In Fact,* Dec. 30, 1946; *Federation News,* Apr. 12, 1947; *New Leader,* Mar. 8, 1947, 5, 19.

117. Proposed Decision in re Applications of WBNX Broadcasting Company, Inc., et al., Apr. 9, 1947, docket 6013, FCC; "FCC Handles Its Hottest FM-TV Case," *Broadcasting,* Apr. 21, 1947, 18.

118. *Variety,* Mar. 5, 1947, Apr. 21, 1948; Toro, "Standing Up for Listeners' Rights," 133.

119. "On the Air: WFDR," *New Republic,* July 4, 1949, 20–21; Elizabeth A. Fones-Wolf, *Selling Free Enterprise: The Business Assault on Labor and Liberalism, 1945–60* (Urbana: University of Illinois Press, 1994), 50–51; "Our 'Laboristic' President," *Fortune,* Dec. 1948, 11.

Chapter 6: Competing Voices

1. *Justice,* July 1, 1949, 1, 3.

2. *Justice,* July 1, 1949, 1, 3; *Variety,* June 22, 1949, 27.

3. It should not be overlooked that throughout the postwar era, Chicago continued to host the only AM labor station in the nation, WCFL. In this period, however,

WCFL was becoming more commercial, and by 1960, as its historian, Nathan Godfried, writes, the station "spoke all too rarely about workers or even trade unionism." Nathan Godfried, *WCFL: Chicago's Voice of Labor, 1926–78* (Urbana: University of Illinois Press, 1997), 268.

4. On the postwar ideological struggle, see Elizabeth A. Fones-Wolf, *Selling Free Enterprise: The Business Assault on Labor and Liberalism, 1945–1960* (Urbana: University of Illinois Press, 1994); Howell John Harris, *The Right to Manage: Industrial Relations Policies of American Business in the 1940s* (Madison: University of Wisconsin Press, 1982); Sanford M. Jacoby, *Modern Manors: Welfare Capitalism since the New Deal* (Princeton, N.J.: Princeton University Press, 1997).

5. Fones-Wolf, *Selling Free Enterprise*, 33–73; "Weir Calls Plant City Symbol of Opportunity," *Iron Age*, May 12, 1949, 168; Ernest Weir, "Which Way America?" *Commercial and Financial Chronicle*, May 2, 1946; Research Division, Special Services, Bureau of the Budget, Current Opinions, Dec. 12, 1945, box 1719, RG 44, U.S. Information Service, Bureau of Special Services, OWI Research Division, NARA.

6. On the postwar business mobilization, see Fones-Wolf, *Selling Free Enterprise*; Harris, *Right to Manage*.

7. National Industrial Information Committee, Annual Report, 1943, box 842, series III, Acc. 1411, NAM (hereafter Acc. 1411, NAM III/842); Preliminary Report on the National Media, n.d., National Industrial Information Committee, *Interpreting Free Enterprise to Grass Roots America*, Acc. 1411, NAM III/845; Jan. 14, 1946, *Salesletter*, Jan. 17. 1949, Acc. 1411, NAM I/110

8. Fones-Wolf, *Selling Free Enterprise*, 158–80; Morrell Heald, *The Social Responsibilities of Business: Company and Community, 1900–1969* (Cleveland: Press of Case Western Reserve University, 1970), 221–30.

9. *Public Relations News*, Dec. 22, 1947; *Exchange*, Feb. 1949, Acc. 1411, NAM I/122.

10. *Community Relations: Telling the Company's Story* (New York: Metropolitan Life Insurance Co., 1949), 20.

11. Frank H. Blumenthal, "Anti-Union Publicity in the Johnstown 'Little Steel' Strike of 1937," *Public Opinion Quarterly* 3 (October 1939): 682; *Variety*, Dec. 5, 1945; Walter H. Uphoff, *Kohler on Strike: Thirty Years of Conflict* (Boston: Beacon Press, 1966), 147, 340–41, 356. On public relations during strikes, see Karen S. Miller, "National and Local Public Relations Campaigns during the 1946 Steel Strike," *Public Relations Review* 21 (Winter 1995): 305–23.

12. *Community Relations*, 17–18; E. T. Gardner, "Clarity Is the Keynote in Our Communications," *Advanced Management*, Nov. 1951, 8.

13. Hugh Higley, "Tested Community Relations," *Public Relations Journal*, Apr. 1951, 9.

14. "Low-Cost Local Radio Program," *Factory Management and Maintenance*, Sept. 1949, 98–99; *Exchange*, Feb. 1950, Acc. 1411, NAM I/122; *Billboard*, Oct. 4, 1947.

15. *NAM News*, Dec. 15, 1951, 20; *Exchange*, Sept. 1949, 5, Acc. 1411, NAM I/122; "Putting More Life into Small-Town Community Relations," *Modern Industry*, Apr. 15, 1953, 93–98; F. C. Minaker, "Novel Idea in Community Relations," *American Business*, June 1953, 24; "Serve and Tell—to Make Friends for Your Plant," *Factory Management and Maintenance*, Aug. 1956, 112.

16. "Successful Community Relations in Eight Companies," *Factory Management and Maintenance,* Dec. 1948, 70; Youngstown Sheet and Tube Company Radio Editorials, transcripts, box 5, Youngstown Sheet and Tube Company Records, Ohio Historical Society, Columbus.

17. Proceedings, Committee on Cooperation with Community Leaders of the National Association of Manufacturers, May 17, 1950, Acc. 1411, NAM I/270.

18. Fones-Wolf, *Selling Free Enterprise,* 82, 94–96, 176, 272.

19. *The State of the Company* (Canton, Ohio: Timken Roller Bearing Co., 1947), 204.

20. "The Timken Message Reaches Its Employees and the General Public by Radio," *Broadcasting,* Sept. 29, 1952, 29, 108; *Community Relations,* 18.

21. *The State of the Company* (Canton, Ohio: Timken Roller Bearing Co., 1948), 198–201; *The State of the Company* (Canton, Ohio: Timken Roller Bearing Co., 1949), 90–92, 196–99, 259–64; "The Timken Message Reaches Its Employees and the General Public by Radio," 29, 108.

22. *The Fabricator,* Sept. 1948, R. L. Wolfe to John S. Bugas, Nov. 24, 1948, "Detroit's Mark Adams Has Been 'Unique,'" flyer, n.d., box 1, Mark Adams Collection, ALUA.

23. "Abretha and the Horsewhip," script, Mar. 8, 1949, "The Great Reform," script, Feb. 14, 1949, box 2, Mark Adams Collection, ALUA.

24. "Security Island," script, July 26, 1949, box 2, Mark Adams Collection, ALUA.

25. Gerd Horten, *Radio Goes to War: The Cultural Politics of Propaganda during World War II* (Berkeley: University of California Press, 2002), 3; Robert H. Zieger, *American Workers, American Unions, 1920–1985* (Baltimore: Johns Hopkins University Press, 1986), 91; Alan Brinkley, *The End of Reform: New Deal Liberalism in Recession and War* (New York: Alfred A. Knopf, 1995), 256.

26. Research Division, Special Services, Bureau of the Budget, Current Opinions, Dec. 12, 1945, box 1719, RG 44, U.S. Information Service, Bureau of Special Services, OWI Research Division, NARA.

27. "Labor on the Air," *New Republic,* Dec. 15, 1947, 35; Allen W. Sayler to Walter P. Reuther and Geo. F. Addes, Mar. 12, 1947, box 146, Walter Reuther Papers, ALUA.

28. *CIO News,* Dec. 16, 1946, Feb. 17, 24, Dec. 15, 1947, Mar. 15, 1948; *Guild Reporter,* Jan. 11, 1946; *Pennsylvania Labor News,* June 11, 1948; *Ford Facts,* May 29, Sept. 25, 1948.

29. T. J. Slowie to New Jersey State Industrial Council, Mar. 8, 1945, box 213, General Corr. File, 1927–46, FCC; *Ammunition,* Jan. 1947, 36; I. Keith Tyler and Nancy Dasher, *Education on the Air* (Columbus: Ohio State University, 1947), 136.

30. "AFL Bodies Start Drive on Unfair Radio Commentators," July 16, 1947, reel 9112, FP; Minutebook, Oct. 21, 1948, 187, Geneva Federation of Labor Papers, KLMDC.

31. Susan J. Douglas, *Listening In: Radio and the American Imagination, from Amos 'n' Andy and Edward R. Murrow to Wolfman Jack and Howard Stern* (New York: Times Books, 1999), 219–22.

32. *Quarterly Report of the UAW,* Jan. 1. 1946, ALUA; *United Automobile Worker,* Feb. 1947; Robert H. Stinson to William Kemsley, Feb. 17, 1950, clipping, attached to Tom Jones to Bill Friedland, Jan. 10, 1951, box 188, Michigan AFL-CIO Papers, ALUA; UE, *Proceedings* (1946), 44, reel 53, ALUCP; *UE News,* Mar. 13, Apr. 10, 1948.

33. *CIO News,* Mar. 31, 1947; Sam Sweet to Ivan E. Brown, Dec. 30, 1946, "Voice of Local 51," scripts, Oct. 27, Dec. 8, 1946, Feb. 2, Sept. 21, 1947, "Local Has Radio Jackpot Quiz," clipping, n.d., box 20, UAW Local 51 Papers, AULA.

34. August Scholle, et al., to All CIO Locals and City Council Affiliated with the Michigan CIO Council, Oct. 29, 1952, box 25, Michigan AFL-CIO, Lansing Office Papers, Bill Kemsley to John Crosby, box 188, Michigan AFL-CIO Papers, ALUA; *Michigan CIO News,* Feb. 8, 1951.

35. Ohio CIO Council, *Proceedings* (1947), 64, SHSW; Michigan CIO Council, *Proceedings* (1948), 175, ALUA; *CIO Radio Activator,* Apr. 1951, box 16, Michigan AFL-CIO Papers, ALUA. See also other issues of this newsletter, sponsored by the Michigan CIO and UAW Education Departments, in box 14, Michigan AFL-CIO Papers, and box 25, Michigan AFL-CIO, Lansing Office Papers, and "Suggested Outline for Remarks on the Work of the Radio and Press Councils," n.d., ca. 1951, box 188, Michigan AFL-CIO Papers, ALUA.

36. *Michigan CIO News,* Apr. 27, July 13, 1950; *The CIO Radio Activator,* Apr. 1951, box 16, Mildred Jeffrey Papers, ALUA.

37. CIO-PAC Scripts, 1946, box, A4–33, Philip Murray Papers, Department of Archives and Manuscripts, Catholic University of America; *Ammunition,* Apr. 1947, 35, Nov. 1947, 36, Aug. 1946, 17; Suggestions on Radio Scripts, Mar. 10, 1950, Yellow Acc., box 95, Radio Scripts, 1955–56, box 665, Red Acc., UE Archives; "IAM Programs," *Broadcasting,* Apr. 24, 1950, 38; Suggestions for the Drive for Voluntary Contributions, n.d., ca. 1948, box 125, David McDonald Papers, HCLA; Albert Hamilton to Joseph Rogers, May 23, 1950, box 3, Labor's League for Political Education, Department of Public Relations Report, May 9, 1950, box 3, Morris S. Novik Papers, GMMA.

38. "The Songs of Bill Friedland and Joe Glazer," History in Song, Jan. 24, 2006, http://www.fortunecity.com/tinpan/parton/2/friedland.html; Bill Friedland to Marjorie Morris, Dec. 28, 1951, box 179, Michigan AFL-CIO Papers, "Summary" Comments on Radio and Television and the CIO, enclosed with Bill Kemsley to Barbara Wertheimer, May 28, 1951, box 188, Michigan AFL-CIO Papers, ALUA.

39. Michigan CIO Radio Council Script File, Flint Labor Talks, FEPC, n.d., box 14, Mildred Jeffrey Papers, ALUA.

40. Bill Kemsley to Edward Baughn, Feb. 9, 1951, box 188, Michigan AFL-CIO Papers, ALUA; Ohio CIO Council, *Proceedings* (1951), 53; *Variety,* Mar. 24, Apr. 7, 1948; *Justice,* May 15, 1949; Minutes, Conference of Eastern Pennsylvania Central Labor Unions, Oct. 30, 1949, Mar. 5, 1950, AUF, box 31, *A History in Words and Pictures of Amalgamated Local 686, UAW, 40th Anniversary,* Aug. 26, 1979, box 11, UAW Local 686 Papers, KLMDC; *The Reporter,* June 1948; *New Era,* Aug. 9, 1951; *CIO News,* Feb. 18, 1951; *Steel Labor,* July 1949; G. W. Johnstone to R. T. Compton, Apr. 6, 1956, Acc. 1411, NAM I/155.

41. UE, *Proceedings* (1951), 190–91; Script, ca. 1954, Local 124, Lancaster, Pa., Red Acc., box 667, script, "News on the Niagara Frontier," July 4, 1953, Red Acc., box 666, UE Archives; "Indiana CIO Had 3 Radio Shows, June 10, 1948, Kentucky AFL Sponsor Weekly Radio Broadcast," reel 9112, FP; Al Hamilton to Victor Reuther, Jan. 14, 1959, box 337, Walter Reuther Papers, ALUA.

42. *CIO News,* Feb. 18, Nov. 11, 1946; Saul Carson, "Labor Forum," *New Republic,* Dec. 8, 1947, 32.

43. Summary Comments on Radio, Television, and the CIO, Report on PAC Activities: The New York Office, Aug. 24, 1945, box 212, pt. 14, Miscellaneous Documents, ACWA; Ben Segal to Larry Rogin, May 13, 21, 1947, box 11, series 8A-1, Textile Workers Union of America Papers, SHSW; Memo from Allan L. Swim, Sept. 4, 1946, reel 20, *Operation Dixie: The CIO Organizing Committee Papers, 1946–1953* (Sanford, N.C.: Microfilm Corporation of America, 1980).

44. David S. Burgess, *My Life Journey* (Benicia, Calif.: David S. Burgess, 1994), 120; Godfried, *WCFL,* 247; "It's Labor," scripts, Akron, Ohio, box 118, Michigan AFL-CIO Papers, ALUA; *Billboard,* Jan. 24, 1948.

45. *Variety,* Jan. 18, 1950; "Iowa Gets Football Broadcasts with Labor Plugs," Oct. 31, 1947, reel 9112, FP; Robert Ross, "Why Teamsters Union Is New Sponsor for Notre Dame Football, *Printers' Ink,* Nov. 16, 1951, 80–81.

46. Barbara S. Griffith, *The Crisis of American Labor: Operation Dixie and the Defeat of the CIO* (Philadelphia: Temple University Press, 1988). For Winston-Salem, see Robert Rodgers Korstad, *Civil Rights Unionism: Tobacco Workers and the Struggle for Democracy in the Mid-Twentieth-Century South* (Chapel Hill: University of North Carolina Press, 2003). On Rome, see Michelle Brattain, *Race, Workers, and Culture in the Modern South* (Princeton, N.J.: Princeton University Press, 2003).

47. Korstad, *Civil Rights Unionism,* 232; William Smith to Van A. Bittner, Aug. 8, 1946, reel 1, *Operation Dixie.* Not all organizers were enthusiastic about radio. In early 1950, over the objections of the union's education and research director, who felt that broadcasts had limited influence, the American Federation of Hosiery Workers ran a thirteen-week series in Greensboro, North Carolina, entitled "Your Stake in Unions," which argued that labor unions fought for the good of the "common man" through their collective bargaining activities and anticipated distributing the series throughout the South. At the end of the series, the southern office district manager, John J. McCoy, asserted that the reaction to the programs was "not too great or too enthusiastic" and urged putting any future broadcasting plans on hold. William Rafsky to John J. McCoy, Nov. 9, 1949, "Your Stake in the Union," scripts, McCoy to Rafsky, box 19, series 3, American Federation of Hosiery Workers Papers, SHSW.

48. Burgess, *My Life Journey,* 120; Franz E. Daniel to George Baldanzi, Jan. 23, 1950, reel 16, *Operation Dixie;* Joel B. Leighton to Emil Rieve, June 14, 1949, box 9, series 2A, Textile Workers Union of America Papers, SHSW.

49. Brian Ward, *Radio and the Struggle for Civil Rights in the South* (Gainesville: University Press of Florida, 2004), 58–61; George Baldanzi to David J. McDonald, Jan. 19, 1950, CIO Texas Bill Strength Show, scripts, box 142, David J. McDonald Papers, United Steel Workers of America Collection, HCLA; Randall L. Patton, "Textile Organizing in a Sunbelt South Community: Northwest Georgia's Carpet Industry in the Early 1960s," *Labor History* 39 (1998): 296; William J. Smith to Baldanzi, Feb. 9, 1950, reel 1, *Operation Dixie.*

50. Report by Ruth A. Gettinger on Gaston County, N.C., Oct. 17, 1946, reel 3, David S. Burgess to Franz Daniel, June 12, 1948, reel 16, *Operation Dixie; CIO News,* May 5, 1952.

51. Franz Daniel to Baldanzi, Dec. 12, 1949, Feb. 6, 1950, reel 16, Lloyd Vaughan to John V. Riffe, Sept. 16, 1950, Lloyd P. Vaughan to FCC, Mar. 7, 1951, CIO Radio Program, scripts, WAIM, Anderson, S.C., 1951–52, Jerome A. Cooper to Lloyd Vaughan,

Sept. 18, 1952, Feb. 2, Mar. 11, 1953, reel 18, *Operation Dixie;* Patton, "Textile Organizing in a Sunbelt South Community," 296.

52. UAW President's Report, 1950, 233, UAW President's Report, 1949, 182, ALUA; Morris Novik interview, June 18, 1985, KLMDC.

53. *New York Times,* Apr. 14, 1947; *New York Times,* Apr. 13, 1947; Gus Tyler, *Look for the Union Label: A History of the International Ladies' Garment Workers' Union* (Armonk, N.Y.: M. E. Sharpe, 1995), 196–208.

54. "Six Non-Profit Davids and the Commercial Goliath," ca. May 1950, box 11, Mildred Jeffrey Papers, ALUA.

55. Nelson Lichtenstein, *The Most Dangerous Man in Detroit: Walter Reuther and the Fate of American Labor* (New York: Basic Books, 1995); Kevin Boyle, *The UAW and the Heyday of American Liberalism, 1945–1968* (Ithaca, N.Y.: Cornell University Press, 1995); *Variety,* Apr. 3, 1946; "Six Non-Profit Davids and the Commercial Goliath," ca. May 1950, box 11, Mildred Jeffrey Papers, ALUA.

56. Lichtenstein, *Most Dangerous Man in Detroit,* 300–303; Fones-Wolf, *Selling Free Enterprise,* 137–52; "Six Non-Profit Davids and the Commercial Goliath," ca. May 1950, box 11, Mildred Jeffrey Papers, ALUA.

57. WCFL's founder, Edward Nockels, had voiced many of these same ideas fifteen years earlier. Godfried, *WCFL,* chaps. 1 and 2; "Notes on WEDT-FM," box 11, Walter P. Reuther to Sir and Brother, Apr. 18, 1949, Paul E. Miley to Sirs and Brothers, Aug. 5, 1947, box 14, Mildred Jeffrey Papers, ALUA; Frederick F. Umhey, "Radio Stations Run by Labor," *American Federationist,* Dec. 1945, 11.

58. Untitled flyer on "Community Clinic," ca. Feb. 1949, box 15, Mildred Jeffrey Papers, ALUA; Norman Matthews, "UAW Outlines FM Plans," *FM Business,* Feb. 1947, Walter Reuther to all Local Union Officers in the WDET-FM Reception Area, June 10, 1949, box 146, Walter Reuther Papers, ALUA; *Ammunition,* Nov. 1948, 32.

59. "On the Air: WFDR," *New Republic,* July 4, 1949, 20–21; Interview with Morris Novik, June 18, 1985, KLMDC; UAW Executive Board Minutes, Mar. 1–6, 1948, box 5, ALUA; Morris Novik, "Radio," box 1, Morris S. Novik Papers, Broadcast Pioneers Library, University of Maryland, College Park; M. S. Novik, "Labor Unions in FM," *FM Business,* Dec. 1946, 14.

60. *Ammunition,* July 1948, 12; Pat Peterman report, ca. Nov. 1950, box 8, Mildred Jeffrey Papers, ALUA; KFMV Sept. 1950 Program Schedule, box 41, Joe Siegel to Frederick Umhey, Mar. 16, 1949, box 47, Frederick F. Umhey Papers, ILGWU.

61. Pat Peterman report, ca. Nov. 1950, box 8, Mildred Jeffrey Papers, ALUA; *Variety,* Feb. 5, 1951, Dec. 28, 1949, Jan. 25, 1950; *Justice,* Oct. 1, 1950.

62. WDET News, Jan. 16, 1950, box 9, UAW Public Relations Department Papers, ALUA; Children's Stories, n.d., box 15, Mildred Jeffrey Papers, ALUA; Ben Hoberman to Emil Mazey, Dec. 31, 1949, box 9, UAW Public Relations Department Papers, ALUA; *Variety,* July 26, 1950.

63. *Billboard,* Feb. 19, 1949; *Variety,* Feb. 25, 1948; "Italian, Ukranian Music on WDET-FM," n.d., box 147, Walter Reuther Papers, ALUA; WDET Program Schedule, Mar. 1952, box 53, Emil Mazey Files, UAW Secretary-Treasurer Papers, ALUA.

64. Barbara Dianne Savage, *Broadcasting Freedom: Radio, War, and the Politics of Race* (Chapel Hill: University of North Carolina Press, 1999), 2; Ward, *Radio and the Struggle for Civil Rights in the South;* "Six Non-Profit Davids and the Commercial

Goliath," ca. May 1950, box 11, Mildred Jeffrey Papers, ALUA; *Pittsburgh Courier,* Dec. 18, 1948; "Teenage Commentators," undated *Pittsburgh Courier* clipping, box 9, UAW Public Relations Department Papers, ALUA; Cliff Gill to M. S. Novik, Feb. 17, 1949, box 41, Joe Siegel to Frederick Umhey, Mar. 27, 1949, box 49, Frederick F. Umhey Papers, ILGWU; Ben Hoberman to Emil Mazey, Sept. 6, 1949, box 22, UAW Research Department Papers, ALUA.

65. Mildred Jeffrey to Hardy Merril, Dec. 3, 1948, box 14, Mildred Jeffrey Papers, ALUA; *Ford Facts,* Aug 6, 1949; "Civic and Community Programs Heard Exclusively on WDET in 1949," n.d., box 11, Mildred Jeffrey Papers, ALUA.

66. While the advocates of the co-op development won this hearing, they ultimately failed to overcome the neighborhood association's intense opposition to the building of the housing project. "Detroit Labor Station Airs Controversial City Council Housing Hearing," n.d., box 1, UAW Radio Department Papers, 1984 Acc., ALUA.

67. "Discrimination in Single-Barred Xmas Seals?" *WDET News,* Dec. 14, 1949; *Michigan CIO News,* Dec. 22, 1949.

68. Report on the Progress of KFMV since Opening, n.d., box 3, Morris S. Novik Papers, GMMA; *Variety,* June 29, 1949; *Justice,* Feb. 1, 1950; *Ammunition,* May 1950, 10; *Michigan CIO News,* Jan. 29, 1949, Jan. 5, 1950.

69. "WCUO Publicity: Programs of Interest to Every Union Member," n.d., box 14, Mildred Jeffrey Papers, ALUA; "Voice of the CIO," scripts, Feb. 12, 19, Mar. 12, 1950, box 1, UAW Radio Department Papers, 1984 Acc., ALUA.

70. UAW Press Release, Apr. 11, 1950, box 7, Mildred Jeffrey Papers, ALUA.

71. *Detroit Free Press,* June 6, 1965; *United Automobile Worker,* May 1949; *Detroit Times,* June 2, 1957.

72. *United Automobile Worker,* May 1949, 10; "Labor Views the News," script, undated, ca. May 1950, box 7, Mildred Jeffrey Papers, ALUA.

73. *Ammunition,* May 1950, 10; "Best in Radio," flyer, n.d., box 147, Walter Reuther Papers, ALUA; Jerry Sherman to Millie Jeffrey et al., Feb. 19, 1951, box 16, Mildred Jeffrey Papers, ALUA.

74. "Six Non-Profit Davids and the Commercial Goliath," ca. May 1950, box 11, FM Sound truck flyer, n.d., box 16, Mildred Jeffrey Papers, ALUA; *WDET News,* Feb. 9, 1950; *United Automobile Worker,* Apr. 1950, 10.

75. Al Rightley to Local Union Presidents in WDET Reception Area, Jan. 20, 1950, box 21, UAW Local 212 Papers, ALUA; Mildred Jeffrey and J. A. Rightley to International Representatives and Local Union Presidents in WDET Reception Area, Jan. 28, 1950, box 32, Michigan AFL-CIO Papers, ALUA; FM Ownership in Detroit and Prospects for its Growth, n.d., box 11, Mildred Jeffrey Papers, ALUA; *Justice,* Apr. 15, 1950, Jan. 1, 1951; Joe Siegel to Frederick Umhey, Jan. 30, 1950, box 49, Frederick F. Umhey Papers, ILGWU; Mildred Jeffrey, interview with the author, July 4, 1997.

76. Minutes, Annual Membership Meeting of the UAW-CIO Broadcasting Corporation of Michigan, Jan. 24, 1950, box 10, Mildred Jeffrey to Emil Mazey, Feb. 25, 1949, box 14, Mildred Jeffrey Papers, ALUA.

77. *United Automobile Worker,* Oct. 1949, 10; Emil Mazey to Walter P. Reuther, Sept. 21, 1949, box 9, UAW Public Relations Department Papers, ALUA; *Michigan CIO News,* Oct. 19, 1950; "WDET News: Bob Hope Guests First WDET 'Teen Tempo

Show,'" n.d., box 1, UAW Radio Department Papers, 1984 Acc., ALUA; Joe Siegel to Frederick Umhey, June 10, 1949, box 49, Frederick F. Umhey Papers, ILGWU.

78. Sample of Listeners' Reaction to WDET, Apr. 14, 1949, box 1, UAW Radio Department Papers, 1984 Acc., ALUA; Charles Adrian to Program Director, WDET, Mar. 23, 1950, box 5, Mildred Jeffrey Papers, ALUA; WDET News, Praise from Listeners, Oct. 8, 1949, Marion H. Bemis to Ben Hoberman, Oct. 5, 1949, box 9, UAW Public Relations Department Papers, ALUA; Typical Listener Comments Taken from Letters Received by WDET, ca. 1950, box 146, Walter Reuther Papers, ALUA.

79. Maxwell Fox to Frederick Umhey, Dec. 5, 1949, box 44, Cliff Gill to Frederick Umhey, Mar. 9, 1951, box 40, Clara S. Logan to David Dubinsky, Feb. 28, 1941, box 39, Frederick F. Umhey Papers, ILGWU; *Justice,* Mar. 1, 1950, Apr. 1, 1951; *United Automobile Worker,* June 1950; Pat Peterman report, ca. 1950, box 8, Mildred Jeffrey Papers, ALUA.

80. *Justice,* Feb. 15, 1951, Feb. 15, 1952; *New York Times,* Feb. 7, 1952; "Regrets Passing of FM station," clipping, Apr. 10, 1952, box 14, Mildred Jeffrey Papers, ALUA; Joe Seigel to Frederick Umhey, Aug. 24, 1950, box 49, Frederick F. Umhey Papers, ILGWU.

81. Joseph L. Rauh to T. J. Slowie, Mar. 18, 1952, box 13, Mildred Jeffrey Papers, ALUA; ILGWU, *Proceedings* (1953), 20, reel 48, ALUCP; *Variety,* Jan. 9, 1952; Mildred Jeffrey, interview with the author, June 2, 1999; Analysis of Public Symphony Hour Listeners According to Occupational Groups, n.d., box 14, Mildred Jeffrey Papers, ALUA.

82. In some ways, the FM stations' financial struggles were similar to those of WCFL, which attempted to solve its fiscal stress by reducing labor programming and adopting a more commercial orientation. Godfried, *WCFL,* chaps. 9 and 10; Guy Nunn to Mildred Jeffrey, Aug. 30, 1950, Jeffrey to Ken Robinson, Oct. 18, 1950, box 11, Mildred Jeffrey Papers, ALUA; Ben Hoberman to Morris Novik, May 24, 1949, box 6, Ben Hoberman to Morris Novik, Oct. 24, 1949, box 4, UAW Radio Department Papers, 1984 Acc., ALUA; Mildred Jeffrey to Bob Miller, Nov. 23, 1949, box 4, Mildred Jeffrey Papers, ALUA; Joe Siegel to Frederick Umhey, Apr. 1, 1948, box 49, Frederick F. Umhey Papers, ILGWU.

83. Godfried, *WCFL,* 239–90; "Six Non-Profit Davids and the Commercial Goliath," ca. May 1950, box 11, Mildred Jeffrey Papers, ALUA.

84. "Looking Ahead in Labor," *Factory Management and Maintenance,* May 1952, W-1.

Chapter 7: Union Voices in a "Wilderness of Conservatism"

1. A Progress Report on the Edward P. Morgan and John W. Vandercook Programs Prepared for the AFL-CIO, June 1, 1956, box 3, Morris S. Novik Papers, GMMA.

2. Irving Fang, *Those Radio Commentators!* (Ames: Iowa State University Press, 1977): 208; Norbert Muhlen, "The Canned Opinion Industry," *Common Sense,* Nov. 1945, 14; *Michigan CIO News,* June 29, 1950.

3. David W. Shepard, "An Experiment in Content Analysis: The Radio Addresses of Henry J. Taylor, 1945–1950" (Ph.D. diss., University of Minnesota, 1953), 220–48;

Henry J. Taylor, *Your Land and Mine* (Detroit: General Motors, 1945), no. 24, 26, Special Collections, Bizzell Memorial Library, University of Oklahoma, Norman.

4. An Integrated Public Relations Program for the National Association of Manufacturers, Acc. 1411, box 110, series I, NAM (hereafter NAM I/110); *The Public Relations Program of the National Association of Manufacturers*, n.d. (ca. Oct. 1946), box 10, J. Howard Pew Papers, HML.

5. *Variety*, Jan. 29, 1947, Aug. 4, 1948; *Billboard*, Jan. 17, 1948; *NAM News*, Jan. 14, Apr. 29, Sept. 9, 1950.

6. *NAM News*, July 8, Oct. 21, 1950, Feb. 17, 1951, Mar. 22, 1957; "NAM Scores a Hit on TV," *Business Week*, Apr. 19, 1952, 86–88; G. W. Johnstone to Divisional and Regional Managers, June 4, 1952, Acc. 1411, NAM I/155.

7. William L. Bird, *"Better Living": Advertising, Media, and the New Vocabulary of Business Leadership, 1935–1955* (Evanston, Ill.: Northwestern University Press, 1999), 189–97; George L. Hicks, *The Radio Story of the Industrial Family That Serves the Nation* (n.p.: The Corporation, 1947), 14, 16, 38, 44, 92, 98, 135, 197–97.

8. Bird, *"Better Living,"* 189–205; "Television Audience Acclaims United States Steel Hour," *U.S. Steel News*, Jan. 1954, 20; Arnold G. Leo to George P. Neilson, Oct. 26, 1954, box 8, Acc. 1803, Du Pont Advertising Department Papers, HML; Bohm Aluminum and Brass Corp. Advertisements, transcripts, Apr. 13 and June 29, 1952, box 132, NBC; Robert Newcomb and Marge Sammons, *Employee Communications in Action* (New York: Harper, 1961), 107.

9. Bird, *"Better Living,"* 190; *Variety*, Sept. 11, 1946, Sept. 7, 1949, Sept. 13, 1950, Sept. 3, 17, 1952, Sept. 21, 1955, Sept. 26, 1946, Aug. 20, 1947; *Billboard*, Sept. 20, 1947.

10. Evidence of the Impact of "Cavalcade," ca. 1956, box 8, Acc. 1803, Du Pont Advertising Department Papers, HML.

11. Sara U. Douglas, *Labor's New Voice: Unions and the Mass Media* (Norwood, N.J.: Ablex Publishing Corp., 1986), 51–52; *CIO News*, Dec. 26, 1949, Nov. 16, 1953; *Daily Worker*, Feb. 11, 1947.

12. *Variety*, Jan. 21, 1952; *Michigan CIO News*, Jan. 17, 1952; AFL, *Proceedings* (1952), 233; *AFL News-Reporter*, Jan. 9, 1952.

13. *American Federationist*, Nov. 1945, 26; *CIO News*, Apr. 8, 1946; *Daily Worker*, Feb. 11, 1947; *Variety*, Jan. 16, 1946.

14. *CIO News*, Jan. 5, Apr. 12, 1948, Henry C. Fleisher to James B. Carey, Feb. 2, 1948, box 25, CIO Office of the Secretary-Treasurer Papers, ALUA.

15. *Billboard*, Jan. 17, 1948, Jan. 29, 1949; *Variety*, Jan. 16, 1946, Jan. 29, 1947, Jan. 21, 1948; Excerpt from Broadcast of H. V. Kaltenborn, Wednesday, Feb, 2, 1949, box 76, CIO Office of the Secretary-Treasurers Papers, ALUA.

16. Henry C. Fleisher to Walter P. Reuther, Dec. 11, 1952, box 76, CIO Office of the Secretary-Treasurer Papers, ALUA.

17. See the many invitations to James Carey in boxes 25 and 26 in CIO Office of the Secretary-Treasurer Papers, ALUA; CIO, *Proceedings* (1953), 263; M. S. Novik to David J. McDonald, Aug. 21, 1956, box 37, RG1–027, George Meany Papers, GMMA; *CIO News*, Oct. 6, 1947, Mar. 12, 1951; *New Era*, Sept. 1, 1955; *United Automobile Worker*, Feb. 1948; "Matters for Discussion," ca. 1953, box 8, Mildred Jeffrey Papers, ALUA.

18. "Shocking Development in Labor Leadership," Nov. 9, 1959, "WTOP Editorial,"

Nov. 10, 1959, "Agronsky Interviews Reuther," Nov. 11, 1959, box 147, Walter Reuther Papers, ALUA.

19. Robert H. Zieger, *The CIO, 1935–1955* (Chapel Hill: University of North Carolina Press, 1995), 215; *CIO News,* Oct. 15, 1945; CIO Executive Board Minutes, Nov. 1–2 1945, 73–75, reel 8, ALUA; "CIO for America," Oct. 29, 1945, box 33, David J. McDonald Papers, United Steel Workers of America Collection, HCLA.

20. *CIO News,* Mar. 17, 31, Apr. 23, June 9, 16, 1947, Len De Caux to Regional Directors et al., Apr. 10, 1947, box 99, series 2, Michigan AFL-CIO Papers, ALUA; *PM,* May 5, June 11, 1947.

21. *Variety,* Apr. 30, 1947; M. S. Novik, "Labor on the Air," *American Federationist,* June 1947, 8; *PM,* May 9, 1947; Memo for Oliver Saylor, "Entertainment Unions Cooperate with AF of L to Defeat Hartley-Taft Bills," box 1, Morris S. Novik Papers, GMMA.

22. *PM,* June 9, 1947; Novik, "Labor on the Air," 8–9, 15; Steven J. Ross, *Working-Class Hollywood: Silent Film and the Shaping of Class in America* (Princeton, N.J.: Princeton University Press, 1998), 156.

23. Novik, "Labor on the Air," 8–9, 15; *Daily Worker,* May 18, 1947; "Story from the Stars," script, May 8, 1947, AFL Variety Show, script, June 5, 1947, box 1, Morris S. Novik Papers, GMMA.

24. List of Programs, enclosed with minutes of Meeting of Entertainment Unions Committee, July 8, 1947, *The Best Things in Life,* scripts, May 6, 9, 16, 1946, box 1, "Actors in 'All My Sons' to Star in New Radio Show," press release, May 21, 1947, box 5, Morris S. Novik Papers, GGMA; *PM,* May 7, 1947.

25. Ross, *Working-Class Hollywood,* 8; Michele Hilmes, *Radio Voices: American Broadcasting, 1922–1952* (Minneapolis: University of Minnesota Press, 1997), 154–75; John Bodnar, *Blue-Collar Hollywood: Liberalism, Democracy, and Working People in American Film* (Baltimore: Johns Hopkins University Press, 2003), 87–126.

26. "Nothing to Fear," series 2 of *The Best Things in Life,* scripts, May 9–14, 1947, box 1, Morris S. Novik Papers, GMMA.

27. "A Woman's Place," series 3 of *The Best Things in Life,* scripts, May 15–21, 1947, box 1, Morris S. Novik Papers, GMMA.

28. "Story from the Stars," script, May 8, 1947, AFL Variety Show, script, June 5, 1947, Morris Novik to Morton Wishengrad, June 2, 1947, box 1, Morris S. Novik Papers, GMMA.

29. *PM,* May 6, 1947; *Billboard,* May 17, 1947; *Variety,* May 14, June 11, 1947.

30. *New York Times,* May 18, 1947; *Variety,* July 2, 1947; "No NAM Fools!" *New Republic,* May 26, 1947, 35.

31. Postcard from Charles and Shirely Vinning, May 11, 1947, Mrs. Vitilakes to WJZ, May 8, 1947, M. Poret to AFL, May 8, 1947, Arline Baum to Cast, May 21, 1947, Lorena M. Keefe to Miss Francis, ca. May 9, 1947, box 1, Morris S. Novik Papers, GMMA.

32. D. A. Lindsay to Entertainment Union Committee, June 6, 1947, Edith A. Lockard to AFL, May 29, 1947, Norman Nash to "Pursuit of Happiness," May 8, 1947, E. Dasch to *Best Things in Life,* May 15, 1947, Donald Shoemaker to Program Director, May 11, 1947, box 1, Morris S. Novik Papers, GMMA.

33. Harrison B. Summers, ed., *A Thirty-Year History of Programs Carried on Na-*

tional Radio Networks in the United States, 1926–1956 (New York: Arno Press, 1971), 149, 155; C. E. Hooper Ratings, May 1947, box 8, Hooper Collection, SHSW; *Variety,* June 4, Sept. 3, 1947; David McCullough, *Truman* (New York: Simon and Schuster, 1992), 566.

34. "Unions on the Air," *Business Week,* Apr. 19, 1947, 95; *CIO News,* May 26, 1947. The UE Archives has a complete collection of transcripts of Gaeth's programs. "Who Is Loyal to America," Apr. 7, 1948, "The Packinghouse Strike," May 10, 1948, "American Justice and the Negro," Feb. 14, 1949, UE; "On the Air," *New Republic,* Jan. 3, 1950, 50.

35. Nathan Godfried, *WCFL: Chicago's Voice of Labor, 1926–78* (Urbana: University of Illinois Press, 1997), 252–55; Gerald Pomper, "The Public Relations of Organized Labor," *Public Opinion Quarterly* 23 (1959–60): 484–85.

36. CIO Executive Board Minutes, Feb. 5, 1953, 66–73, June 4, 1953, 218–22, reel 5, ALUA; Untitled report on television and radio, ca. 1953, box 8, Mildred Jeffrey Papers, ALUA; Susan J. Douglas, *Listening In: Radio and the American Imagination, from Amos 'n' Andy and Edward R. Murrow to Wolfman Jack and Howard Stern* (New York: Times Books, 1999), 220–21; Jim Cox, *Say Goodnight, Gracie: The Last Years of Network Radio* (Jefferson, N.C.: McFarland and Co., 2002), 53–54; Zieger, *CIO 1935–1955,* 351.

37. *CIO News,* Aug. 17, 1953, July 12, 1954; CIO Executive Board Minutes, Sept. 8–11, 1953, 46–49, reel 5, ALUA; "How the CIO Uses Radio to Prove 'Unions Don't Have Horns,'" *Sponsor,* Jan. 11, 1954, 78.

38. Summary of CIO's Vandercook Newscast, Weeks of Sept. 14–18, 21–25, and Nov. 23–27, 1953, box 62, J. W. Hill Papers, SHSW; "How the CIO Uses Radio to Prove 'Unions Don't Have Horns,'" 34; Middle Commercials, Jan. 20, June 26, 1958, box 96, Edward P. Morgan Papers, SHSW.

39. Morgan Show, Commercial no. 3, Jan, 5, 1955, box 1, Morris S. Novik Papers, SHSW; Commercial, June 17, 1958, box 96, Edward P. Morgan Papers, SHSW.

40. Morgan Show, commercials, Jan. 21, June 18, 23, 24, 27, 1958, box 96, Edward P. Morgan Papers, SHSW.

41. Summary of CIO's Vandercook Newscast, Weeks of Sept. 21–25, Sept. 28–Oct. 2, Nov. 16–20, Nov. 30–Dec. 4, 1953, box 62, J. W. Hill papers, SHSW; Frank P. Graham to Leonard Goldenson, Mar. 9, 1959, box 37, RG1–027, George Meany Papers, GMMA.

42. Brian Ward, *Radio and the Struggle for Civil Rights in the South* (Gainesville: University Press of Florida, 2004), 76–78.

43. Edward P. Morgan and the News, script, Oct. 13, 1955, box 37, RG1–027, George Meany Papers, GMMA; *AFL-CIO News,* Apr. 21, 1956, 11.

44. Cleveland Jones to Edward P. Morgan, Feb. 24, 1956, box 1, 1968 Acc., Edward P. Morgan Papers, SHSW; V. R. Bowman to George Meany, n.d., box 37, RG1–027, George Meany Papers, GMMA; unsigned to Edward P. Morgan, Oct. 3, 1961, box 38, Edward P. Morgan Papers, SHSW.

45. I would like to thank Kathy Newman for bringing Edwards's autobiography to my attention and for sharing a paper entitled, "*My First 10,000,000 Sponsors:* Frank Edwards and the Radio Culture of the Post-War Labor Movement," presented at the American Studies Association meeting, Washington, D.C., Nov. 8–11, 2001; *Detroit*

Labor News, Nov. 18, 1949; Frank Edwards, *My First 10,000,000 Sponsors* (New York: Ballantine Books, 1956), 141–44; "Sponsor Trouble—AFL Style," *Business Week,* Aug. 21, 1954, 32; *Philadelphia Evening Bulletin,* June 24, 1952; Godfried, *WCFL,* 255; "The Urgent Voices," *Time,* Aug. 28, 1950, 47.

46. *United Automobile Worker,* July 1950; "Edwards the Great," *New Republic,* Feb. 11, 1952, 8; Report on AFL Radio News Program, Aug. 1953, box 2, Morris S. Novik Papers, GMMA; Booton Herdon, "Labor Tells Its Story," *Nation's Business,* June 1954, 66.

47. *Labor World,* Mar. 8, 1950; *United Automobile Worker,* July 1950; Ellsworth Green to William Green, Nov. 3, 1951, L. J. Decker to William Green, Apr. 3, May 12, 1951, box 18, AFL Papers, SHSW.

48. Monroe Sweetland to William A. Green, Feb. 8, 1952, Claude R. Wickard to William Green, May 31, 1950, box 18, AFL Papers, SHSW; Newman, *"My First 10,000,000 Sponsors."*

49. H. E. Barker to William Green, July 17, 1951, and similar letters in box 18, AFL Papers, SHSW; E. C. Bateman to George Meany, Oct. 18, 1954, Leonard T. Smith to Earl C. Bohr, Feb. 14, 1953, Fred Bugby to George Meany, Mar. 8, 1953, Fred J. Schrader to George Meany, Sept. 5, 1954, box 37, RG1–027, George Meany Papers, GMMA.

50. Don Connery to Edward Morgan, Jan. 3, 1955, box 37, Edward P. Morgan Papers, SHSW; James R. Jones to Frank Edwards, Sept. 19, 1953, box 37, RG1–027, George Meany Papers, GMMA; S. H. Wetzler to Frank Edwards, June 14, 1950, box 18, AFL Papers, SHSW; Walter B. Stiles to Chairman FCC, Sept. 19, 1950, box 60, General Corr., 1947–56, FCC.

51. Pomper, "Public Relations of Organized Labor," 485; Godfried, *WCFL,* 255; Earl Jimerson to William Green, Sept. 6, 1950, box 18, AFL Papers, SHSW.

52. Morris Novik to Harry Flannery, Aug. 29, 30, Sept. 10, 1951, Flannery to Novik, Sept. 16, Nov. 4, 1951, box 2, Morris S. Novik Papers, GMMA; Donald Montgomery to Frank Winn, June 30, 1952, box 67, Donald Montgomery Papers, UAW Washington Office Collection, ALUA; Godfried, *WCFL,* 255; George W. Dean to William Green, Aug. 25, 1952, and similar letters and telegrams in box 18, AFL Papers, SHSW; Newman, *"My First 10,000,000 Sponsors"*; "Edwards Off the Air," *The Nation,* August 21, 1954, 141.

53. *CIO News,* Aug. 31, 1953, Mar. 15, 1954; Adam Ooms to AFL-CIO Executive Committee, Jan. 23, 1956, Helen Fahey to George Meany, box 37, RG1–027, George Meany Papers, GMMA; Henry Fleisher to Reuther, undated report on CIO Radio Program, box 76, CIO Office of the Secretary-Treasurer Papers, ALUA; Donald Kehoe, interview with the author, Oct. 24, 2000.

54. Margaret Nordfeldt to George Meany, Dec. 13, 1957, box 37, RG1–027, George Meany Papers, GMMA; Arthur J. Knodel to Edward P. Morgan, July 7, 1959, box 38, Douglas Watson to William F. Schnitzler, Sept. 6, 1958, box 36, Edward P. Morgan Papers, SHSW; "Edward P. Morgan Speaks," *American Federationist,* Feb. 1955, 7.

55. Francine Millier to George Meany, Nov. 18, 1957, box 37, George Meany to James F. Kelley, Nov. 17, 1955, RG1–027, George Meany Papers, GMMA; *New York Times,* Feb. 28, 1965; George Meany to John Meany, Oct. 19, 1961, box 38, Edward P. Morgan Papers, SHSW.

56. Ray Denison, "A Decade of Edward P. Morgan and the News," *AFL-CIO Ameri-*

can Federationist, Feb. 1965, 13; Godfried, *WCFL,* 255; Undated clipping, review of "Edward P. Morgan and the News," box 3, Morris S. Novik Papers, GMMA; Priscilla Fox to George Meany, Nov. 21, 1957, A. L. Spradling to George Meany, Sept. 2, 1954, C. S. Benjamin to George Meany, Jan. 12, 1955, E. C. Bateman to George Meany, Oct. 18, 1954, Mary Barnett Gilson to Joe, Feb. 7, 1959, Francine Millier to George Meany, Nov. 18, 1957, Edward P. Morgan and the News-Letter Excerpts, enclosed in Morgan to Meany, Mar. 16, 1959, box 37, RG1–027, George Meany Papers, GMMA.

57. "Merchandising Verbal Poison," *Business Week,* Sept. 29, 1951, 156; *The Advocator,* UAW Chrysler Local 371, Feb. 1953; Report on AFL Radio News Program, Aug. 1953, box 2, Morris S. Novik papers, GMMA; "Labor on the Air," *Newsweek,* Aug. 28, 1950, 50; "Listen to Guy Nunn," undated clipping, box 7, Mildred Jeffrey Papers, ALUA; *United Automobile Worker,* Mar. 1956; Paul Christopher to Ed Lashman, Apr. 7, 1954, box 1912, AFL-CIO Region 8 Papers, Southern Labor Archives, Georgia State University, Atlanta.

58. John W. Hill to John C. Long, Oct. 27, 1953, box 26, J. W. Hill Papers, SHSW; CIO Executive Board Minutes, July 20, 1955, reel 5, ALUA; G. W. Johnstone to R. T. Compton, Apr. 6, 1956, Acc. 1411, NAM I/155.

59. Vera Barnes to Jack Kroll, Mar. 4, 1947, box 1, CIO Political Action Committee Papers, ALUA; *Michigan CIO News,* May 11, 1950; Thomas M. Hampson to Edward P. Morgan, May 12, 1967, box 1, 1968 Acc., Edward P. Morgan Papers, SHSW; Herbert Scott to Walter Reuther, Sept. 4, 1964, box 147, Walter Reuther Papers, ALUA; *AFL-CIO News,* Aug. 4, 1962.

60. *New York Times,* Nov. 6, 1957; UAW International Executive Board Minutes, May 7–11, 1951, box 8, 361, ALUA.

61. "Labor Views the News," script, ca. 1953, box 7, Mildred Jeffrey Papers, ALUA; *UAW President's Report* (1955), 117D-18D, ALUA; James Caldwell Foster, *The Union Politic: The CIO Political Action Committee* (Columbia: University of Missouri Press, 1975), 185–89. For a detailed description of the UAW television program see Billie Joe Langston, "A Historical Study of the UAW Television Program *Telescope*" (Ph.D. diss., University of Michigan, 1969).

62. UAW International Executive Board Minutes, Apr. 25–29, 1955, 46, box 10, ALUA; "Does Your Company Sell Ideas as Well as This Union?" ca. 1956, box 22, UAW Research Department Papers, ALUA; Guy Nunn to Bob Rice, Nov. 19, 1958, box 9, Guy Nunn to Paul Schrade, Apr. 18, 1955, box 11, UAW Radio Department papers, 1984 Acc., ALUA; "Eye Opener," scripts, Sept. 15, Oct. 13, 1955, box 4, UAW Radio Department Papers, ALUA; "Eye Opener," scripts, Oct. 25, 26, 1955, box 1, Brendan Sexton Papers, ALUA.

63. Michael Berg to Dear Friends, Aug. 4, 1964, box 147, Walter Reuther Papers, ALUA; Douglas Fraser, interview with the author, June 3, 1997; *UAW President's Report* (1957), 123–D, ALUA; UAW International Executive Board Minutes, May 13–17, 1957, 90–91, box 11, ALUA.

64. Guy Nunn to Emil Mazey, June 16, 1955, box 27, Roy Reuther Papers, UAW PAC Collection, ALUA; *Detroit Free Press,* Mar. 1, 1955, Dec. 11, 1964; Lanston, "Historical Study of the UAW Television Program *Telescope*," 378, 102; "Labor Views the News," audio tape, Oct. 17, 1956, ALUA; Random Proofs of "Eye Opener" Impact or

Influence, enclosed in Guy Nunn to Walter P. Reuther, Jan. 21, 1959, box 337, Walter Reuther Papers, ALUA.

65. *Variety,* Nov. 3, 1954; *New York Times,* Aug. 8, Oct. 10, 1956; *Detroit Free Press,* Mar. 1, 1955; "Eye Opener," script, July 7, 1955, box 4, UAW Radio Department Papers, ALUA.

66. For a detailed recounting of this case, see Langston, "Historical Study of the UAW Television Program *Telescope,*" 207–71. *United Automobile Worker,* July 1955; *Detroit Free Press,* July 21, 1955; UAW International Executive Board Minutes, July 6–8, 1955, 18–19, Jan. 9–11, 1956, 76, box 10, ALUA.

67. *New York Times,* Oct. 30, Oct. 31, Nov. 1, 7, 1957.

68. Nelson Lichtenstein, *The Most Powerful Man in Detroit: Walter Reuther and the Fate of American Labor* (New York: Basic Books, 1995), 319–40; Kevin Boyle, *The UAW and the Heyday of American Liberalism, 1945–1968* (Ithaca, N.Y.: Cornell University Press, 1995), 90–91; Thomas J. Sugrue, *The Origins of the Urban Crisis: Race and Inequality in Postwar Detroit* (Princeton, N.J.: Princeton University Press, 1996).

69. *New York Times,* July 14, 19, 1949; "Must Propaganda be the Monopoly of Our Leftists?" *Saturday Evening Post,* Mar. 4, 1950, 10; Jack Metzgar, *Striking Steel: Solidarity Remembered* (Philadelphia: Temple University Press, 2000), 55.

Epilogue

1. *Variety,* Jan. 6, 1954.

2. *Variety,* Jan. 6, 1954; Morris Novik, "Labor Turns to Radio," *Broadcasting,* Sept. 19, 1955, 174–75; Novik to George, Apr. 28, 1955, and strike broadcast scripts, G. E. Leighty to George Meany, July 15, 1955, box 3, Morris S. Novik Papers, GMMA.

3. *Variety,* Jan. 6, 1954.

4. Robert Oliver to Walter P. Reuther, Feb. 2, 1954, box 26, CIO Washington Office Papers, ALUA; IUD Public Relations Committee Meeting, May 28, 1959, box 1, RG 1, Subject Files of James B. Carey, President's Office, International Union of Electrical Workers Archives, Special Collections, Rutgers University Libraries, New Brunswick, N.J.; Nelson Lichtenstein, *State of the Union: A Century of American Labor* (Princeton, N.J.: Princeton University Press, 2002), 142–48.

5. Guy Nunn to Alan Henry, June 11, 1958, box 11, 1984 Acc., UAW Radio Department Papers, ALUA; *UAW President's Report* (1959), 134–D, ALUA; *Detroit Free Press,* Dec. 11, 1964; *Detroit News,* Dec. 10, 1964; *UAW President's Report* (1964), pt. 3, 144–45, *UAW President's Report* (1966), pt. 3, 123, Irving Bluestone to L. Cordell Washington, Jan, 14, 1965, box 147, Walter Reuther Papers, ALUA.

6. Louis F. Suda to UAW, Aug. 4, 1964, V. V. Roe to UAW, July 31, 1964, Michael Berg to Dear Friends, Aug. 4, 1964, V. V. Roe to UAW-CIO, July 31, 1964, A. Hewitt to Walter Reuther, Feb. 1, 1965, box 147, Walter Reuther Papers, ALUA; Lisa McGirr, *Suburban Warriors: The Origins of the New American Right* (Princeton, N.J.: Princeton University Press, 2001).

7. Ruth E. Miller to Walter Reuther, July 31, 1964, Lewis Waldrup to UAW, Aug. 8, 1964, box 147, Walter Reuther Papers, ALUA.

8. Billie Joe Langston, "A Historical Study of the UAW Television Program *Tele-*

scope" (Ph.D. diss., University of Michigan, 1969), 337; Oscar Paskal, interview with the author, Dec. 5, 2000; John D'Agostino, interview with the author, May 10, 1999.

9. Nelson Lichtenstein, *The Most Dangerous Man in Detroit: Walter Reuther and the Fate of American Labor* (New York: Basic Books, 1995), 326; Langston, "Historical Study of the UAW Television Program *Telescope*," 381, 377; Oscar Paskal, interview with the author, Dec. 5, 2000.

10. Victor G. Reuther and Paul Sifton to Roy L. Reuther et al., Nov. 8, 1957, box 7, 1984 Acc., UAW Radio Department Papers, ALUA; Report of Public Relations Committee, AFL-CIO Executive Council Meeting, May 1957, box 2, RG 2–07, Office of the Secretary-Treasurer, Wm. F. Schnitzler Files, GMMA; Elizabeth Fones-Wolf, *Selling Free Enterprise: The Business Assault on Labor and Liberalism, 1945–1960* (Urbana: University of Illinois Press, 1994), 258–70.

11. Robert H. Zieger, *American Workers, American Union* (Baltimore: Johns Hopkins University Press, 1994), 158–63; UAW International Executive Board Minutes, Sept. 8–11, 1959, 57, ALUA; "Says Labor's Image Is Deteriorating," Radio-TV Monitoring Service, Sept. 3, 1966, box 49, RG 1–38, George Meany Papers, GMMA.

12. Sara U. Douglas, *Labor's New Voice: Unions and the Mass Media* (Norwood, N.J.: Ablex Publishing Corp., 1986), 38–41; Report of the Public Relations Department to the Public Relations Committee of the Executive Council (AFL-CIO), ca. 1967, box 99, RG 1–38, George Meany Papers, GMMA.

13. AFL-CIO Executive Council Minutes, Aug. 15, 1957, GMMA; William Pollock to Edward P. Morgan, box 37, RG 1–27, Emil Mazey to Edward P. Morgan, Nov. 18, 1966, box 49, RG 1–38, George Meany Papers, GMMA; "The Last Big Voice," *Newsweek*, Sept. 19, 1966, 98.

14. Alan G. Clive to Edward P. Morgan, May 10, 1967, Sidney Siefer to Edward P. Morgan, June 21, 1967, Lawrence C. Sullivan to Federal Communications Communication, box 1, 1968 Acc., Edward P. Morgan Papers, SHSW.

15. Nathan Godfried, *WCFL: Chicago's Voice of Labor, 1926–1978* (Urbana: University of Illinois Press, 1997), 281–90; *Machinist*, Apr. 16, 1964; Douglas, *Labor's New Voice*, 80–81, 39–40.

16. Douglas, *Labor's New Voice*, 59–62, 75–77, 97–99; Sam Pizzigati and Kathleen Lyons, "Labor as Advertiser: The Hard Lessons Learned in the 80s and 90s," paper presented at the Social Science History Association Conference, Washington, D.C., Oct. 16, 1997.

17. *Machinist*, Aug. 22, 1963, Jan. 30, 1964; David Vogel, *Fluctuating Fortunes: The Political Power of Business in America* (New York: Basic Books, 1989), 217–18; Thomas Byrne Edsall, *New Politics of Inequality* (New York: W. W. Norton and Co., 1984), 107–40, 151–57.

18. Nelson Lichtenstein, *State of the Union: A Century of American Labor* (Princeton, N.J.: Princeton University Press, 2002), 213; John B. Judis, *The Paradox of American Democracy: Elites, Special Interests, and the Betrayal of Public Trust* (New York: Pantheon Books, 2000), 116.

19. Robert W. McChesney, *Rich Media, Poor Democracy: Communication Politics in Dubious Times* (Urbana: University of Illinois Press, 1999); Susan J. Douglas, *Listening In: Radio and the American Imagination, from Amos 'n' Andy and Edward R. Murrow to Wolfman Jack and Howard Stern* (New York: Times Books, 1999), 293–303.

20. The Century Foundation Task Force on the Future of Unions, *What's Next for Organized Labor?* (New York: The Century Foundation Press, 1999), 49; Michael Eisenscher, "Beyond Mobilization: How Labor Can Transform Itself," *Working USA* 1 (Mar.–Apr. 1998): 37.

21. *Chicago Tribune,* Dec. 18, 1995; Frank Emspak, "WINS: Transforming the Way Workers Relate to the Media," paper presented at the Radio Conference Transnational Forum, University of Wisconsin at Madison, July 30, 2003; Robert W. McChesney and John Nichols, *Our Media, Not Theirs: The Democratic Struggle against Corporate Media* (New York: Seven Stories Press, 2002), 123–28.

PRIMARY SOURCES CONSULTED

Archives and Libraries

Alabama Department of Archives and History, Montgomery
   Charles Durr Papers
Broadcast Pioneers Library, University of Maryland, College Park
   Morris S. Novik Papers
Department of Archives and Manuscripts, The Catholic University of America, Washington, D.C.
   CIO National and International Union Files
   John Brophy Papers
   Philip Murray Papers
Ford Motor Company Archives, Dearborn, Mich.
   Henry Ford Office Papers
Franklin D. Roosevelt Library, Hyde Park, N.Y.
   Franklin D. Roosevelt Papers
   Stephen T. Early Papers
George Meany Memorial Archives, Silver Spring, Md.
   AFL Executive Council Minutes
   AFL-CIO Executive Council Minutes
   George Meany Papers
   Morris S. Novik Papers
   William Green Papers
   William Schnitzler Papers
Hagley Museum and Library, Wilmington, Del.
   National Association of Manufacturers Records
      E. I. Du Pont de Nemours and Company Records
      Du Pont Public Affairs Department Papers
      Du Pont Advertising Department Papers

Walter S. Carpenter Jr. Files
J. Howard Pew Papers
Historical Collections and Labor Archives, Pennsylvania State University, University Park
Meyer Bernstein Papers
United Steelworkers of America Archives
Kheel Center for Labor-Management Documentation and Archives, Cornell University, Ithaca, N.Y.
Amalgamated Clothing Workers of America Papers
Sidney Hillman Correspondence
Joseph Potofsky Correspondence
General Executive Board Minutes
American Union Files
Greater Buffalo Industrial Union Council Records
Geneva, N.Y., Federation of Labor Minutebook
ILGWU Records
Charles S. Zimmerman Papers
David Dubinsky Papers
Frederick F. Umhey Papers
General Executive Board Minutes
International Workers Order Records
Morris S. Novik Papers
UAW Local 686 Records, Buffalo, N.Y.
Lehman Library, Columbia University, New York
Bureau of Applied Research Papers
Library of Congress, Washington, D.C.
Edward R. Murrow Papers
Jo Davidson Papers
Joseph Rauh Papers
NBC Papers
National Archives and Records Center, College Park, Md.
Federal Communications Commission Records, RG 173
Office of War Information Records, RG 44
Records of the U.S. Senate, RG 46
New York Public Library
Norman Thomas Papers
Ohio Historical Society, Columbus
Youngstown Sheet and Tube Company Records
Rare Book and Manuscript Library, Butler Library, Columbia University, New York
Federated Press Papers
James Fly Papers
Paul Lazarsfeld Papers
Seeley G. Mudd Library, Princeton University, Princeton, N.J.
ACLU Papers

Southern Labor Archives, Georgia State Univesity, Atlanta
AFL-CIO Region 8 Papers
Special Collections and University Archives, Rutgers University Libraries, New Bruns-
wick, N.J.
International Union of Electrical Workers Archives
Special Collections Department, University of Iowa Libraries, Iowa City
C. B. Baldwin Papers
Tamiment Library and Robert F. Wagner Labor Archives, New York University
Mark Starr Papers
United Electrical Workers Archives, University of Pittsburgh Libraries
Red Accession
Yellow Accession
UE Executive Board Minutes
District 1 Records
Walter P. Reuther Library for Labor and Urban Affairs, Wayne State University, De-
troit
Brendan Sexton Papers
Carl Haessler Papers
CIO Executive Board Minutes
CIO Office of Secretary-Treasurer Papers
CIO Political Action Committee Papers
CIO Washington Office Papers
Edward Levinson Papers
Henry Kraus Papers
Homer Martin Papers
Katherine Ellickson Papers
Len De Caux Papers
Maurice Sugar Papers
Michigan AFL-CIO Records
Mildred Jeffrey Papers
Norman Smith Papers
Richard Frankensteen Papers
R. J. Thomas Papers
UAW Citizenship Department Papers
UAW Education Department Papers
UAW International Executive Board Minutes
UAW Local 51 Papers
UAW Local 212 Papers
UAW Political Action Committee Papers
UAW Public Relations Department Papers
UAW Radio Department Papers
UAW Region 2A Papers
UAW Research Department Papers
UAW Washington Office Papers
Walter P. Reuther Papers

Wayne County AFL-CIO Papers
West Virginia and Regional History Collections, West Virginia University Libraries,
  Morgantown
  West Virginia Industrial Union Council Records
Wisconsin Historical Society, Madison
  American Federation of Labor Papers
  American Federation of Hosiery Workers Records
  American Legion Papers, Department of Wisconsin
  Adolph Germer Papers
  Bruce Barton Papers
  C. E. Hooper, Inc. Records
  Dane County Labor Defense Council Papers
  Edward S. Morgan Papers
  Harry W. Flannery Papers
  H. V. Kaltenborn Papers
  John W. Hill Papers
  Leland Stowe Papers
  Morris S. Novik Papers
  National Broadcasting Company, Inc., Records
  National Association of Broadcasters Papers
  Pulse, Inc. Report Papers
  Textile Workers Union of America Papers
  United Packinghouse Workers Papers
  William S. Hedges Papers

Microfilm Collections

American Labor Unions' Constitutions and Proceedings (Glen Rock, N.J.: Microfilm-
  ing Corporation of America, 1975).
CIO Files of John L. Lewis (Frederick, Md.: University Publications of America,
  1988)
Operation Dixie: The CIO Organizing Committee Papers, 1946–1953 (Sanford, N.C.:
  Microfilming Corporation of America, 1980)
Southern Tenant Farmers' Union Papers, 1934–1970 Microfilm (Glenlock, N.J.: Micro-
  filming Corporation of America, 1971)

Newspapers and Periodicals

ACLU Bulletin
Advance
Advanced Management
AFL-CIO Federationist
American Federation of Labor Weekly News Service
Akron Times-Press
Atlantic Monthly
American Business

Ammunition
Billboard
Broadcasting
Business Week
Chicago Industrial Worker
Christian Century
CIO News
CIO News—Wisconsin Edition
Civil Liberties News
Common Sense
Daily Worker
Detroit Free Press
Detroit News
Evening Public Ledger
Exchange
Factory Management and Maintenance
Federation News (Chicago)
Federated Press Labor Letter
Ford Facts
Fortune
In Fact
Journal of Commerce
Justice
Labor Herald (San Francisco)
Labor Herald and Citizen (Rochester, N.Y.)
Labor Review (Portsmouth, Ohio)
Labor's Daily
Labor's News (New York)
Labor World (Chattanooga, Tenn.)
Los Angeles Citizen
Machinist
Michigan CIO News
NAB Reports
NAM Newsletter
NAM News
The Nation
Nation's Business
New Leader
New Republic
New York Herald Tribune
New York Post
New York Times
Newsweek
Pennsylvania Labor Record
PM
Printers' Ink

Public Opinion Quarterly
Public Relations Journal
Public Relations News
Radio Daily
Sales Management
Saturday Evening Post
Socialist Call (New York)
Steel Labor
Time
United Automobile Worker
United Rubber Worker
Union Labor Record (Philadelphia)
Variety
Voice of Freedom
Wall Street Journal
West Side Conveyor
Wisconsin CIO News

INDEX

ELIZABETH FONES-WOLF is a professor of history at West Virginia University. She is also the author of *Selling Free Enterprise: The Business Assault on Labor and Liberalism, 1945–60*.

The History of Communication

The University of Illinois Press
is a founding member of the
Association of American University Presses.

Composed in 10.5/13 Adobe Minion
by Jim Proefrock
at the University of Illinois Press
Manufactured by Thomson-Shore, Inc.

University of Illinois Press
1325 South Oak Street
Champaign, IL 61820-6903
www.press.uillinois.edu